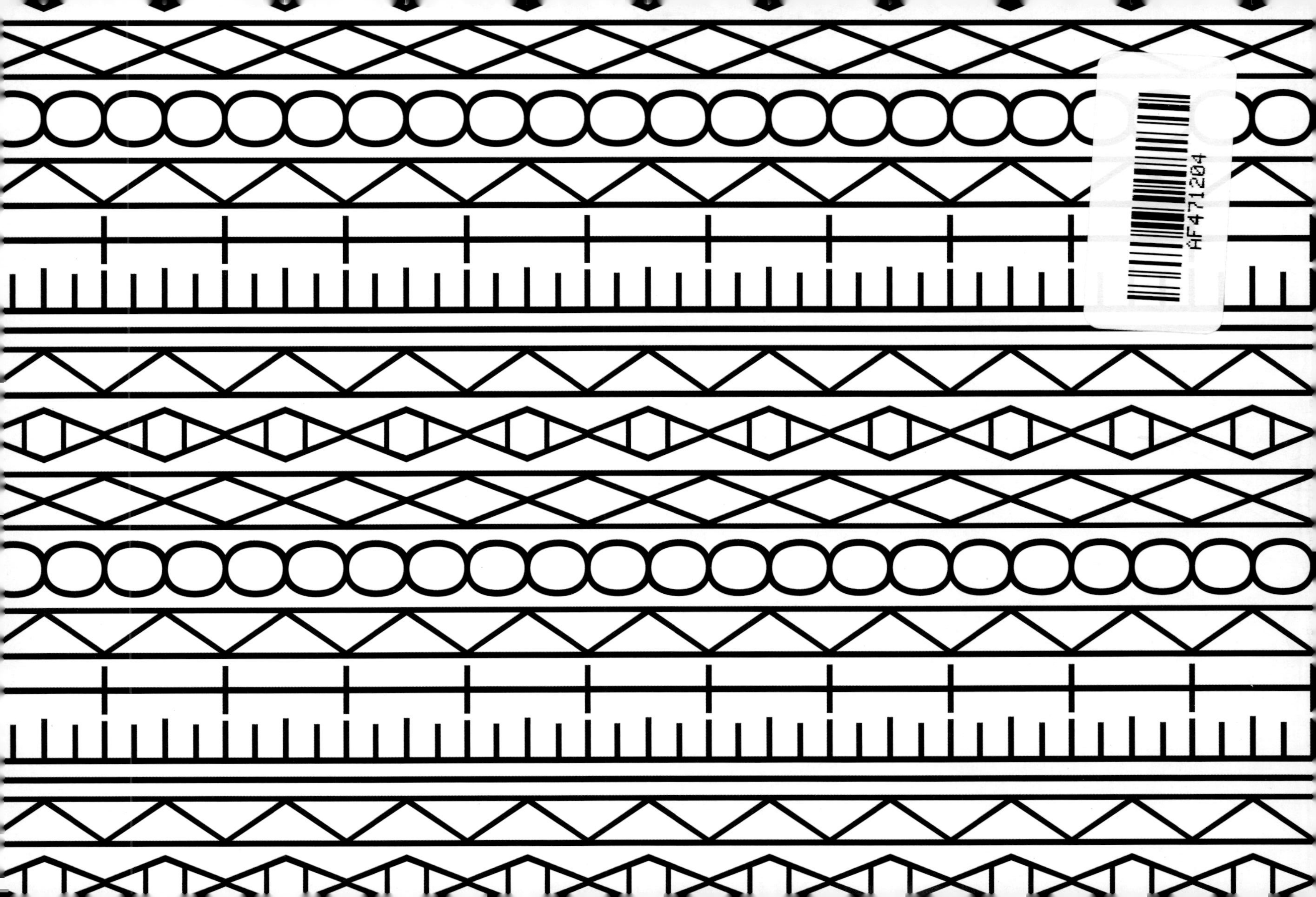

AF471204

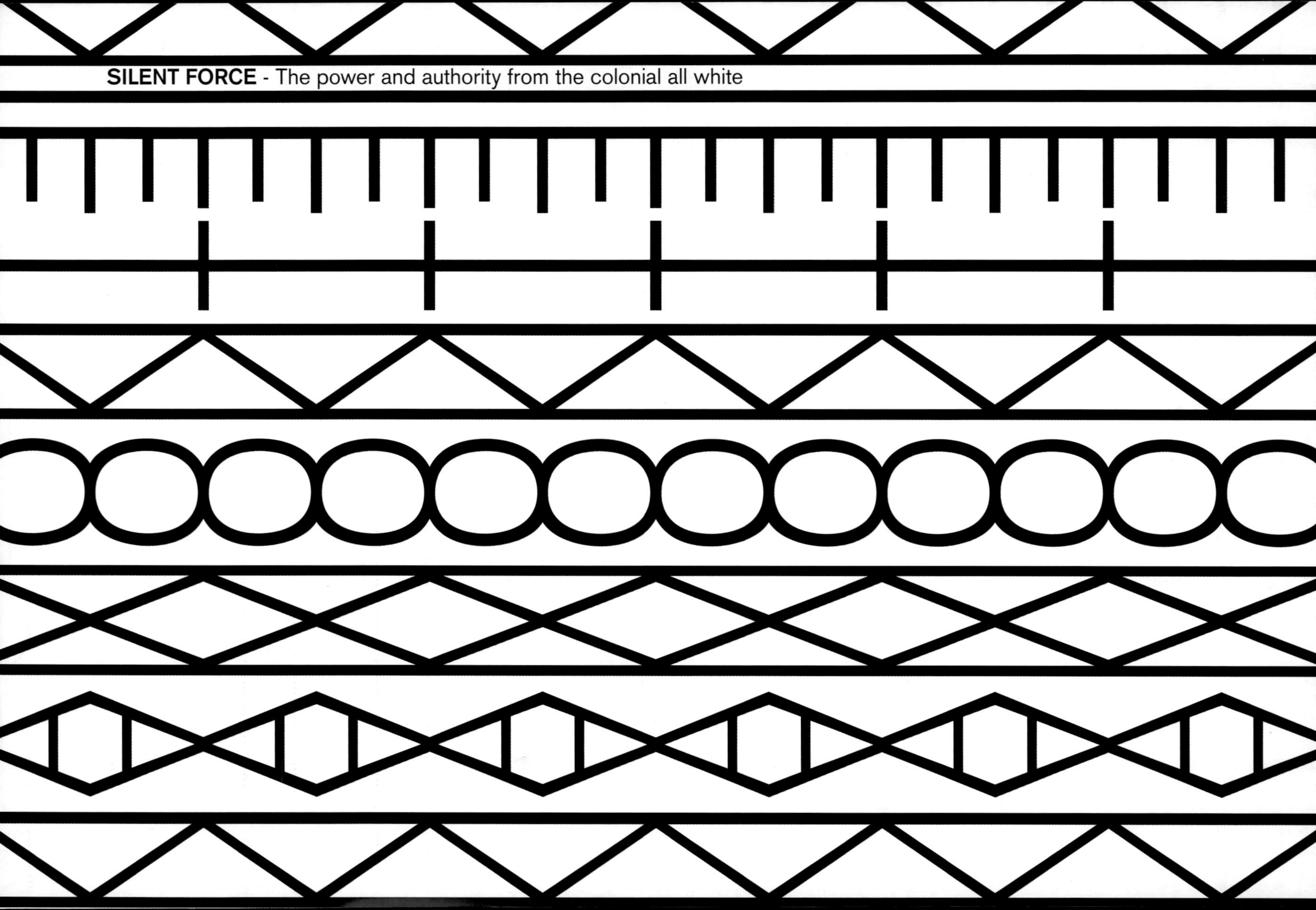

SILENT FORCE - The power and authority from the colonial all white

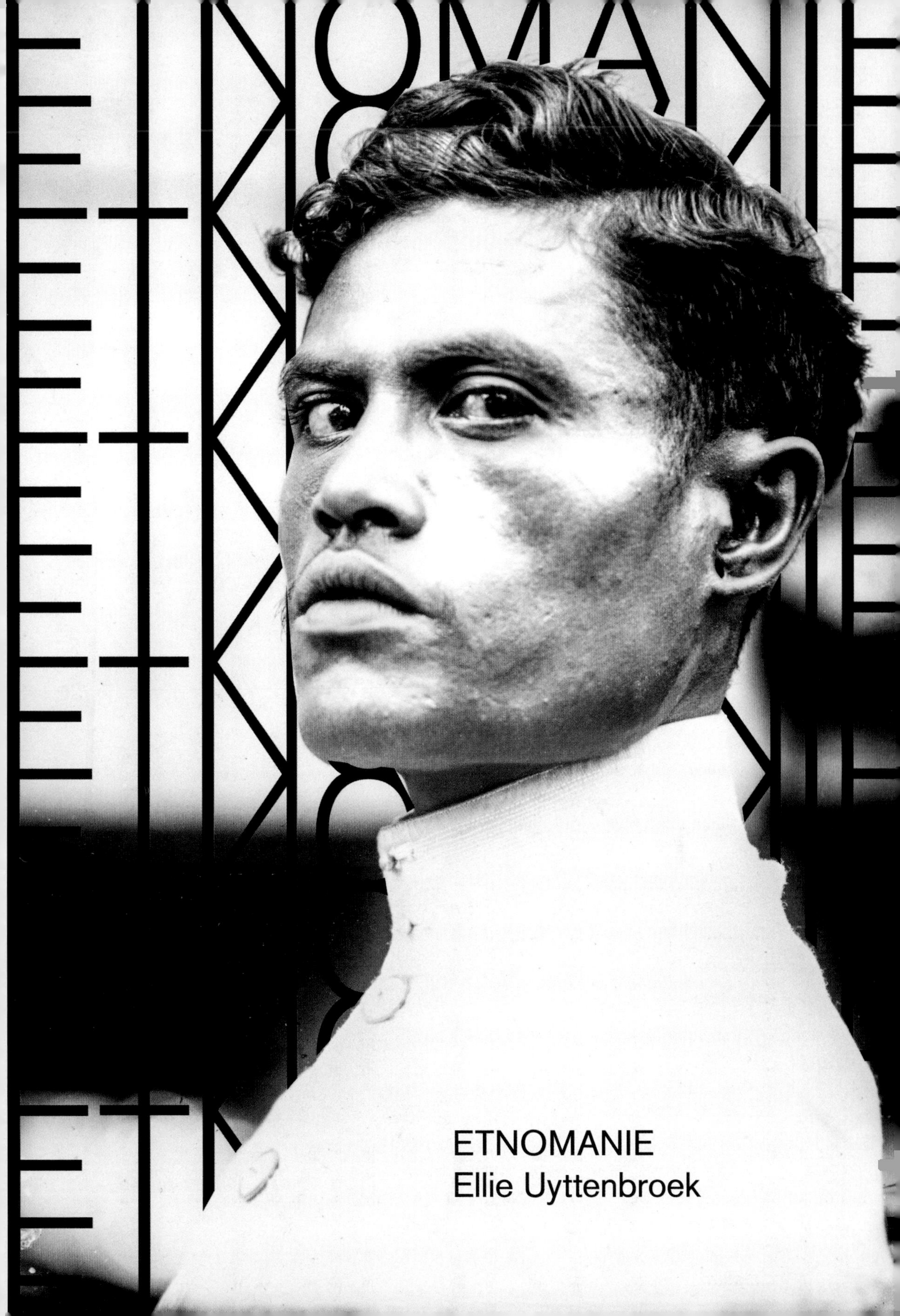
ETNOMANIE
Ellie Uyttenbroek

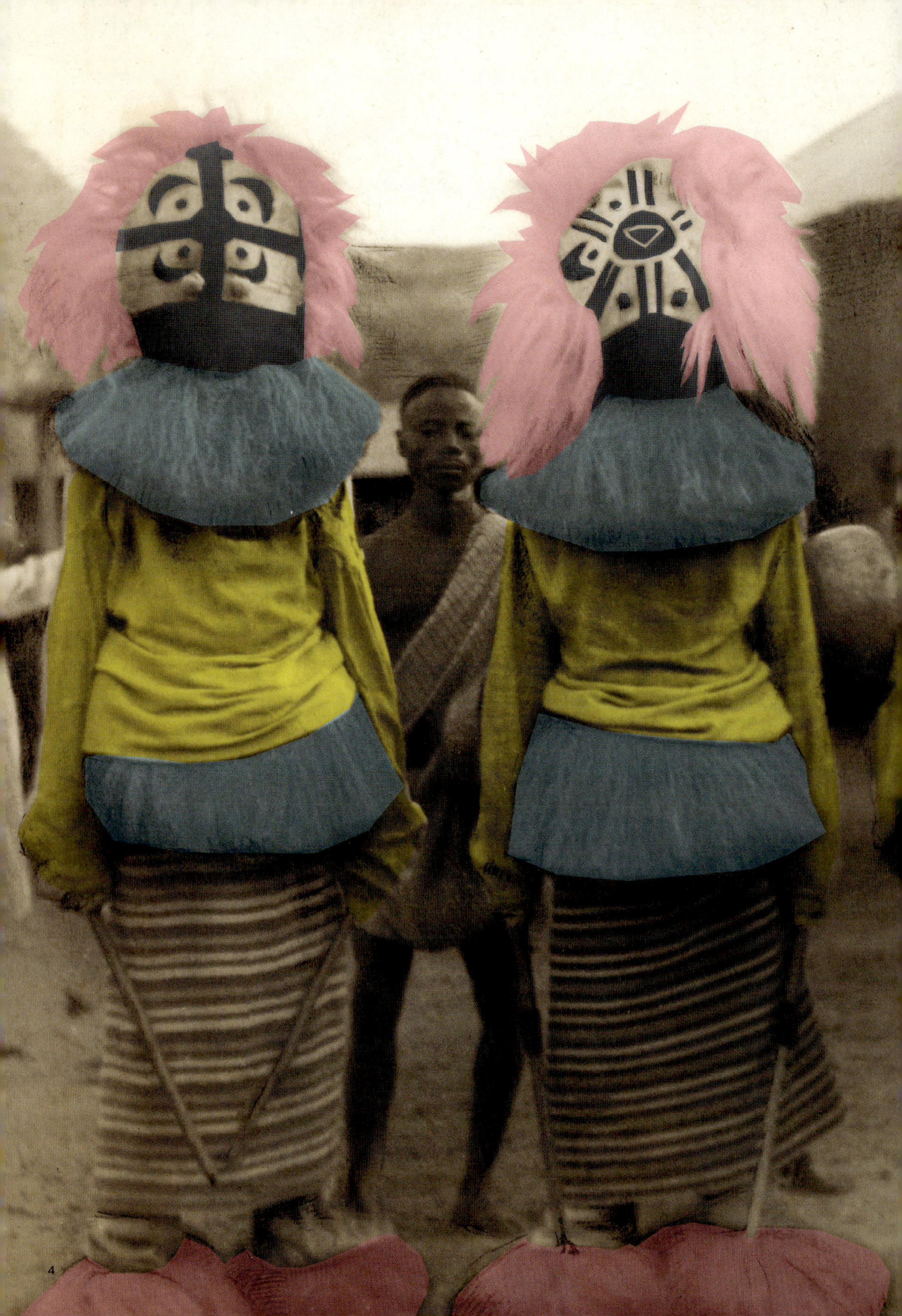

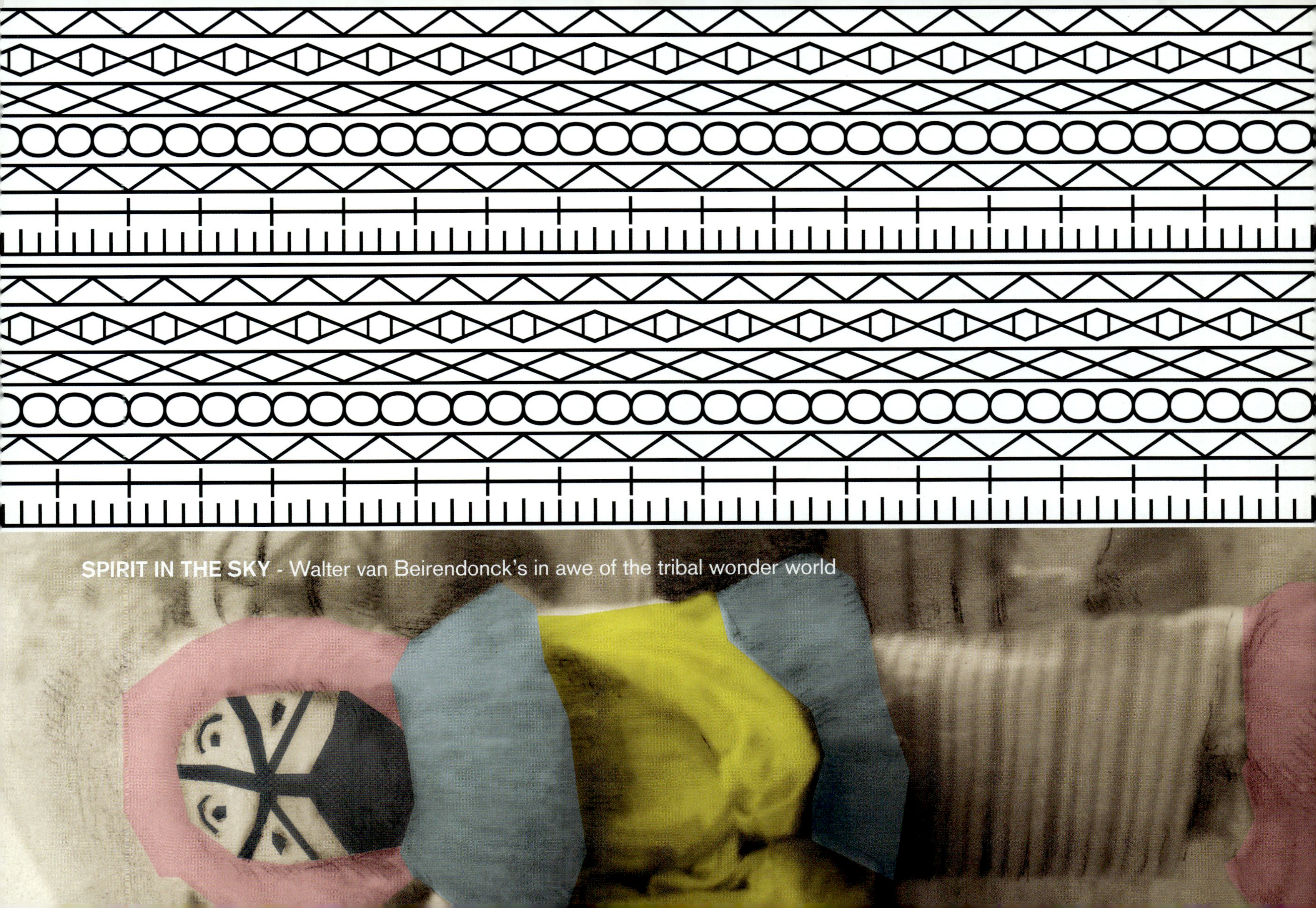
SPIRIT IN THE SKY - Walter van Beirendonck's in awe of the tribal wonder world

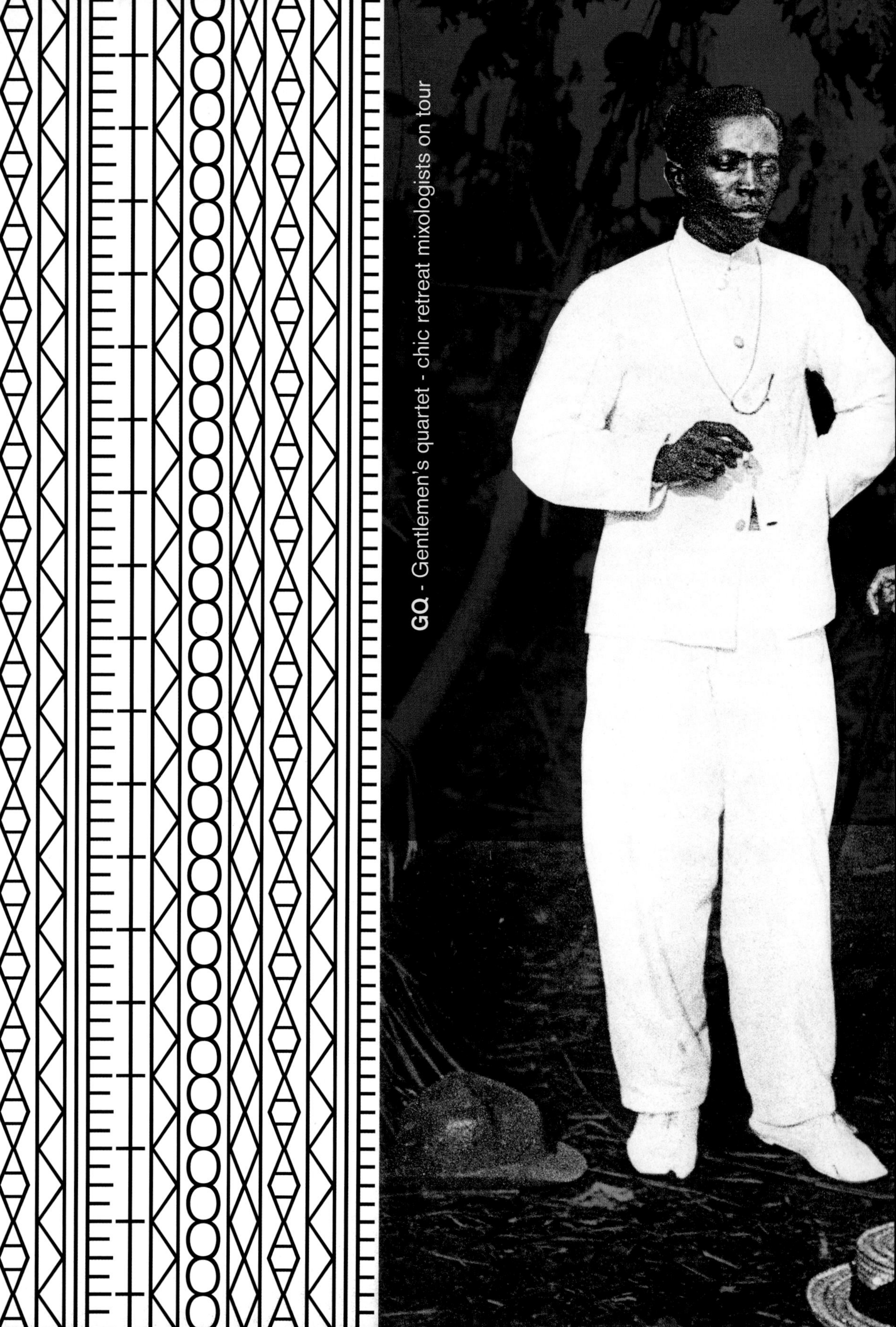

GQ - Gentlemen's quartet - chic retreat mixologists on tour

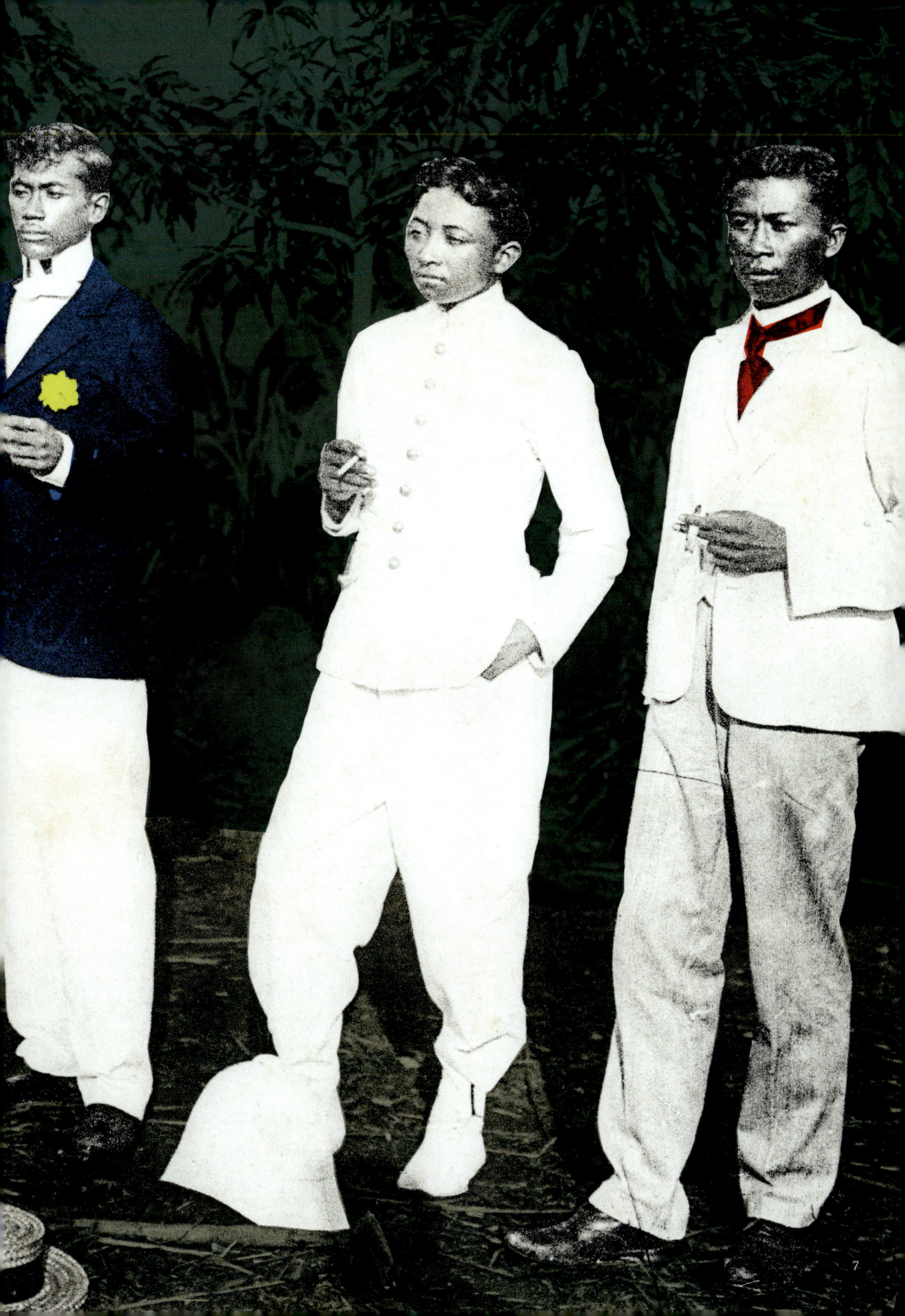

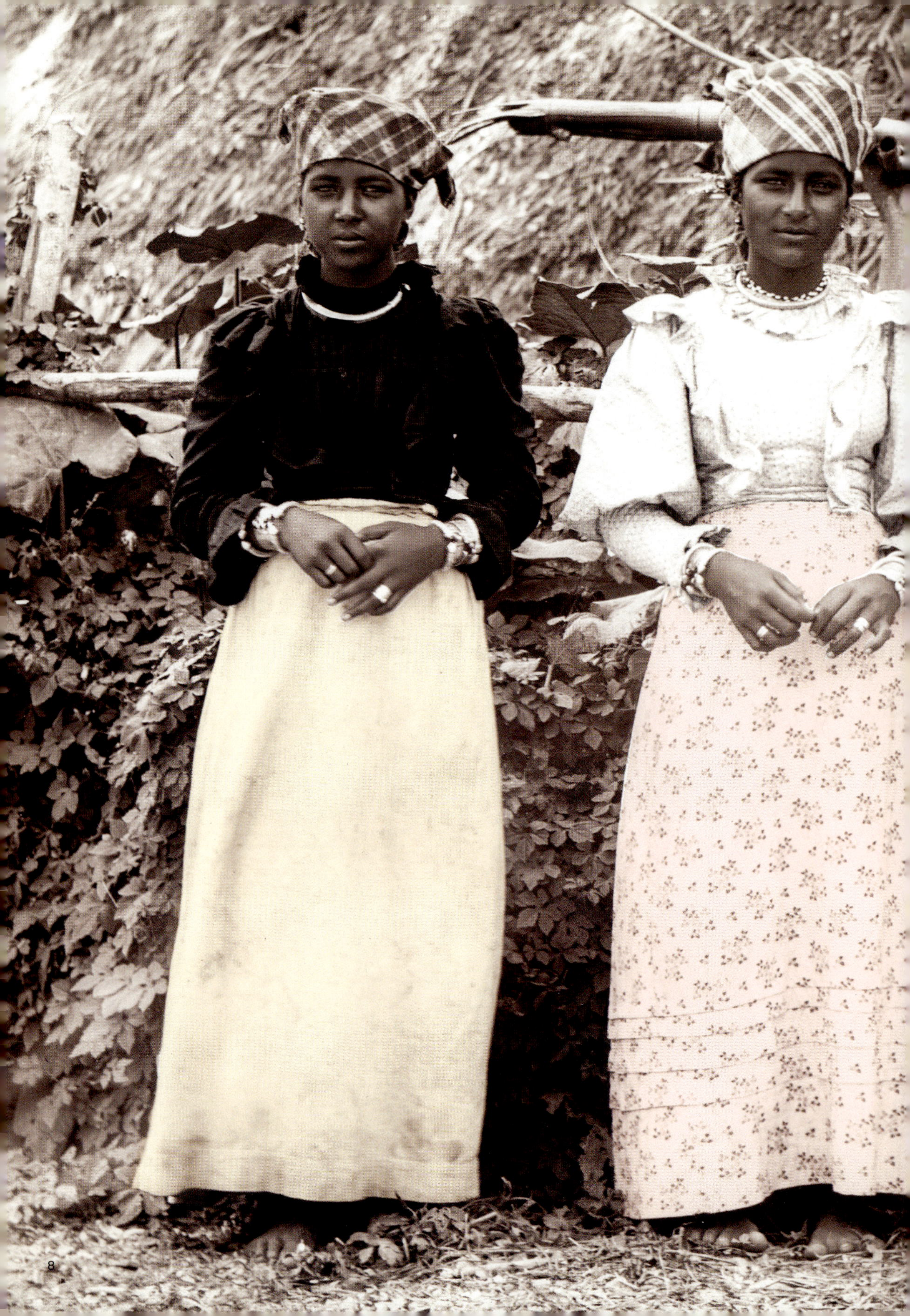

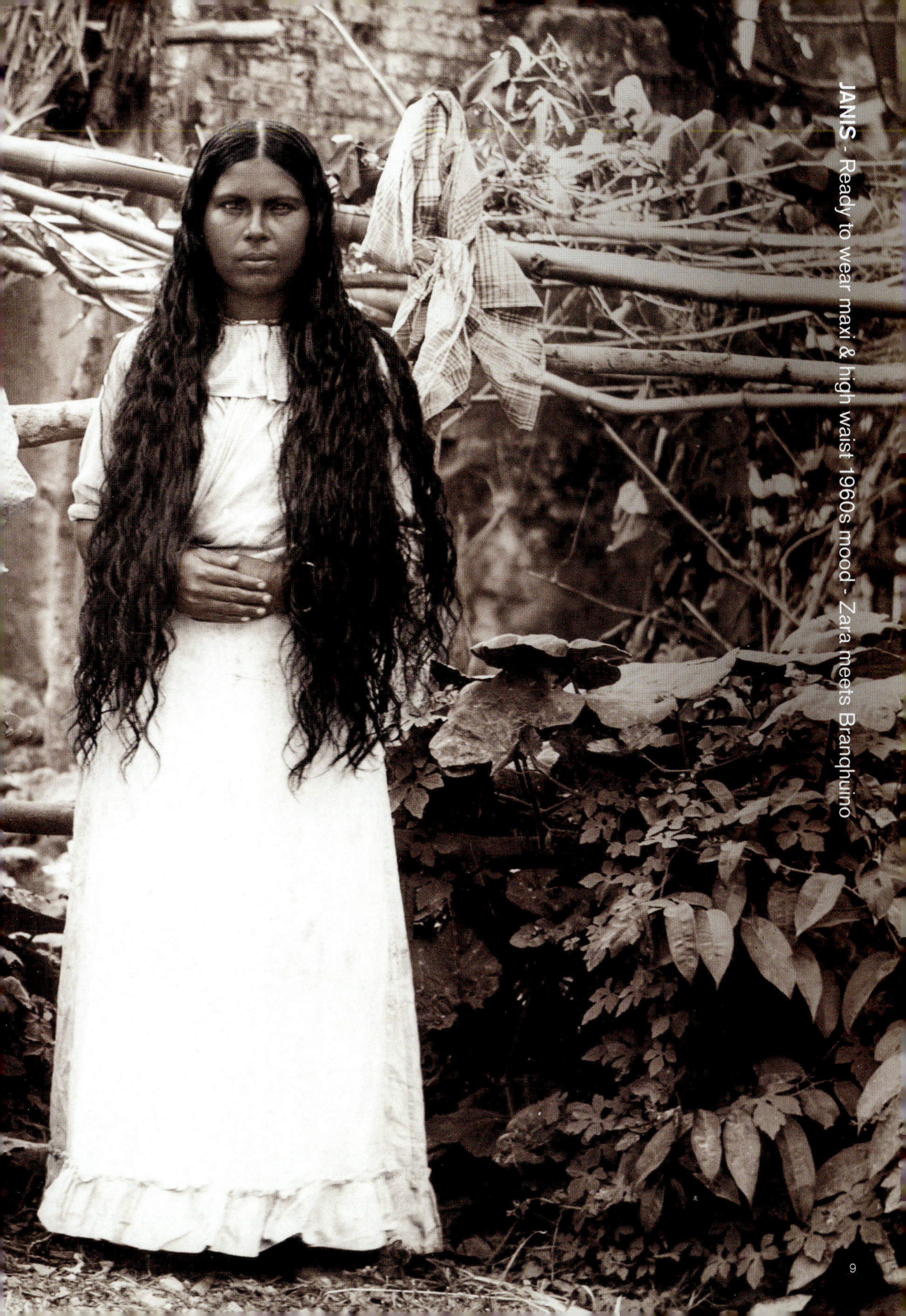

JANIS - Ready to wear maxi & high waist 1960s mood - Zara meets Branghuino

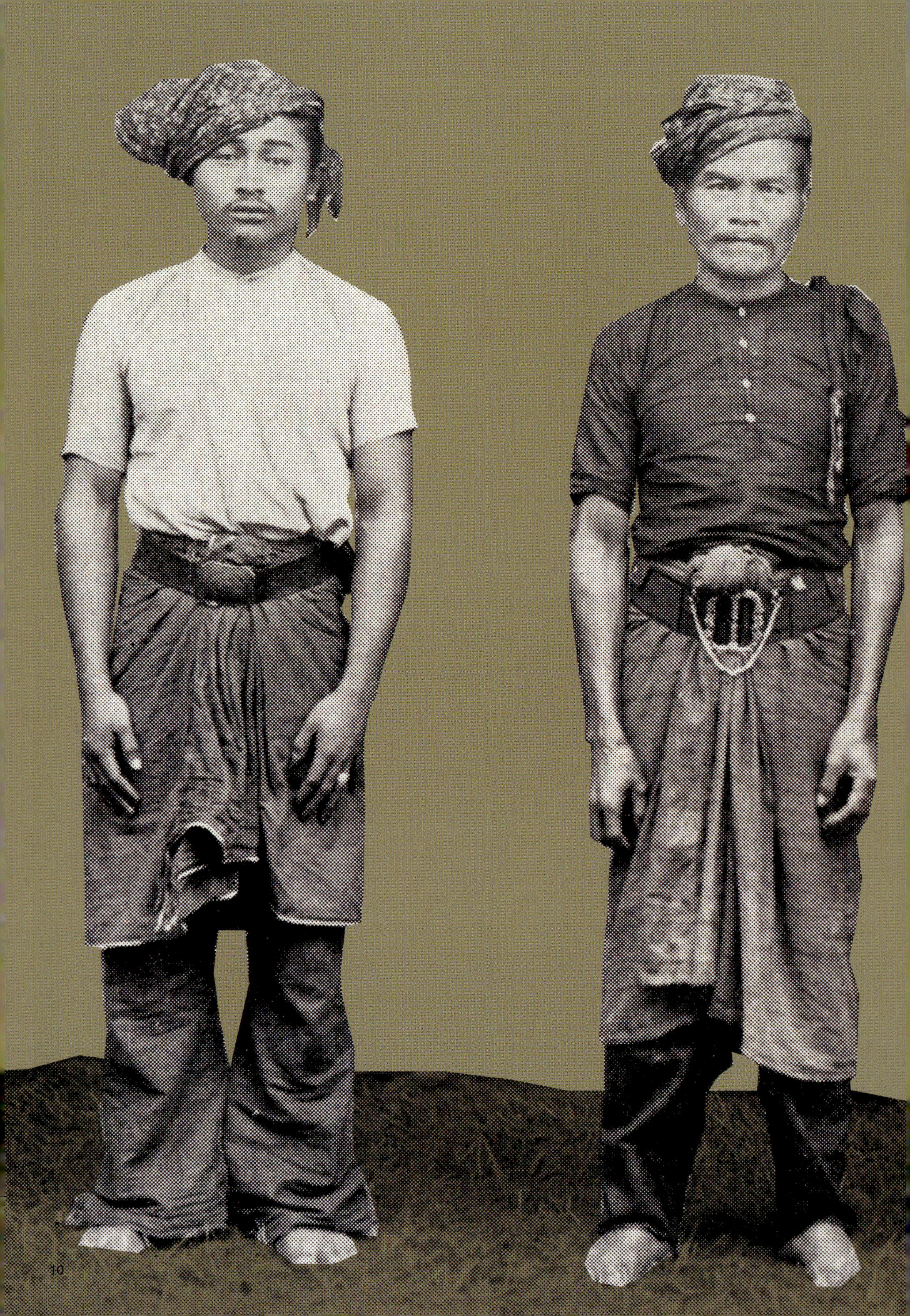

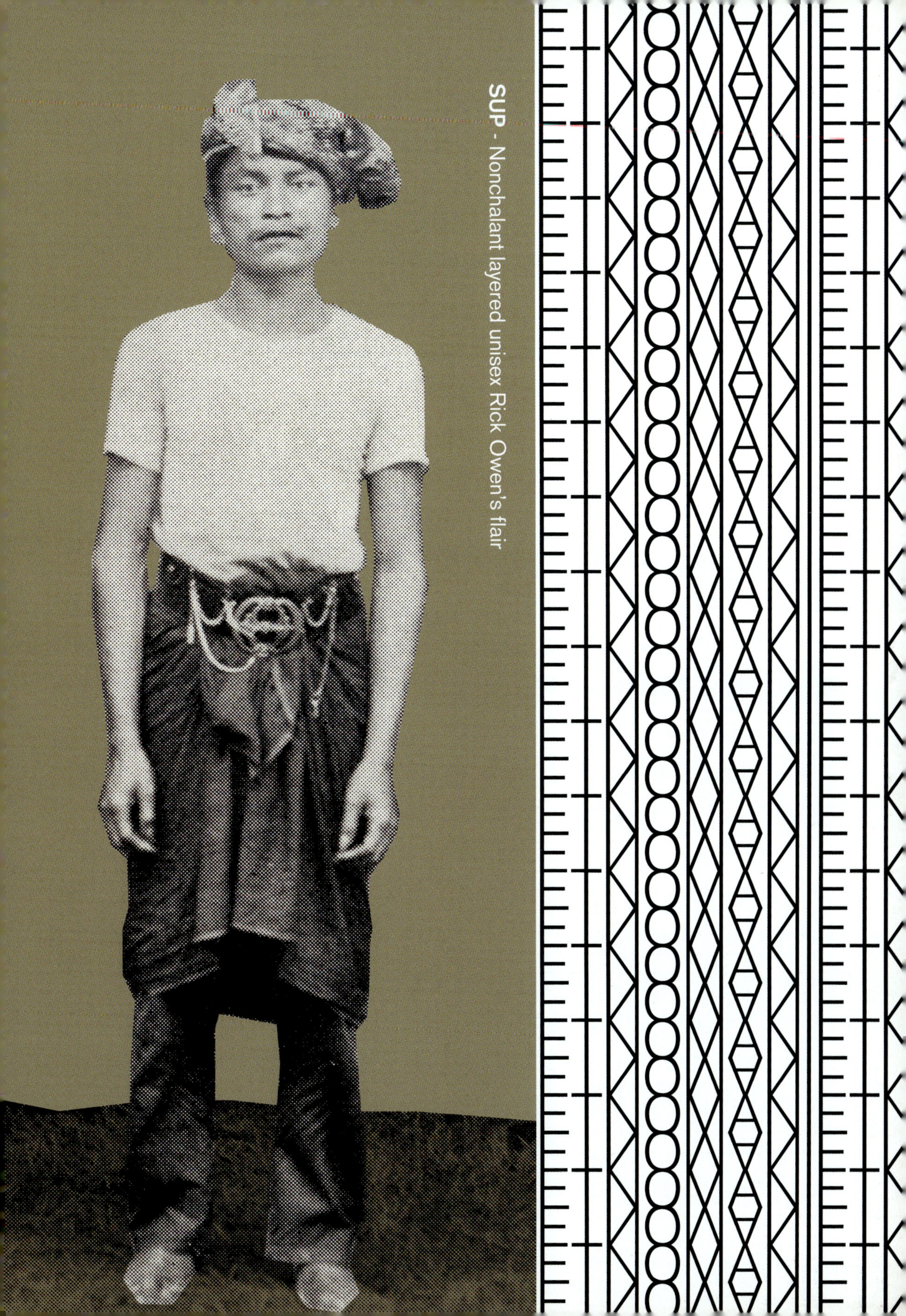

SUP - Nonchalant layered unisex Rick Owen's flair

With ETNOMANIE Ellie Uyttenbroek goes to the heart
of her extensive artistic career: as a 'style profiler' she
has been focusing on the relationship between subcultures and fashion for over 20 years. With an excellent
eye for style, she manages to spot recurring patterns,
visualize style profiles, and map out the tension
between trendsetters and trend followers. The strength
of her work lies in making visible the dynamics between
fashion and style: fashion seems to be tied to time and
rules, while style can be ascribed to active users who
personalize these rules of fashion.

Uyttenbroek's method of working is almost
anthropological. Starting off with an impartial eye, she
investigates diverse cultures and subcultures, and the
associated expressions of style. By juxtaposing various
people in style profiles, she makes remarkable patterns discernible. In this way, she provides insight into
the workings of style and renders the invisible visible.
Furthermore, her work makes it abundantly clear that
style crosses all generations and bridges various eras.
Therefore, it seems only logical that she would at some
point work with photographic documents amassed
for anthropological purposes, as her impeccable and
unprejudiced eye for fashion would invite the beholder
to look at these historical images from a different
perspective.

The portraits used for ETNOMANIE originate from

the World Collection, the ethnografic photo collection
of the Nederlands Fotomuseum, and were photographed in the late nineteenth and early twentieth
centuries. Merchants, missionaries and globetrotters
brought back these images from their voyages.
These photos were not so much produced for aesthetic
considerations, but functioned as evidence to show
people back home what 'the other' looked like. Every
portrait tells its own story, but nowadays the meanings
of those stories are subject to change. The shift in
the meaning of the photos demonstrates the period-
specific perspective on ethnocultures and reveals the
timelessness of style. With ETNOMANIE Uyttenbroek
is therefore offering a welcome new perspective that
highlights the invisible dynamism between culture and
style. This makes the collection quite topical.

As a graduate in fashion design from Rotterdam's
Academy of Art, Uyttenbroek knows all too well how
the past is a great source of inspiration. Fashion con-
stantly makes use of the ethnohistorical past as a
source of inspiration to reinvent itself. What makes
guest curation by a Fashion Stylist so relevant is the
aversion to traditionally established ideals of beauty.
The selection of images for ETNOMANIE actually
demonstrates that this constant quest for ideals of
beauty is of all time and that all of us are always search-
ing for opportunities to express our personal identity.

In her selection Uyttenbroek has therefore intentionally chosen portraits in which the 'object of study' stares directly into the camera, so the people in the photos acquire a certain form of autonomy. It is not entirely coincidental that the stylist is seeking out parallels with another form of photography that captures its subjects in a similar manner: contemporary Fashion Photography. By placing the anthropologically amassed material for ETNOMANIE in the aesthetic context of a fashion magazine, Uyttenbroek draws our attention to the artificial character of the original photos. In this way, she makes us aware of our habituation to such images, which points to our own self-created ideals of beauty. This then, makes the photos transcend their status as historical documents.

The result is highly staged and performative photos: posed portraits with consideration for individual expression, silhouette, outfit, body decoration, accessories and other fashionable details in which style predominates. It is not uncommon to see silhouettes that can be recognized directly in the modern-day street scene. With humour and incongruity, Uyttenbroek's idiosyncratic approach brings these style profiles to life, and allows us to reflect critically upon the ways in which we try to design and style ourselves.

The collaboration with designer Mary Pelders Vos has been essential in this regard: by literally colouring in and bringing the images to life, they metaphorically lend 'colour' to ETNOMANIE. The beholder is intentionally made aware of this image manipulation, so the images no longer only represent what they stood for in the past. Uyttenbroek thus prompts the beholder to reflect actively upon the constant quest for personal style. By employing cultural fields of tension and paradoxes she creates personal images that cause us to briefly enter into a direct relationship with the people in the photos. What effect does it have if something typically black in colour is abruptly supplanted with a cheerful yellow? Why is it interesting to know that crossdressers are an age-old phenomenon? What feeling is prompted by the clothing in a portrait of a man who recently con-verted to Christianity?

The eclectic mix of styles, clothing and people combine into an aesthetic whole, while it is primarily the multitude and diversity of the portraits that emphasizes the universality of humankind. This helps to temporarily lift the distinction between the self and the other, the beholder and the portrait. Now, the beholder becomes part of the work. Moved by a story, a personal connec-tion or a visually coloured-in element, the works have become style profiles that arouse feelings and emotions that can be of every age and of anyone.

Charlotte Dwyer

Charlotte Dwyer is fashion researcher and explores the relationship between contemporary culture and fashion. She critically analyses the presence of fashion in visual media and currently lectures as a media and culture teacher at the University Utrecht and the Amsterdam Fashion Institute.

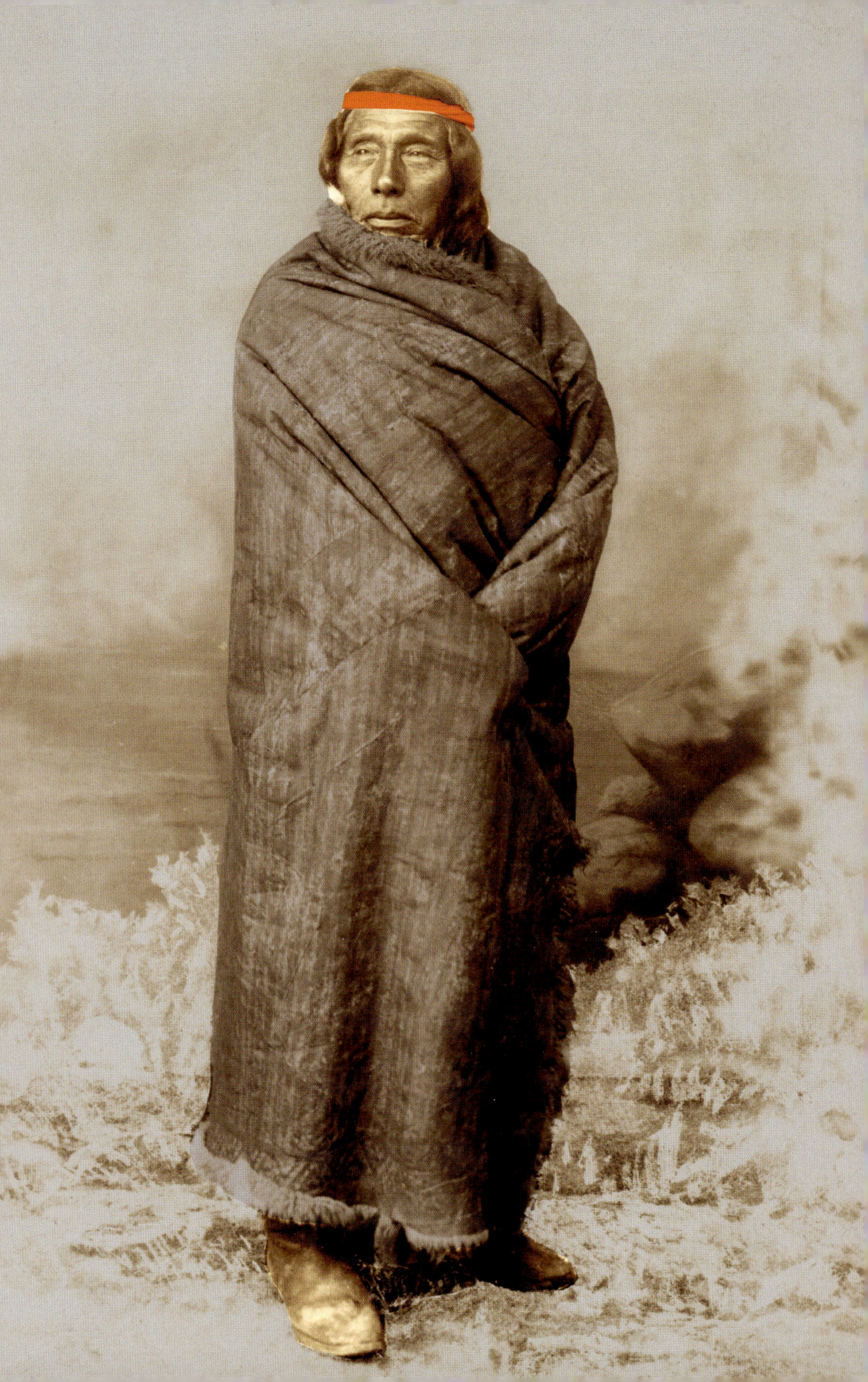

DUVET - All condition gear - grand foulard shelter look - A Martin Margiela 1999 intuition

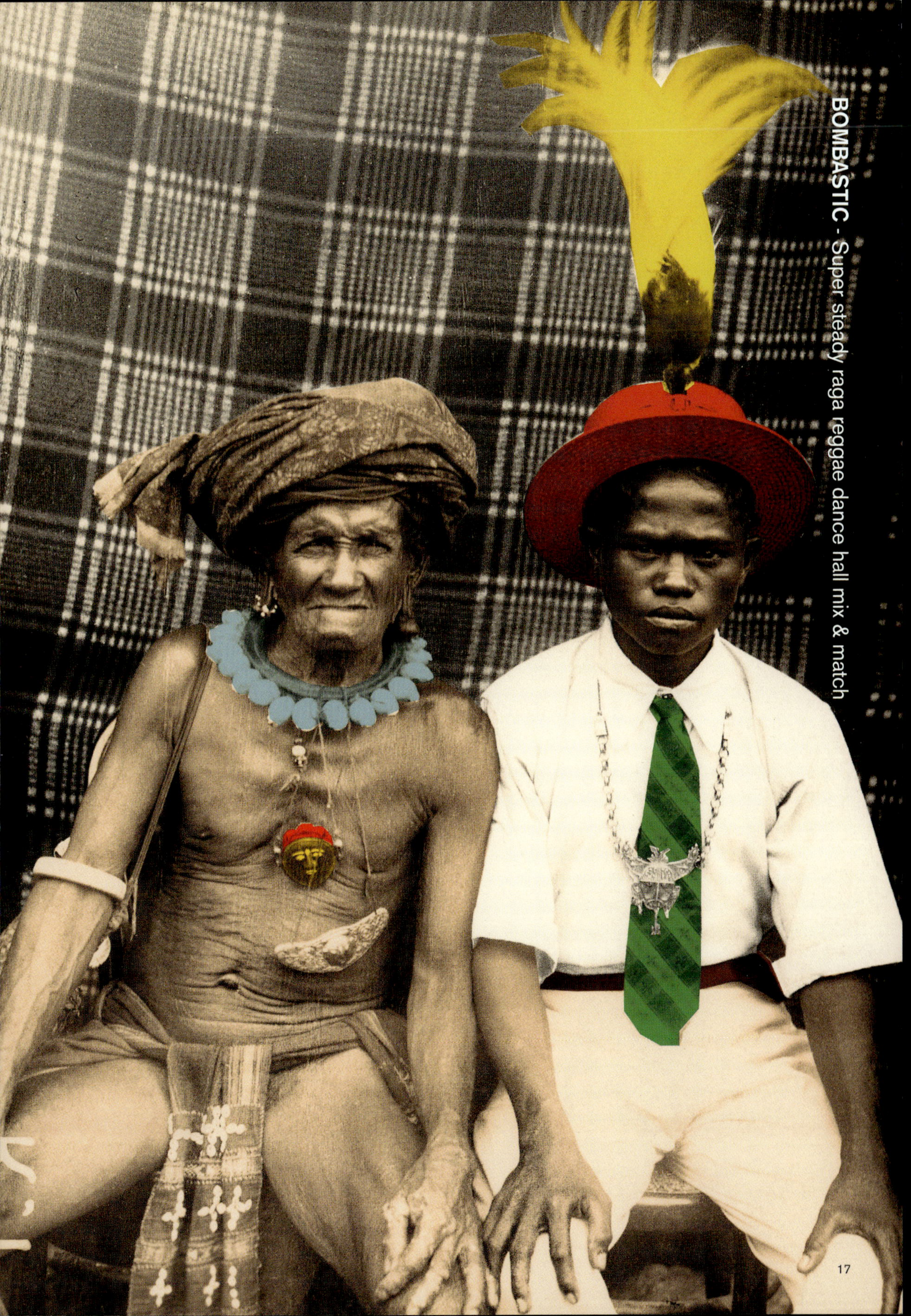

BOMBASTIC - Super steady raga reggae dance hall mix & match
17

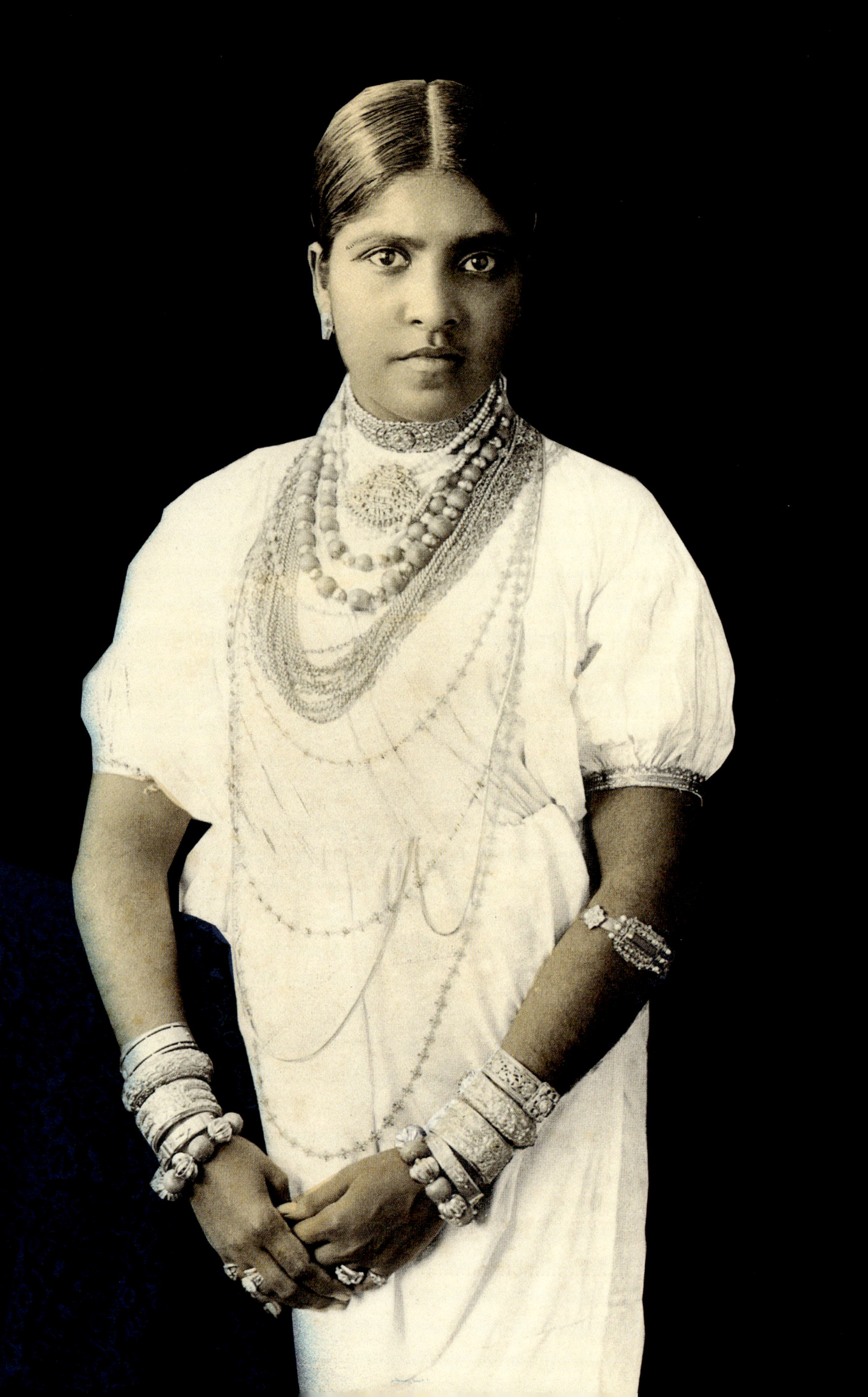

SRI SRI - Bagwan-enlightened Westerners introduced 'more is more' Indian silver jewellery in the 1970s

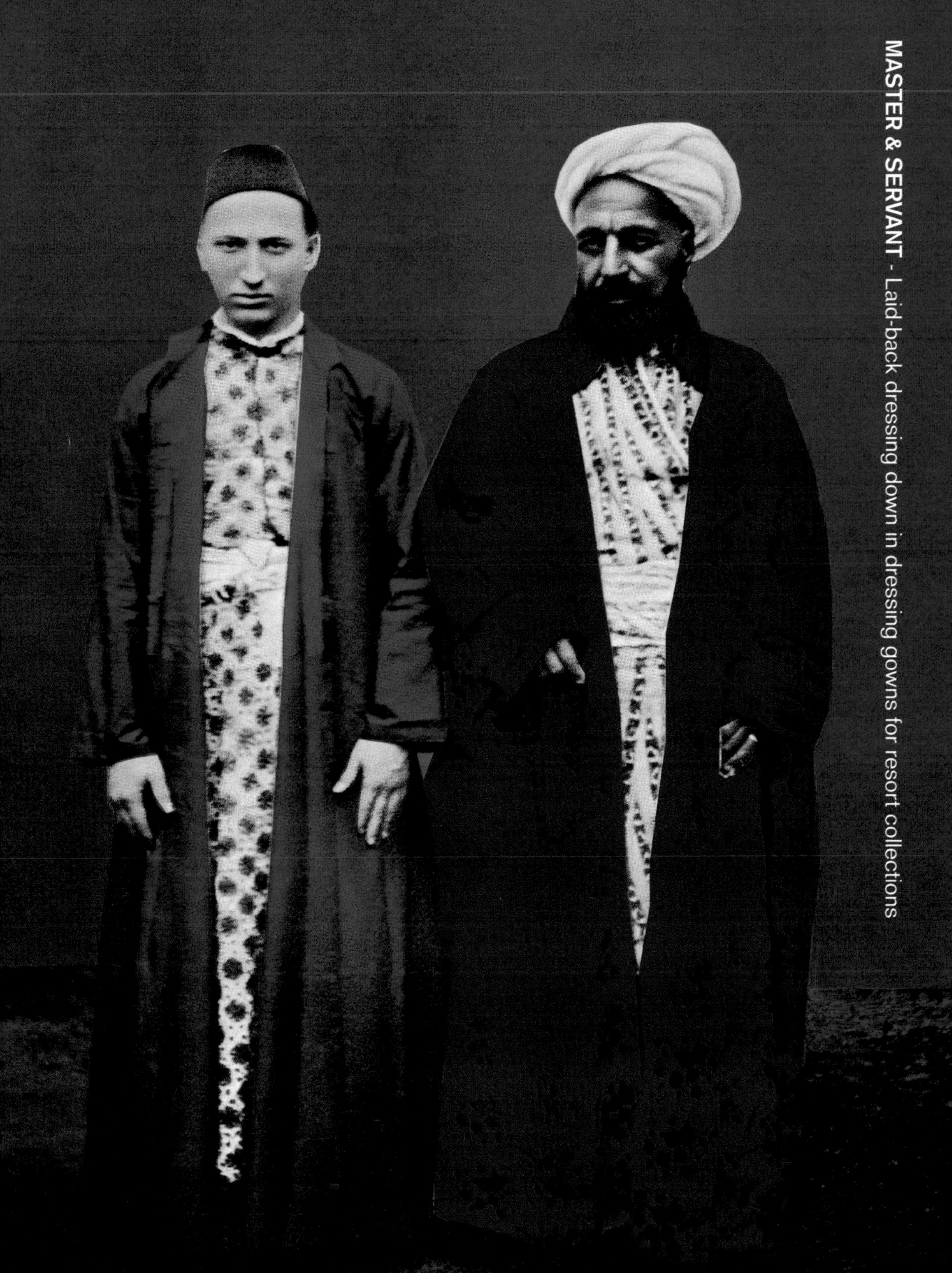

20

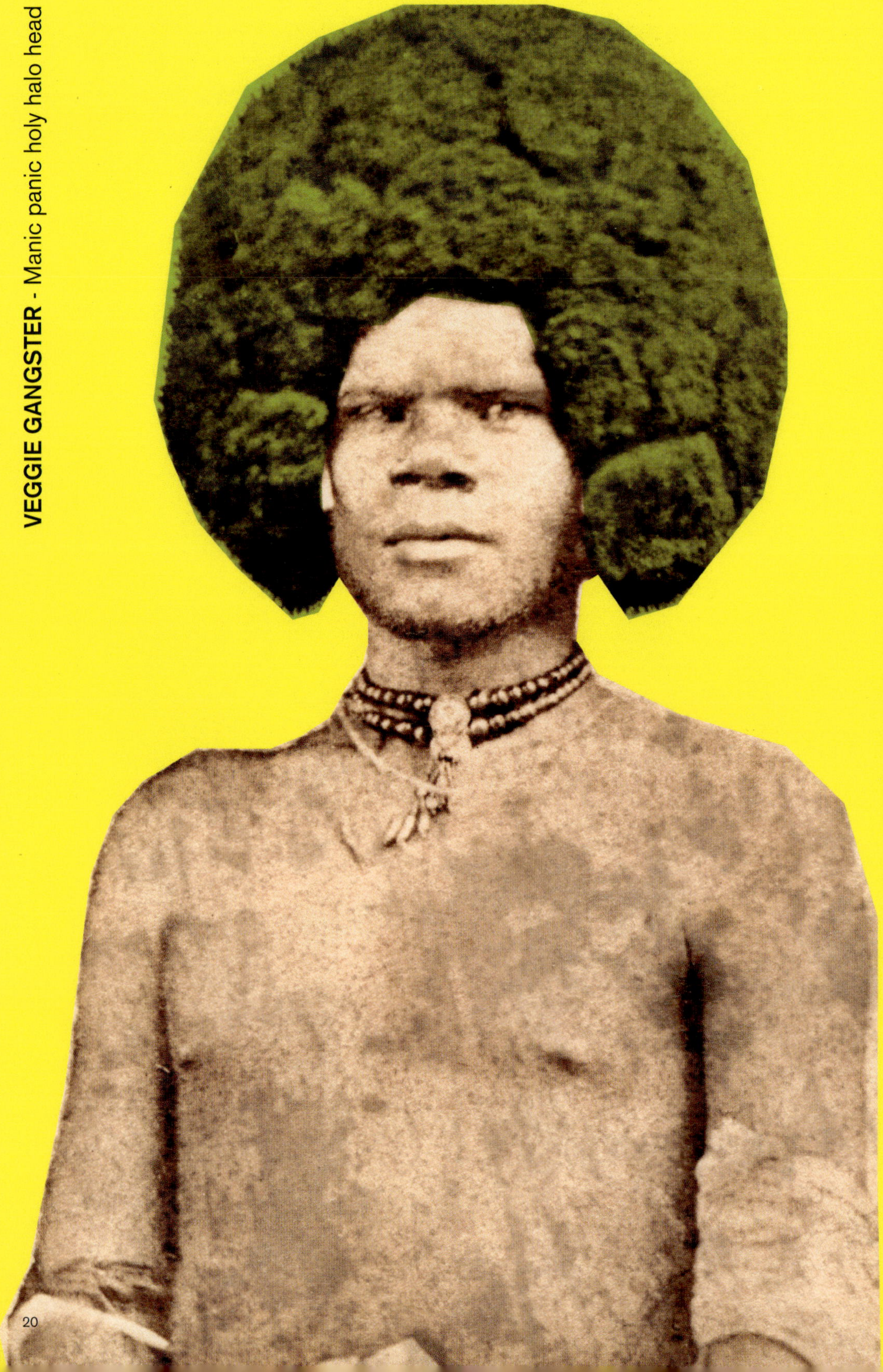

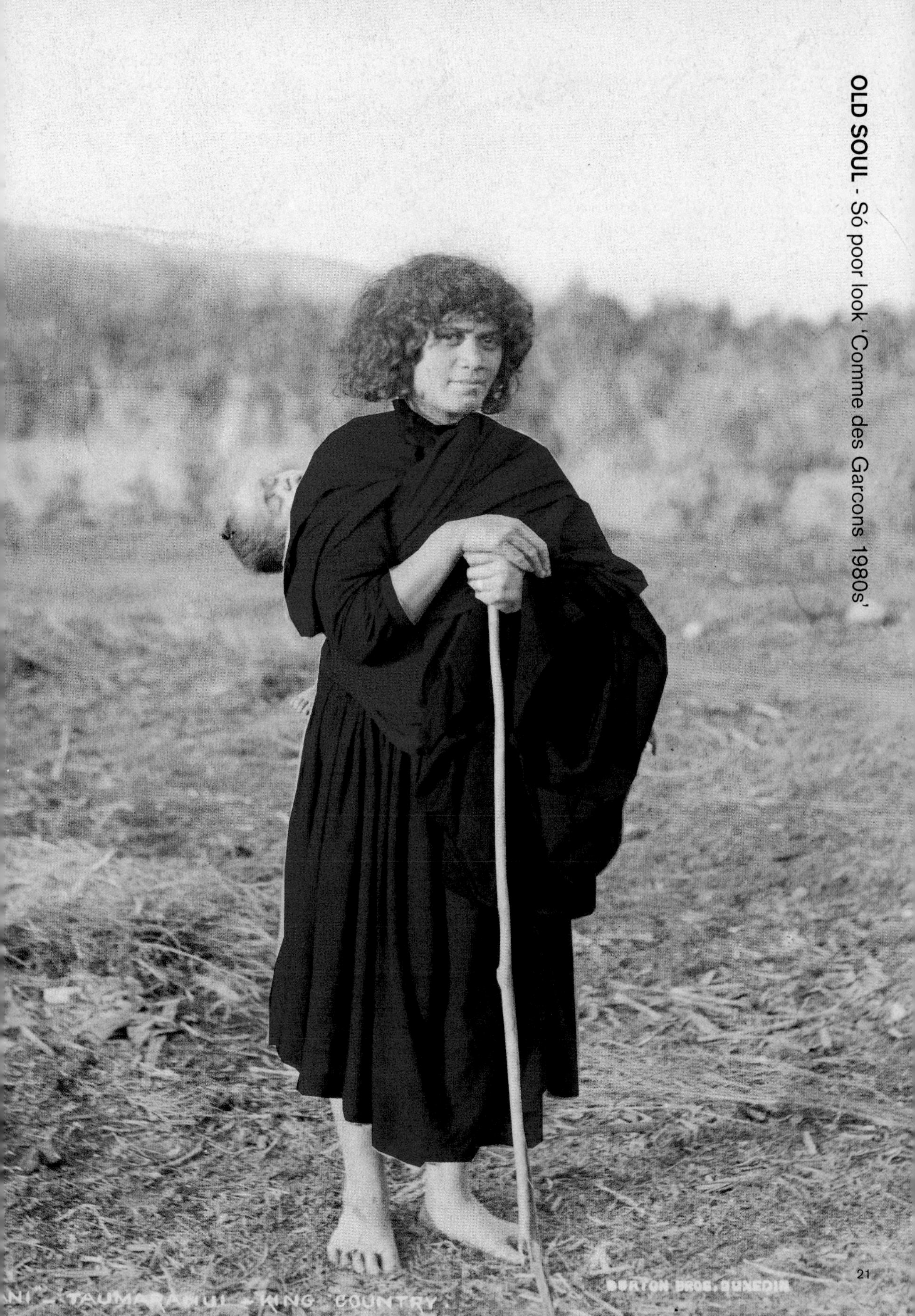

BURTON BROS. DUNEDIN
NI · TAUMARANUI · KING · COUNTRY ·

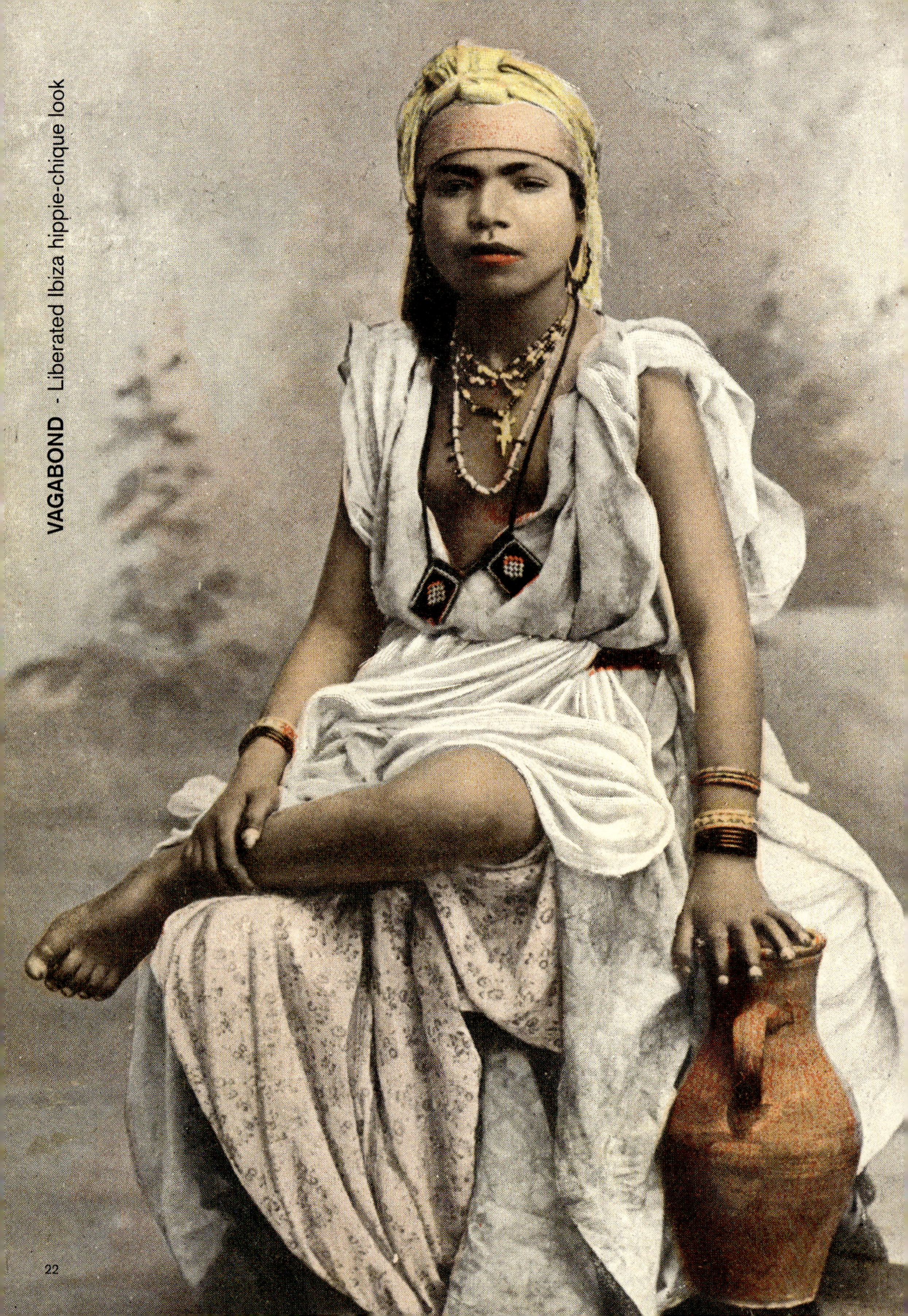

22

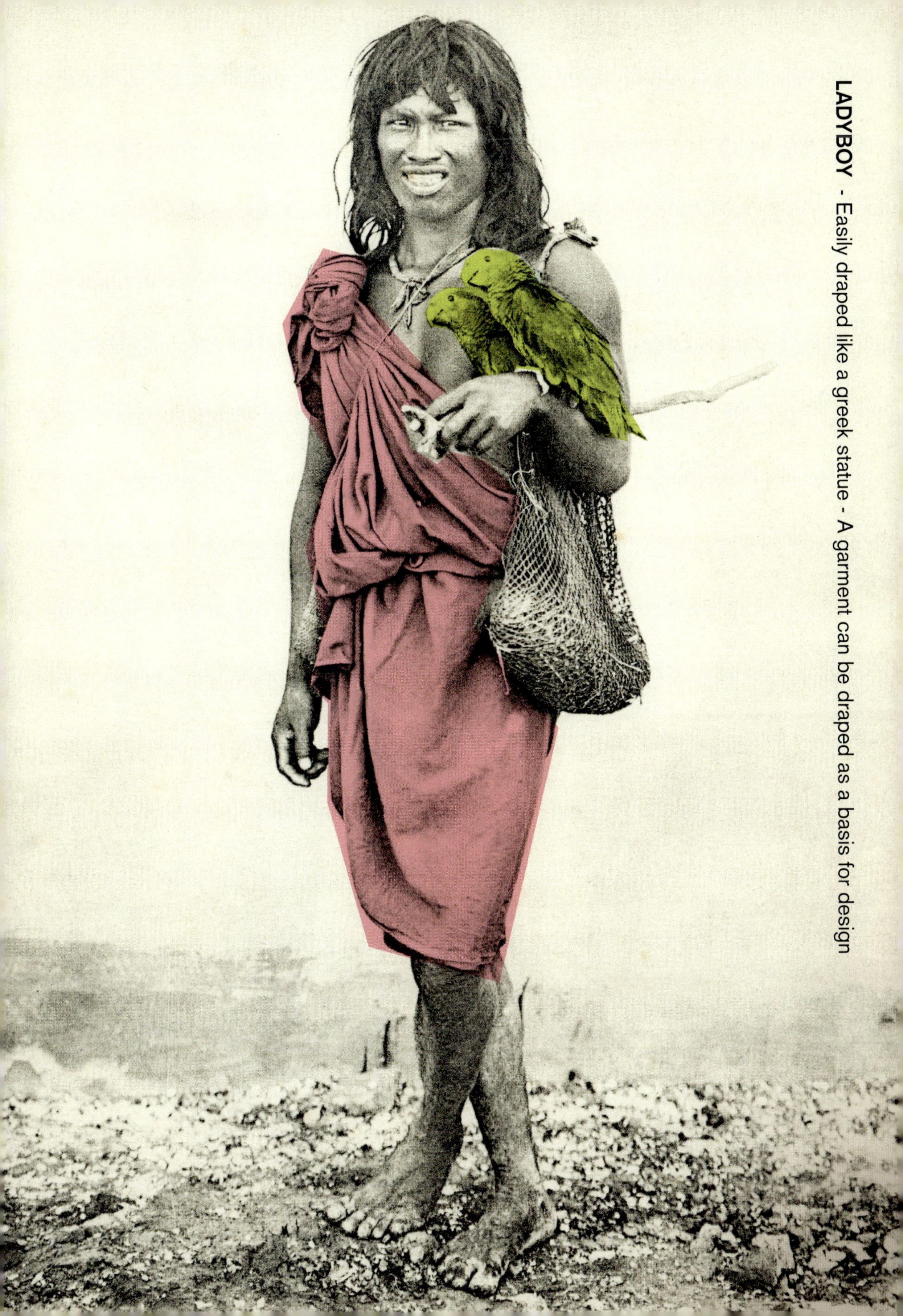

LADYBOY - Easily draped like a greek statue - A garment can be draped as a basis for design

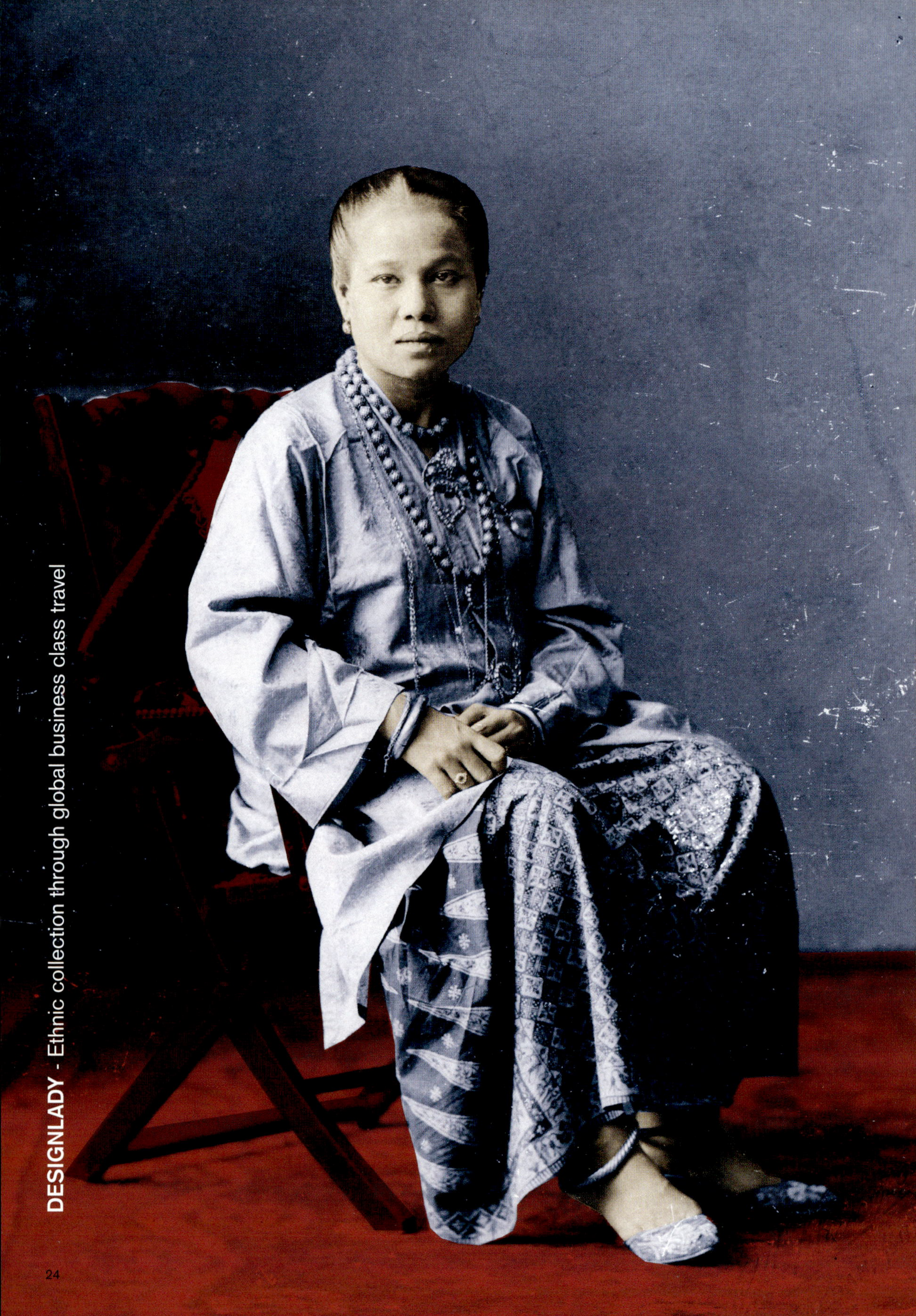
DESIGNLADY - Ethnic collection through global business class travel

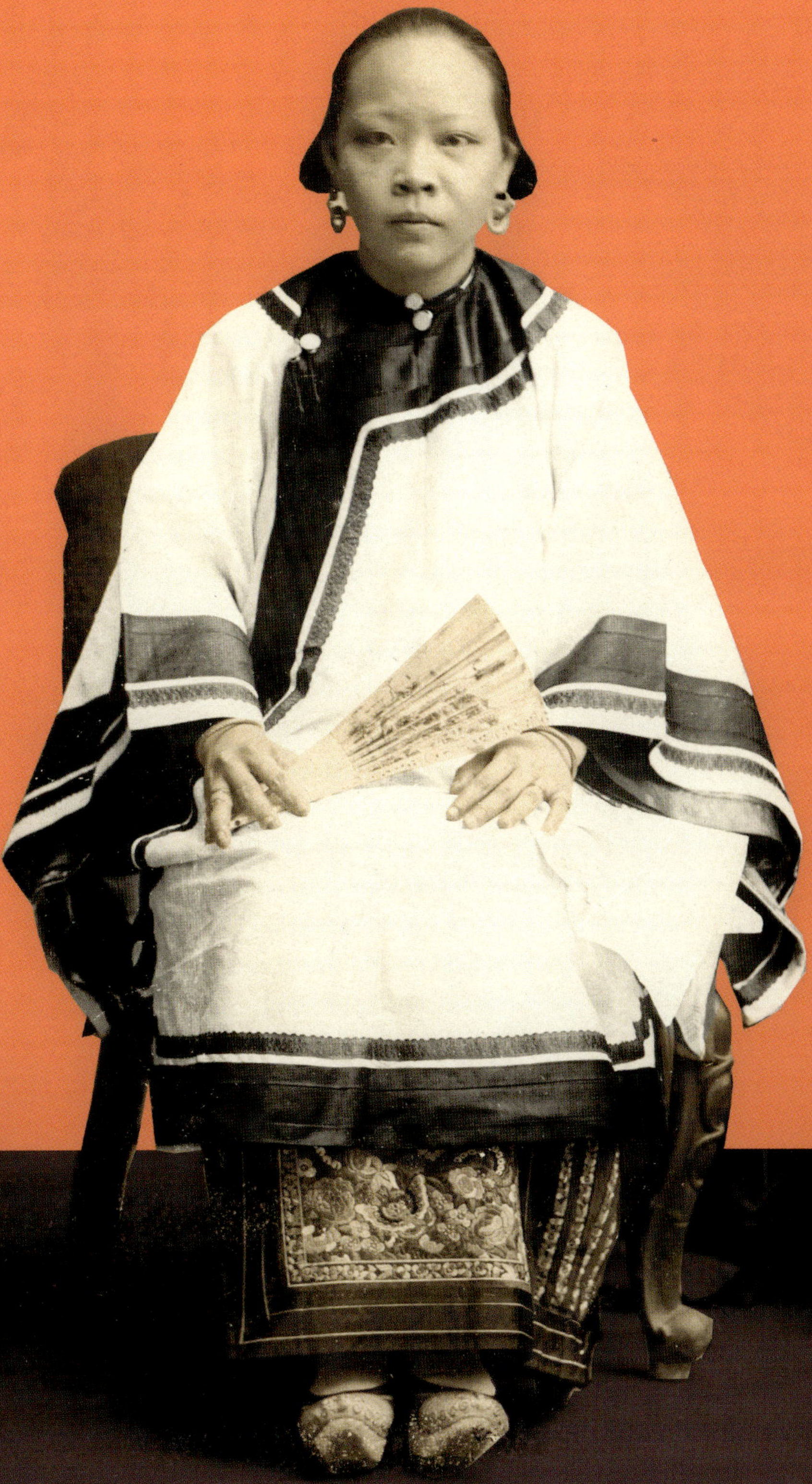

MADAM BUTTERFLY - Tea time & Tai Chi tranquility

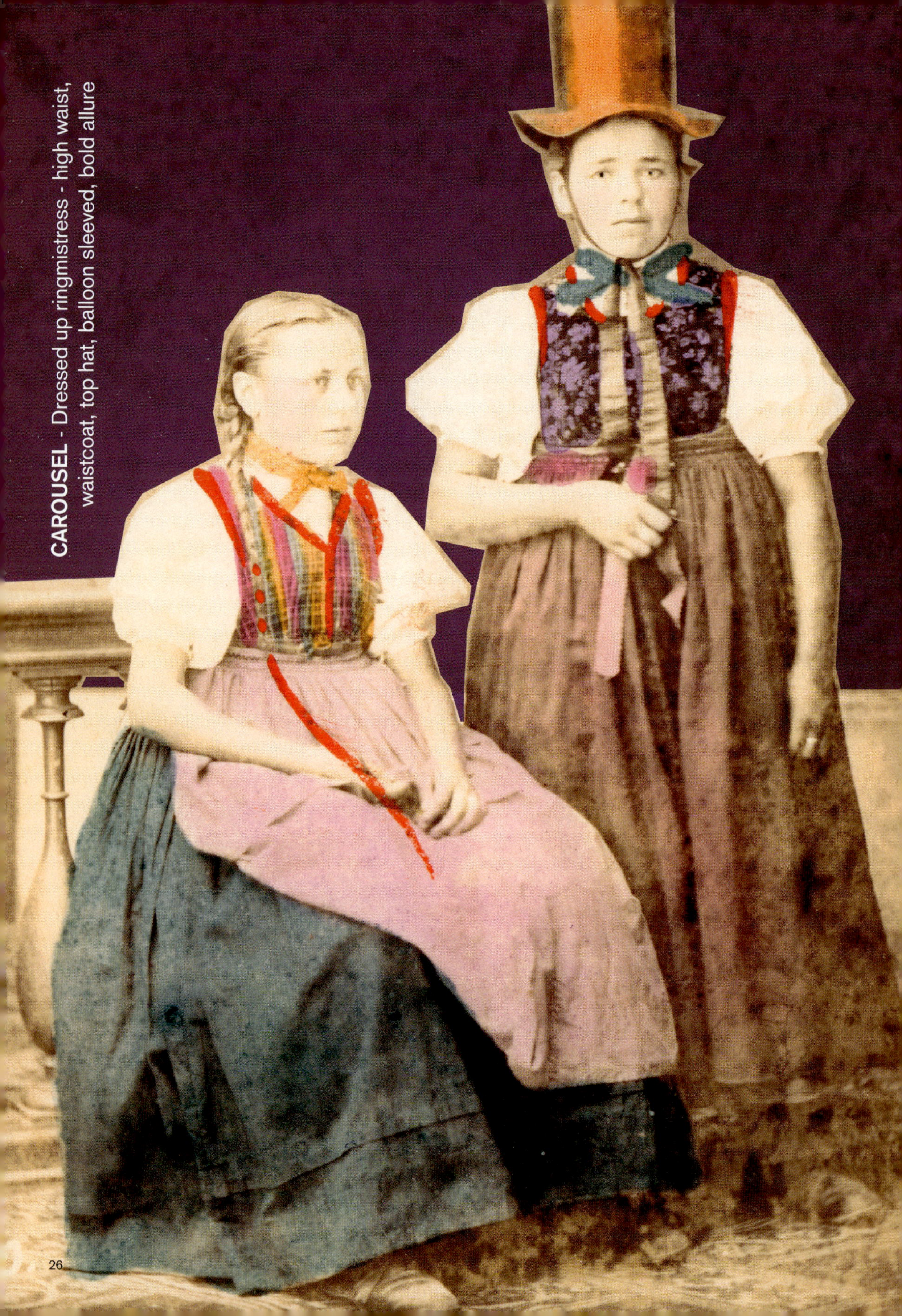

CAROUSEL - Dressed up ringmistress - high waist, waistcoat, top hat, balloon sleeved, bold allure

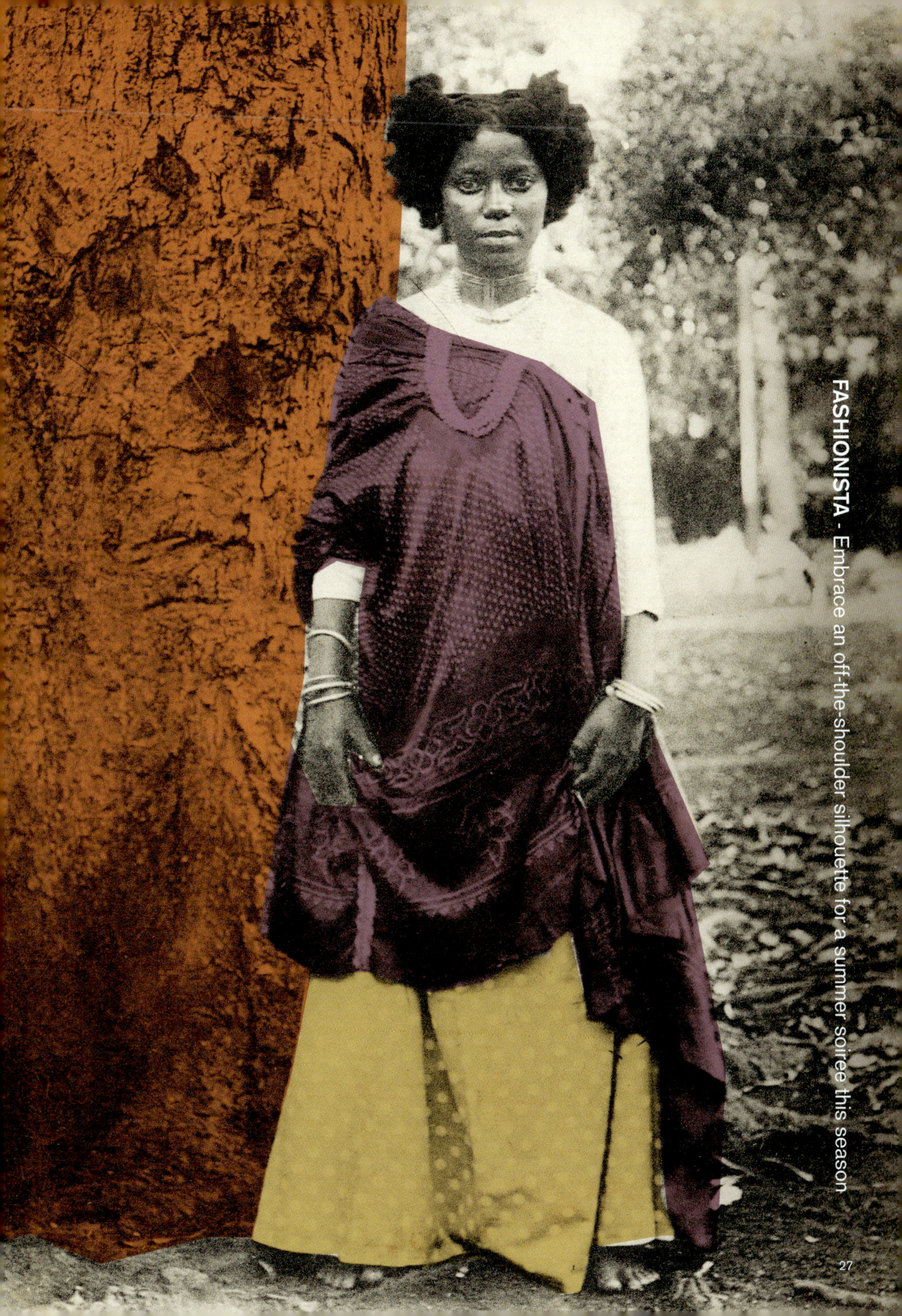

FASHIONISTA - Embrace an off-the-shoulder silhouette for a summer soiree this season

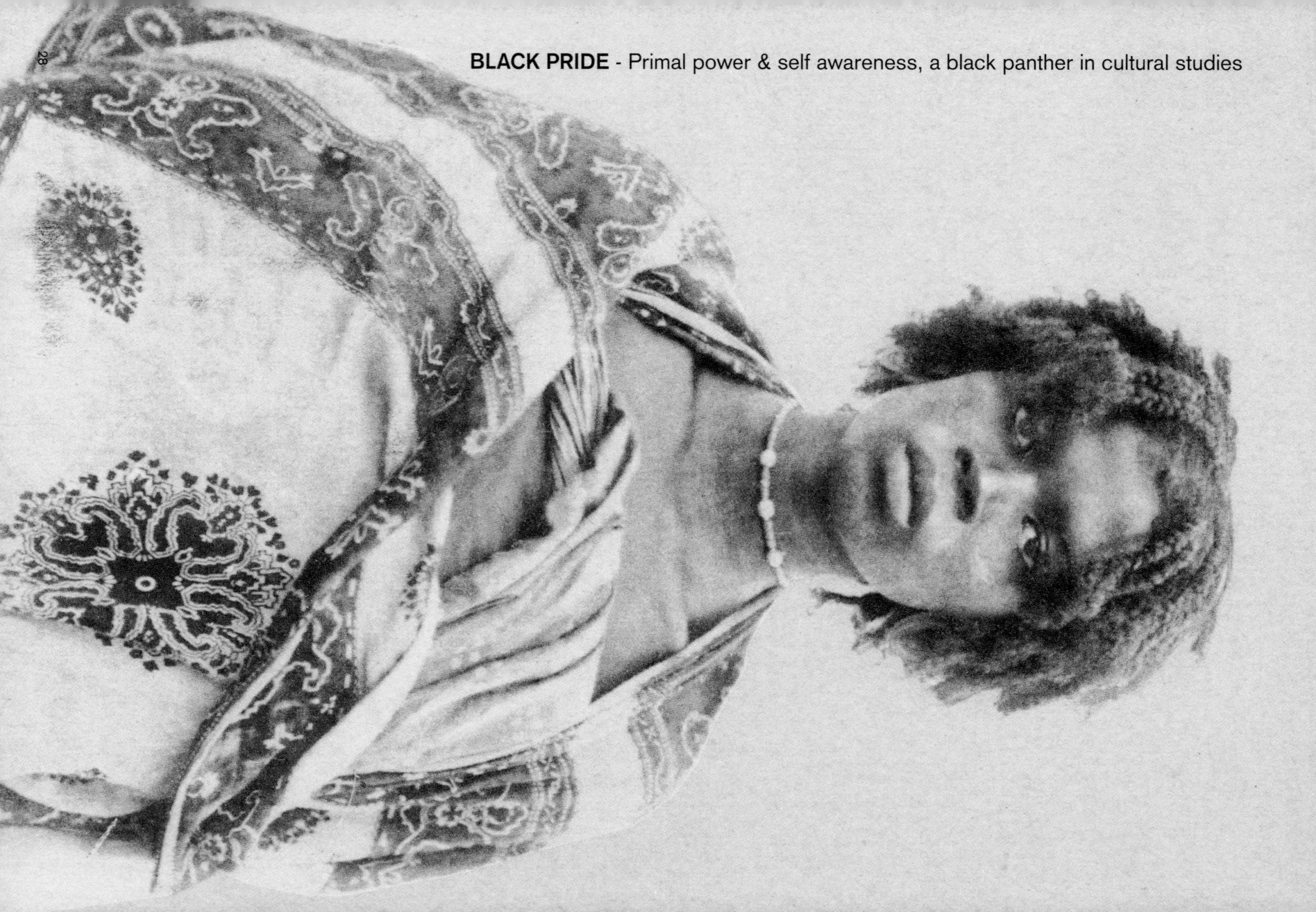

BLACK PRIDE - Primal power & self awareness, a black panther in cultural studies

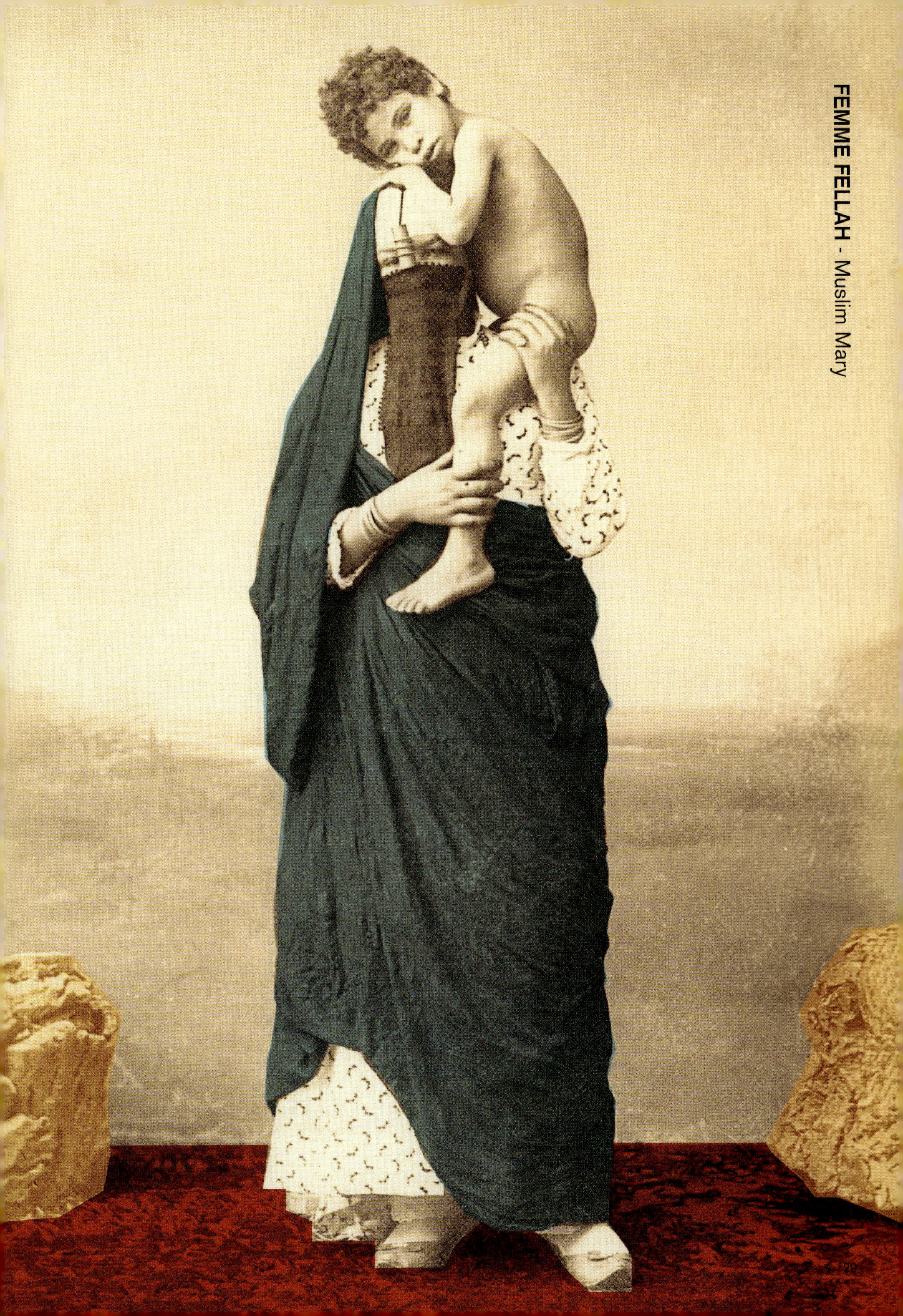

FEMME FELLAH - *Muslim Mary*

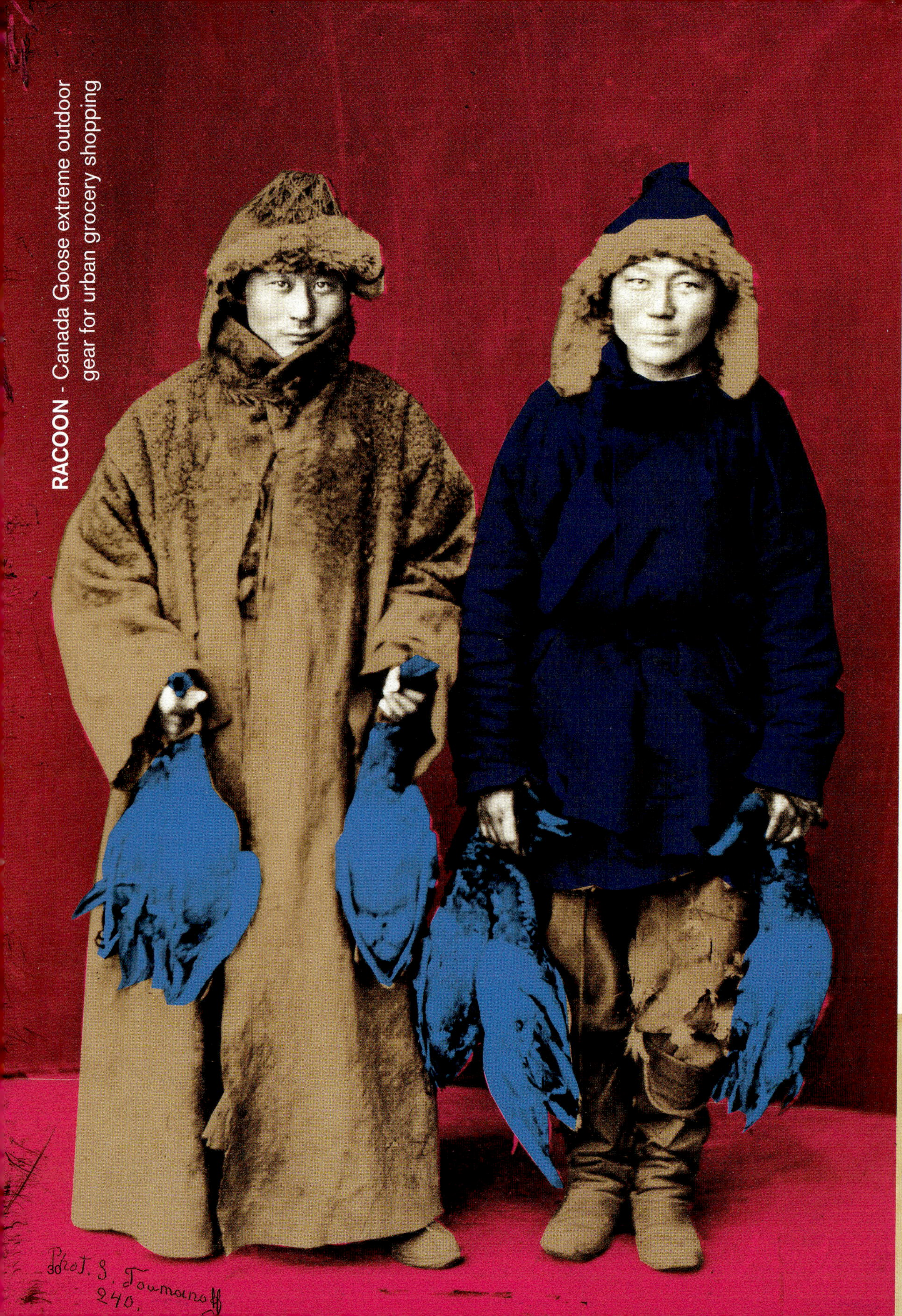

RACOON - Canada Goose extreme outdoor gear for urban grocery shopping

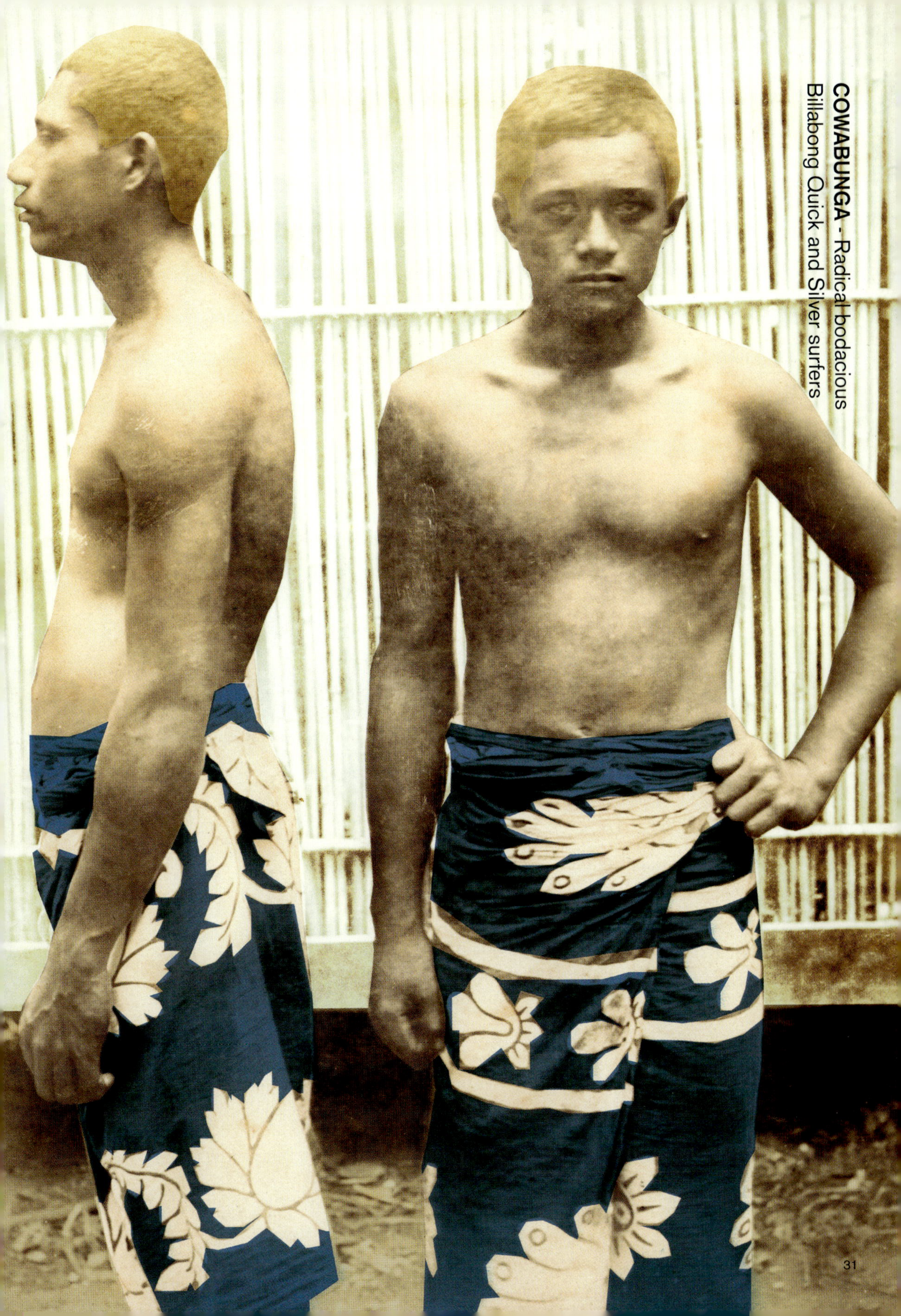

COWABUNGA - Radical bodacious
Billabong Quick and Silver surfers

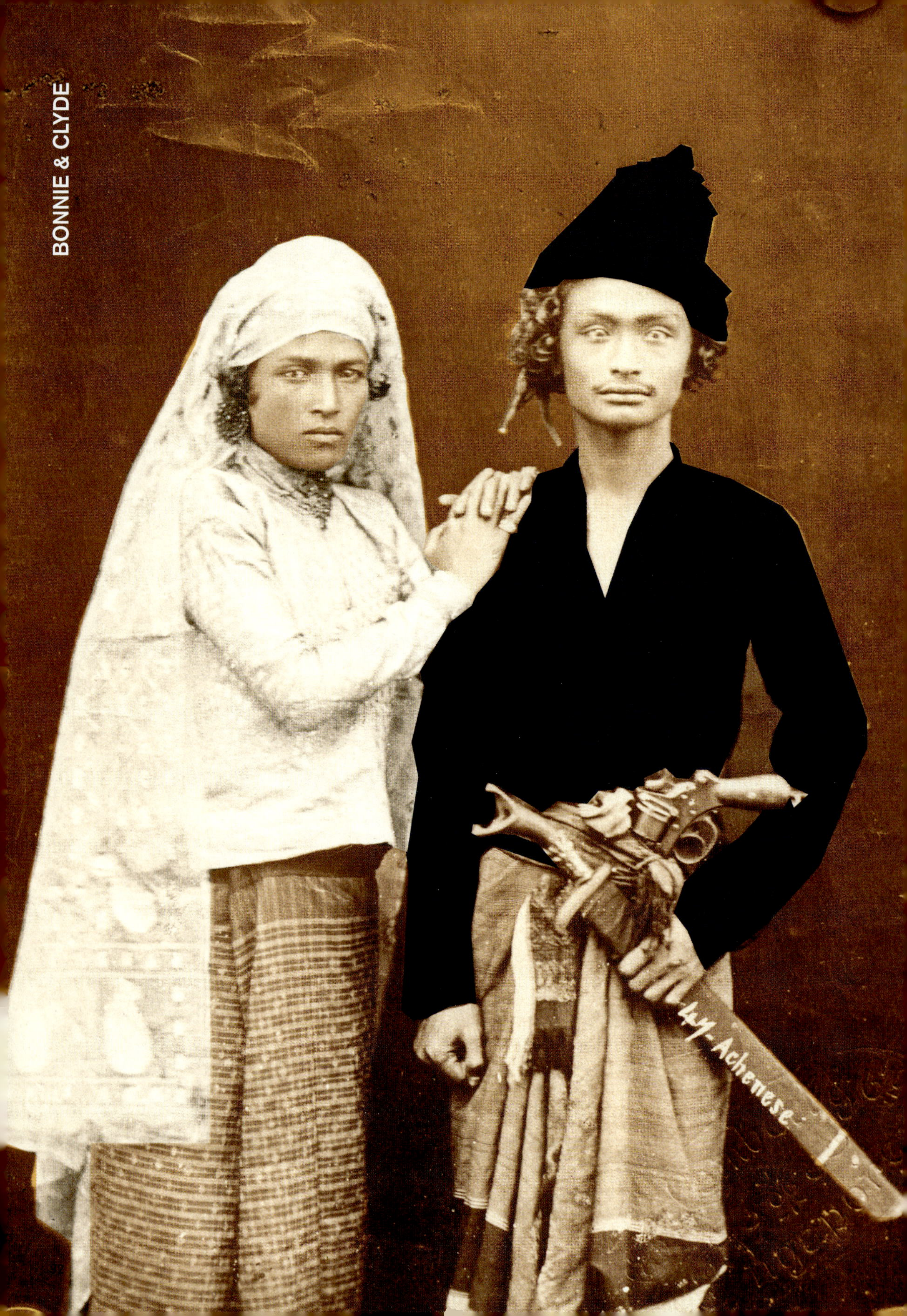
BONNIE & CLYDE
Achenese

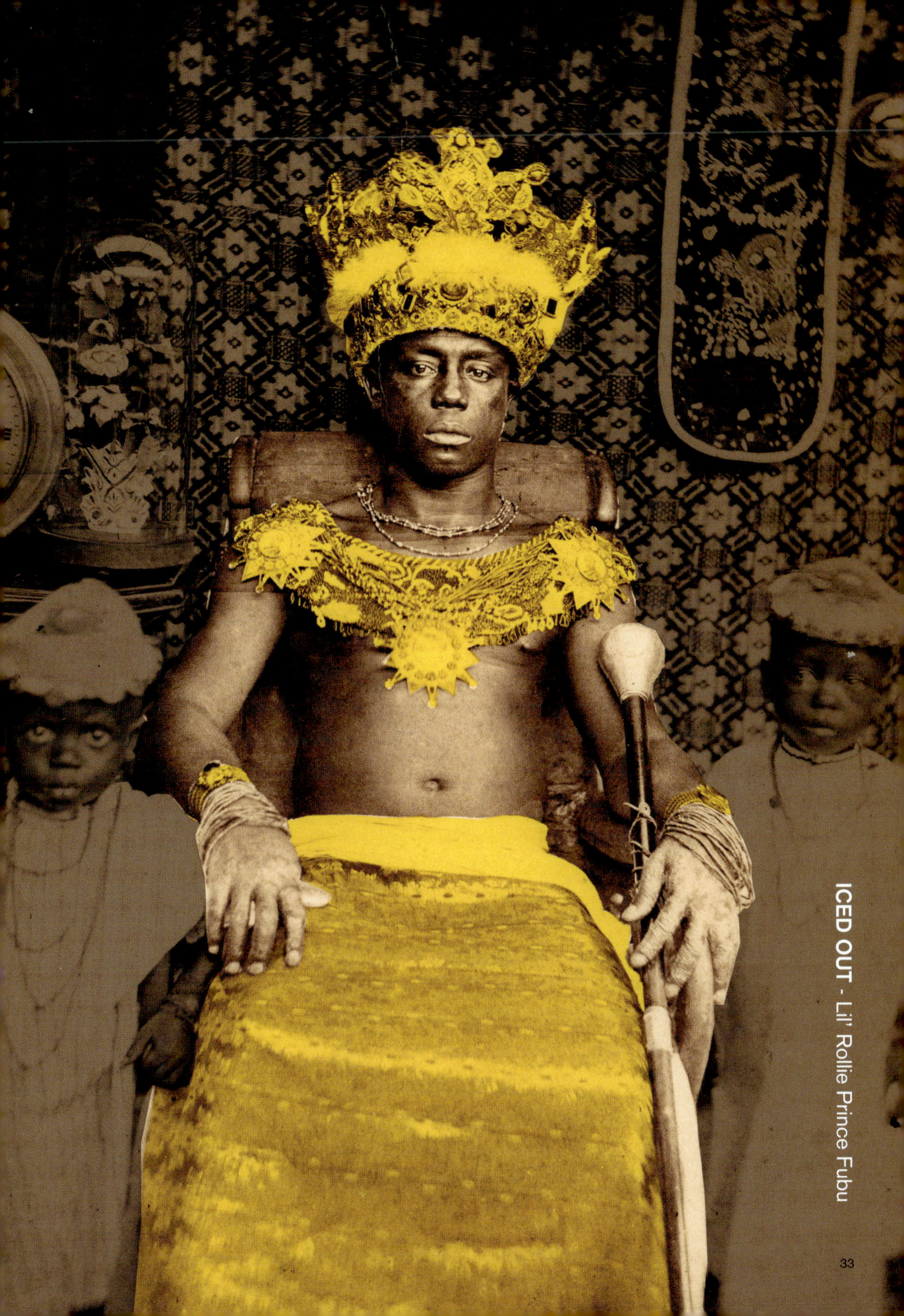

ICED OUT - Lil' Rollie Prince Fubu

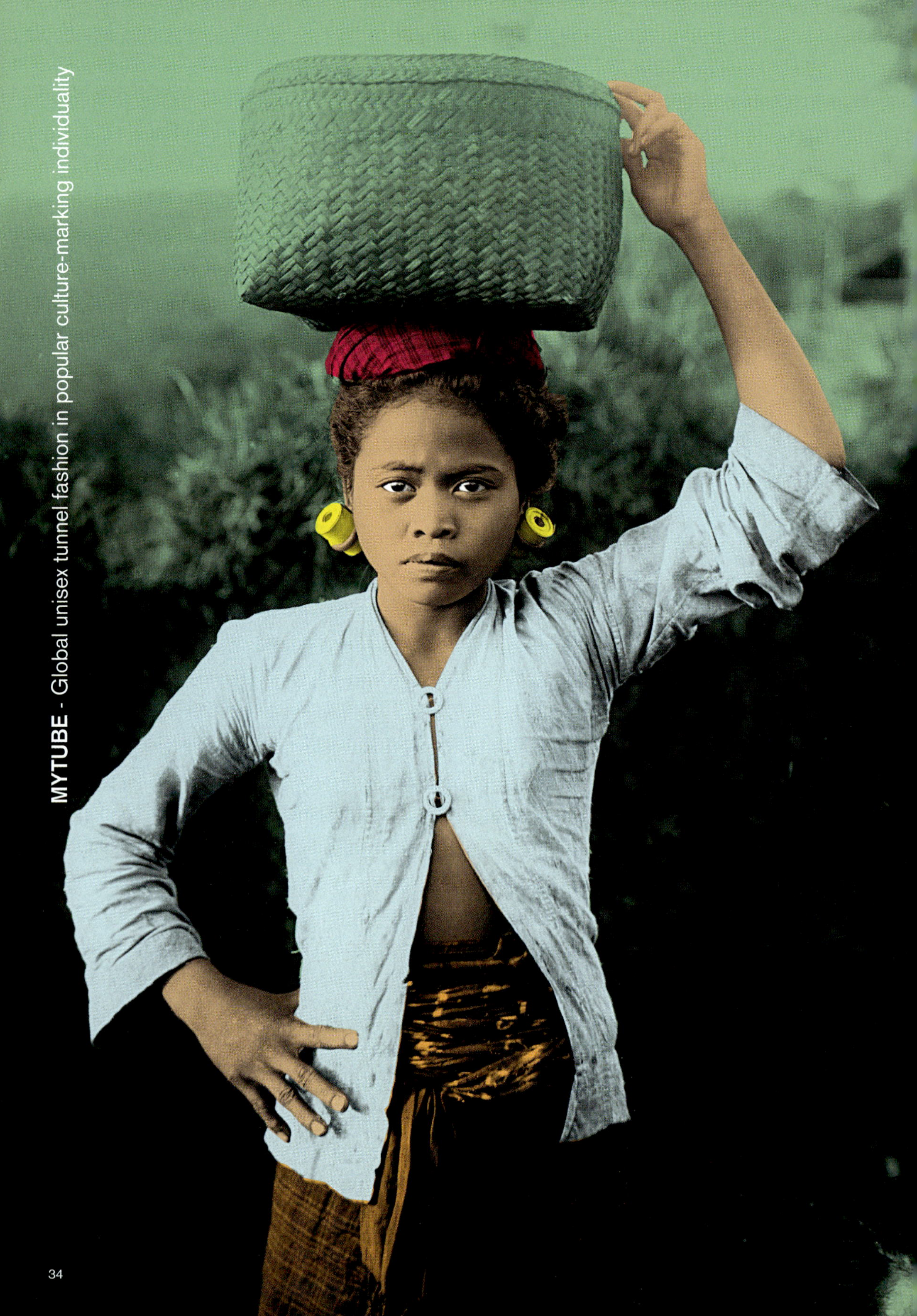

MYTUBE - Global unisex tunnel fashion in popular culture-marking individuality

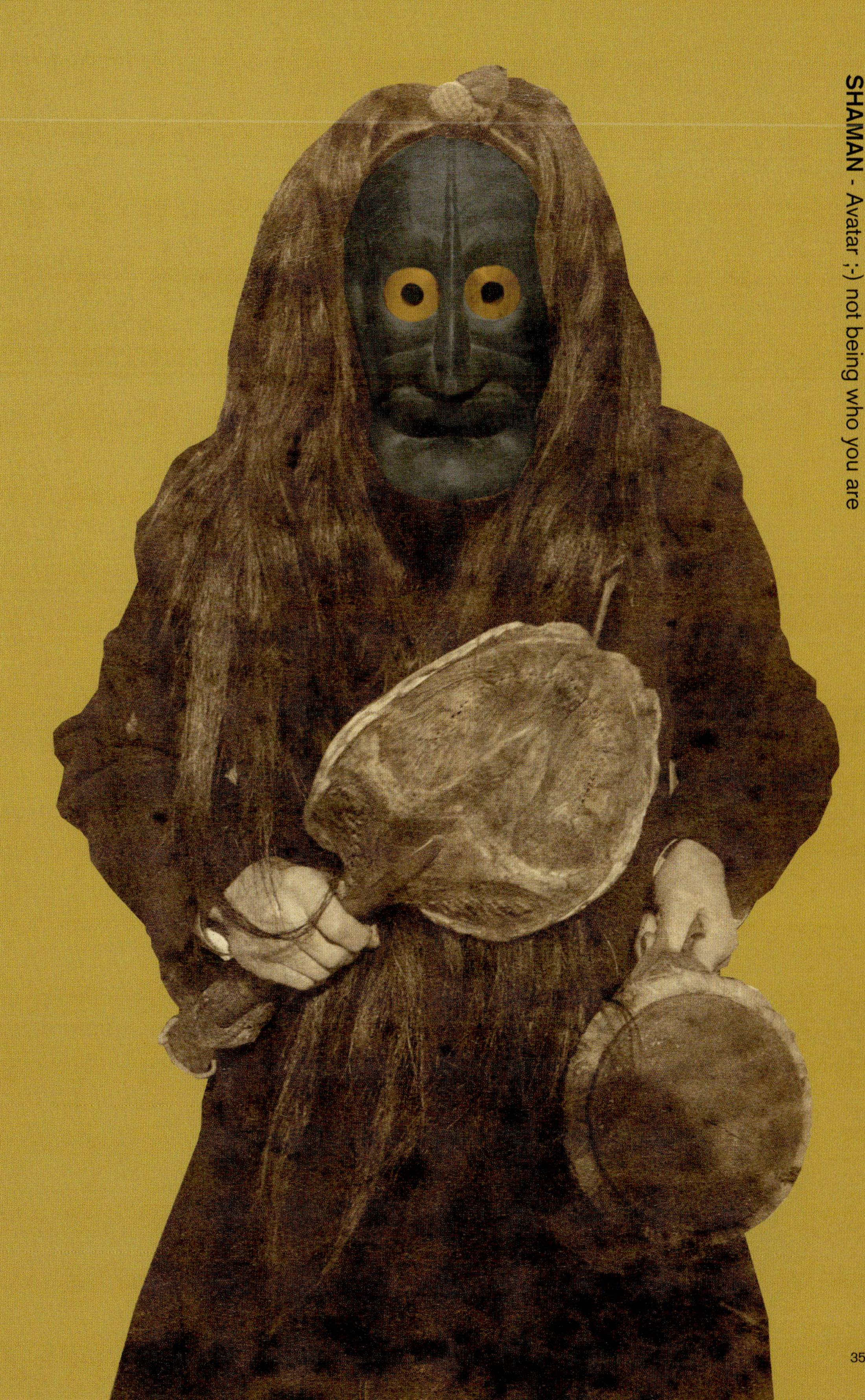

35

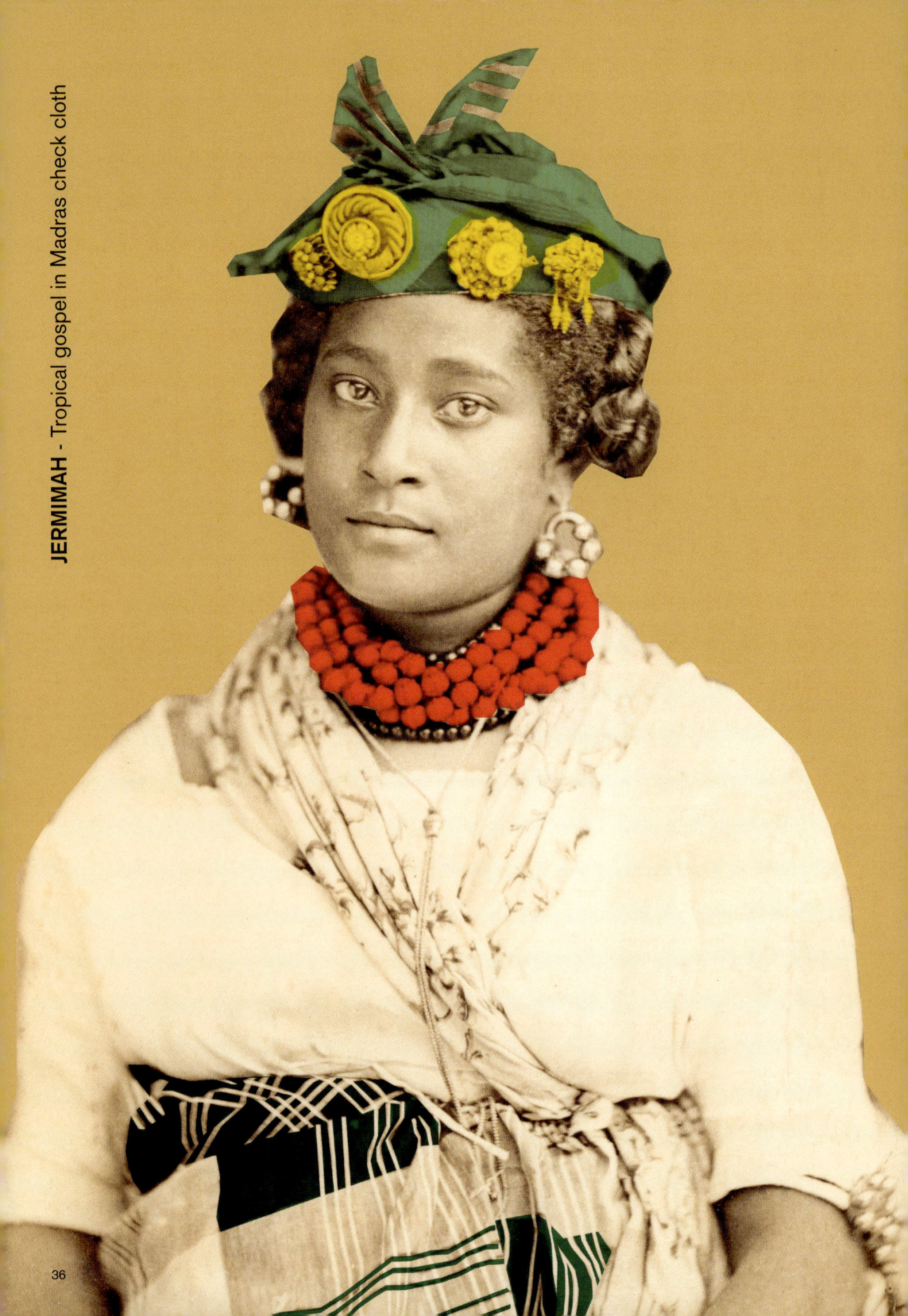

JERMIMAH - Tropical gospel in Madras check cloth

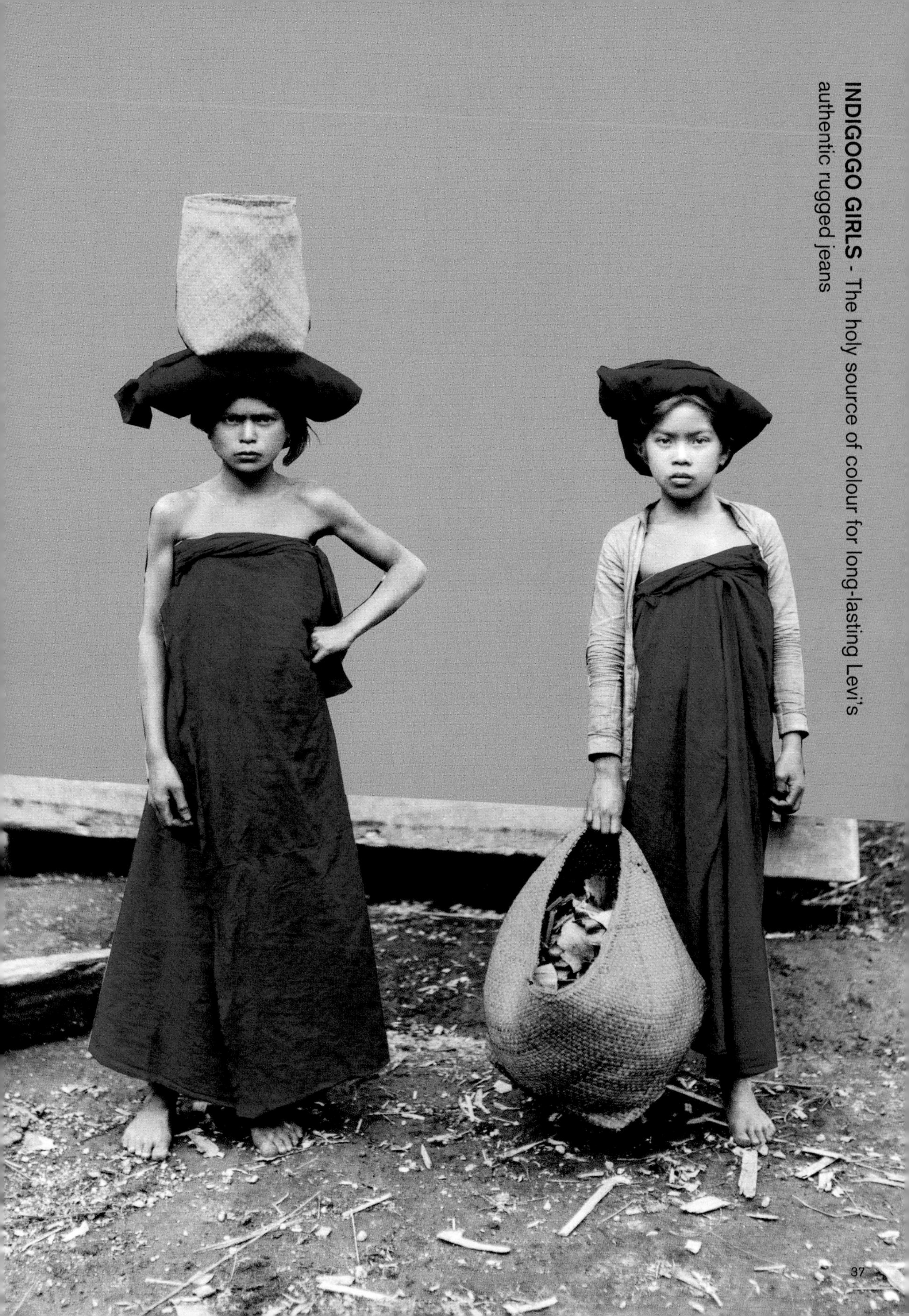

INDIGOGO GIRLS - The holy source of colour for long-lasting Levi's authentic rugged jeans

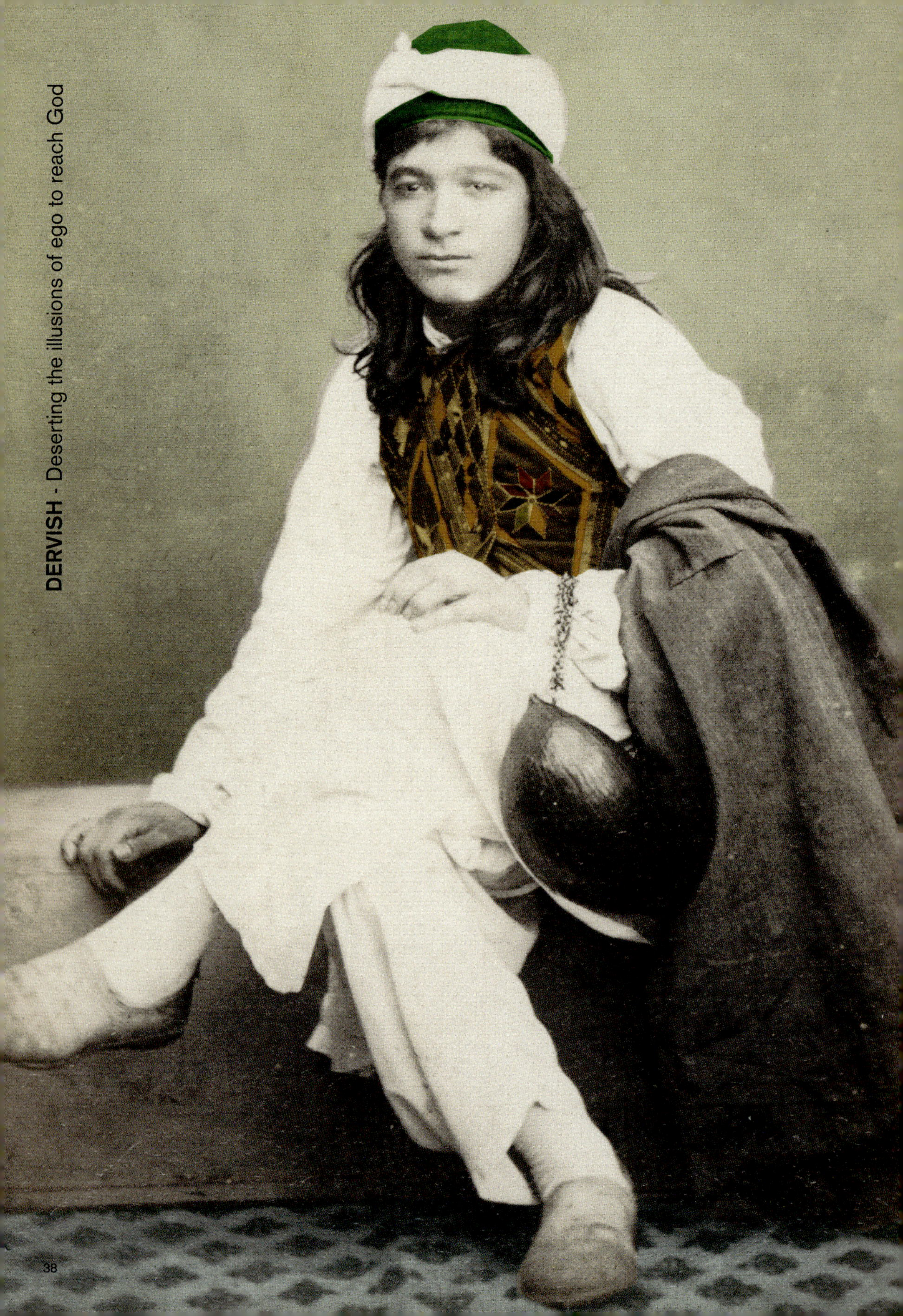

DERVISH - Deserting the illusions of ego to reach God

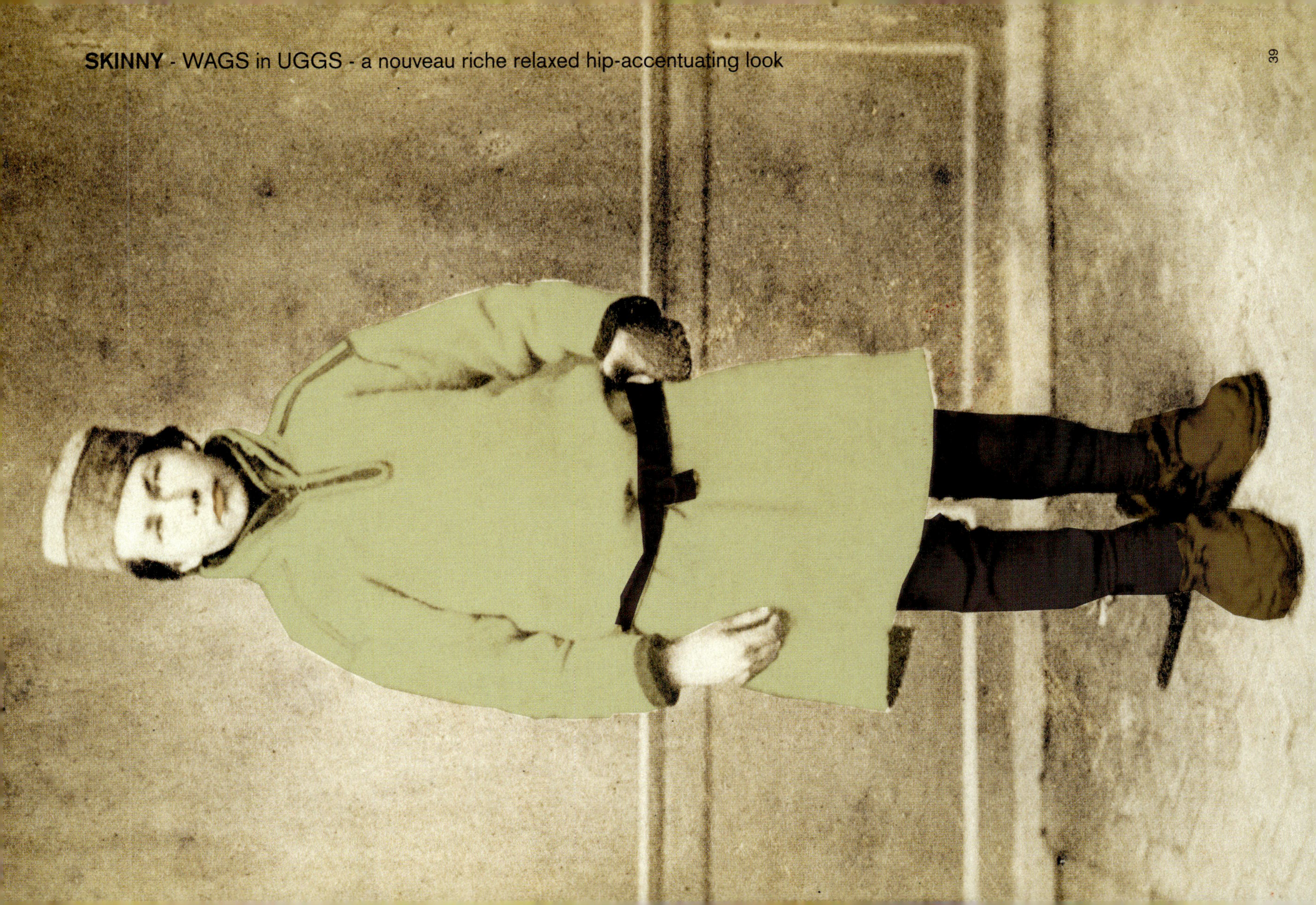

SKINNY - WAGS in UGGS - a nouveau riche relaxed hip-accentuating look

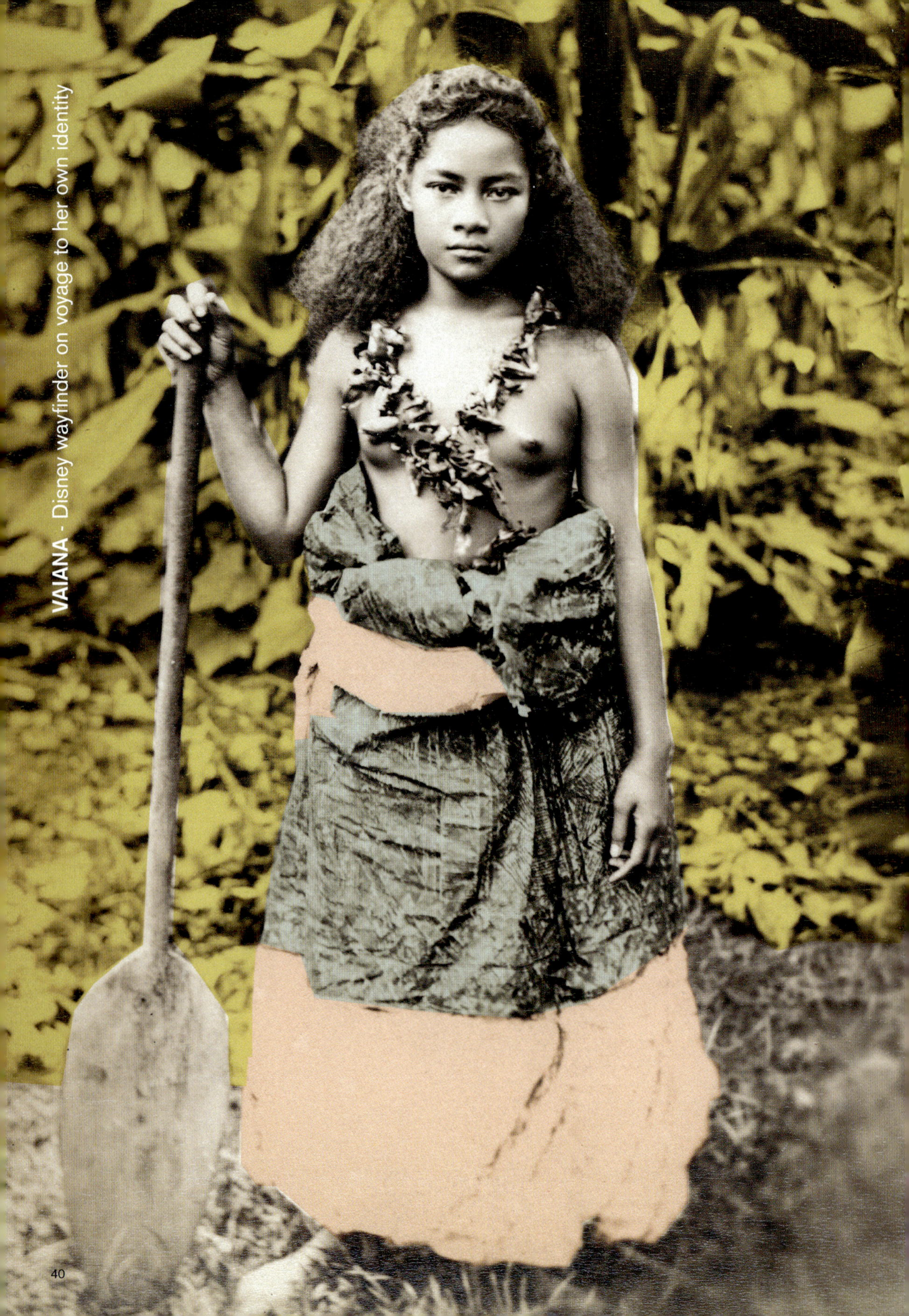
VAIANA - Disney wayfinder on voyage to her own identity

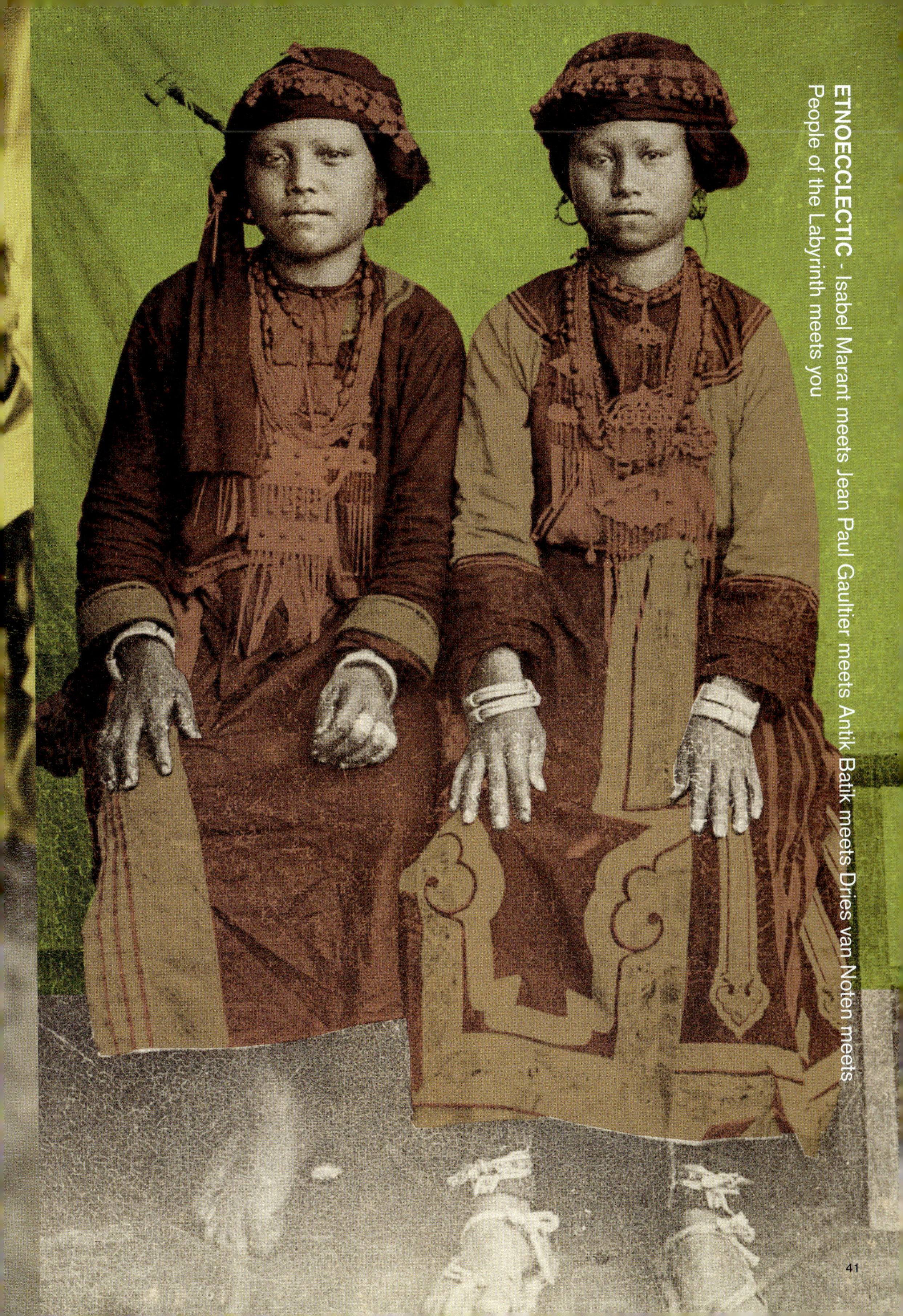
ETNOECCLECTIC - Isabel Marant meets Jean Paul Gaultier meets Antik Batik meets Dries van Noten meets
People of the Labyrinth meets you

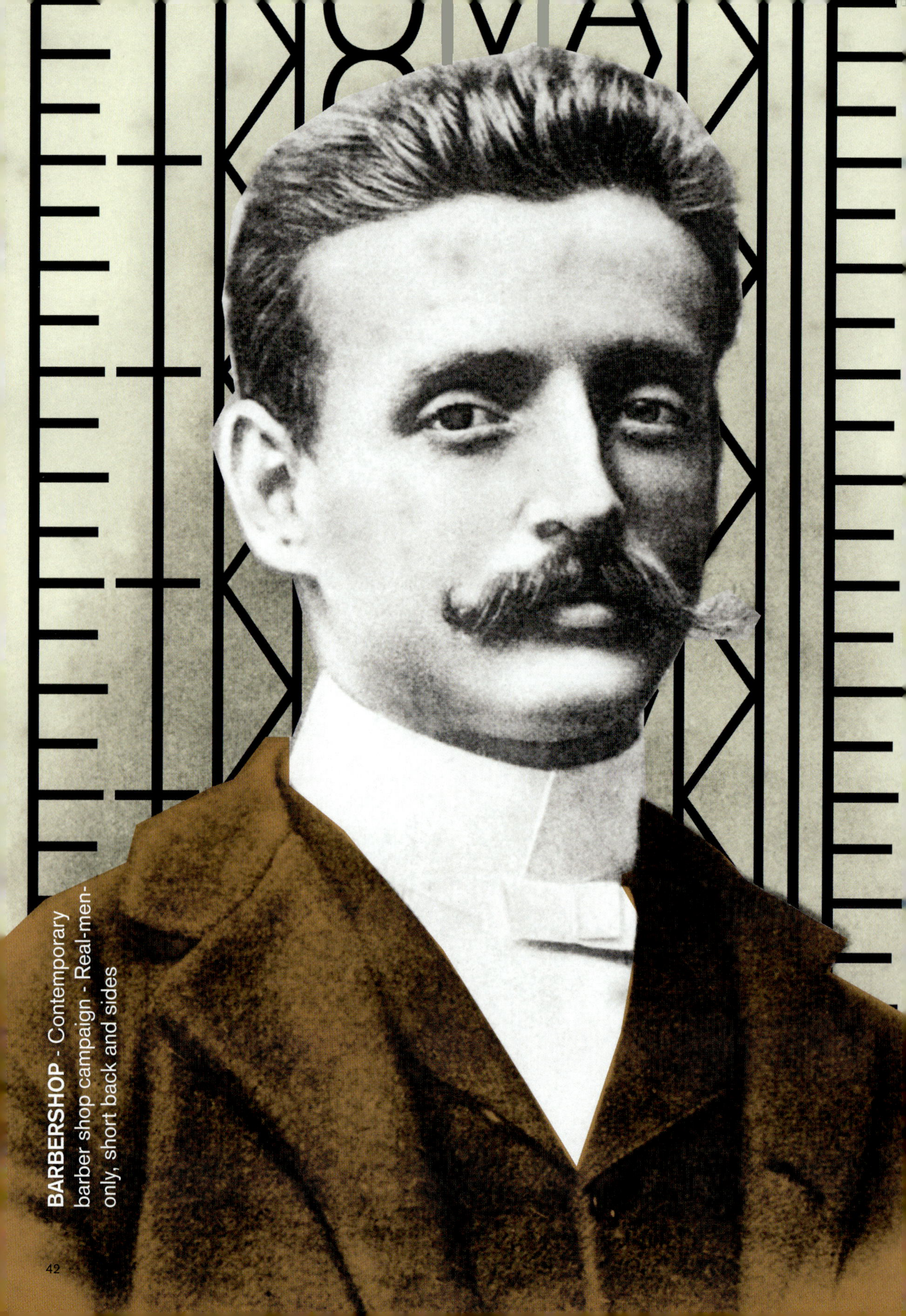

BARBERSHOP - Contemporary barber shop campaign - Real-men-only, short back and sides

42

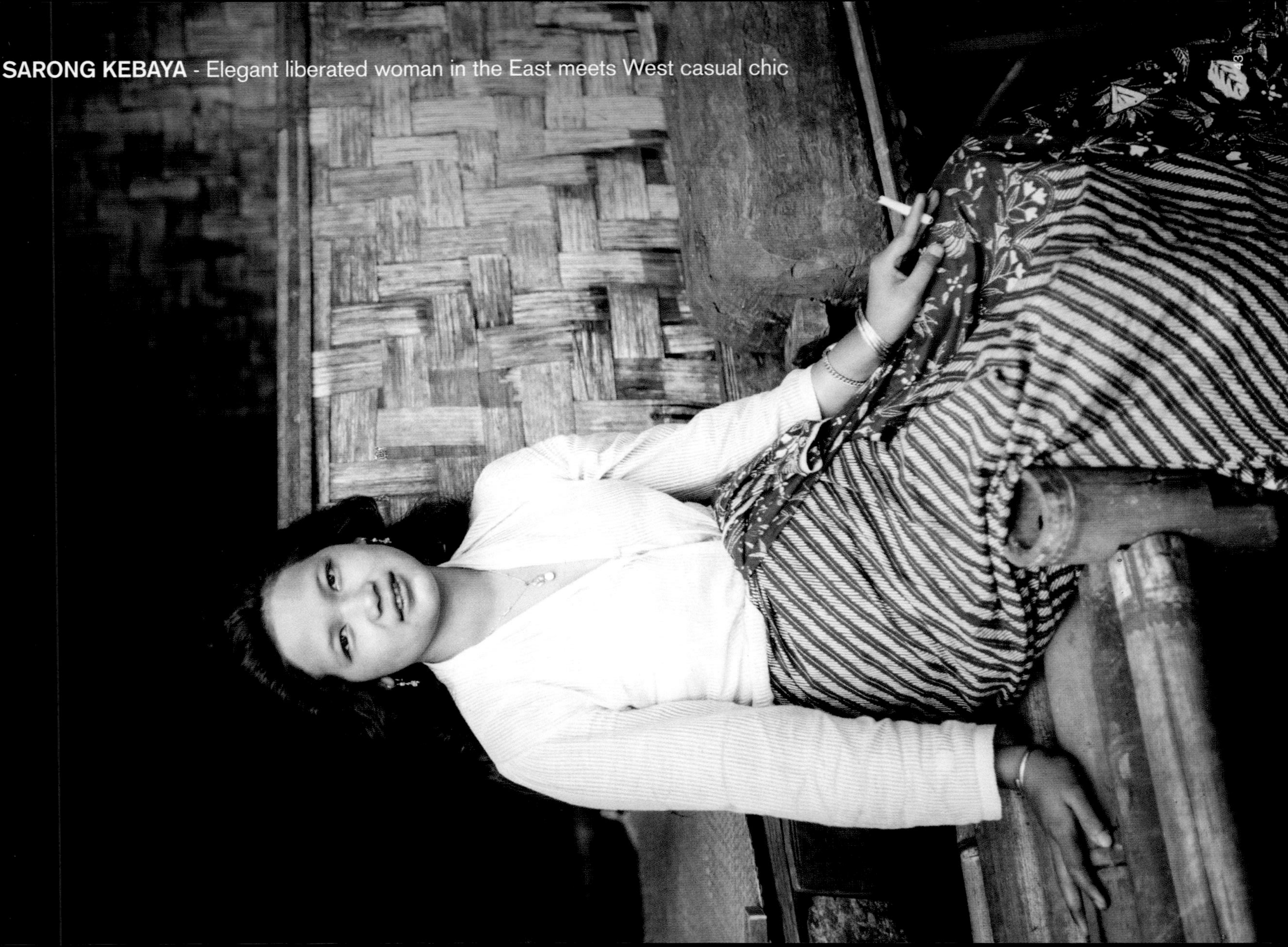

SARONG KEBAYA - Elegant liberated woman in the East meets West casual chic

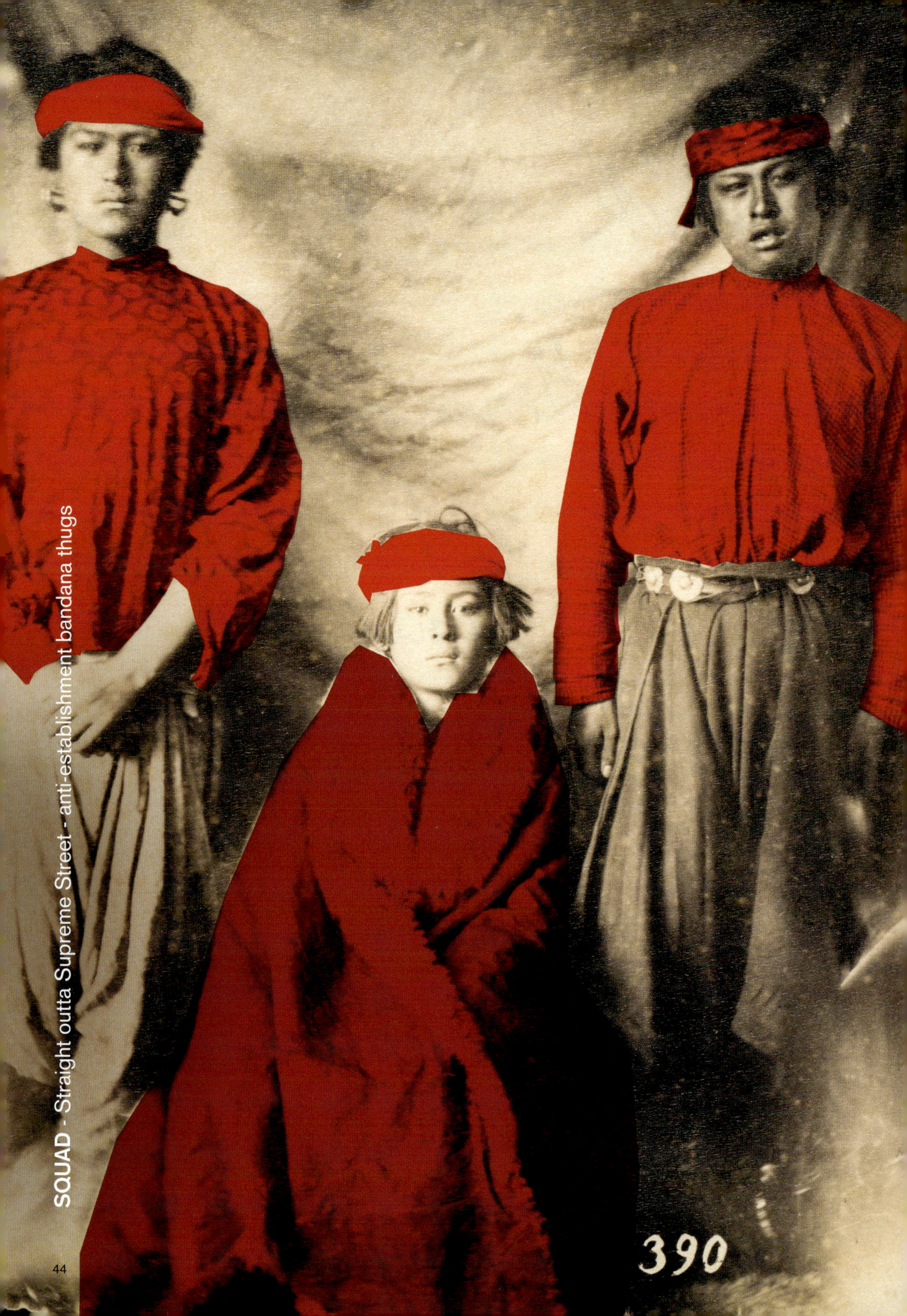

SQUAD - Straight outta Supreme Street - anti-establishment bandana thugs
390

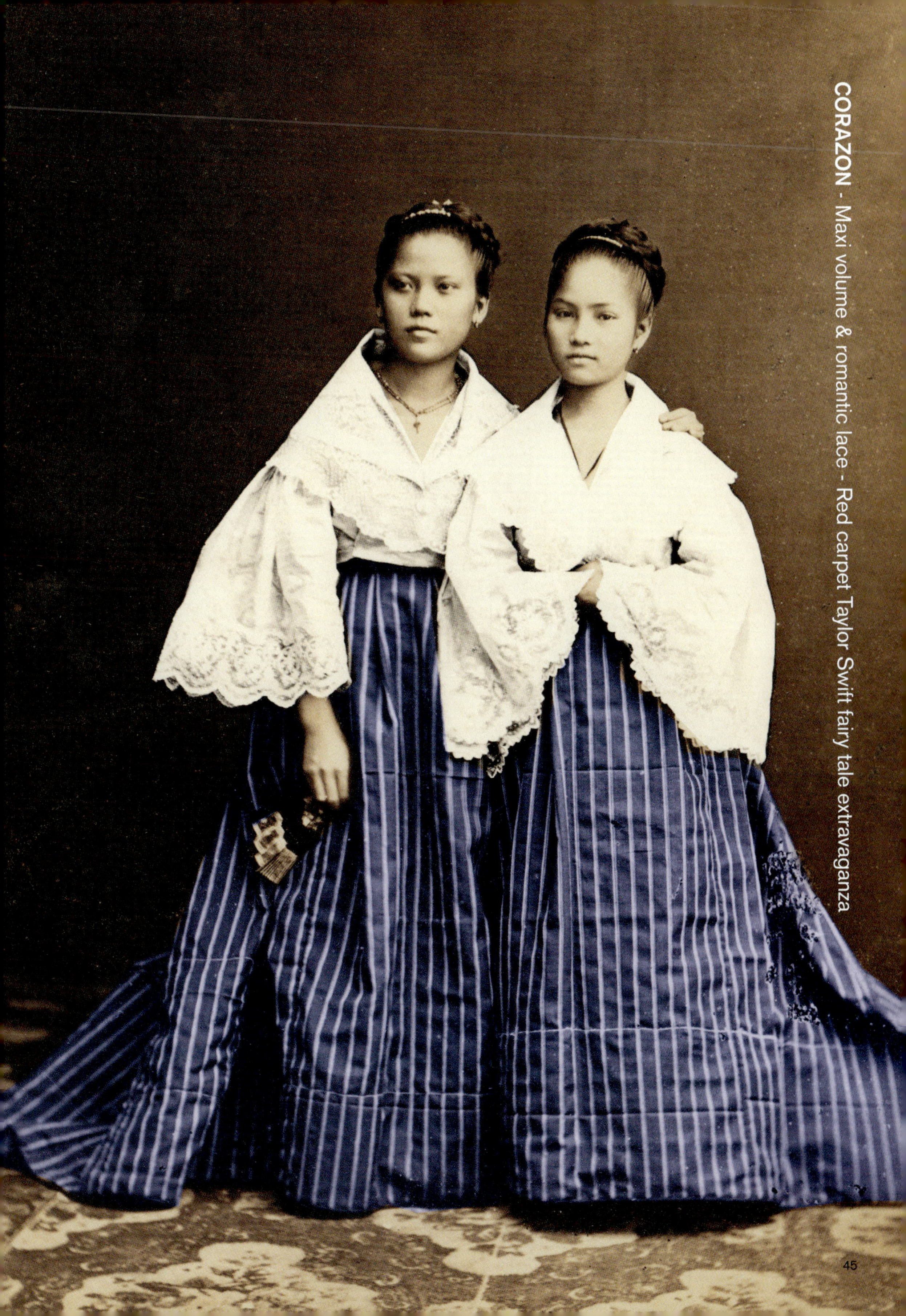

CORAZON - Maxi volume & romantic lace - Red carpet Taylor Swift fairy tale extravaganza

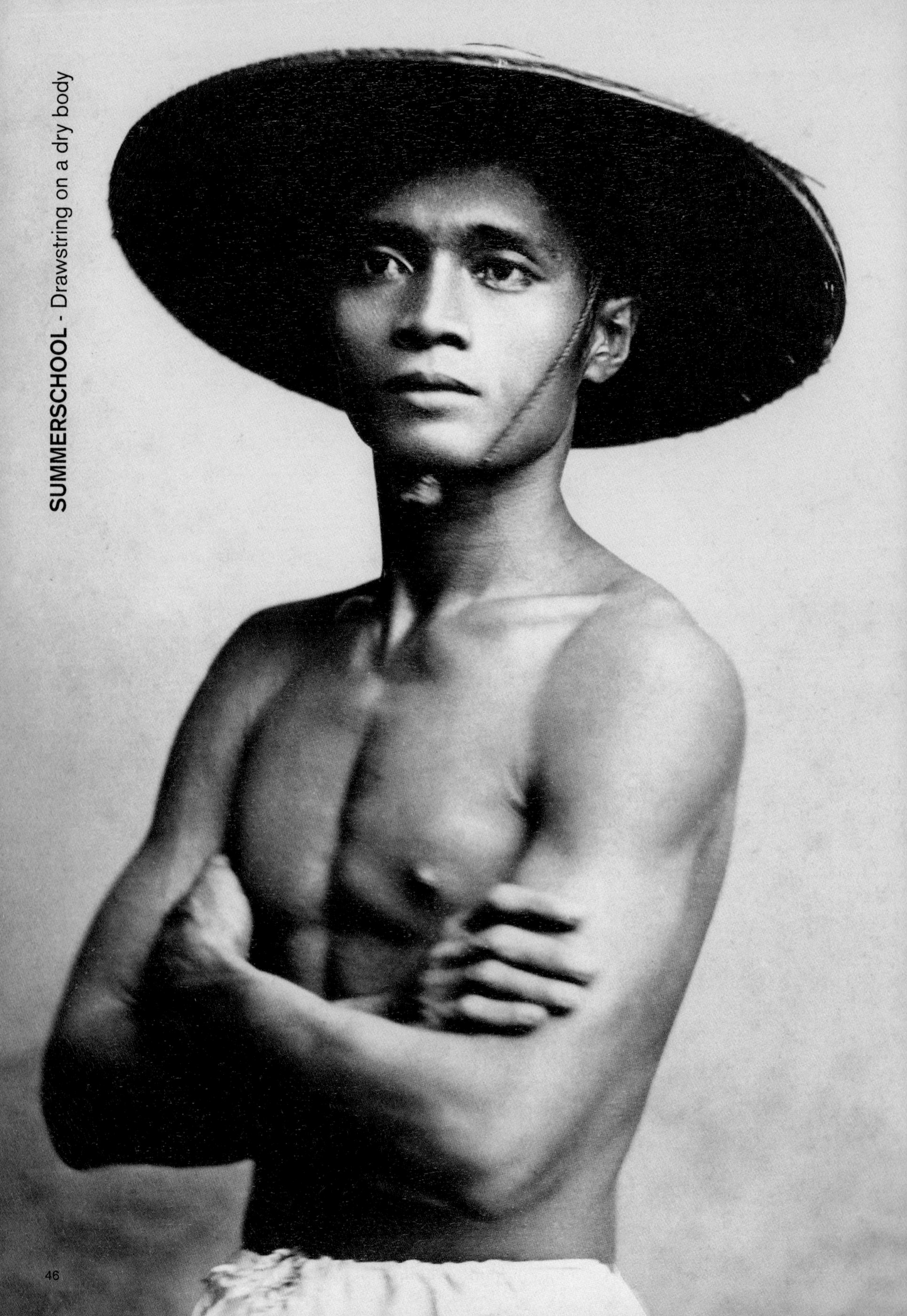
SUMMERSCHOOL - Drawstring on a dry body

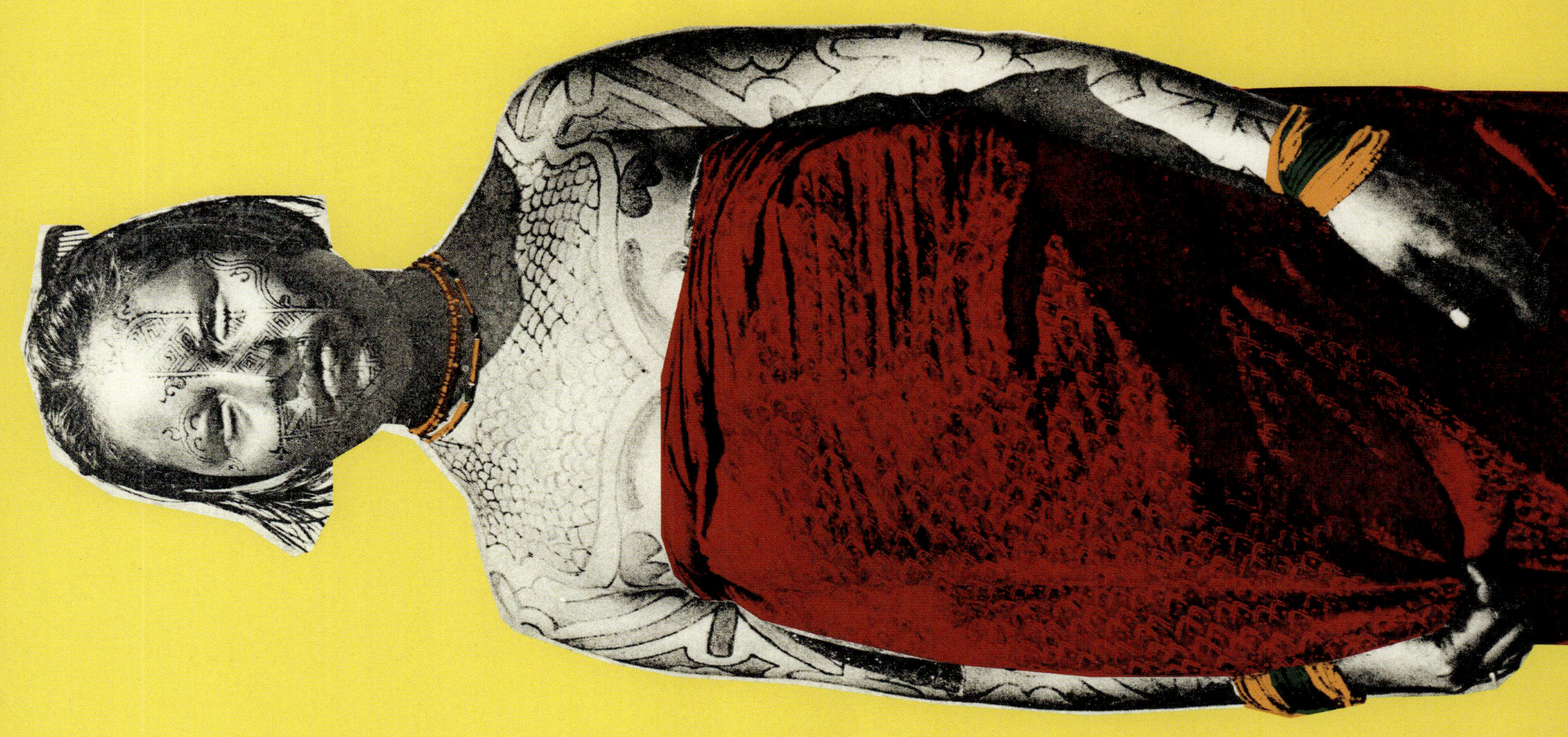

BEACHBABE - Wrap-around ease for exhibition in a body-conscious culture

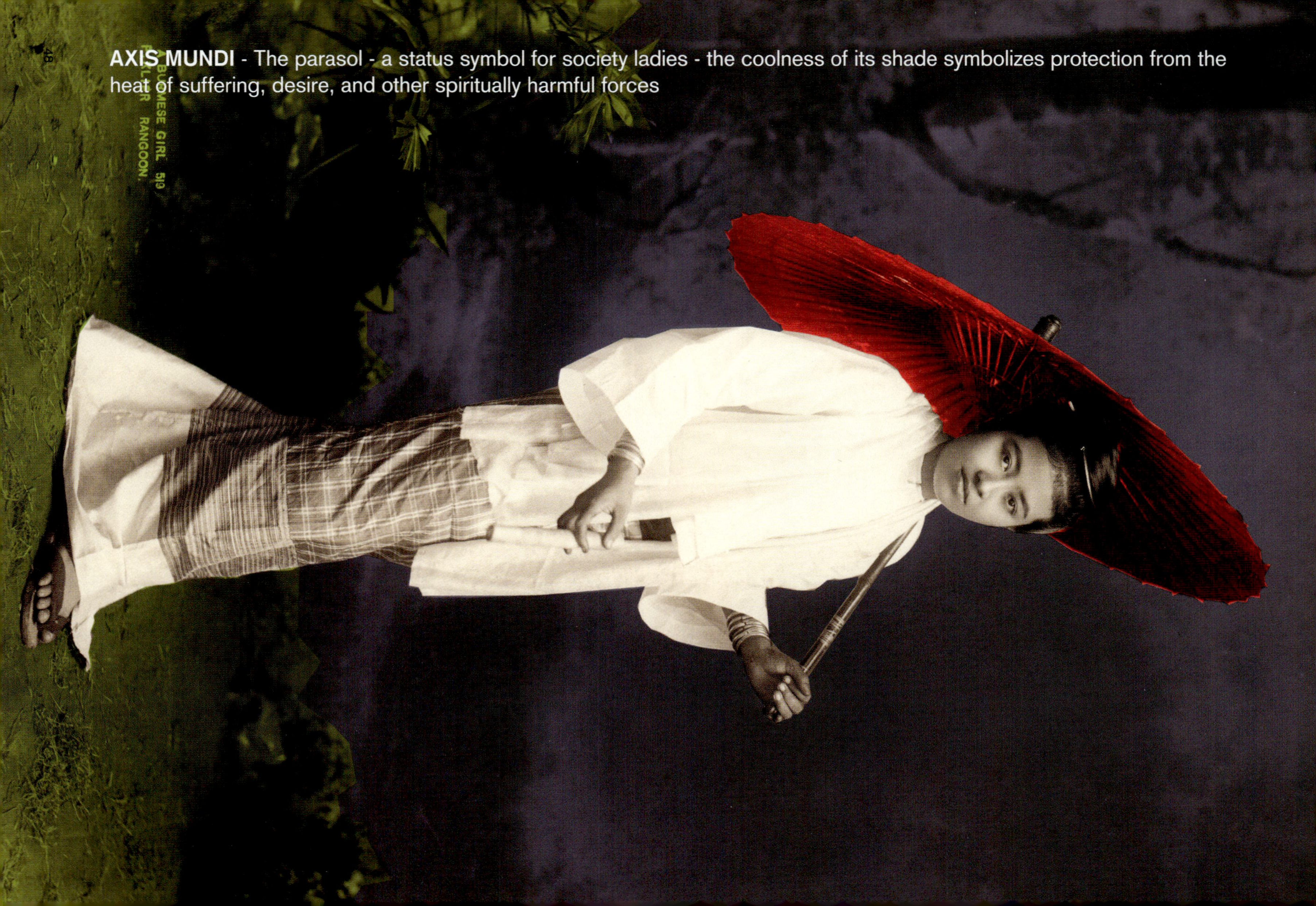

AXIS MUNDI - The parasol - a status symbol for society ladies - the coolness of its shade symbolizes protection from the heat of suffering, desire, and other spiritually harmful forces

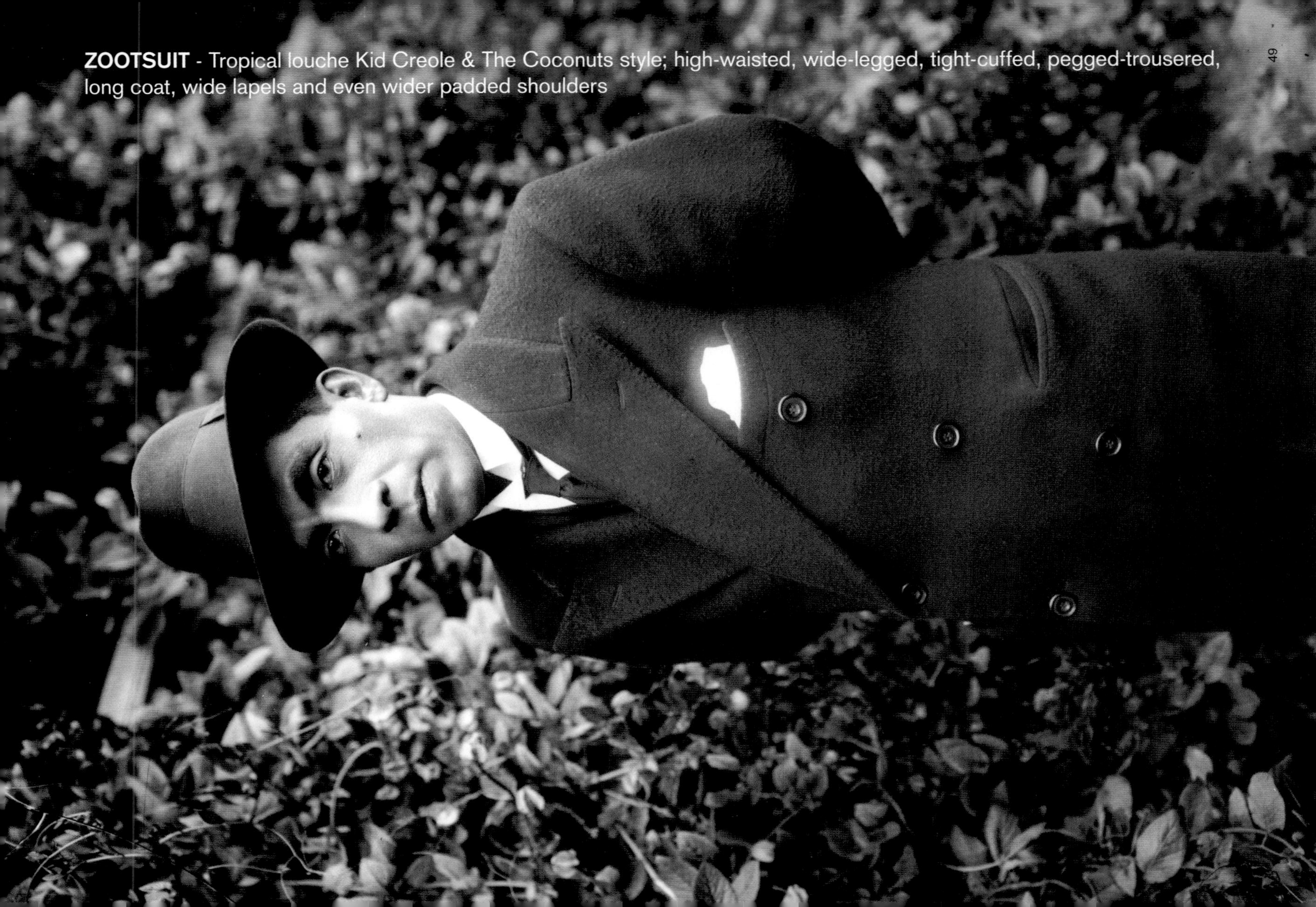

ZOOTSUIT - Tropical louche Kid Creole & The Coconuts style; high-waisted, wide-legged, tight-cuffed, pegged-trousered, long coat, wide lapels and even wider padded shoulders

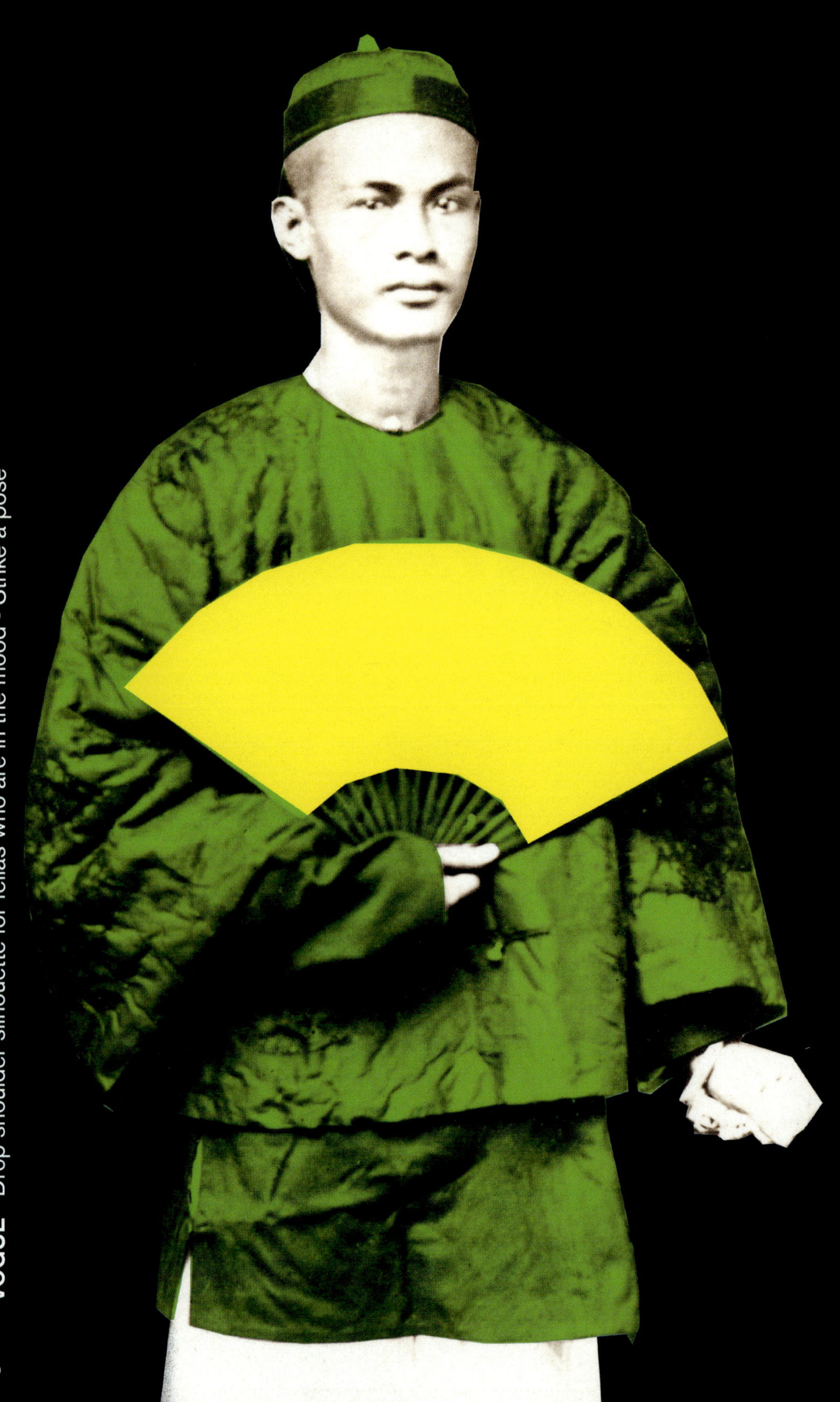

VOGUE - Drop shoulder silhouette for fellas who are in the mood - Strike a pose

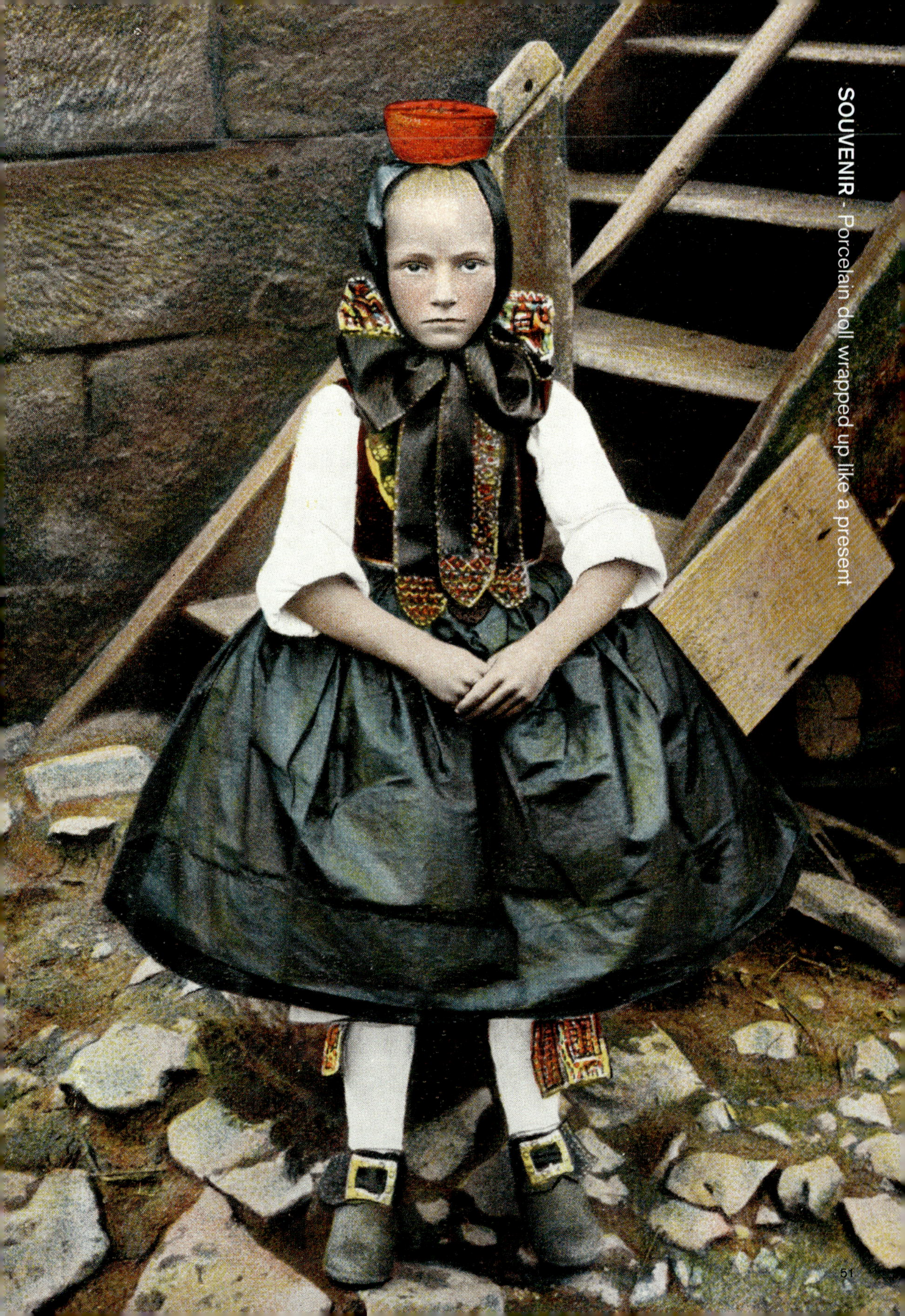

SOUVENIR - Porcelain doll wrapped up like a present

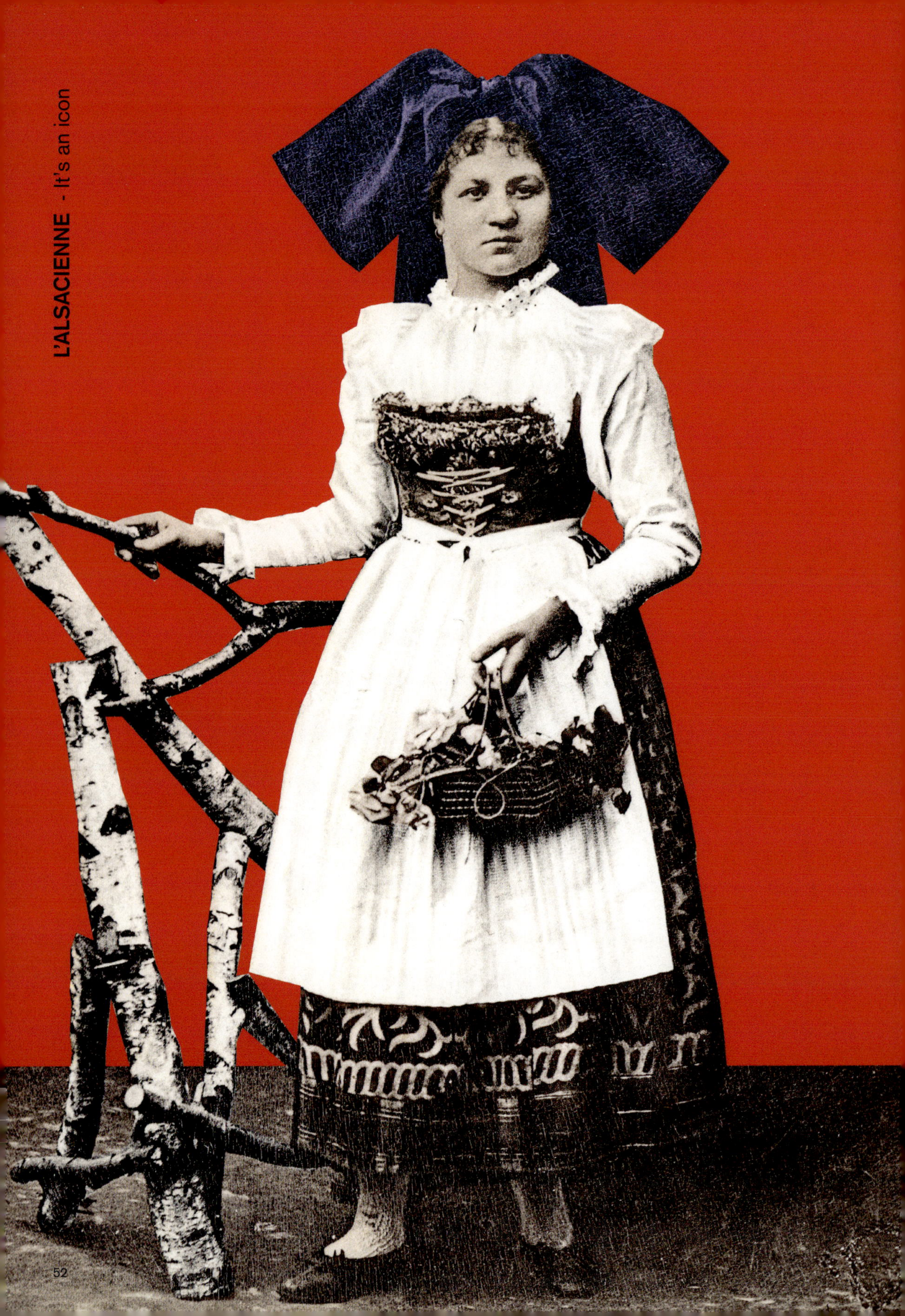

L'ALSACIENNE - It's an icon

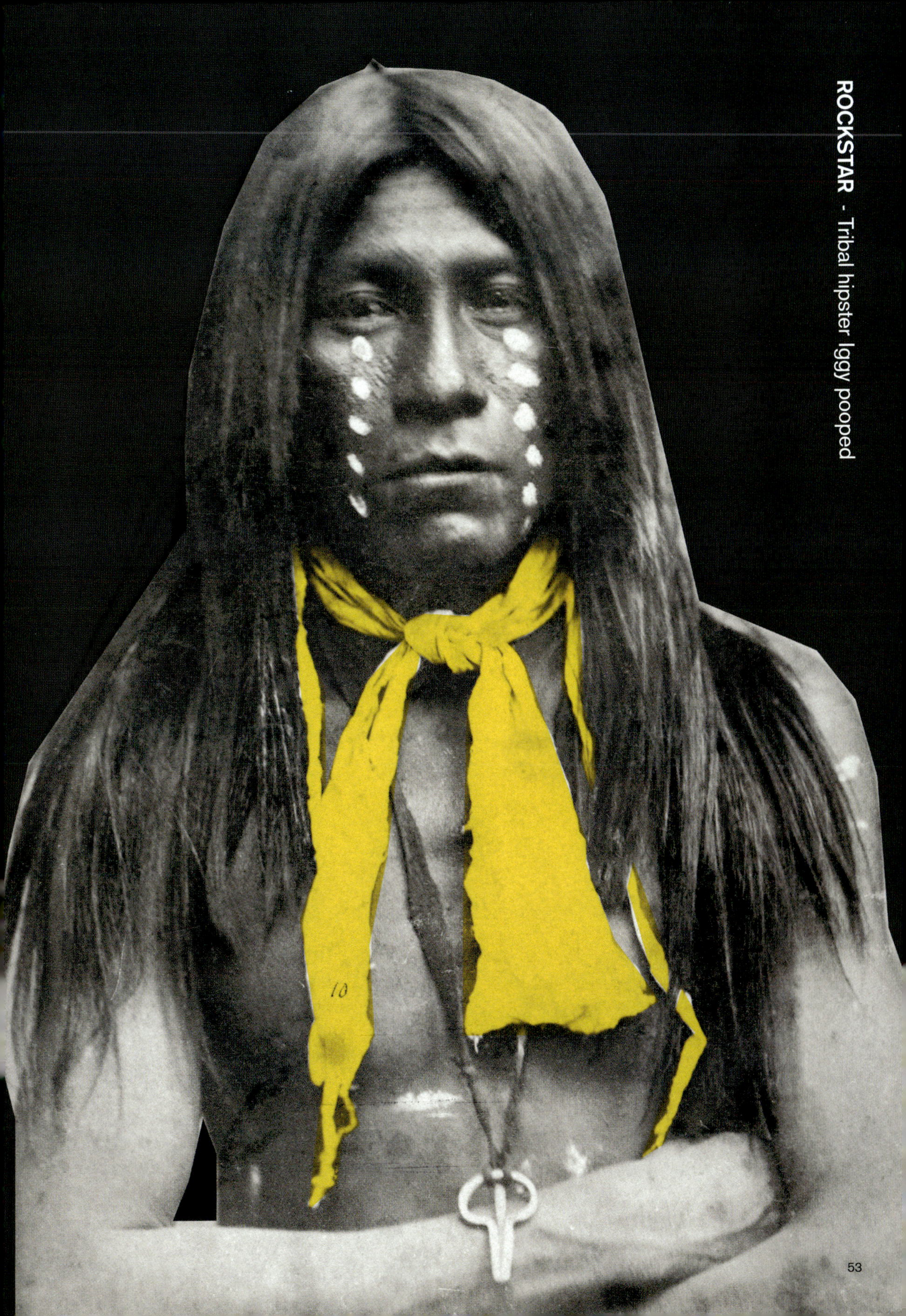

ROCKSTAR - Tribal hipster Iggy pooped

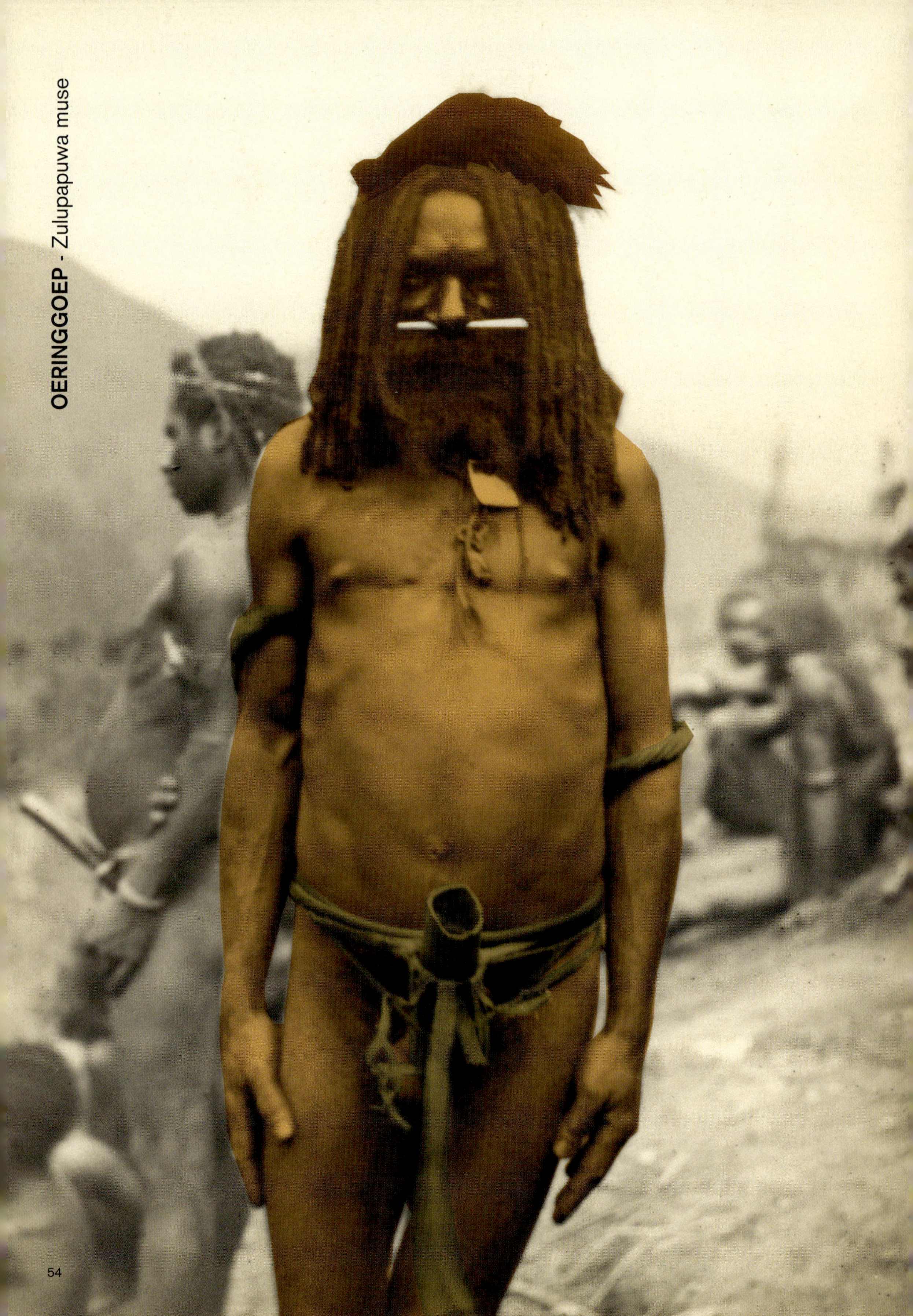

OERINGGOEP - *Zulupapuwa muse*

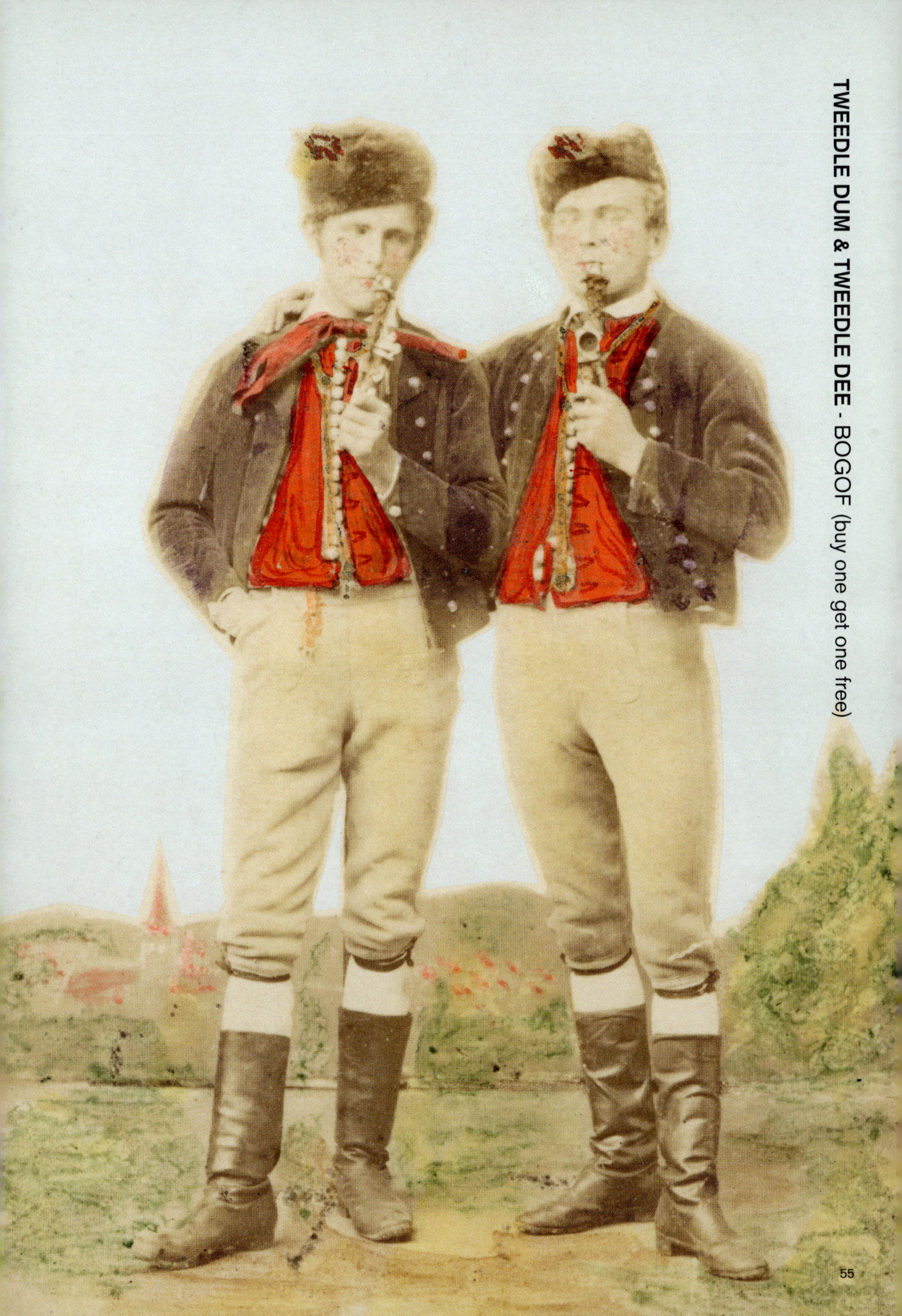

TWEEDLE DUM & TWEEDLE DEE - BOGOF (buy one get one free)

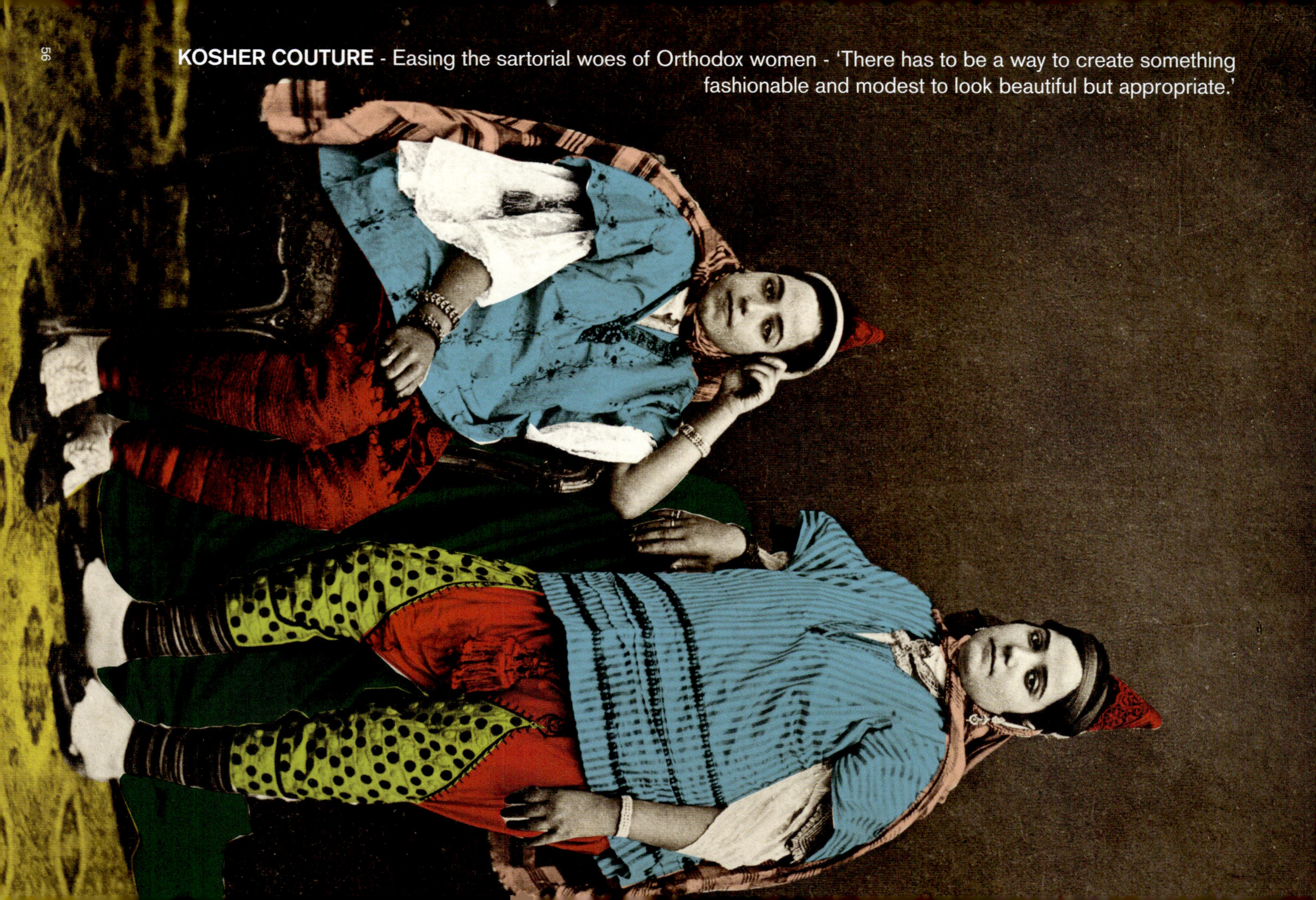

KOSHER COUTURE - Easing the sartorial woes of Orthodox women - 'There has to be a way to create something fashionable and modest to look beautiful but appropriate.'

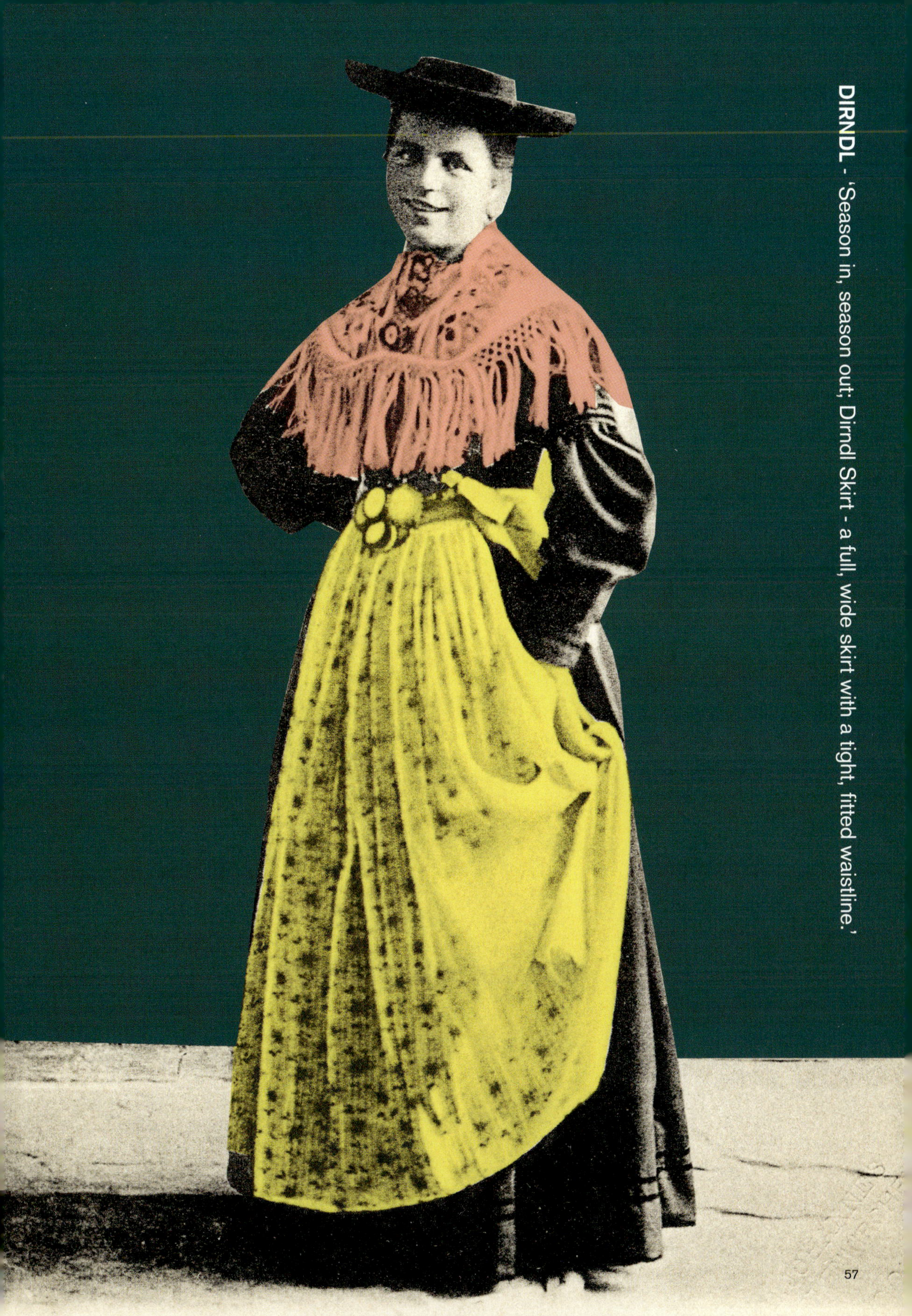

DIRNDL - 'Season in, season out; Dirndl Skirt - a full, wide skirt with a tight, fitted waistline.'

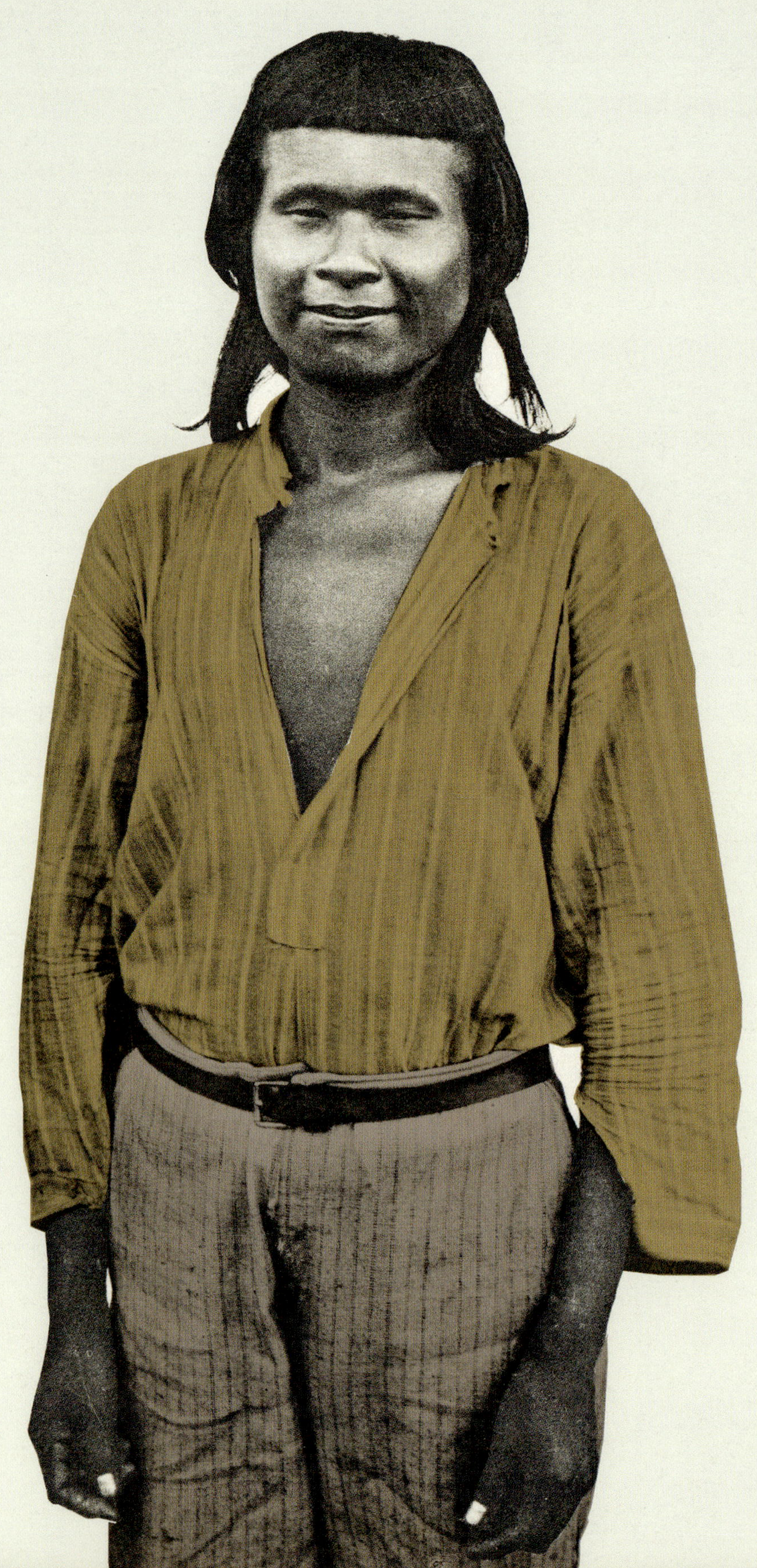

NIRVANA - Grungy saddle & sand, colour coordinated - lived-in luxury

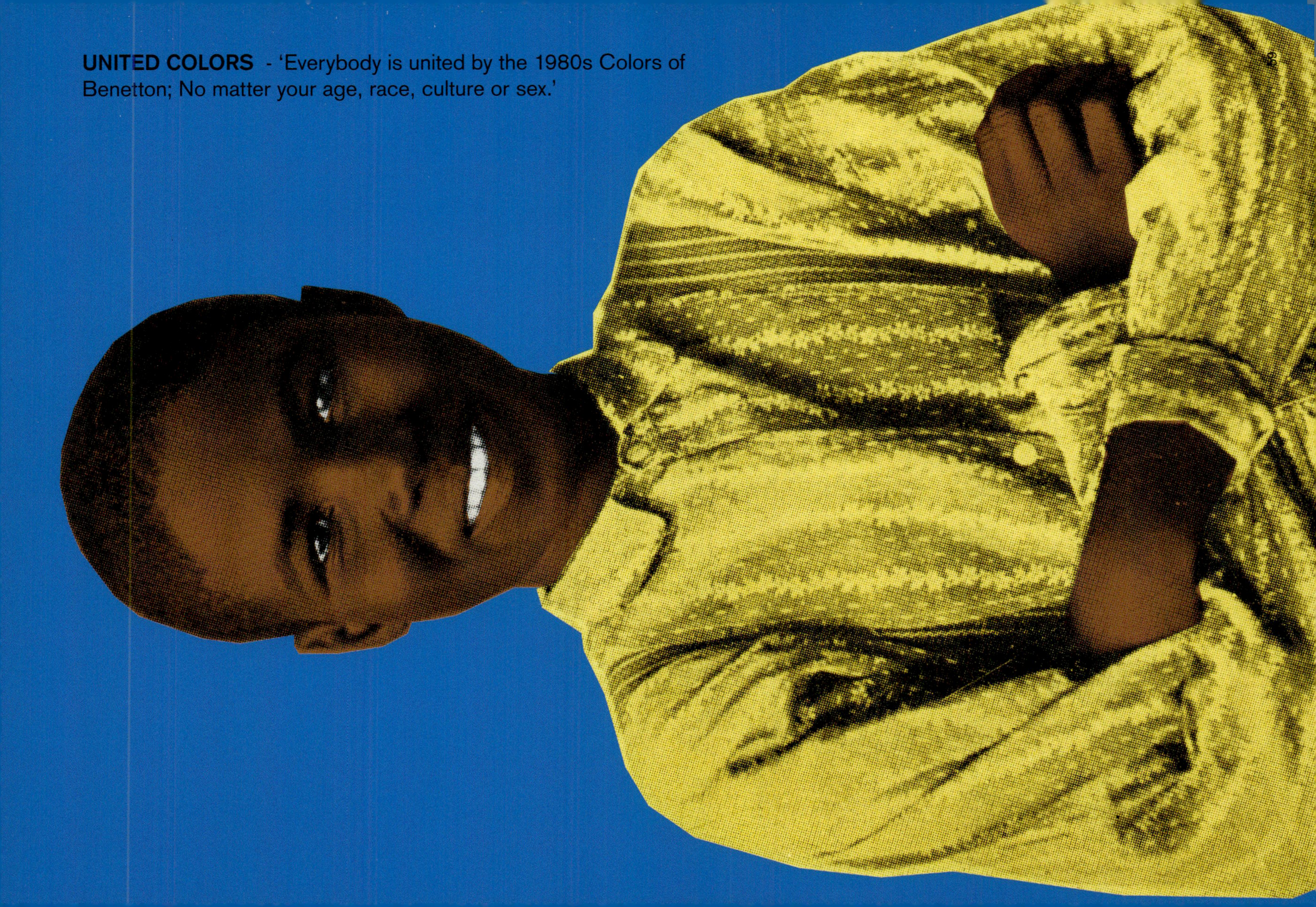
UNITED COLORS - 'Everybody is united by the 1980s Colors of Benetton; No matter your age, race, culture or sex.'

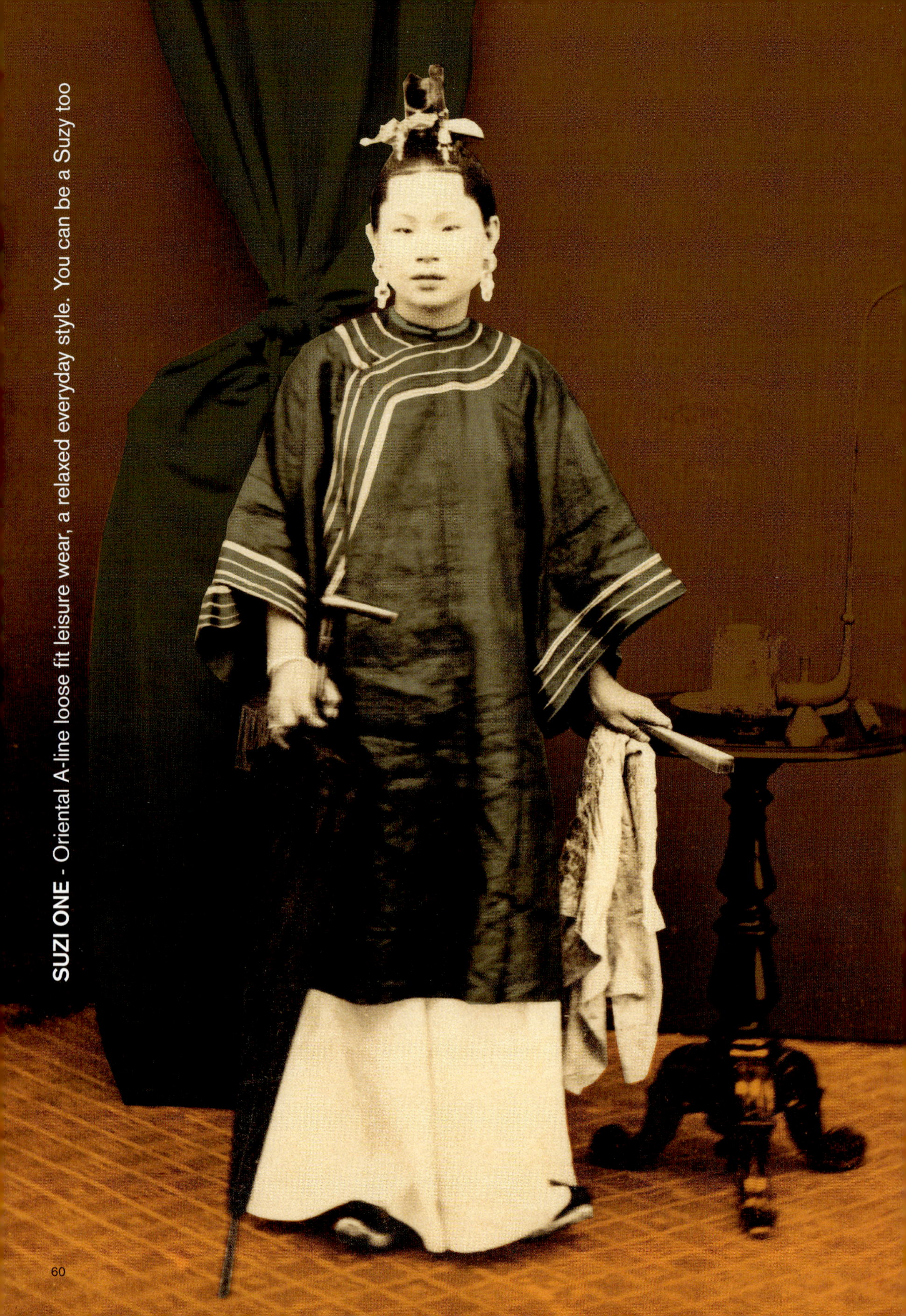

SUZI ONE - Oriental A-line loose fit leisure wear, a relaxed everyday style. You can be a Suzy too

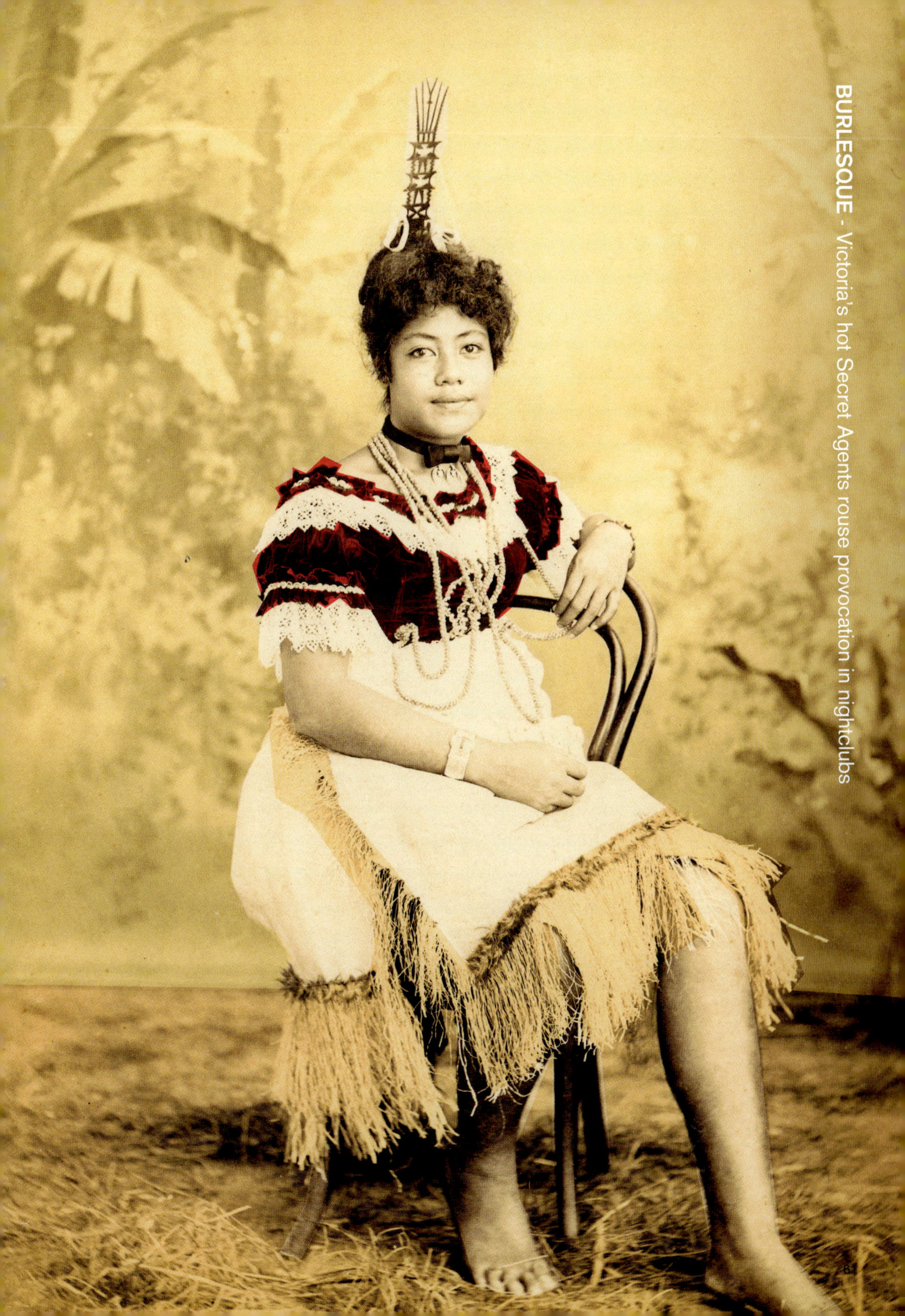
BURLESQUE - Victoria's hot Secret Agents rouse provocation in nightclubs

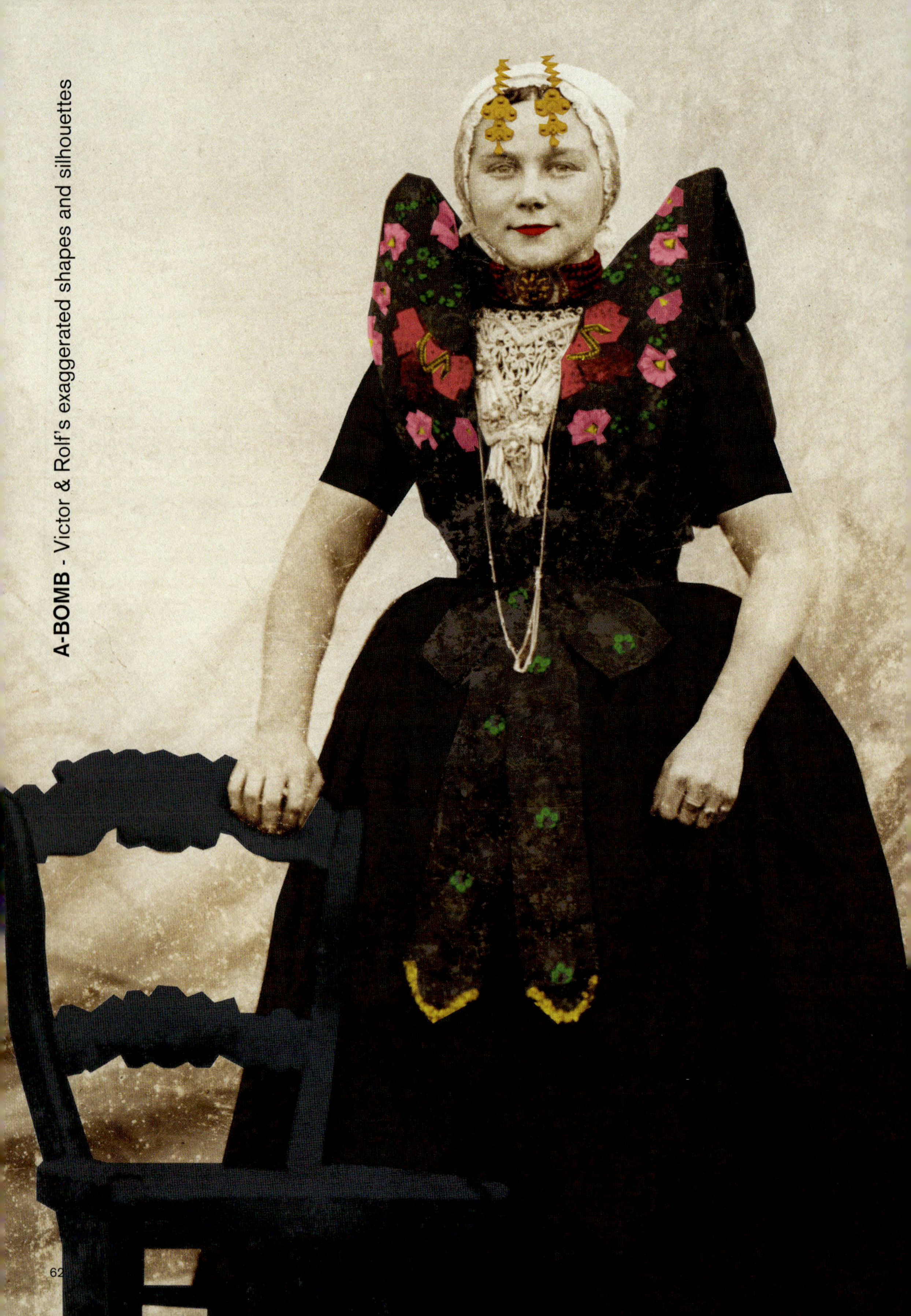

A-BOMB - Victor & Rolf's exaggerated shapes and silhouettes

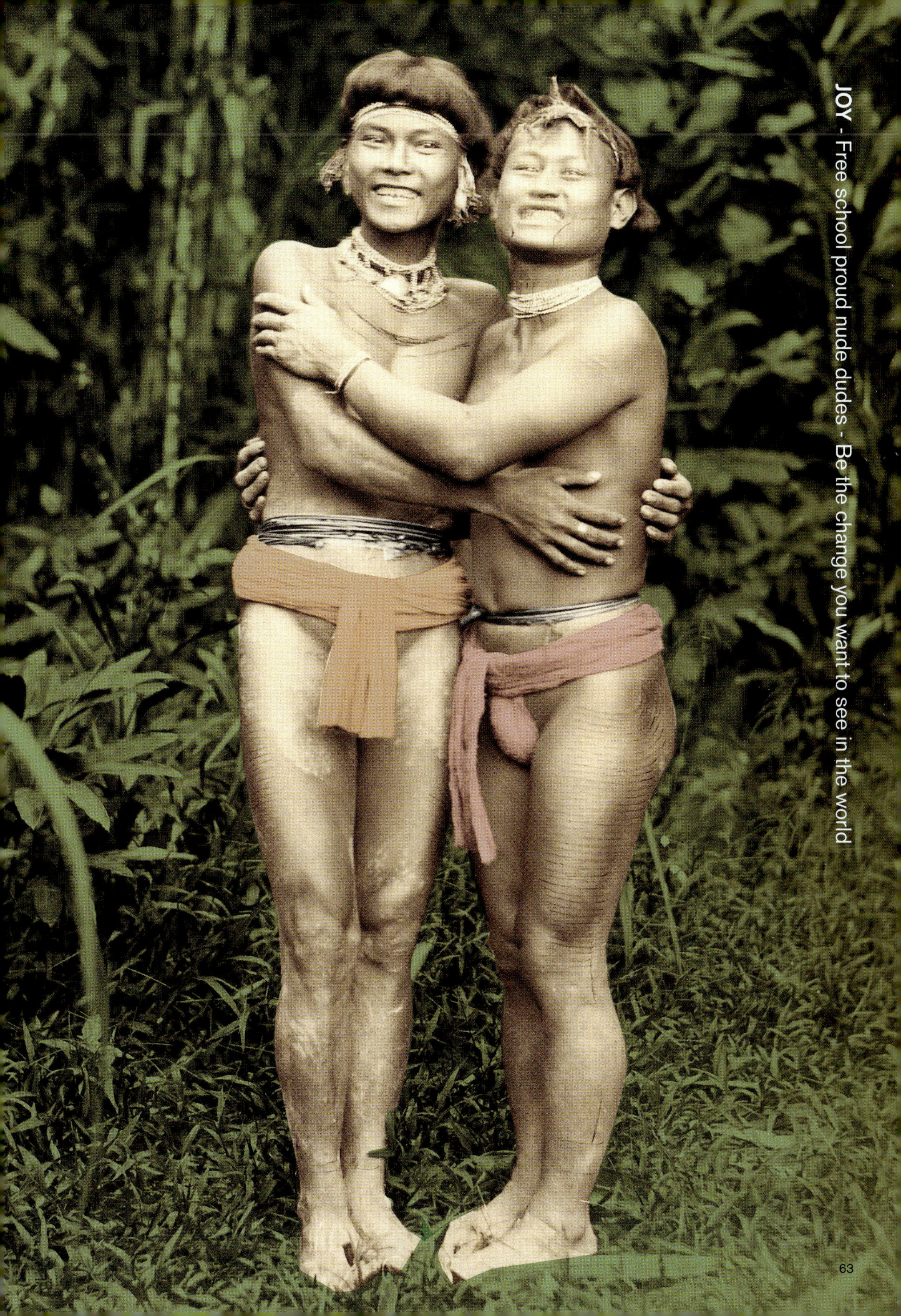

JOY - Free school proud nude dudes - Be the change you want to see in the world

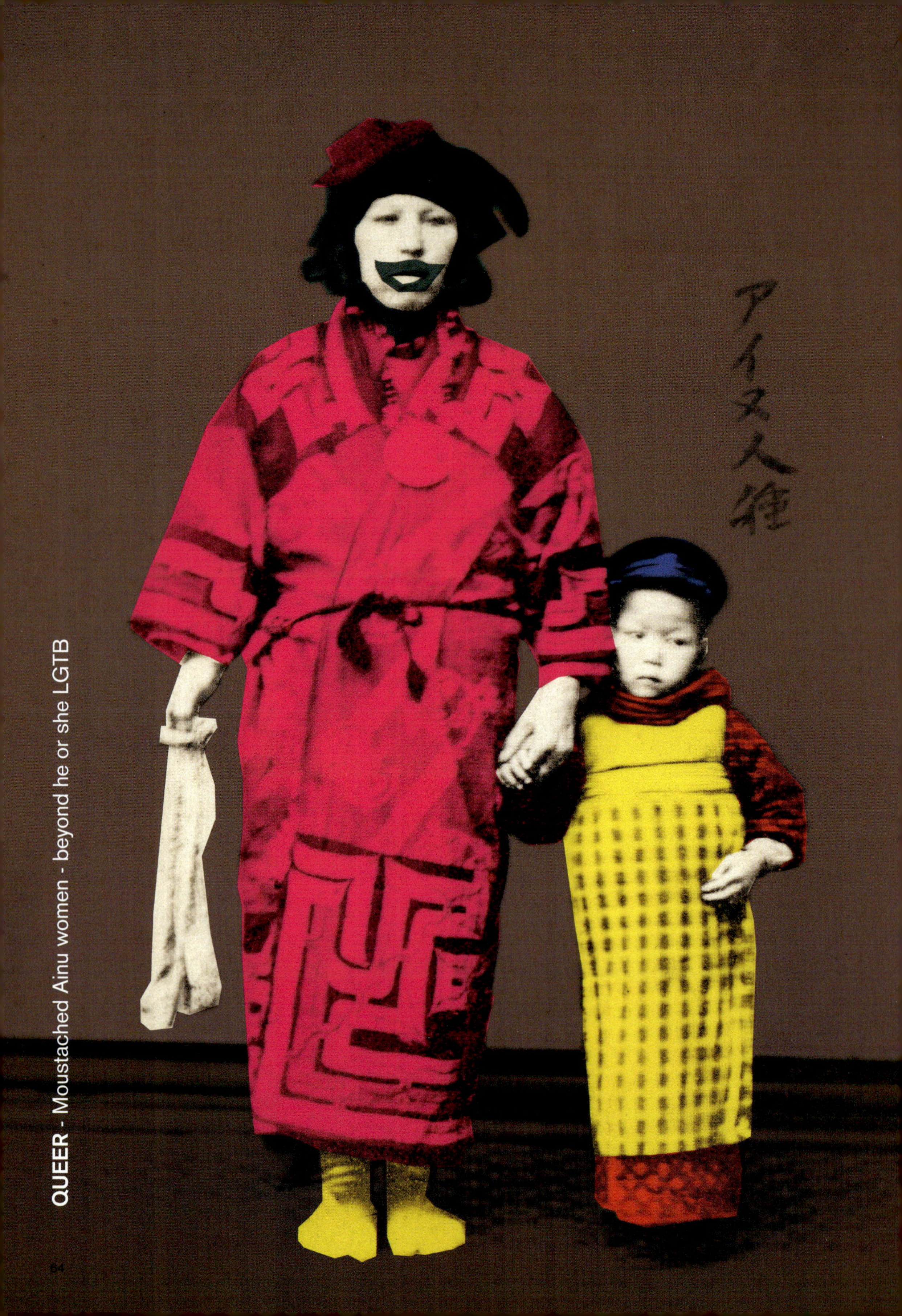

QUEER - Moustached Ainu women - beyond he or she LGTB

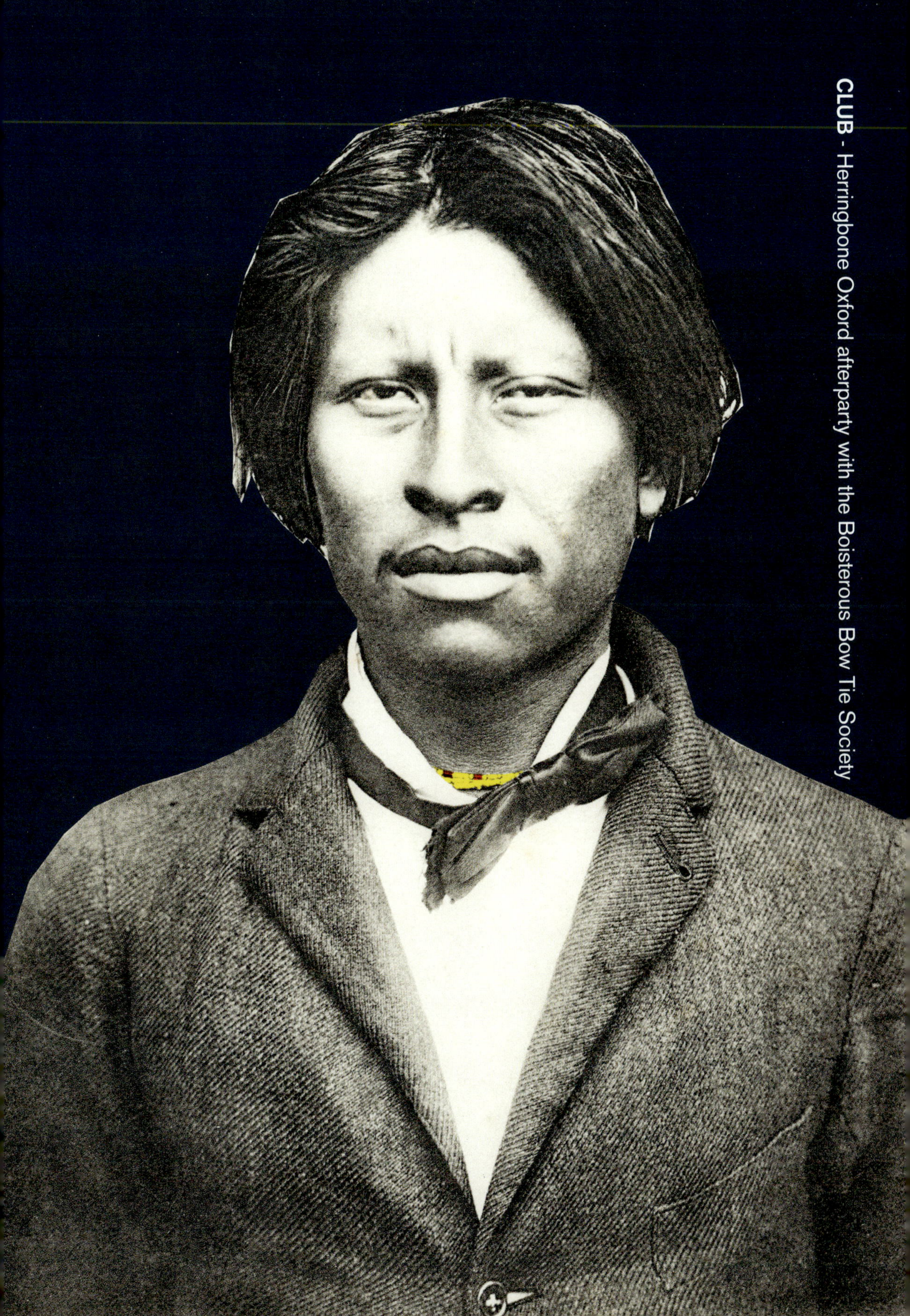
CLUB - Herringbone Oxford afterparty with the Boisterous Bow Tie Society

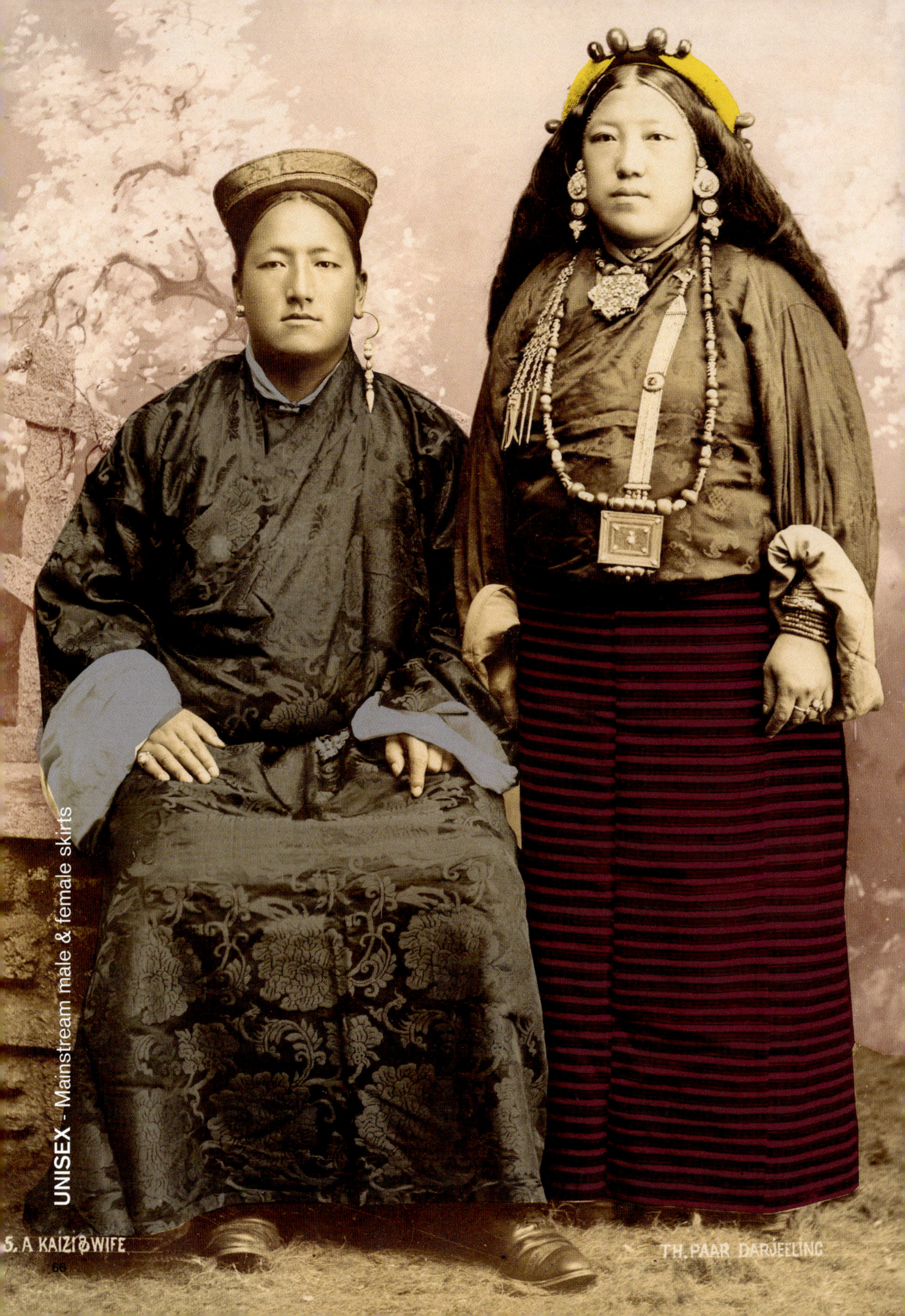

UNISEX - Mainstream male & female skirts
S. A KAIZI & WIFE
TH. PAAR DARJEELING

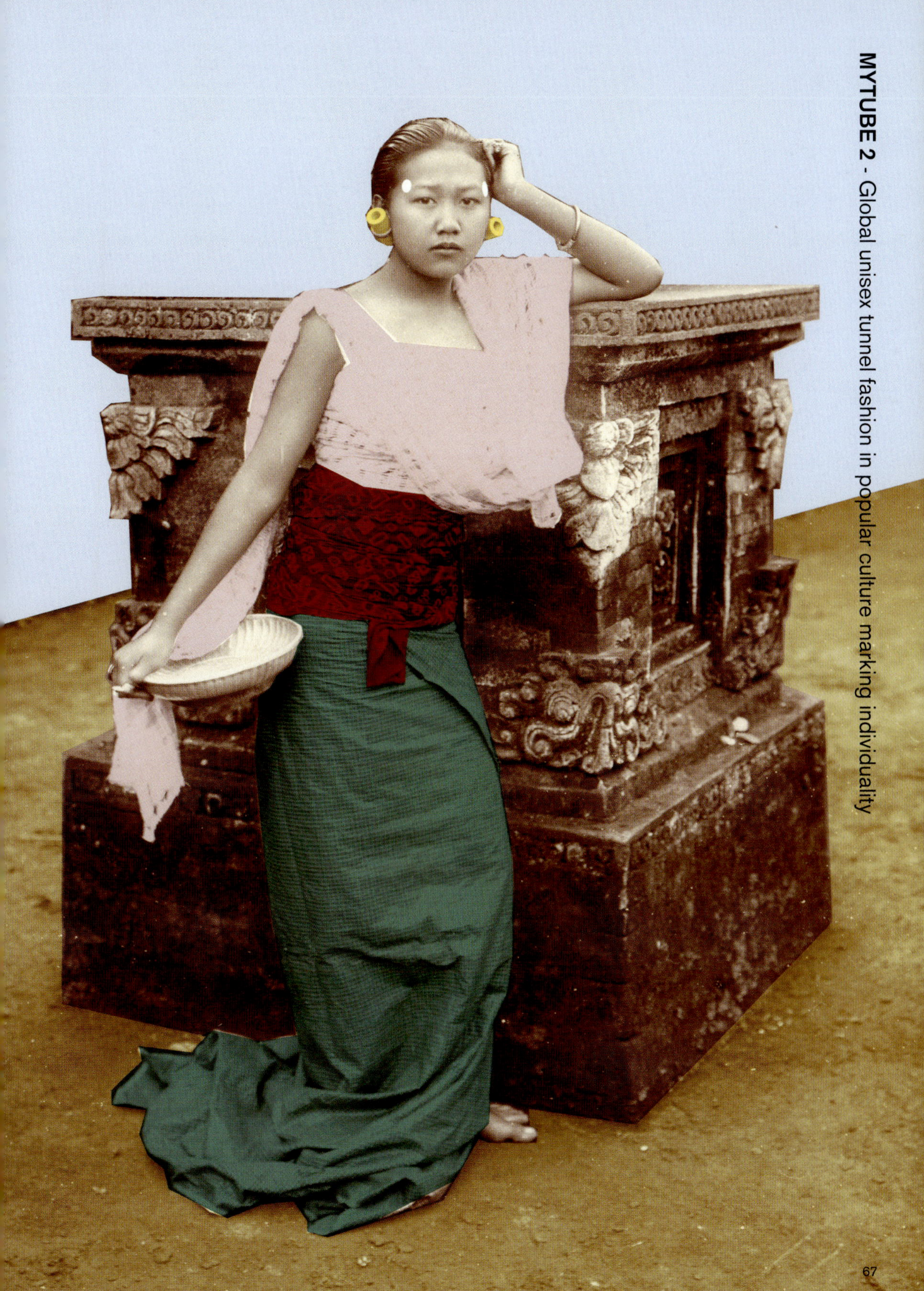

MYTUBE 2 - Global unisex tunnel fashion in popular culture marking individuality

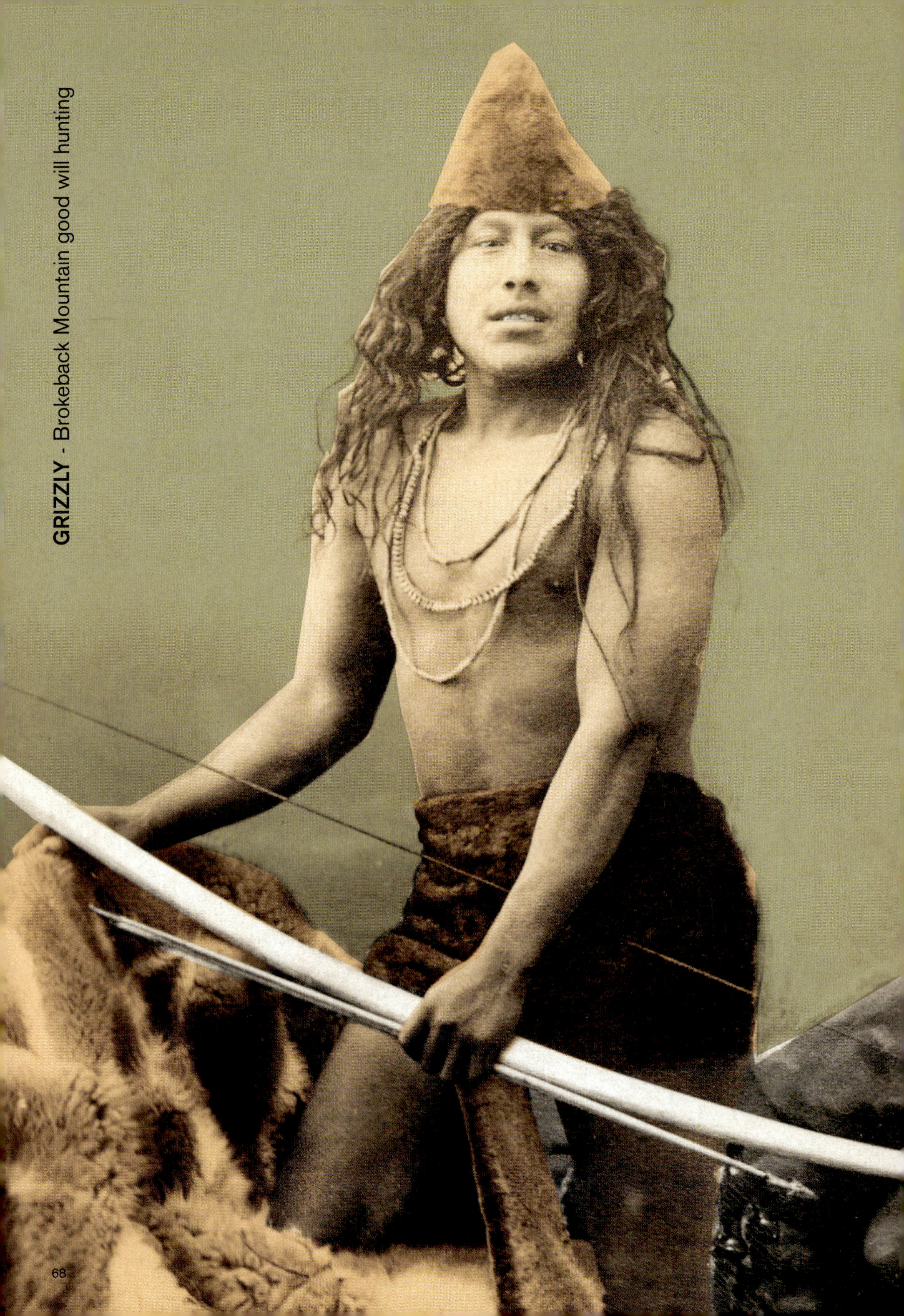

GRIZZLY - Brokeback Mountain good will hunting

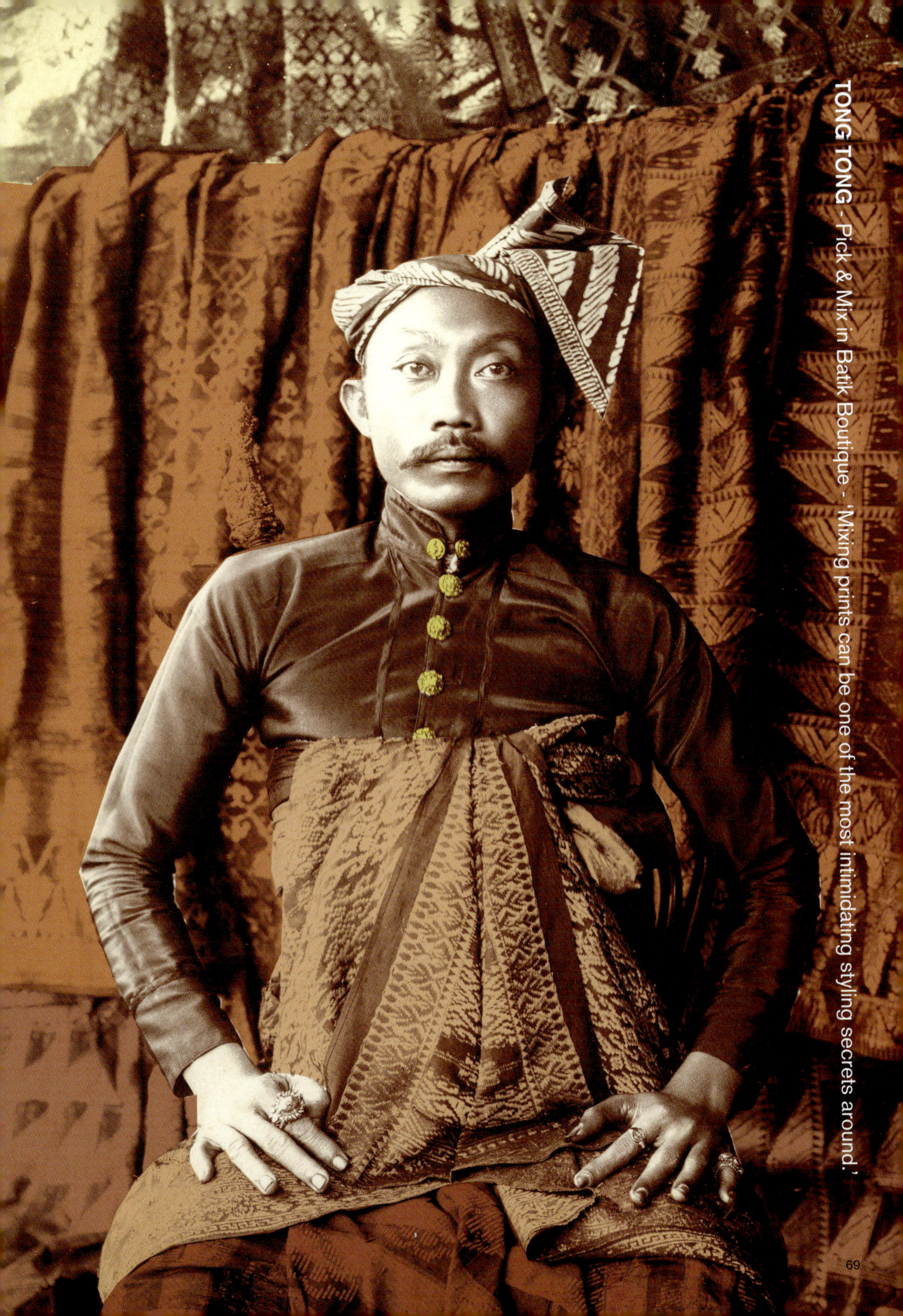

TONG TONG - Pick & Mix in Batik Boutique - "Mixing prints can be one of the most intimidating styling secrets around."

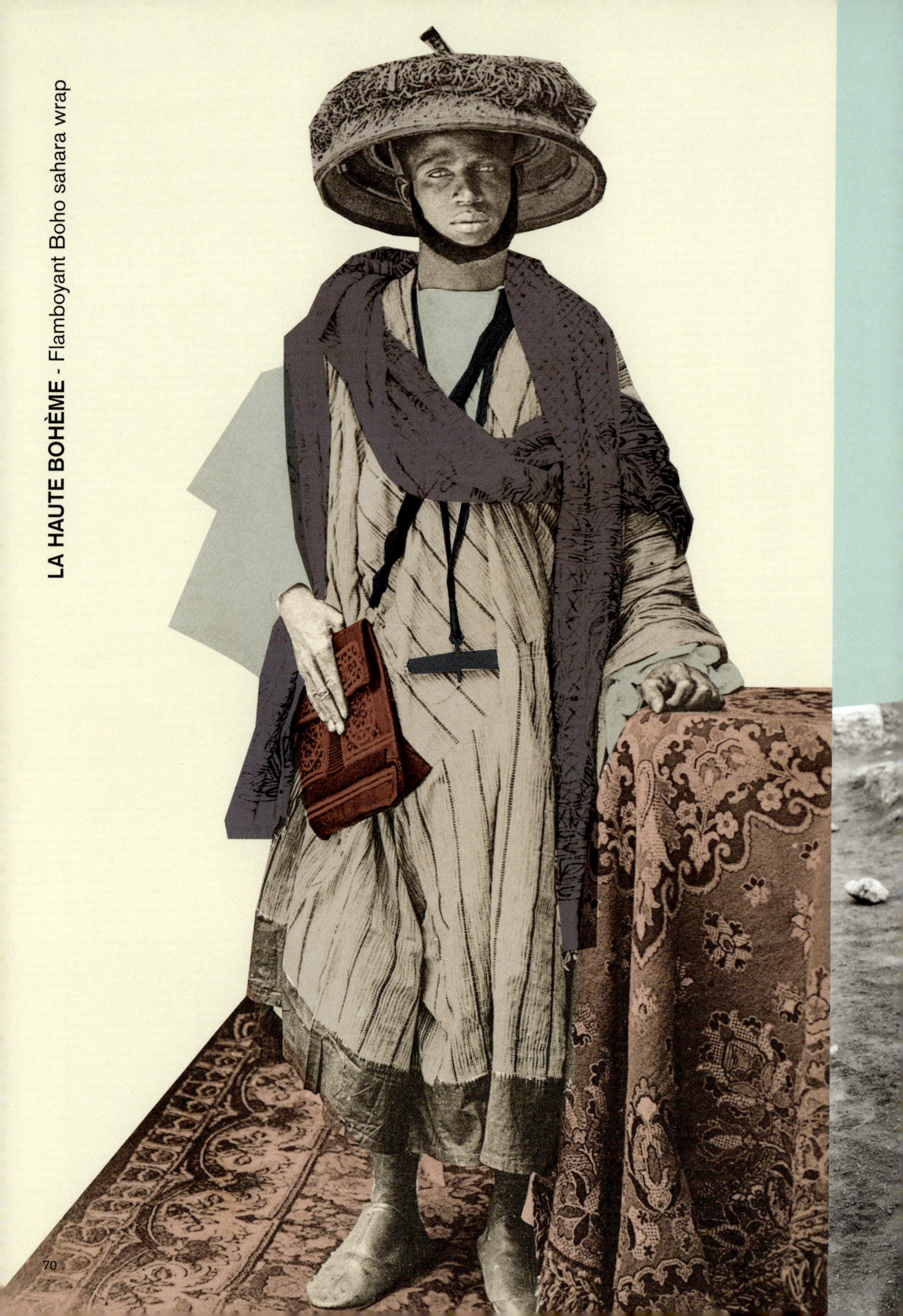

LA HAUTE BOHÈME - Flamboyant Boho sahara wrap

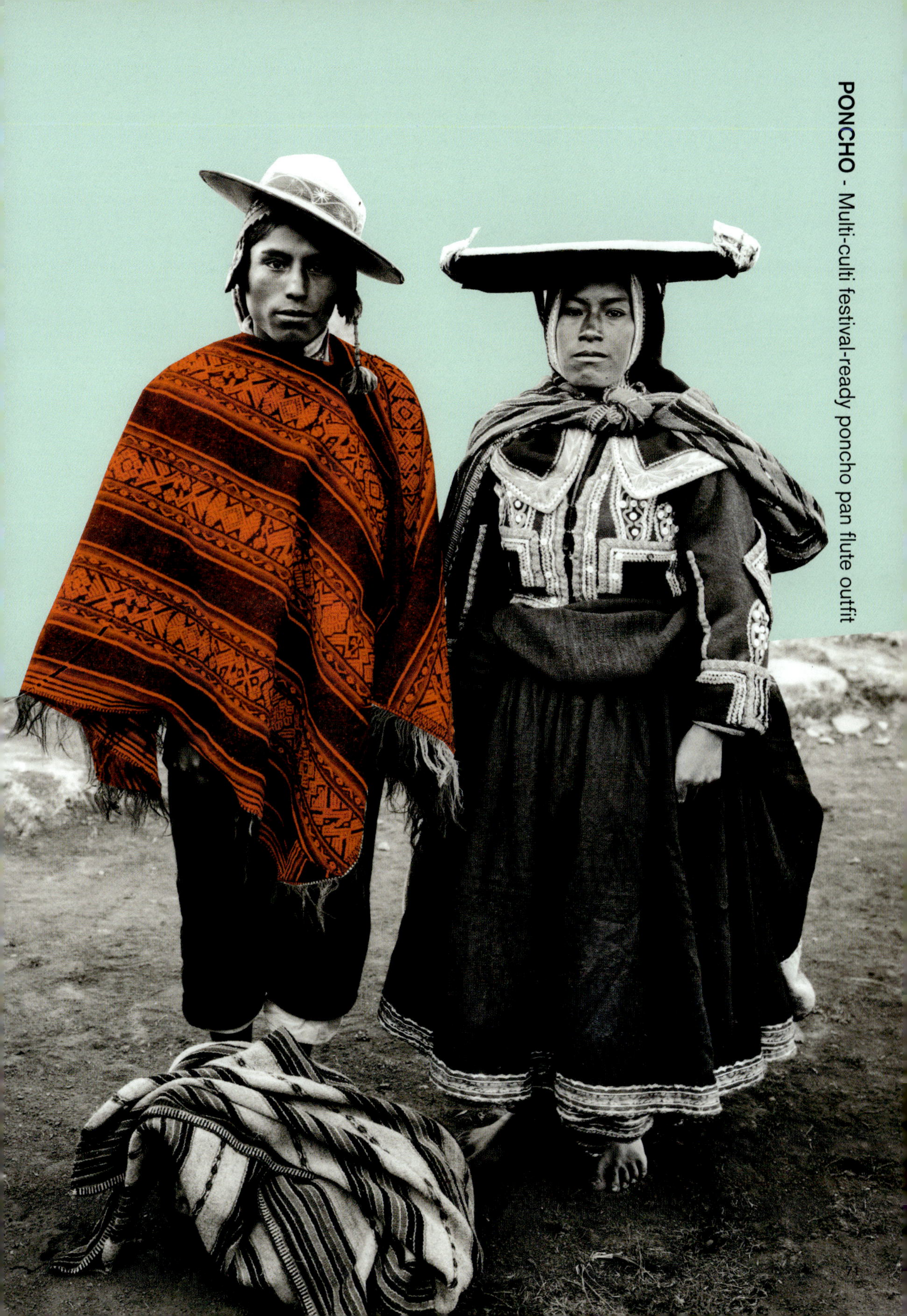

PONCHO · Multi-culti festival-ready poncho pan flute outfit

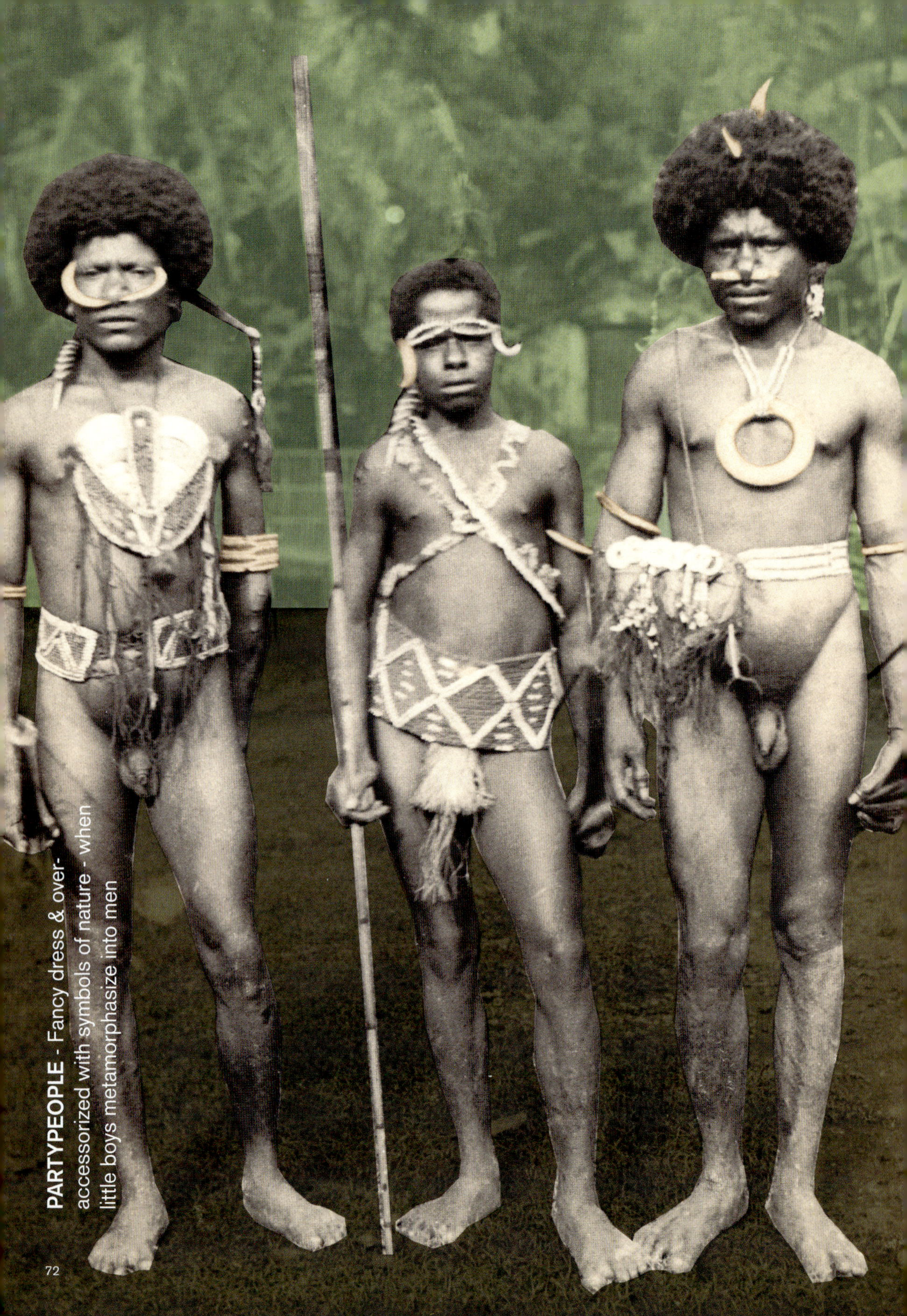

PARTYPEOPLE - Fancy dress & over-accessorized with symbols of nature - when little boys metamorphasize into men

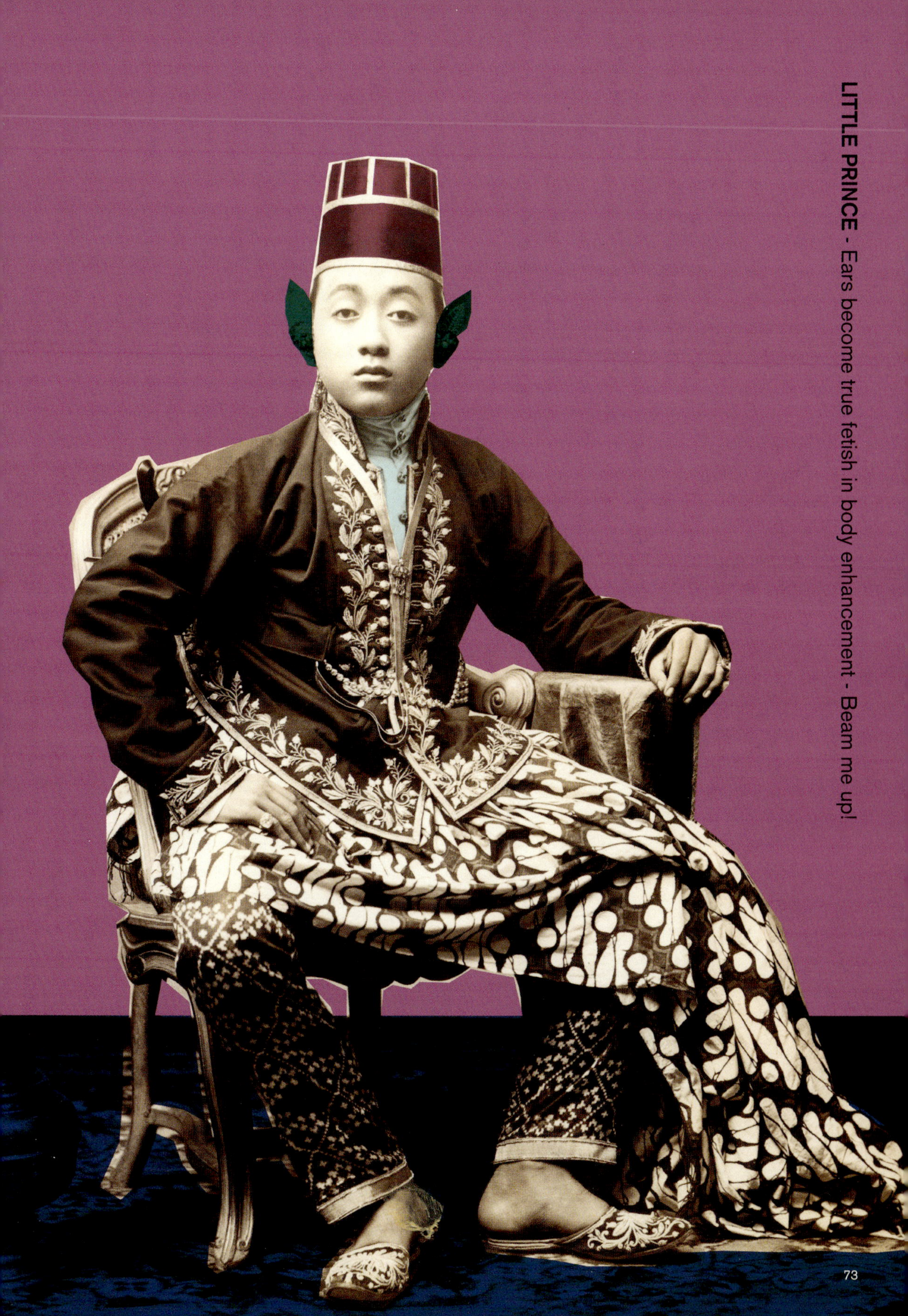

LITTLE PRINCE - Ears become true fetish in body enhancement - Beam me up!

73

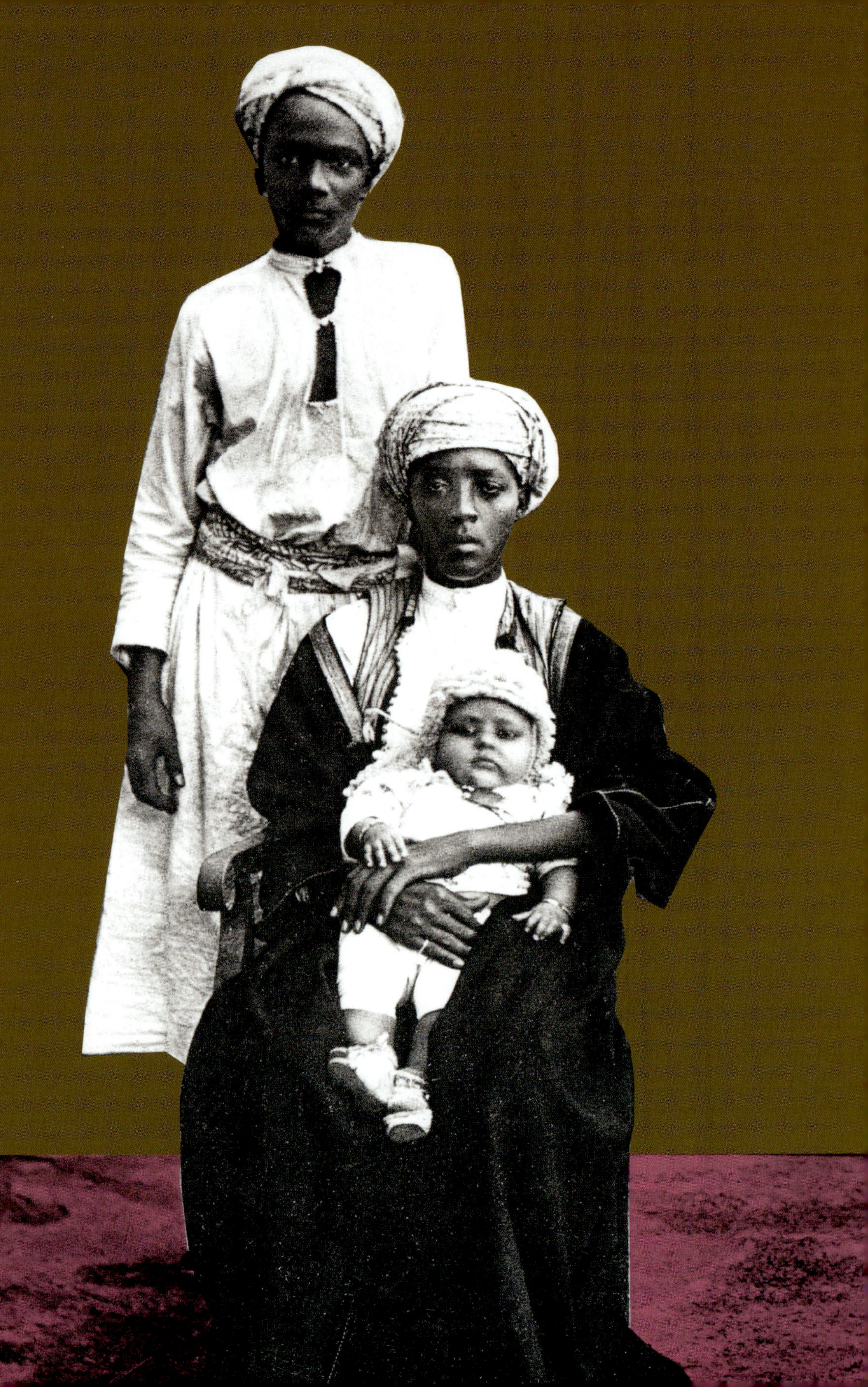

EUNUCH - Eunuch taboo has obscured the meaning of the word throughout history

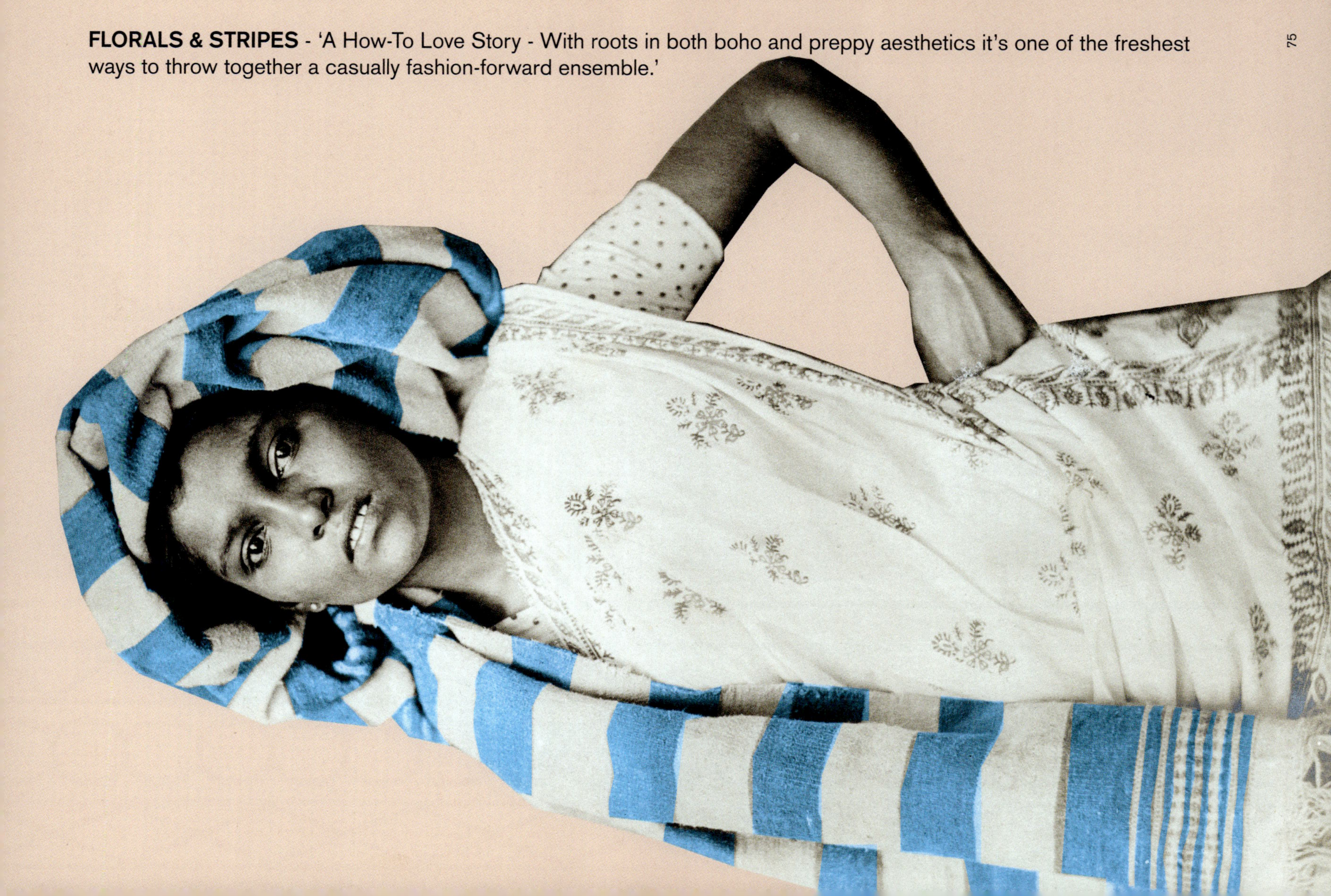

FLORALS & STRIPES - 'A How-To Love Story - With roots in both boho and preppy aesthetics it's one of the freshest ways to throw together a casually fashion-forward ensemble.'

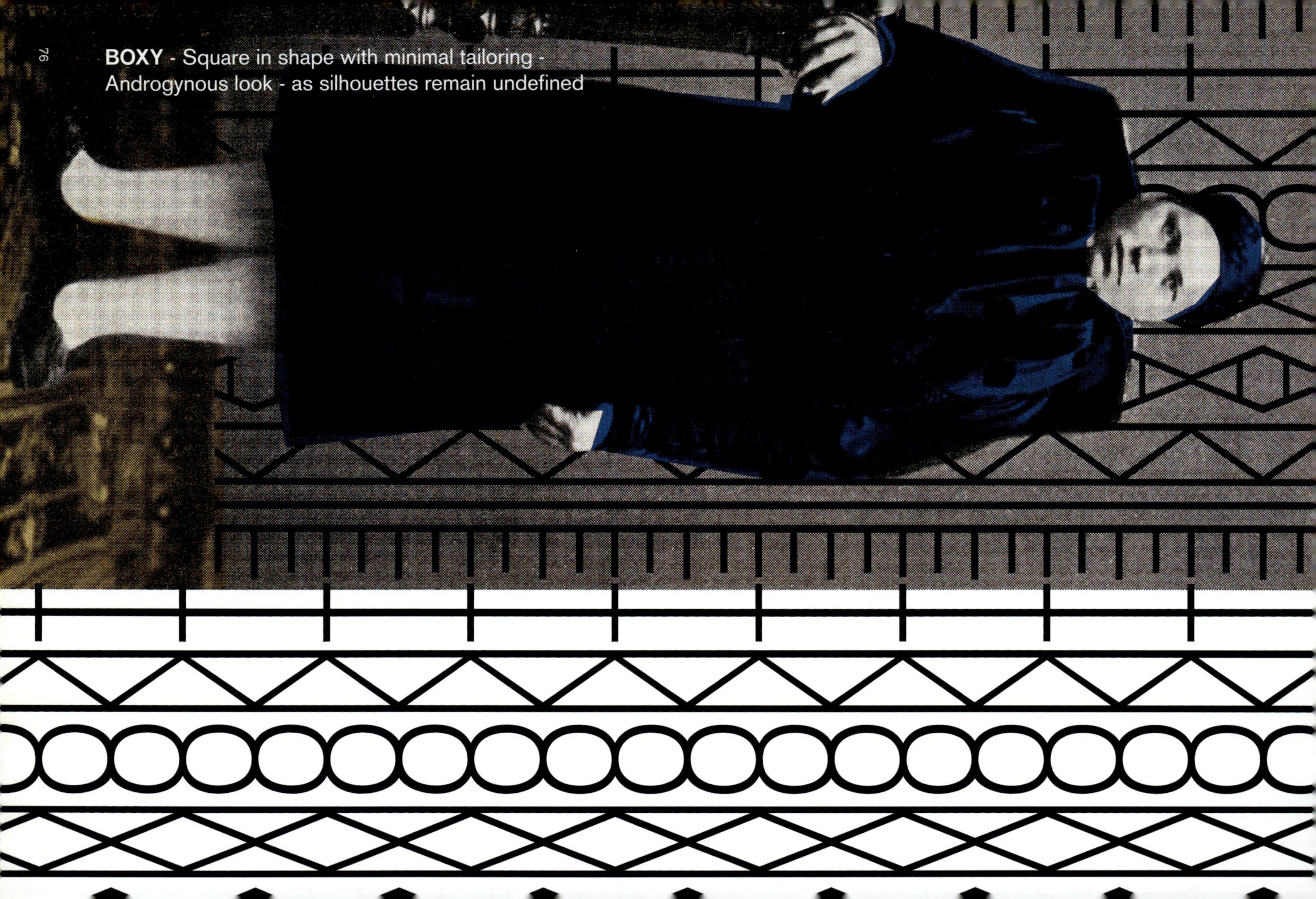

BOXY - Square in shape with minimal tailoring -
Androgynous look - as silhouettes remain undefined

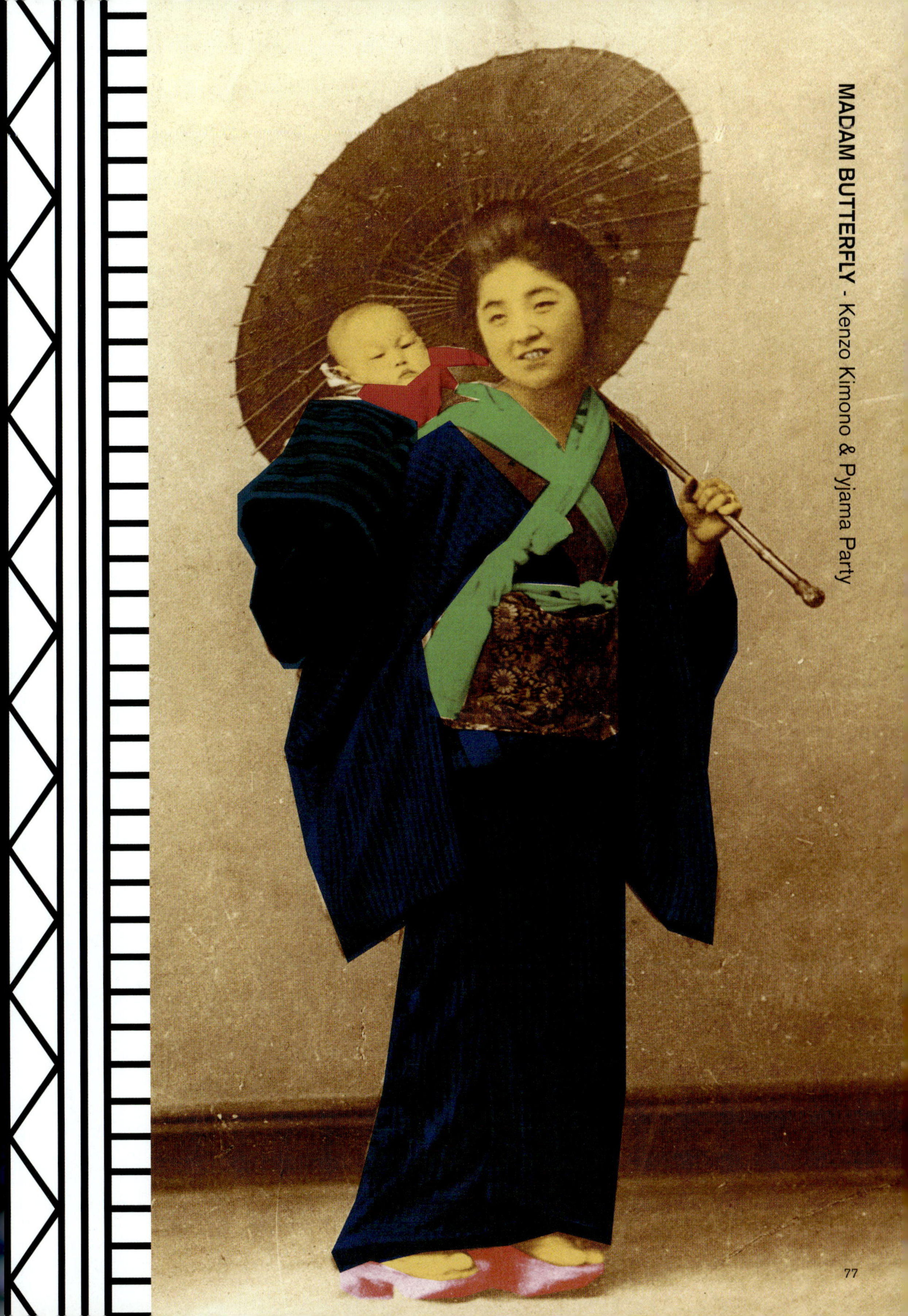

MADAM BUTTERFLY - Kenzo Kimono & Pyjama Party

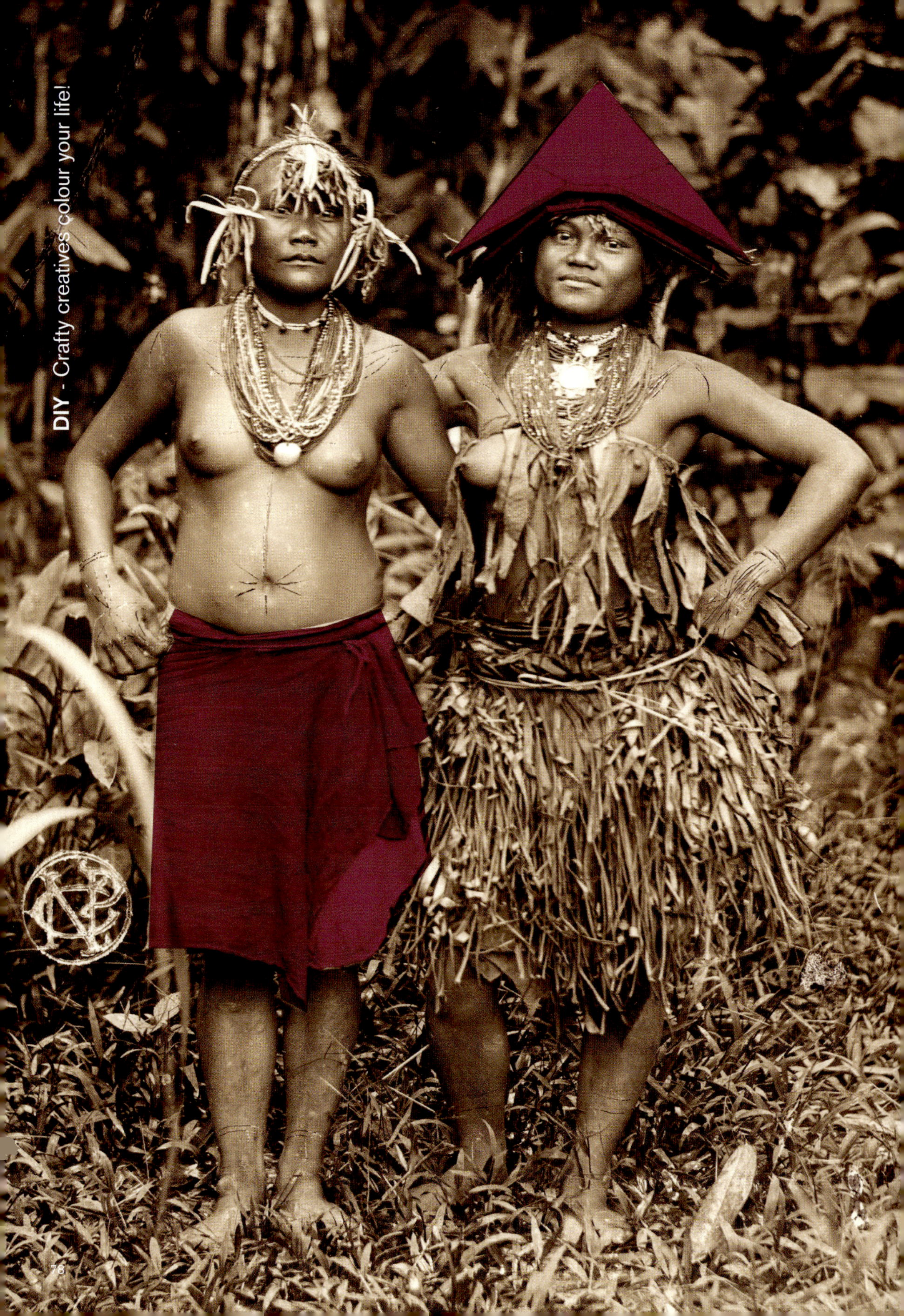
DIY - Crafty creatives colour your life!

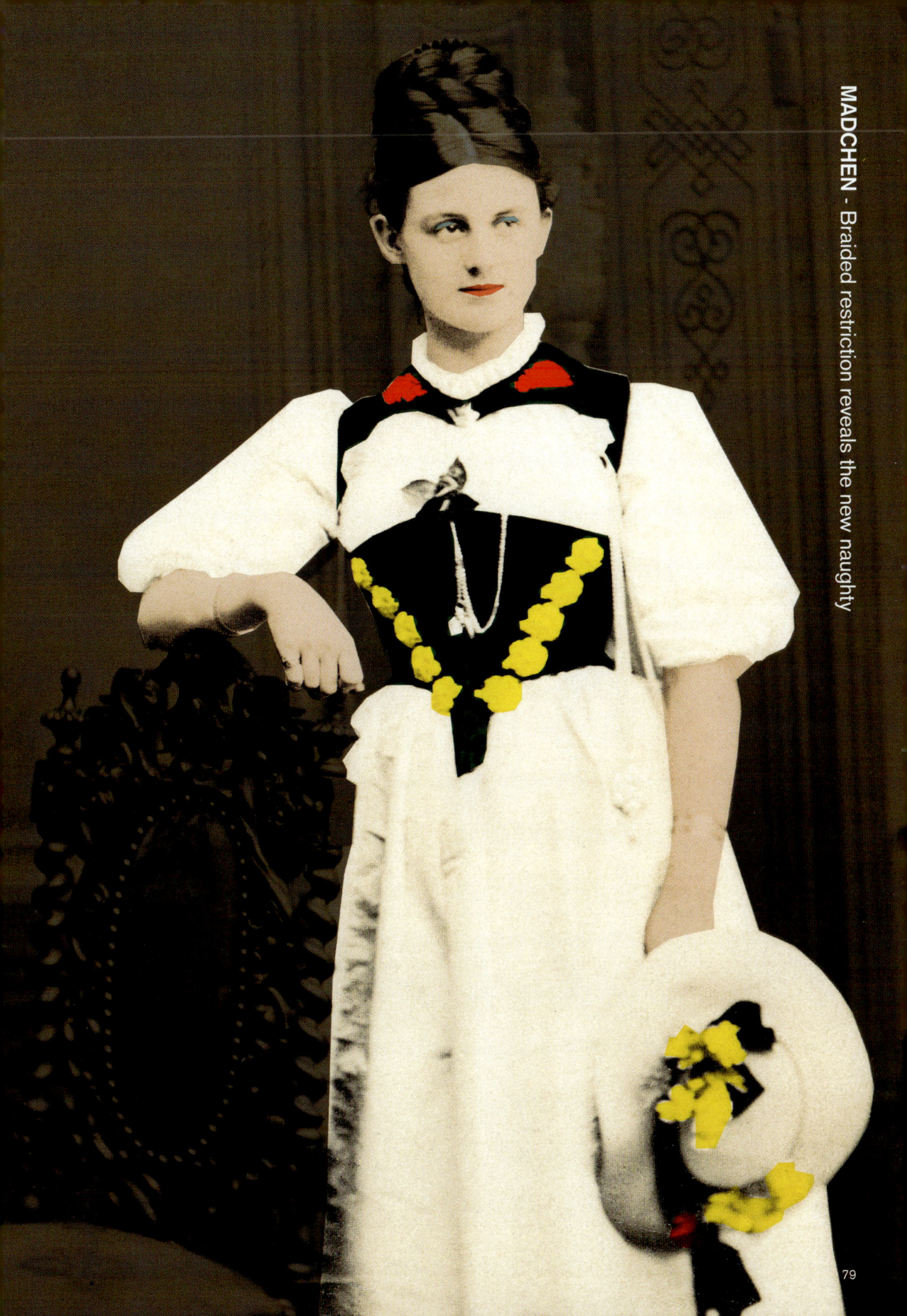
MADCHEN - Braided restriction reveals the new naughty

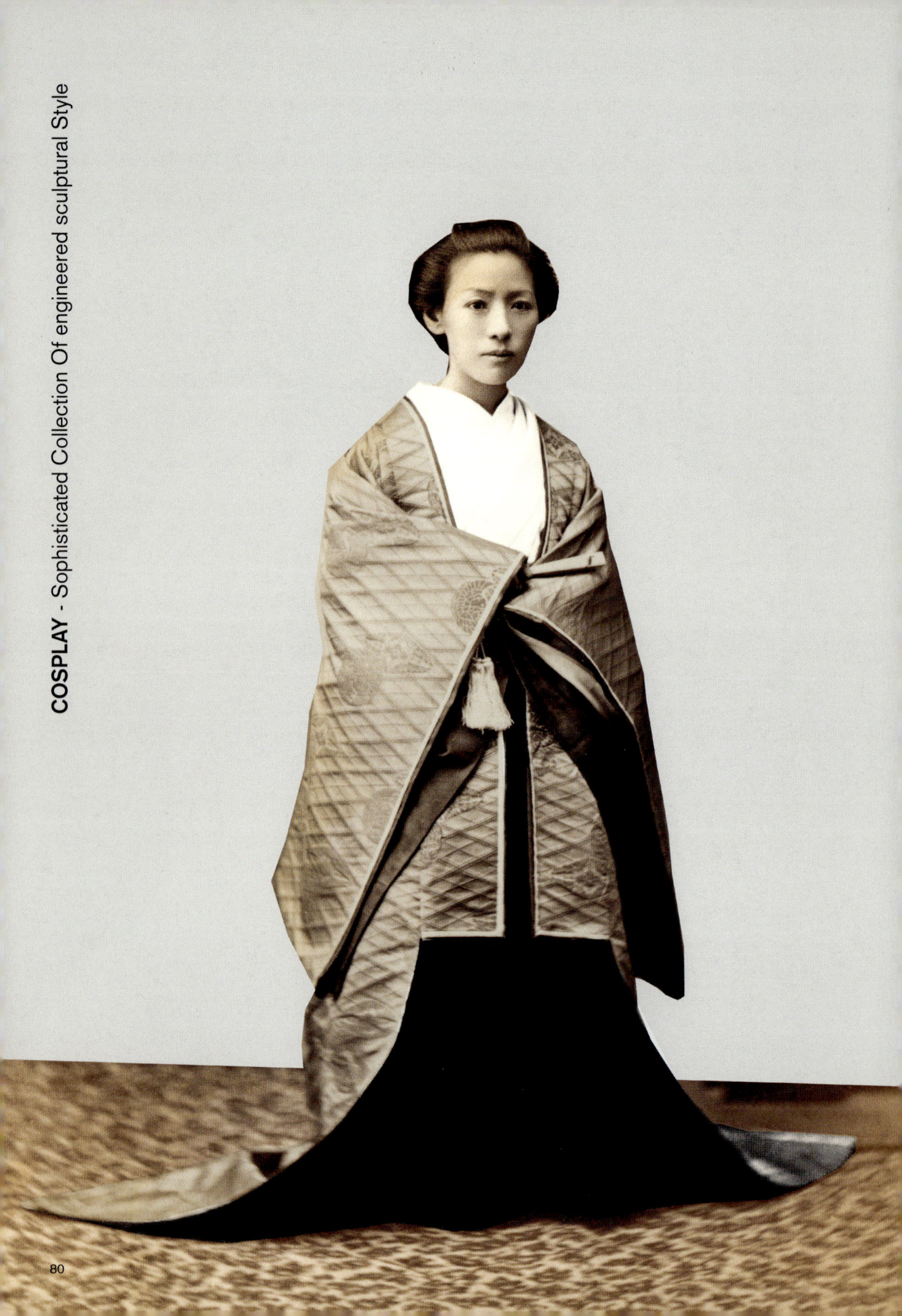

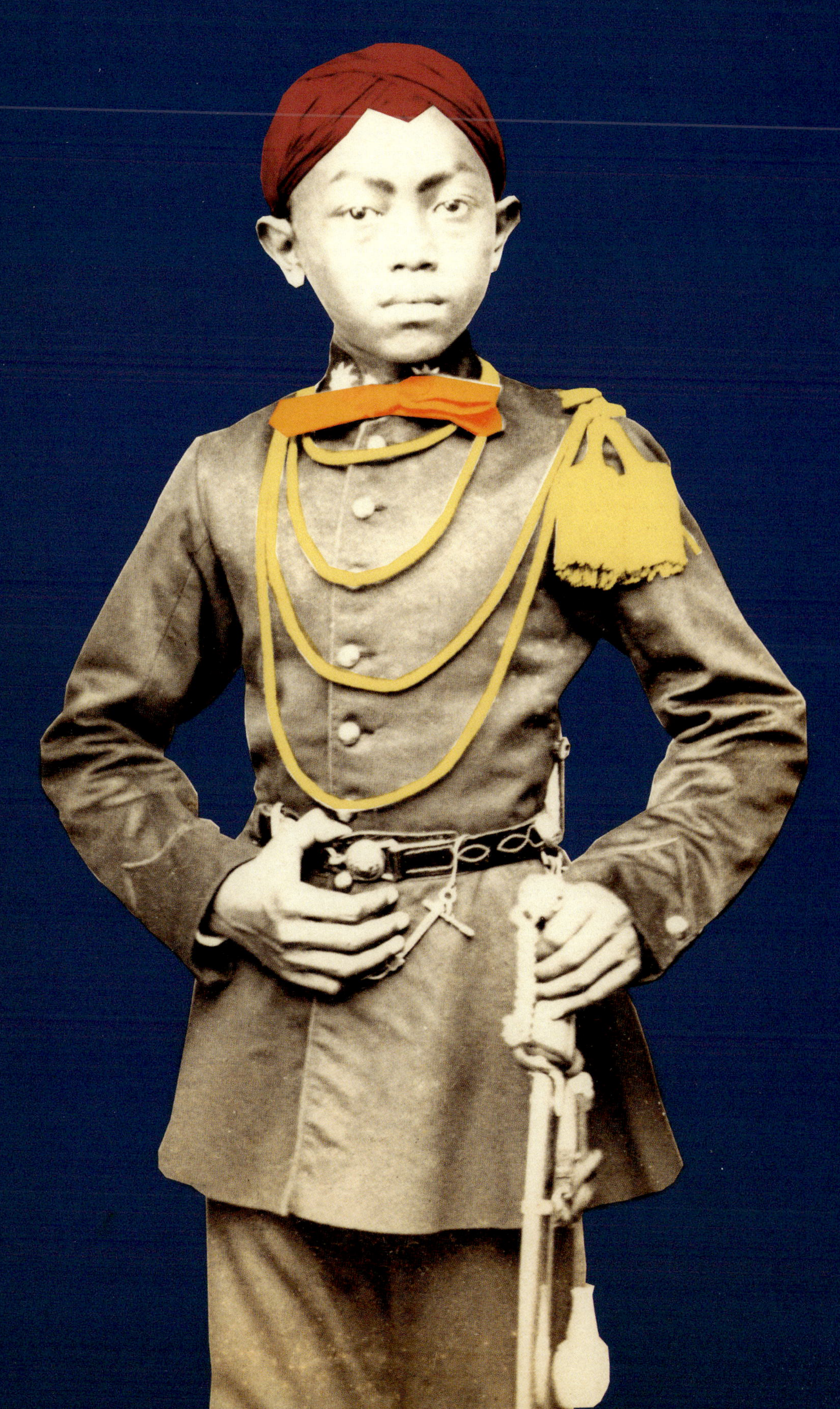

ROYALTY - Playing a prank with Moschino pop power symbols

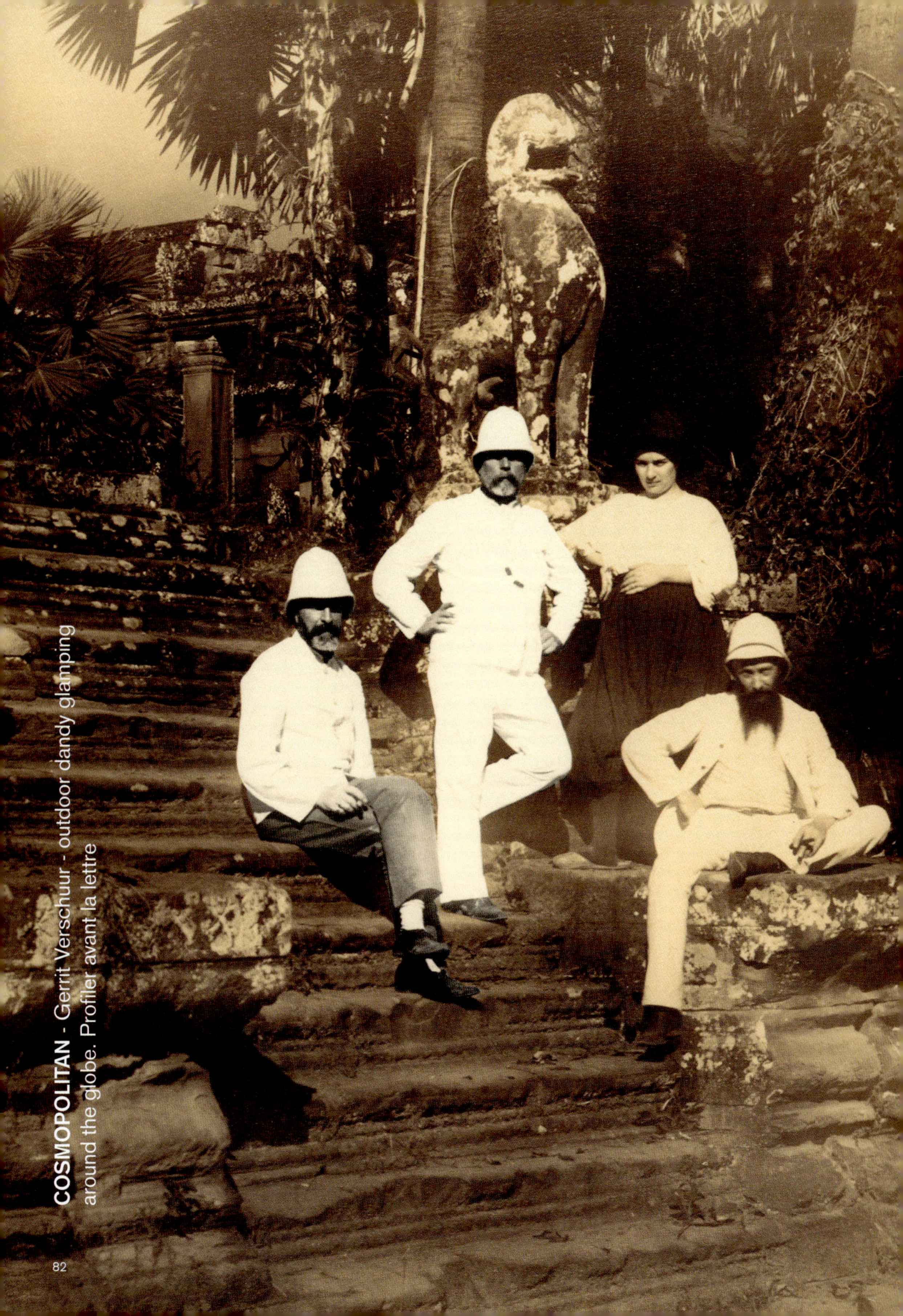
COSMOPOLITAN - Gerrit Verschuur - outdoor dandy glamping around the globe. Profiler avant la lettre

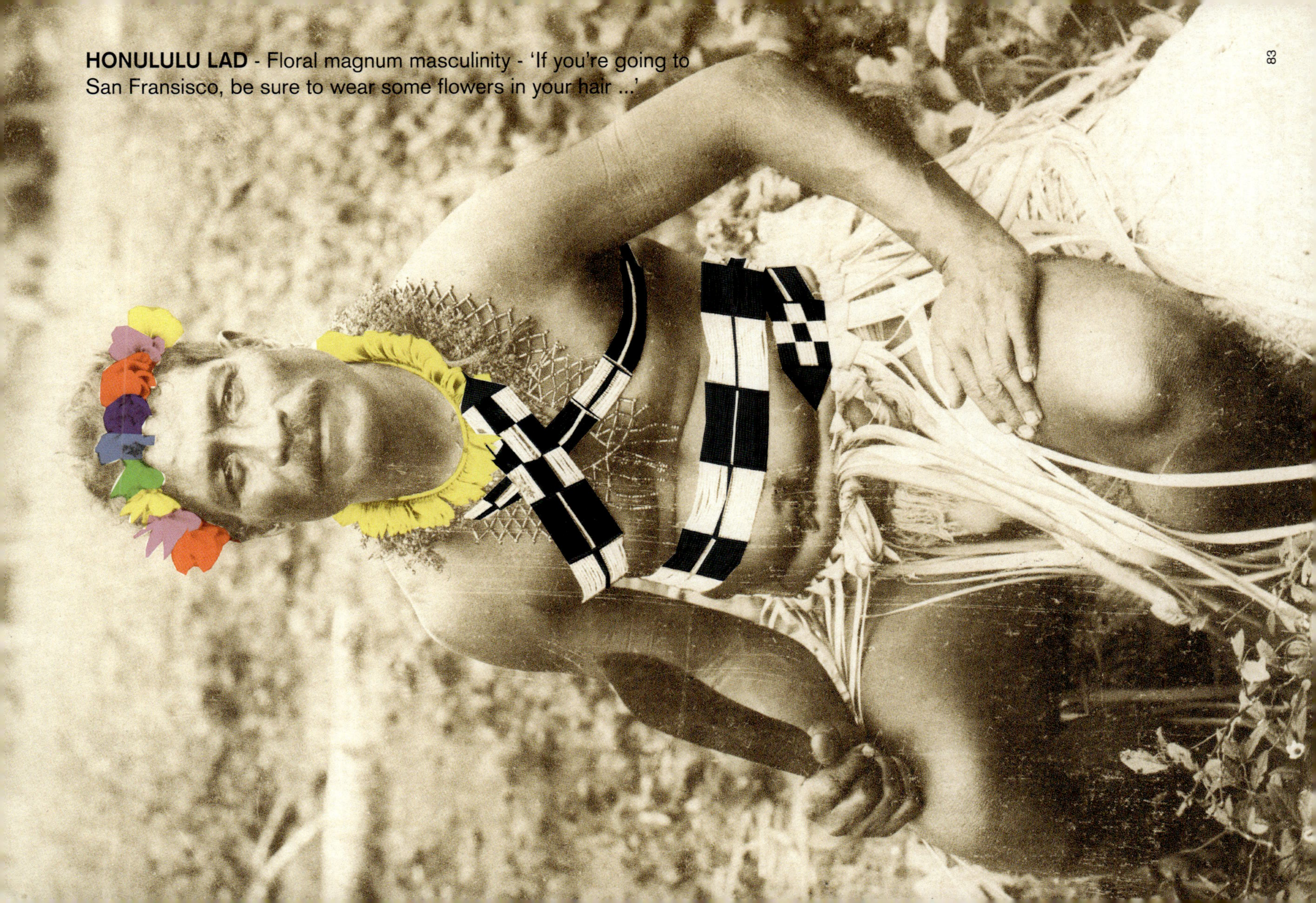

HONULULU LAD - Floral magnum masculinity - 'If you're going to San Fransisco, be sure to wear some flowers in your hair ...'

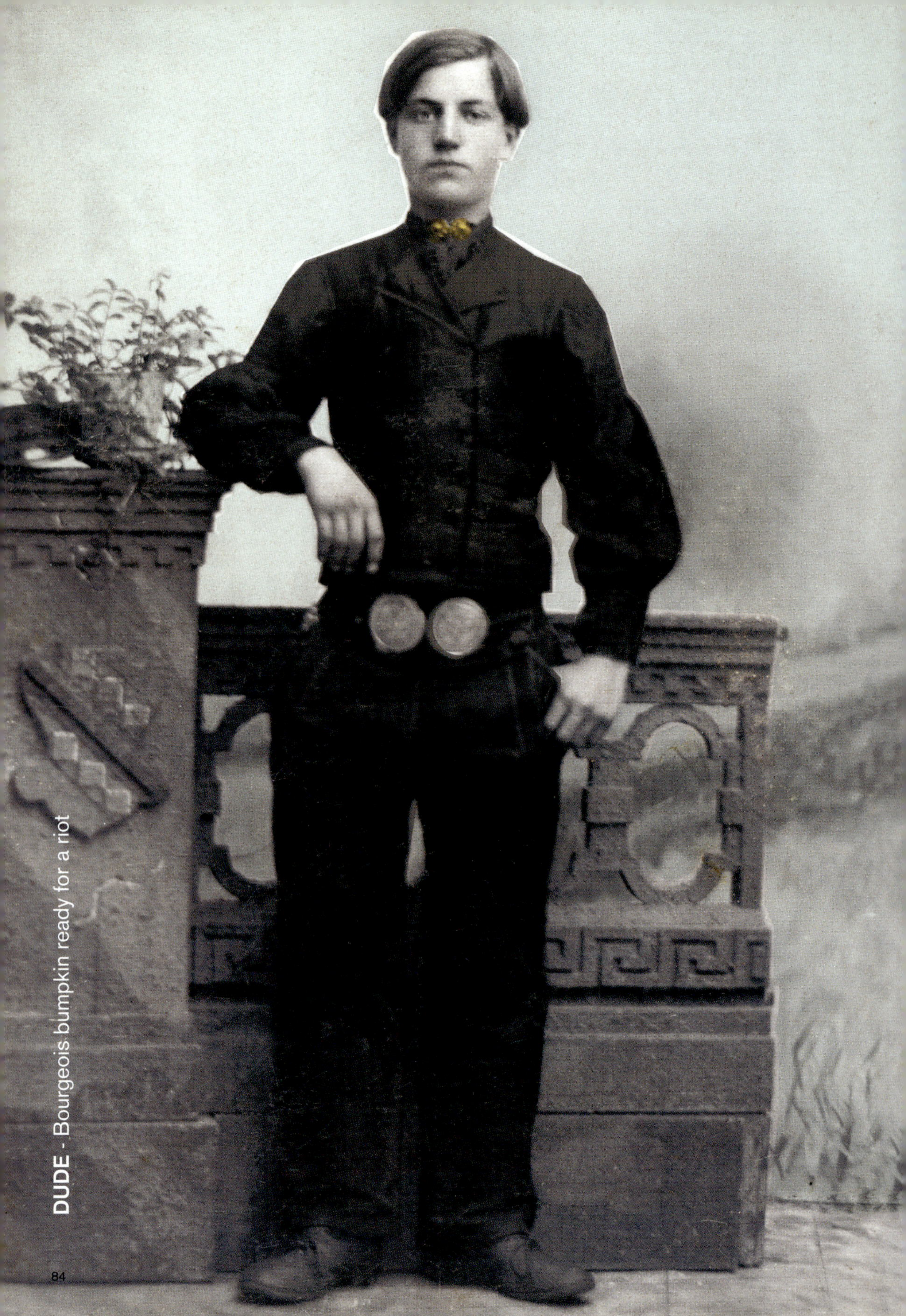

84

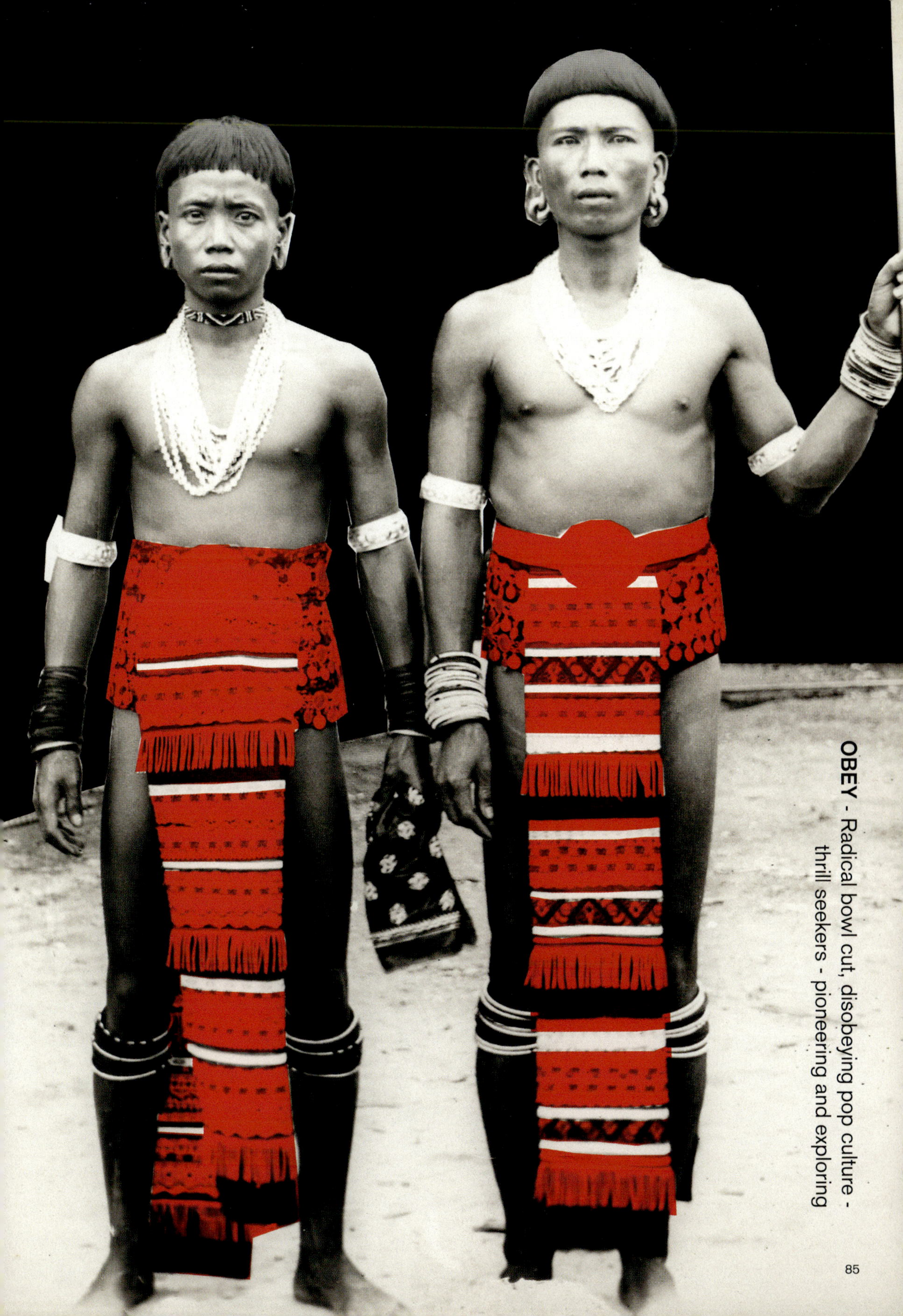

OBEY - Radical bowl cut, disobeying pop culture - thrill seekers - pioneering and exploring

85

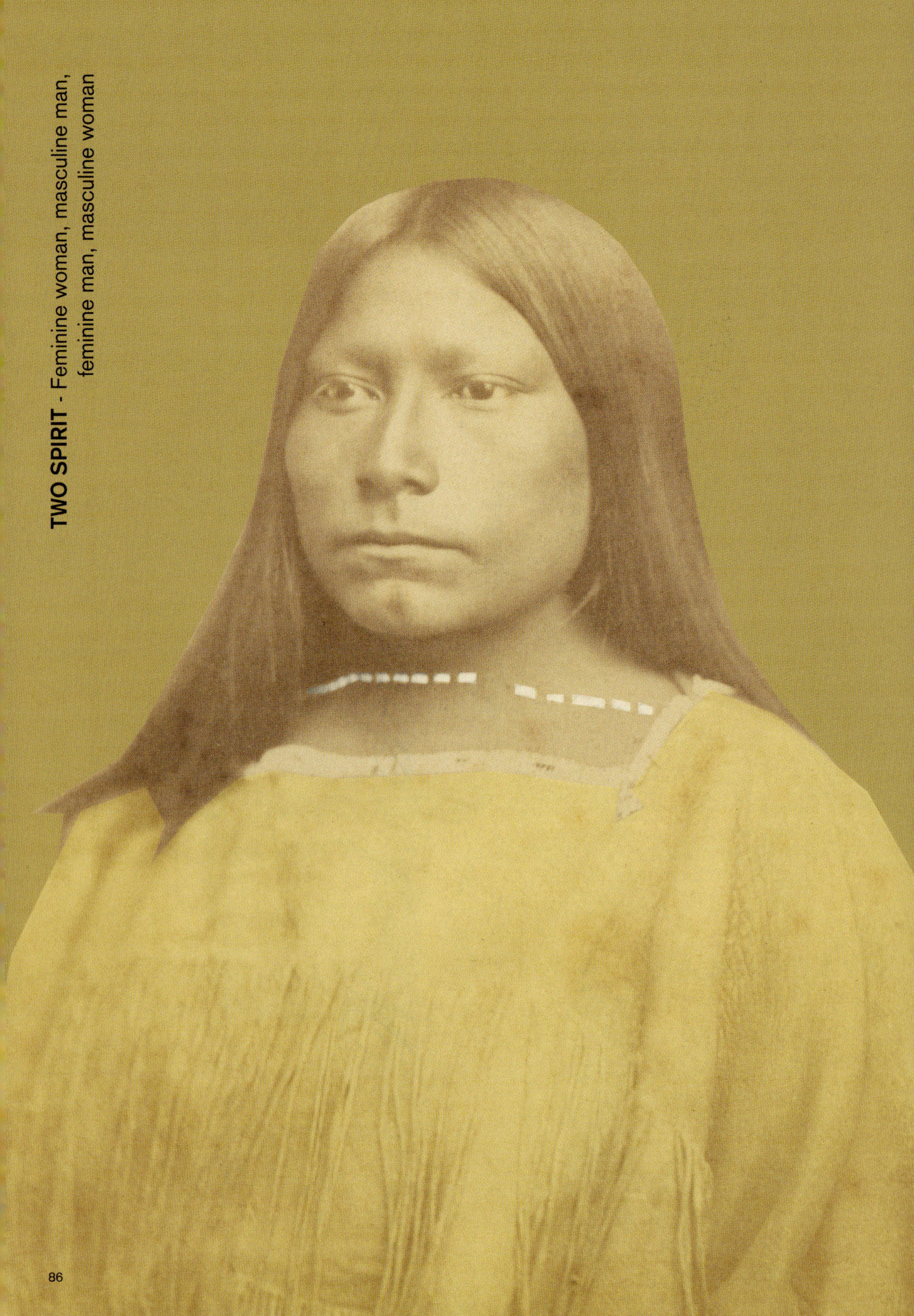

TWO SPIRIT - Feminine woman, masculine man,
feminine man, masculine woman

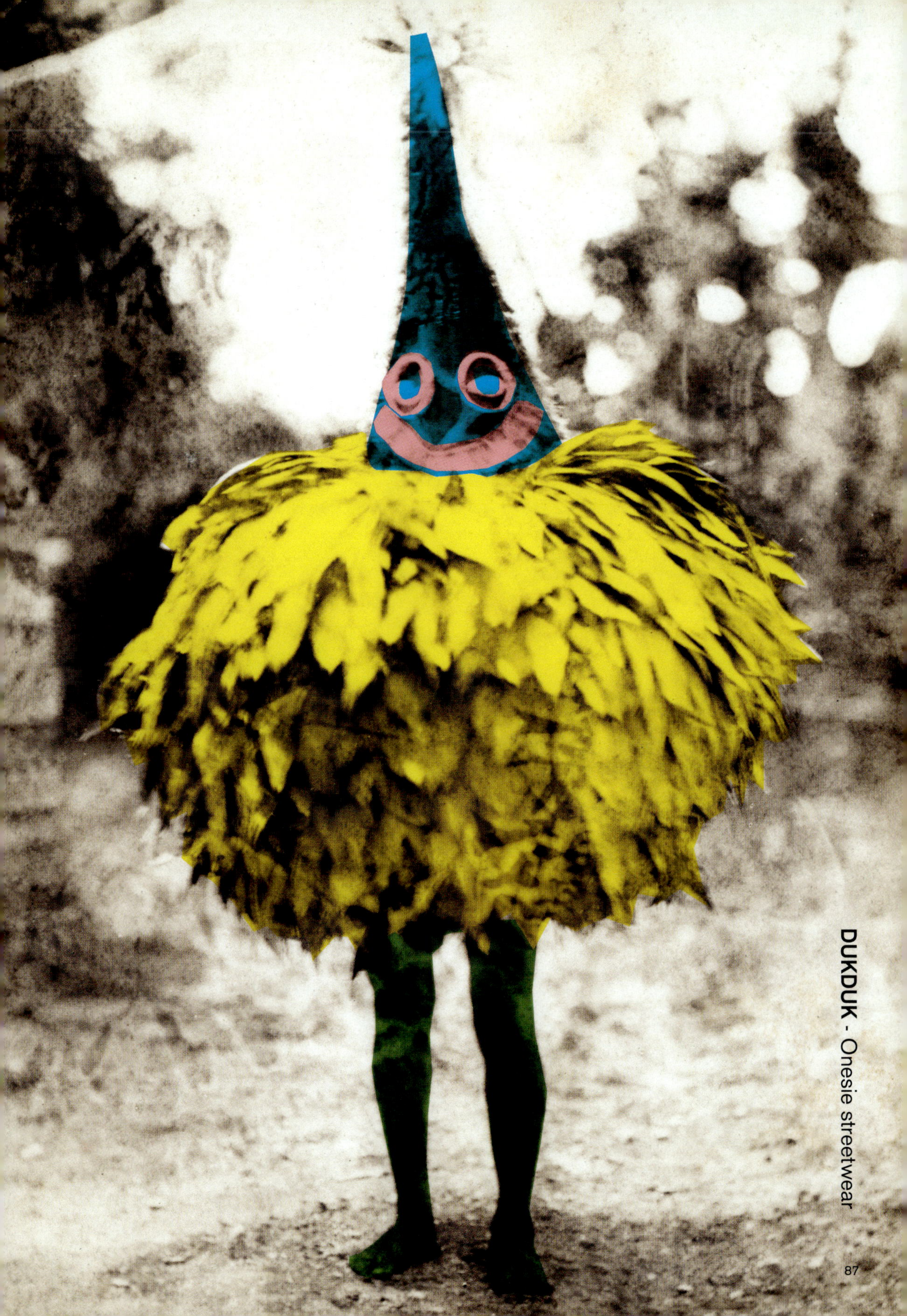

DUKDUK - Onesie streetwear

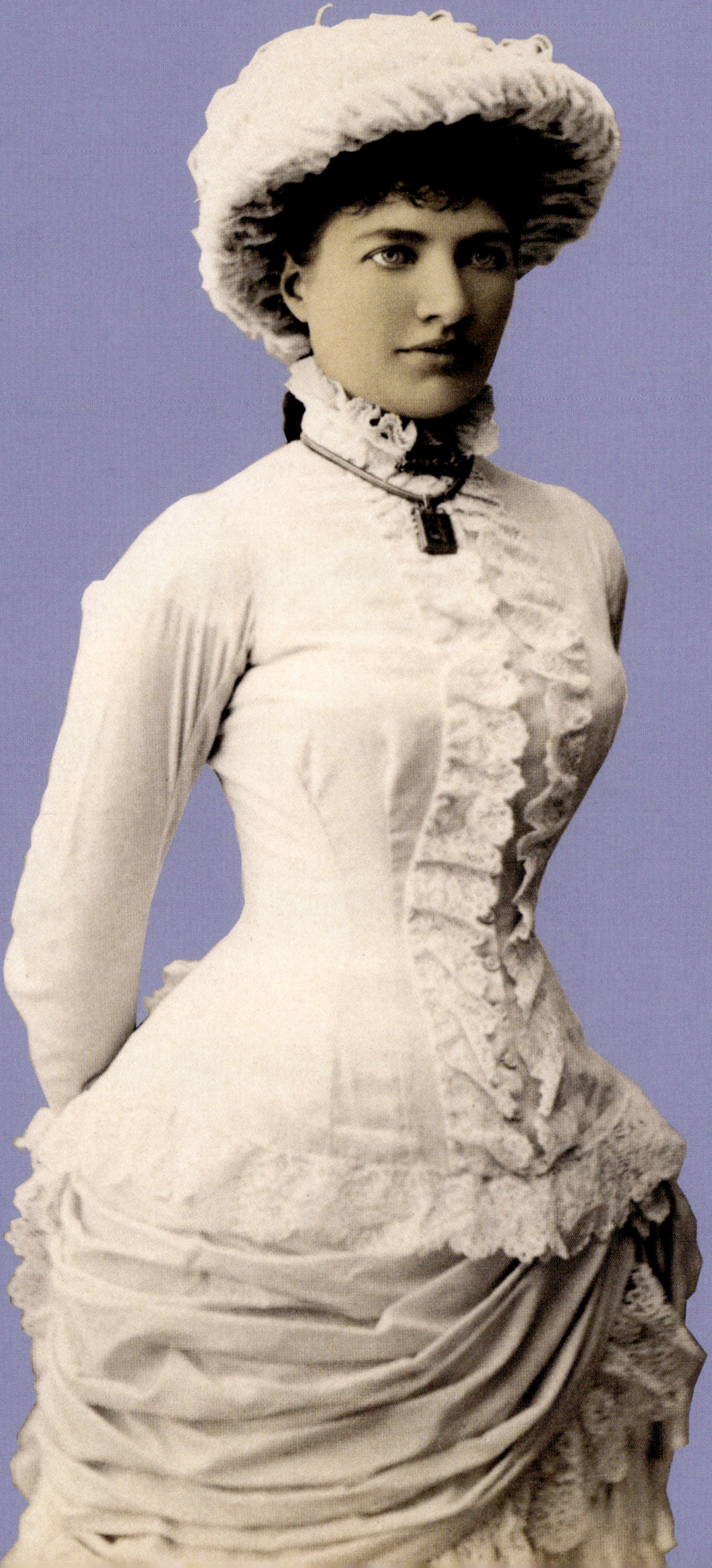

HIGH TEA - Victorian sponge wrapped up tight in a summer corset

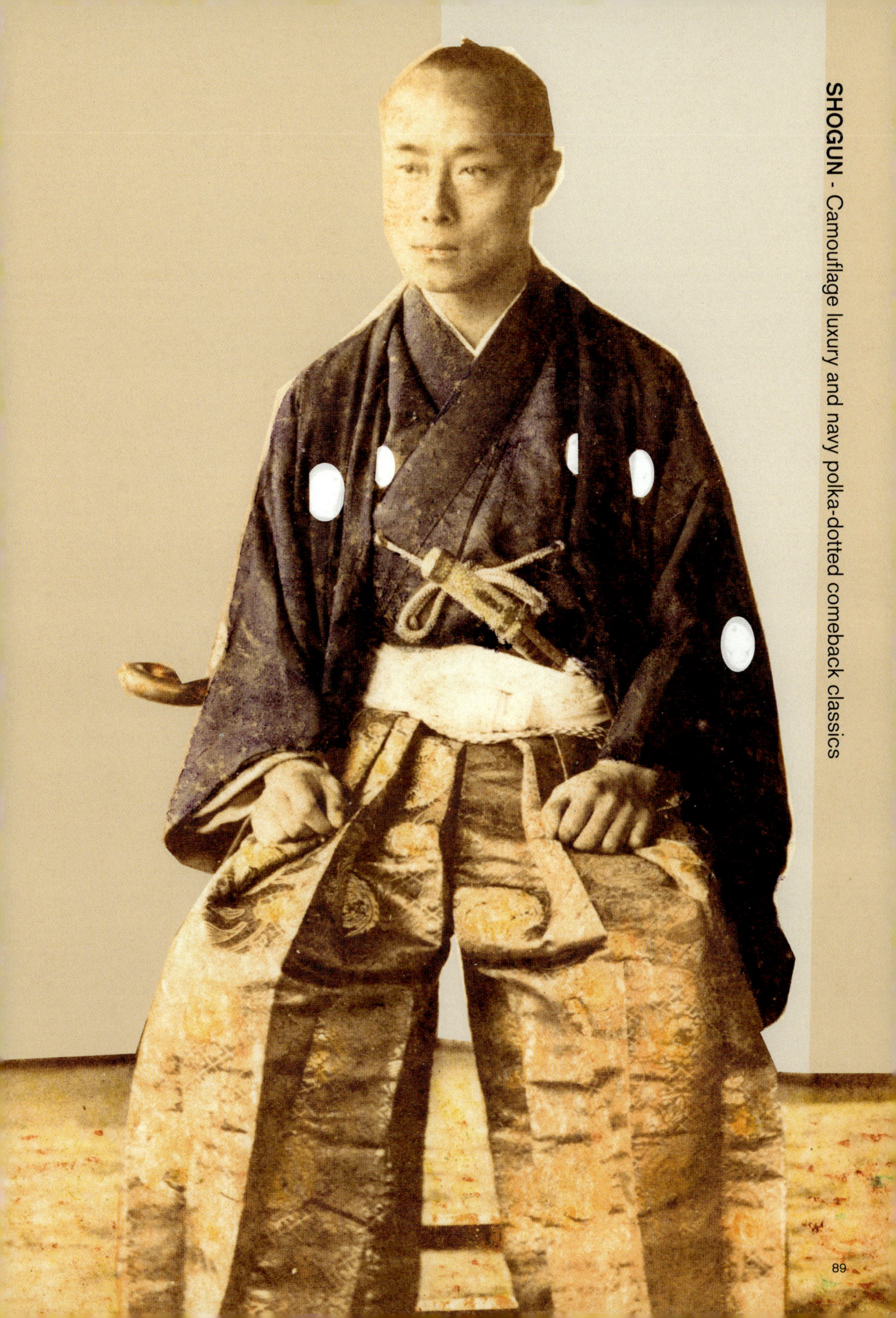

SHOGUN - Camouflage luxury and navy polka-dotted comeback classics

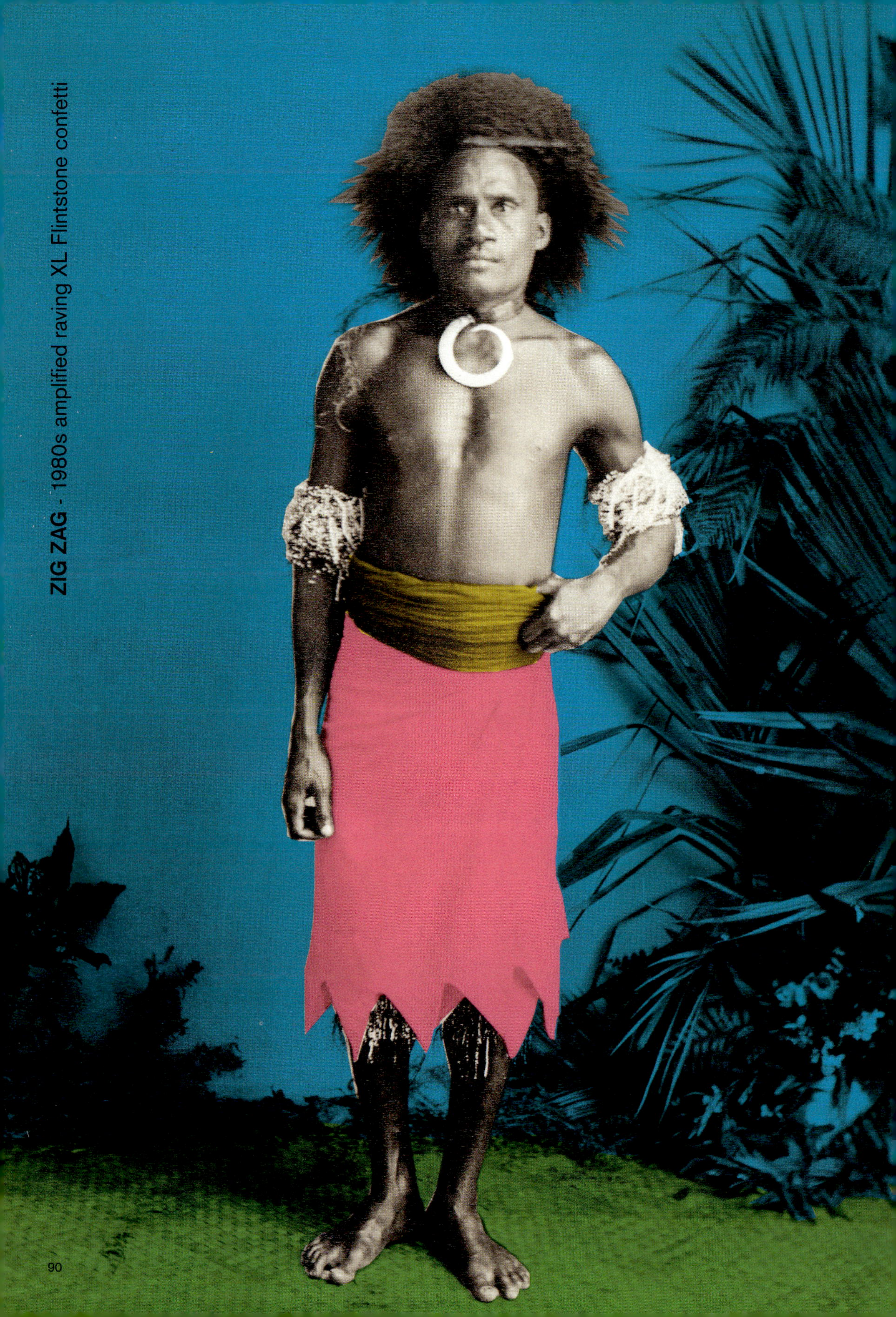

ZIG ZAG - 1980s amplified raving XL Flintstone confetti

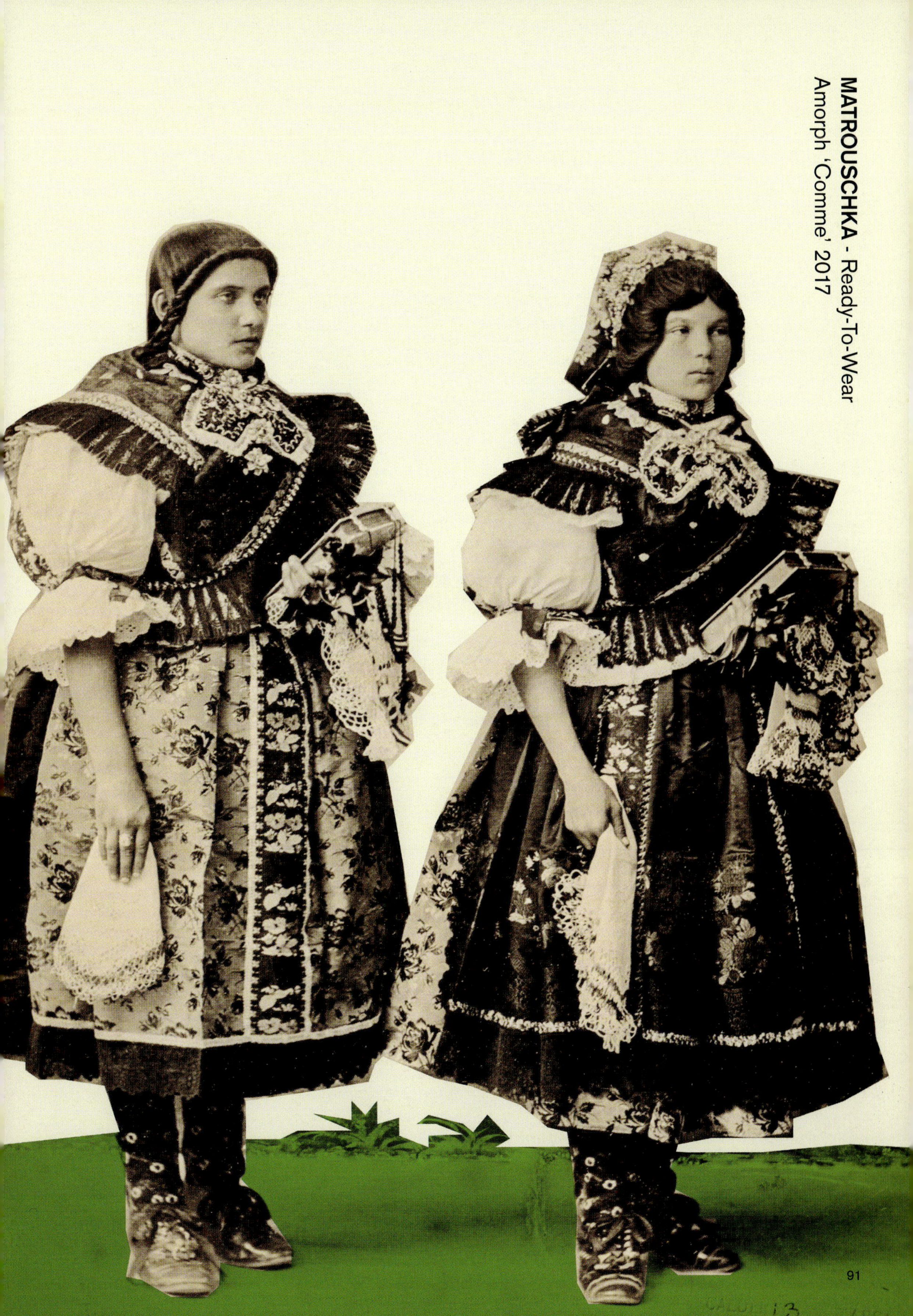

MATROUSCHKA - Ready-To-Wear
Amorph 'Comme' 2017

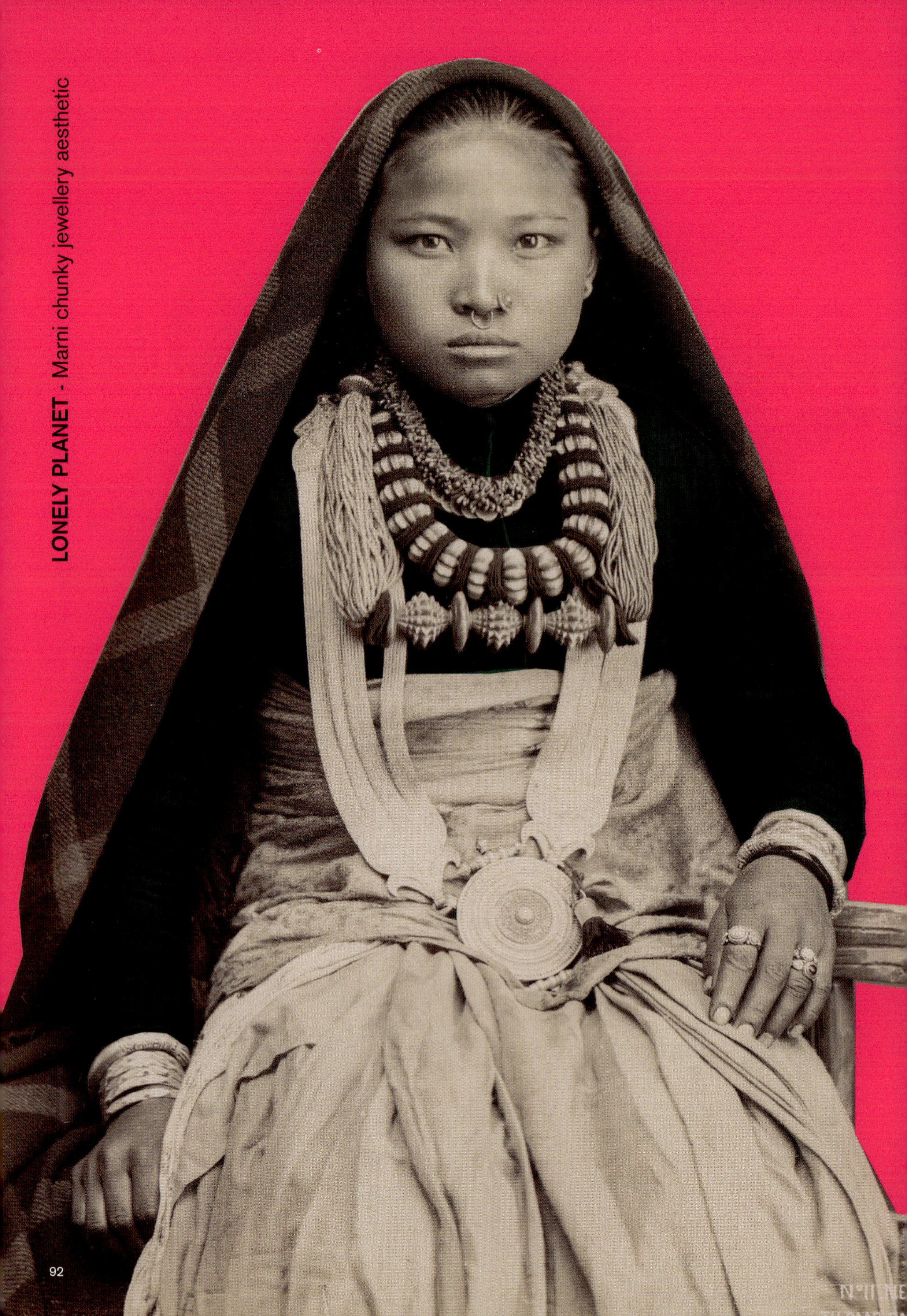

LONELY PLANET · Marni chunky jewellery aesthetic

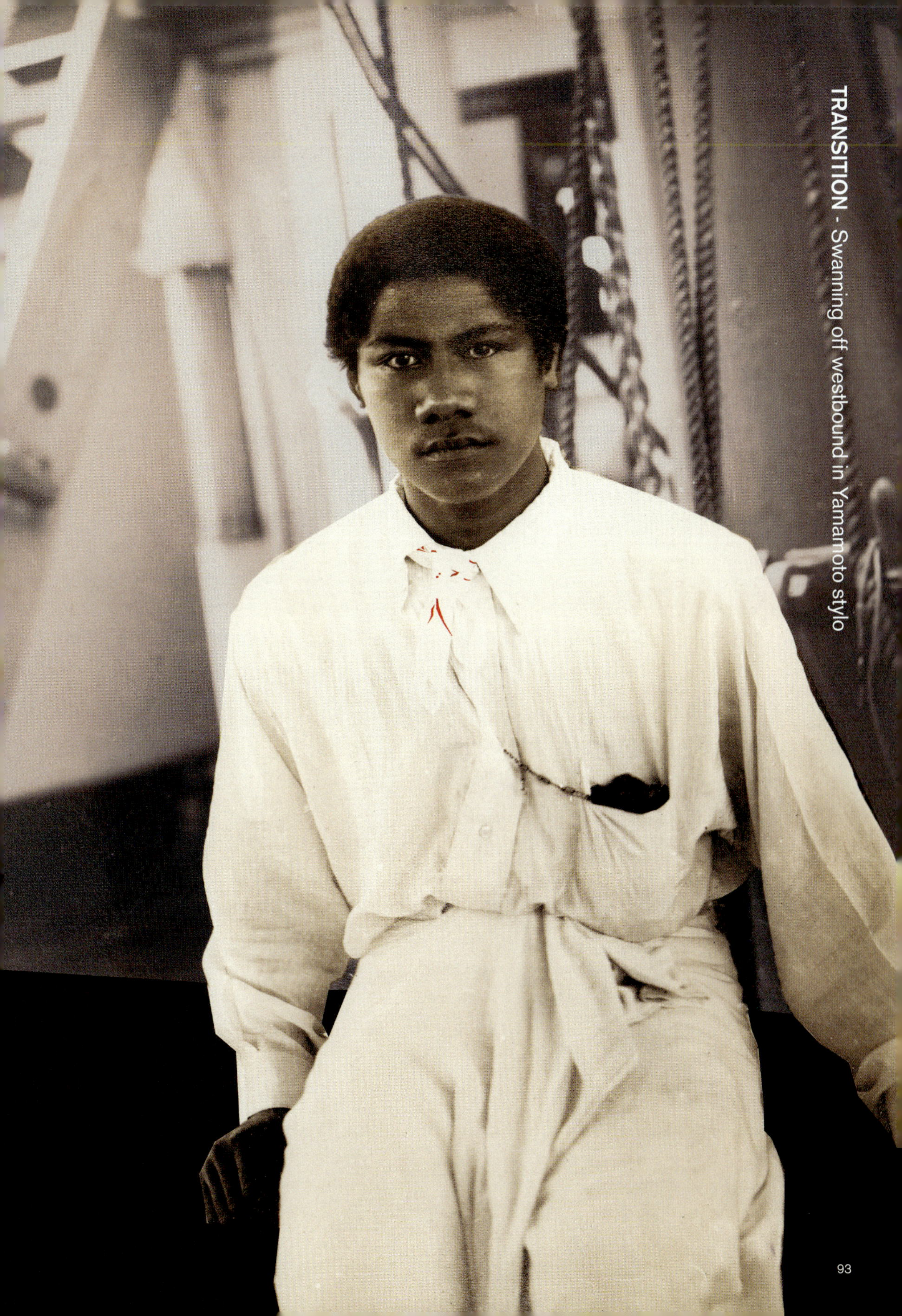

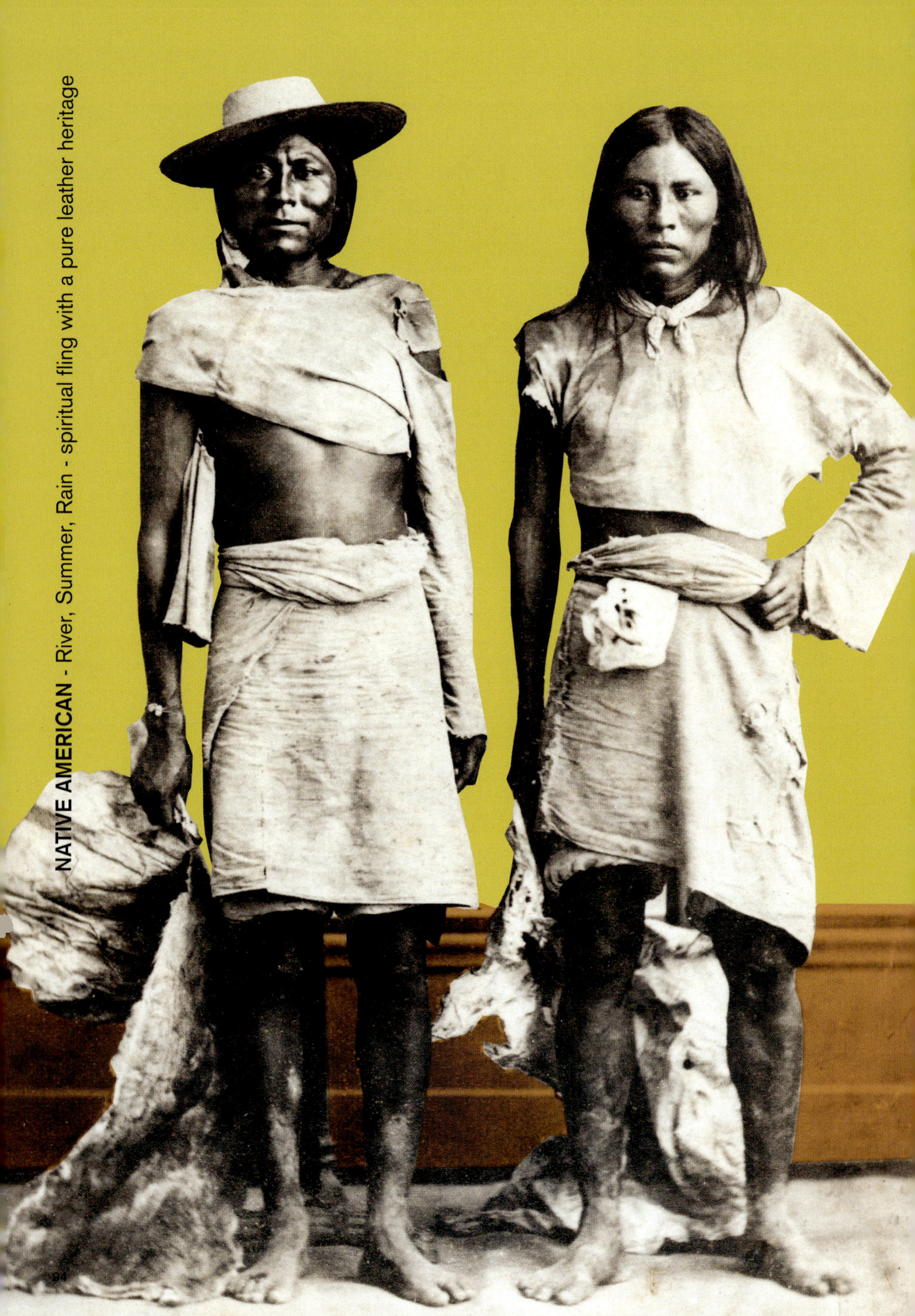

NATIVE AMERICAN - River, Summer, Rain - spiritual fling with a pure leather heritage

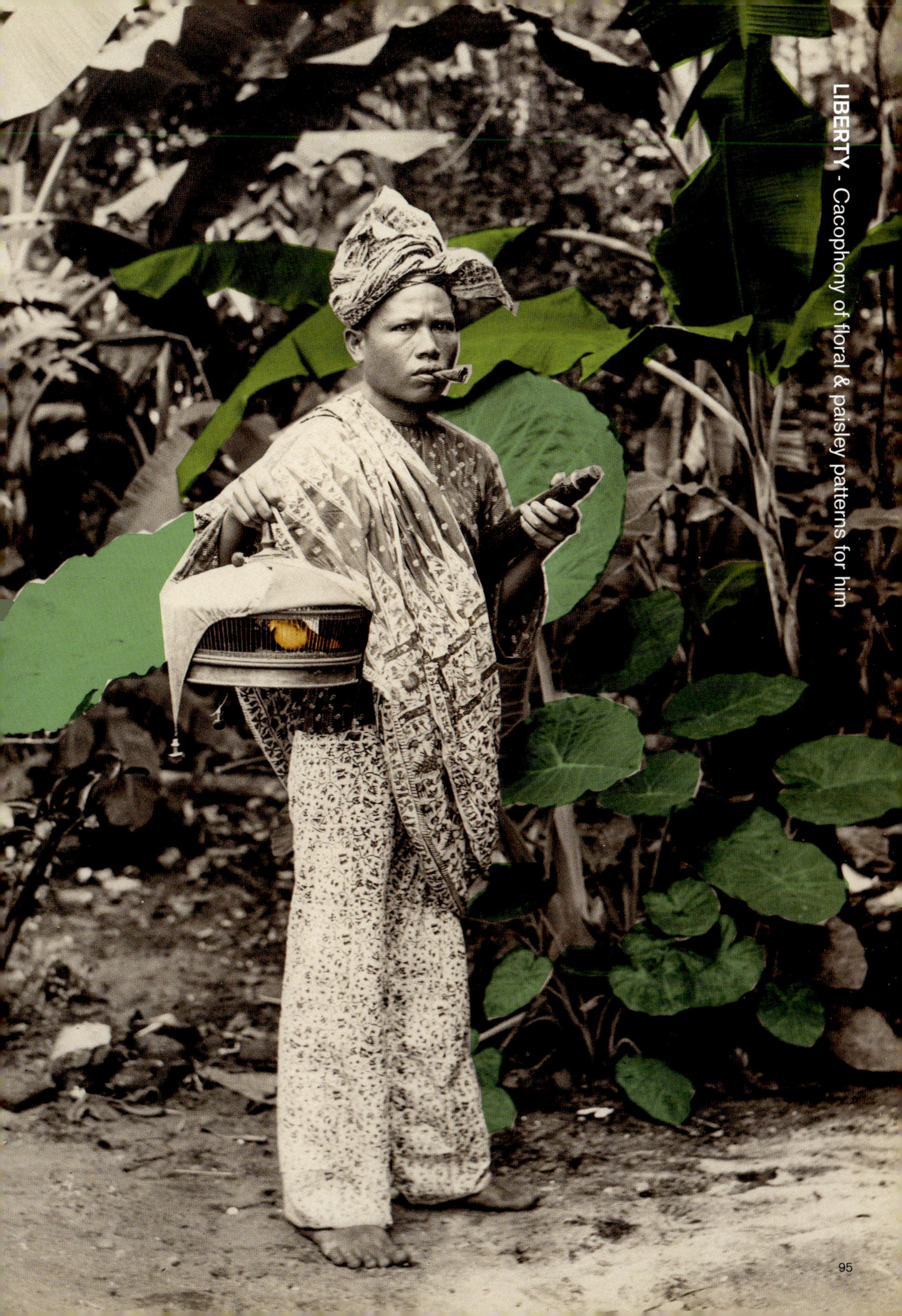
LIBERTY - Cacophony of floral & paisley patterns for him

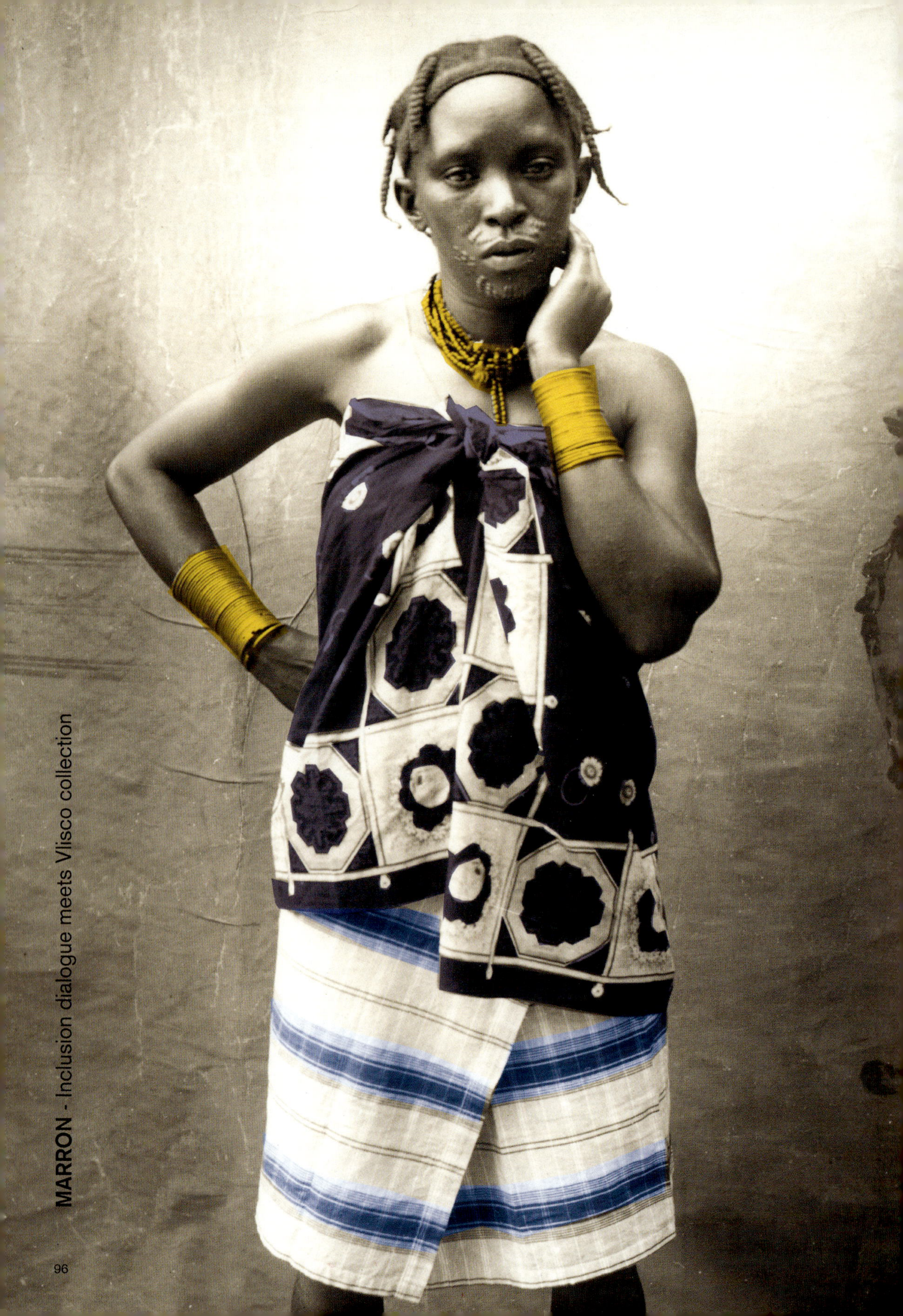

MARRON - Inclusion dialogue meets Vlisco collection

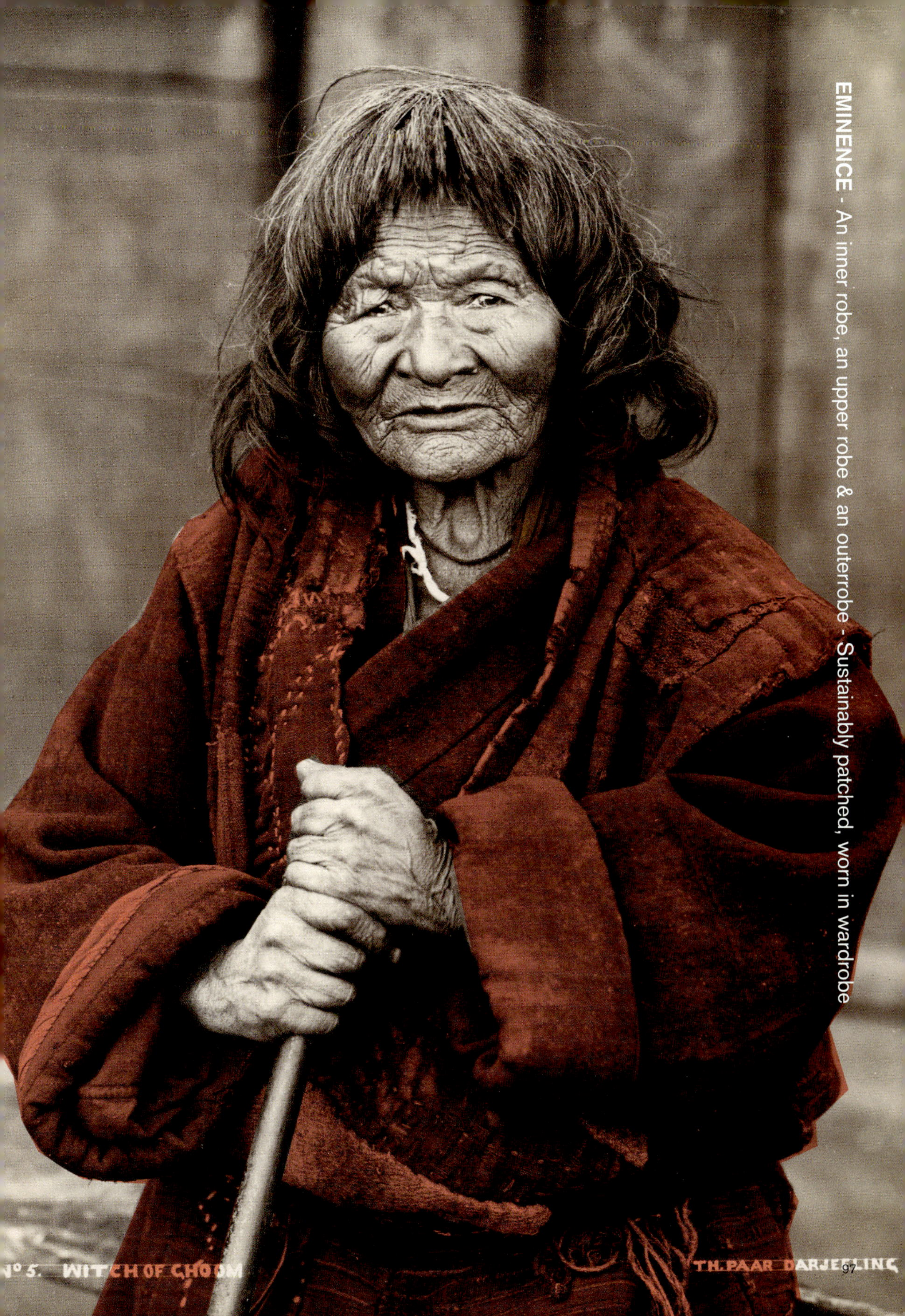

EMINENCE - An inner robe, an upper robe & an outerrobe - Sustainably patched, worn in wardrobe
Nº 5.   WITCH OF CHOOM
TH. PAAR DARJEELING

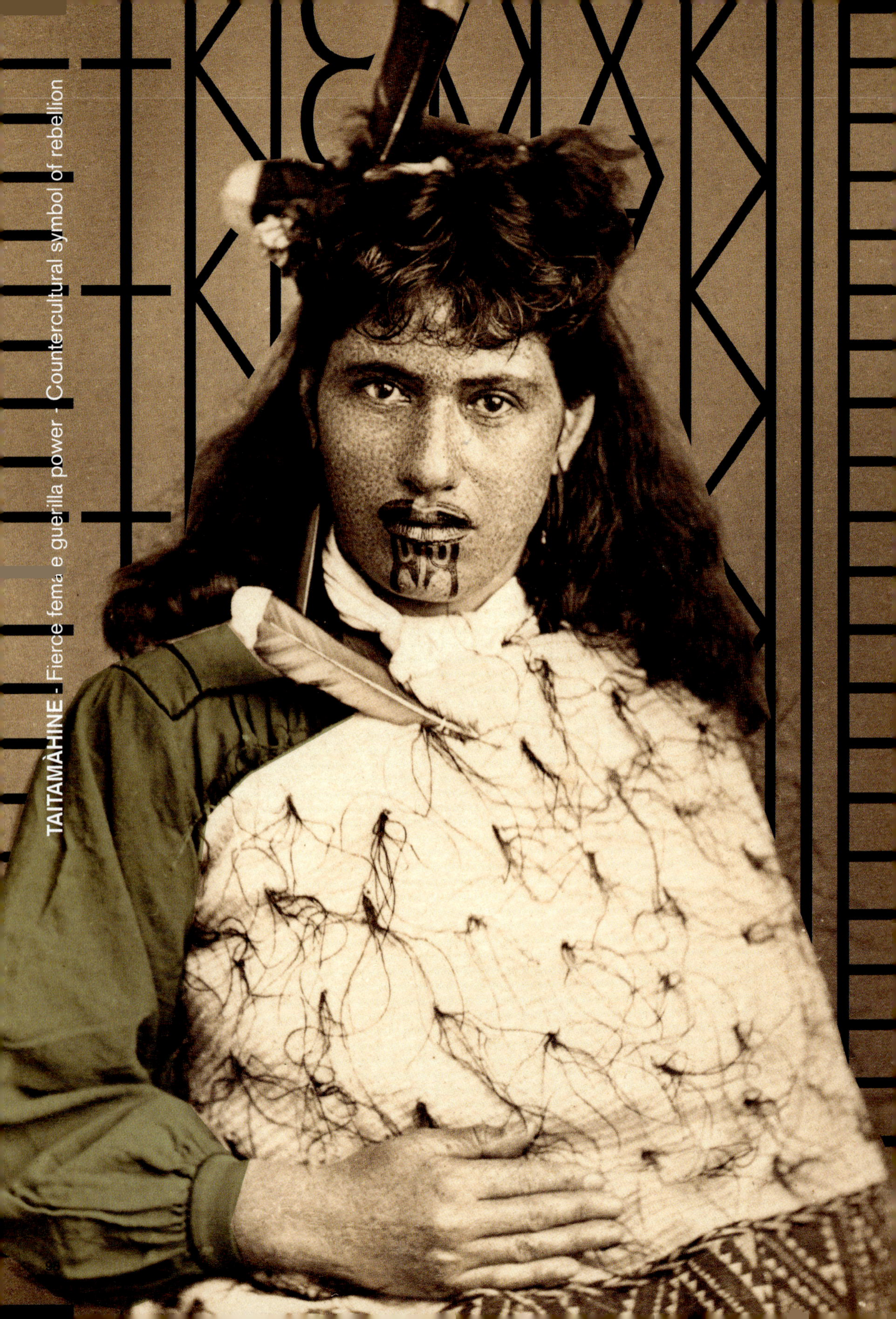
TAITAMÁHINE - Fierce femá e guerilla power - Countercultural symbol of rebellion

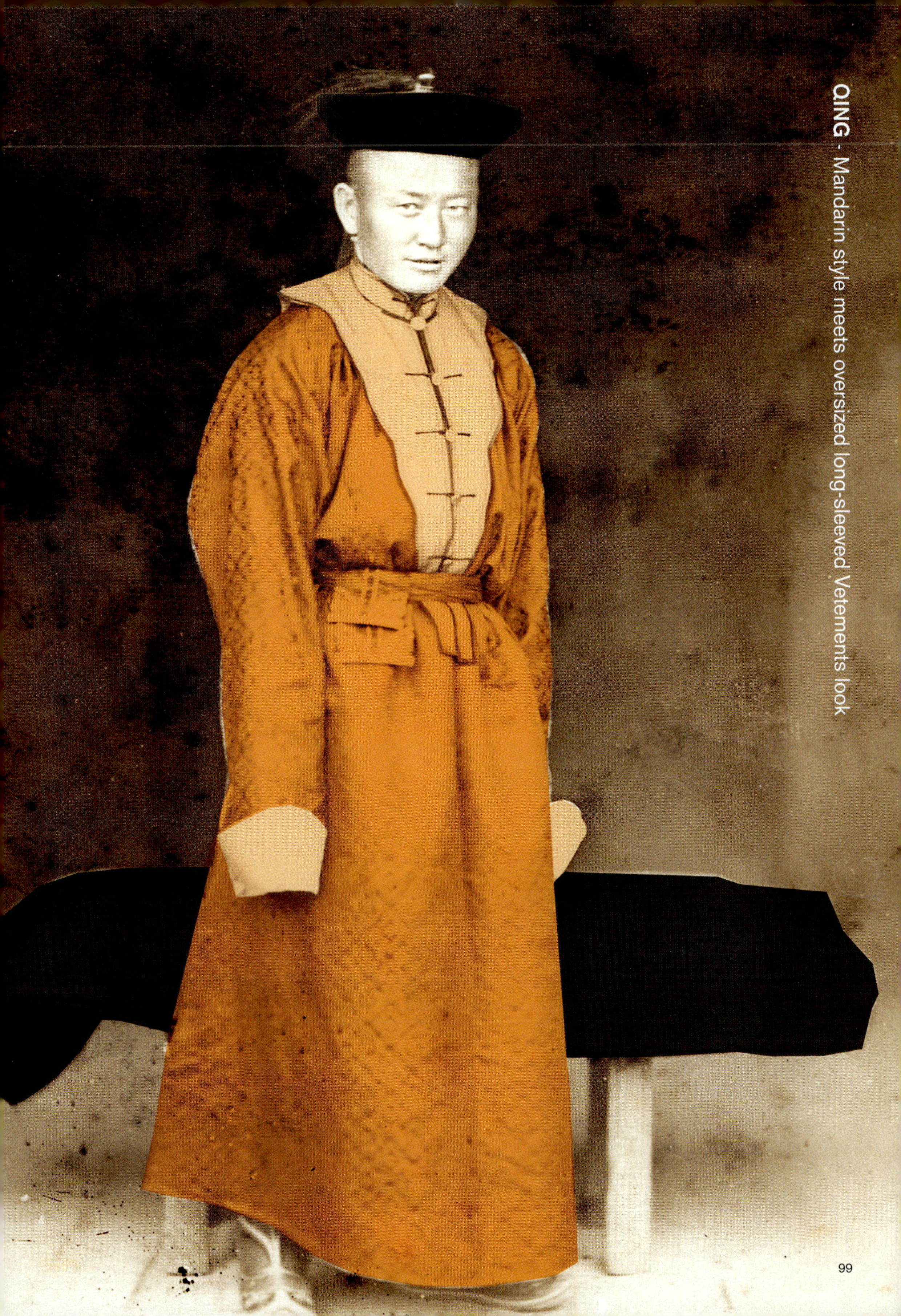

QING - Mandarin style meets oversized long-sleeved Vetements look

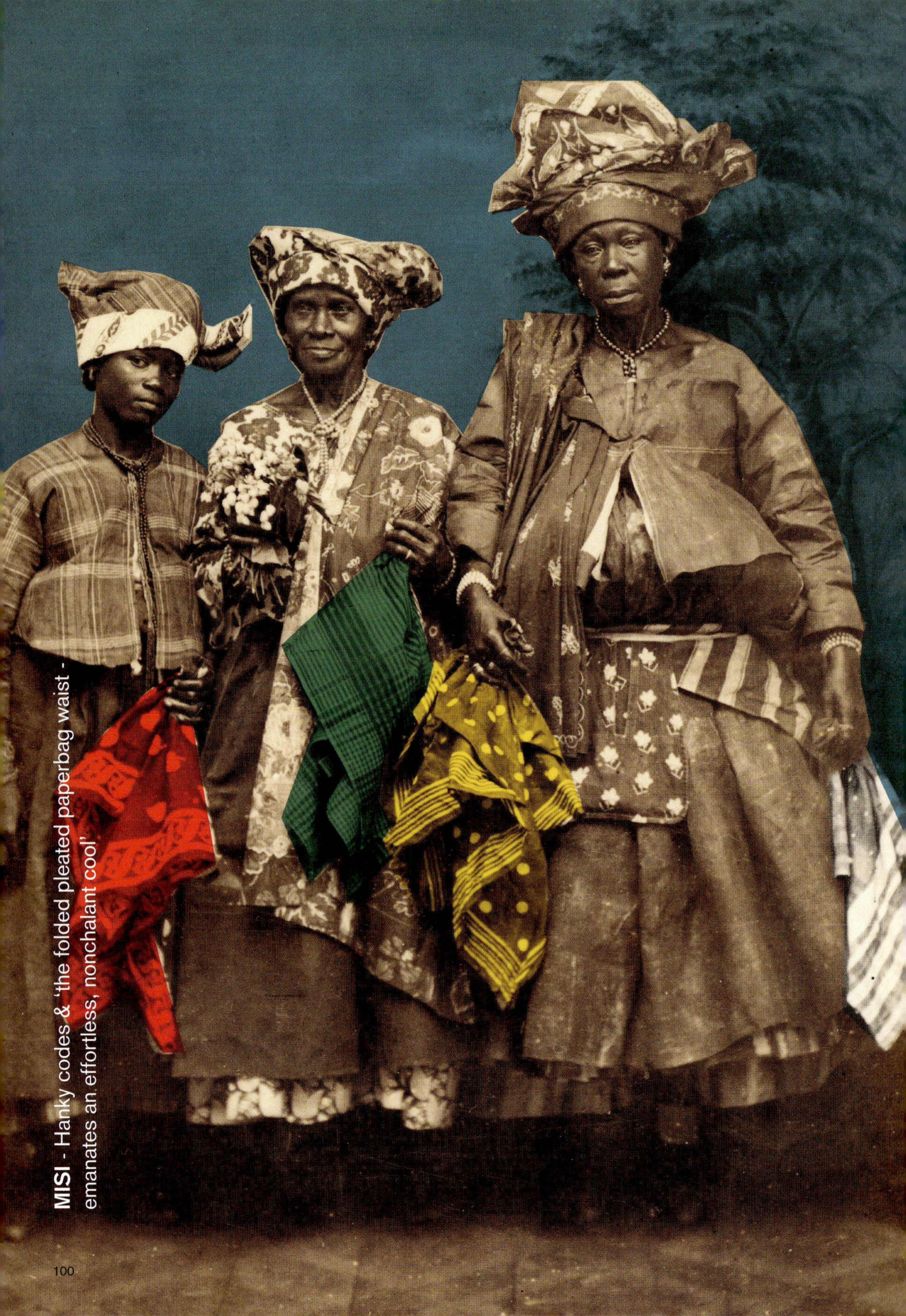

MISI - Hanky codes & "the folded pleated paperbag waist - emanates an effortless, nonchalant cool"

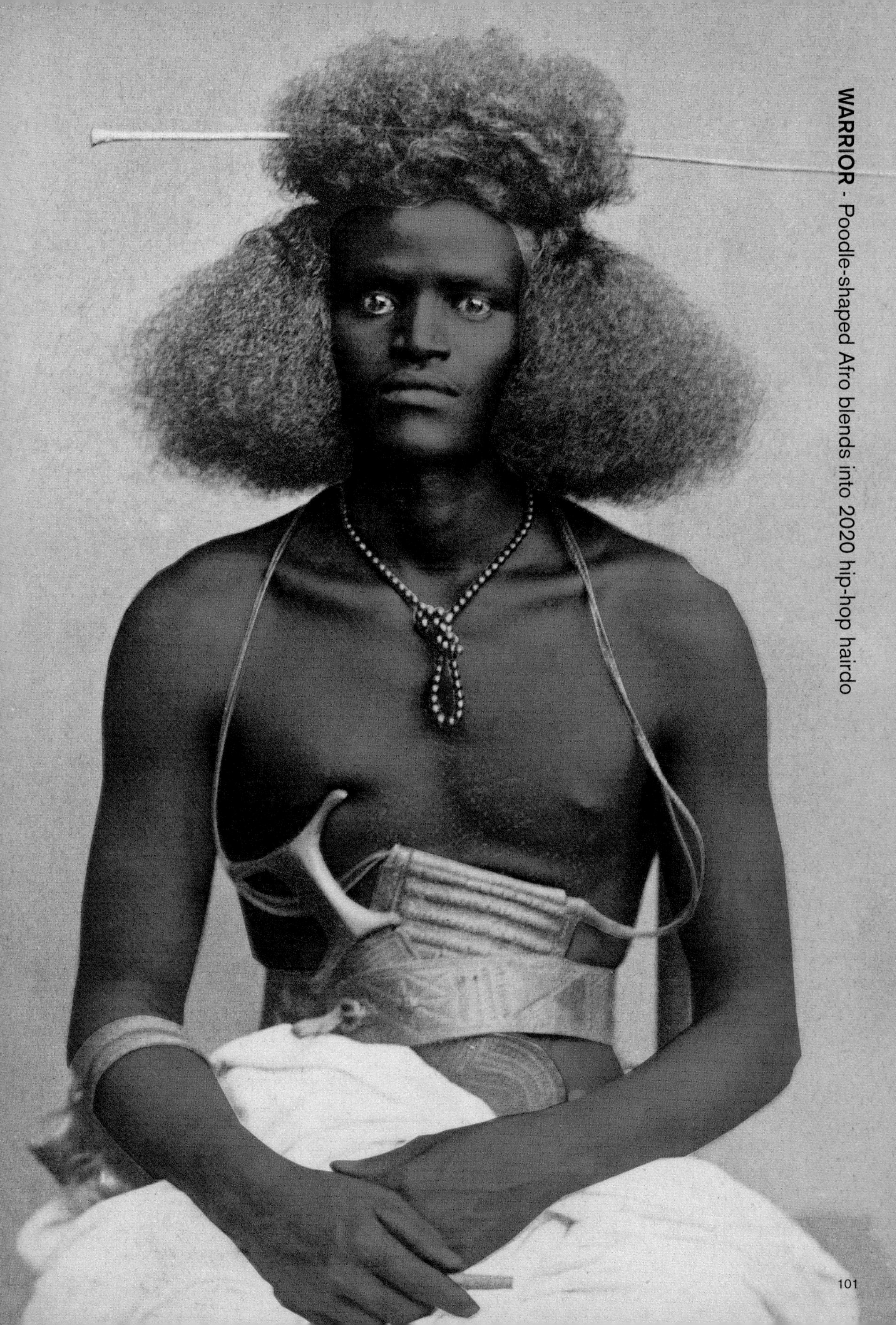

WARRIOR · Poodle-shaped Afro blends into 2020 hip-hop hairdo

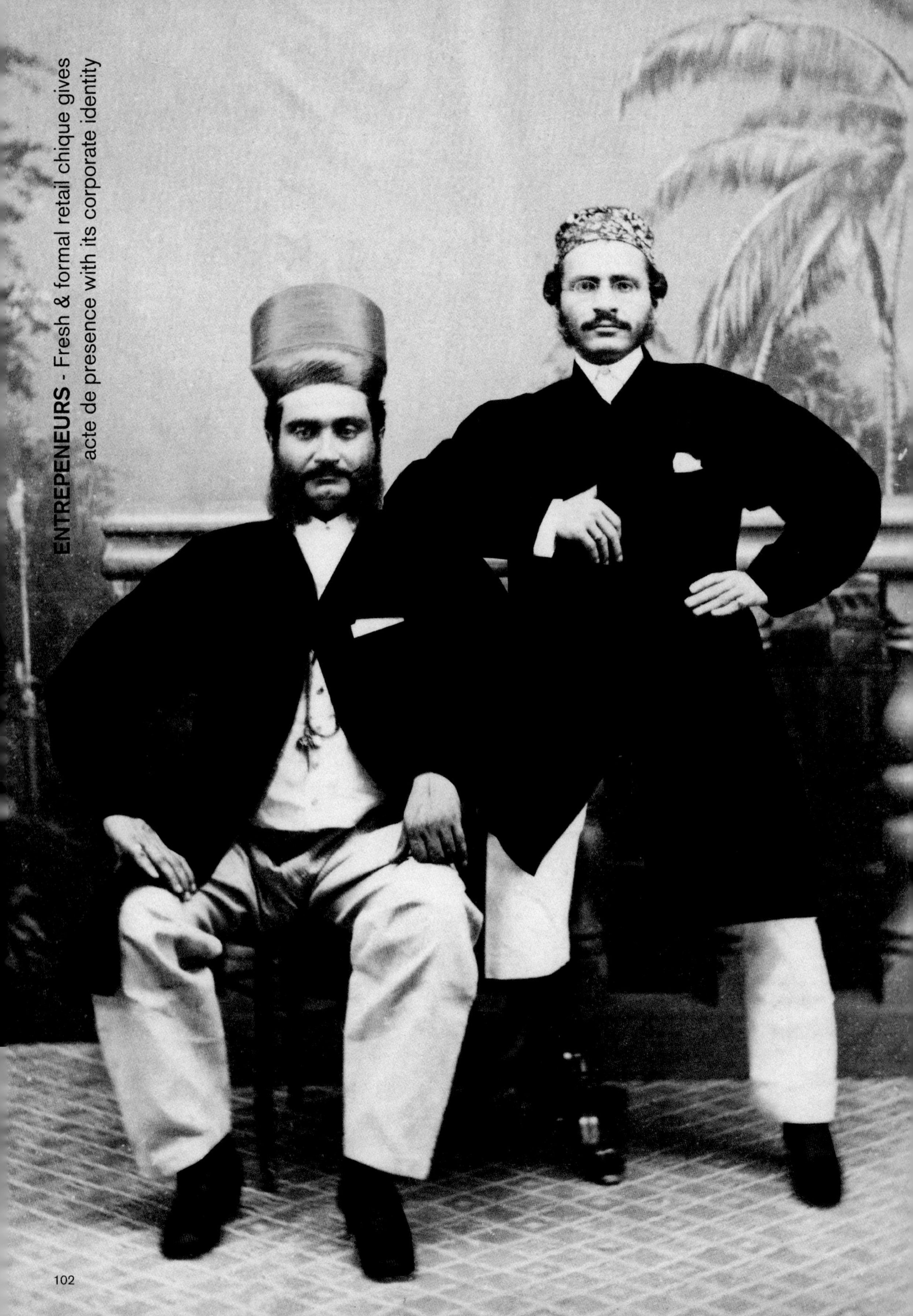

ENTREPENEURS - Fresh & formal retail chique gives acte de presence with its corporate identity

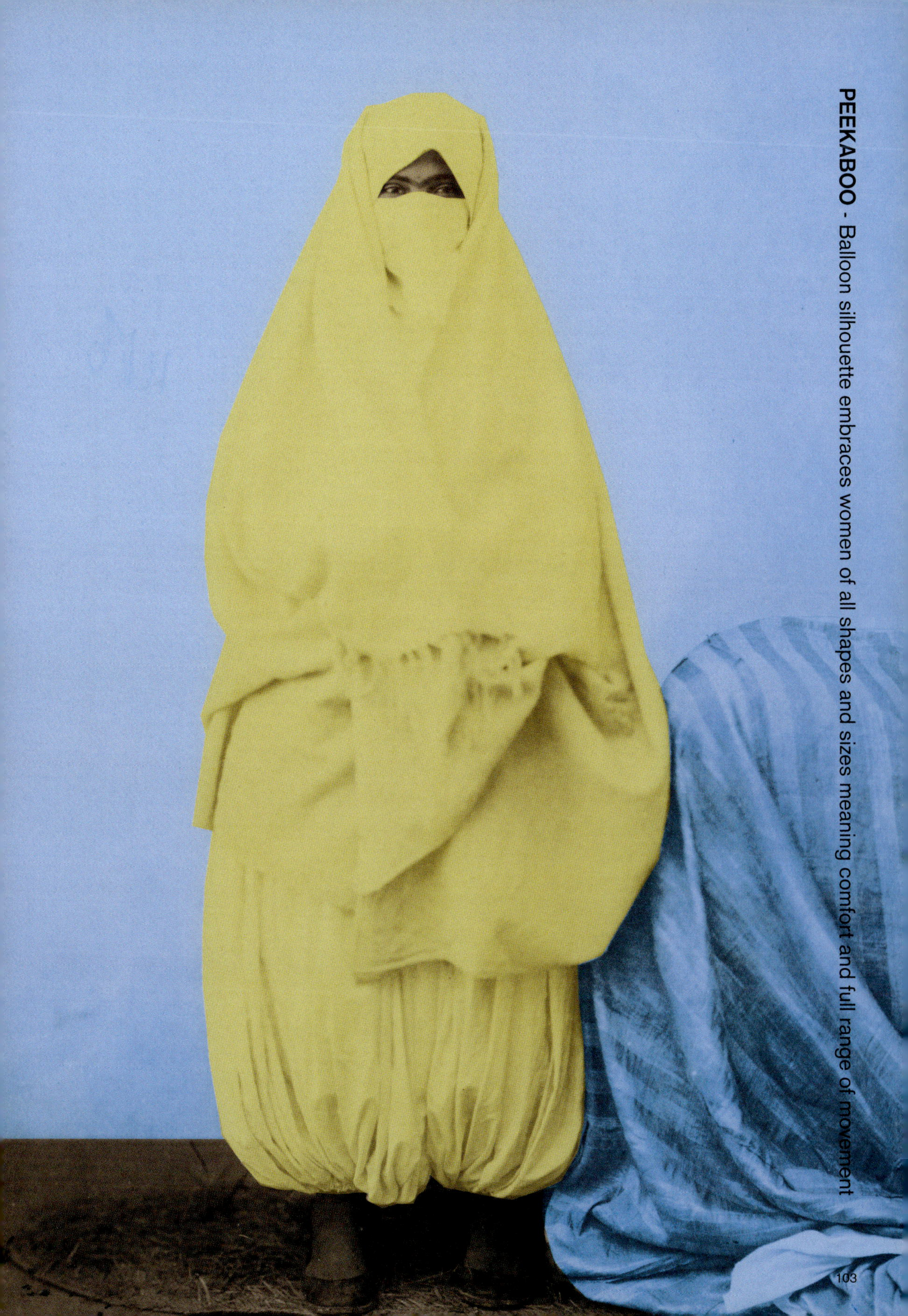

PEEKABOO - Balloon silhouette embraces women of all shapes and sizes meaning comfort and full range of movement

103

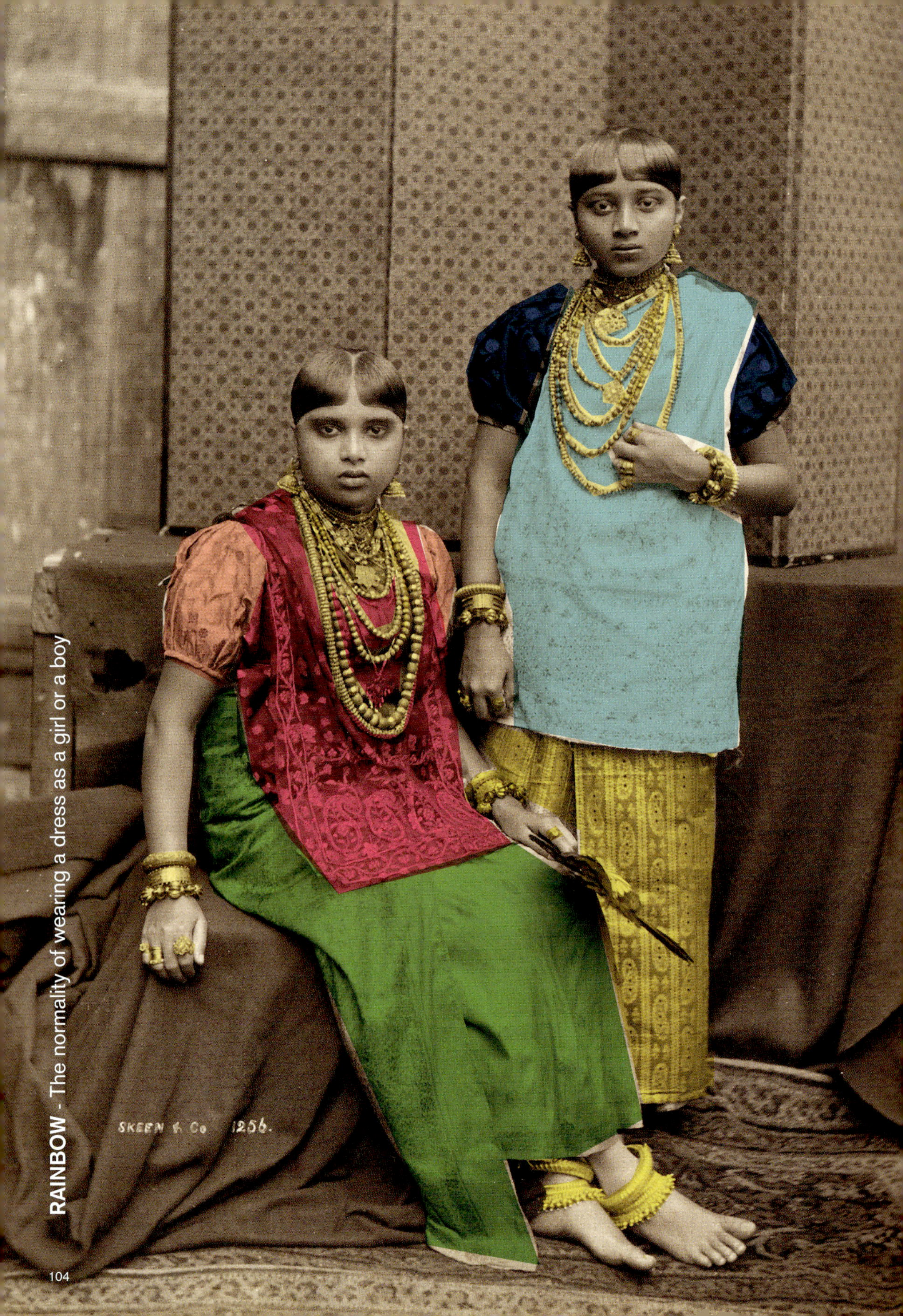

SKEEN & Co 1256.

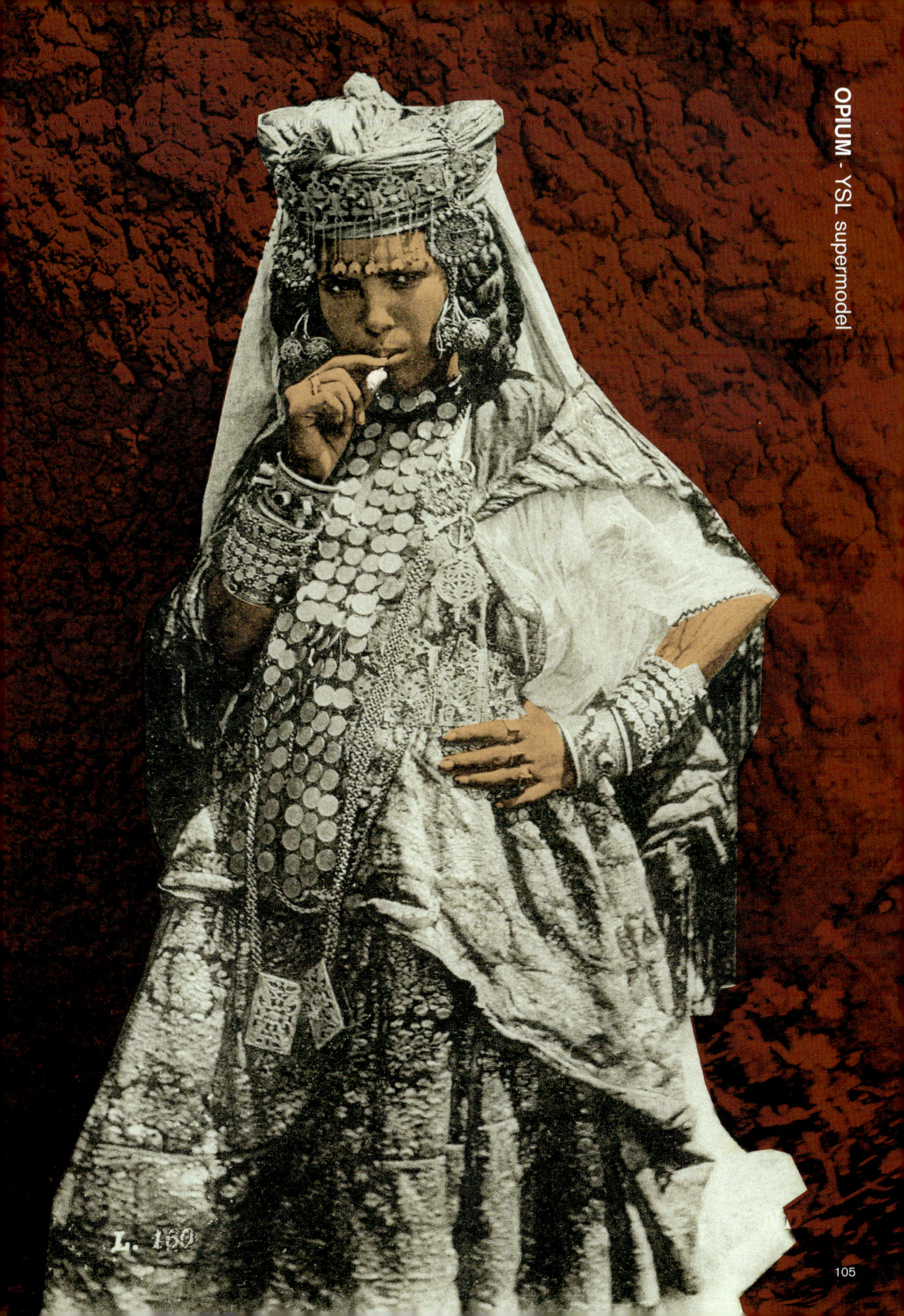

L. 150

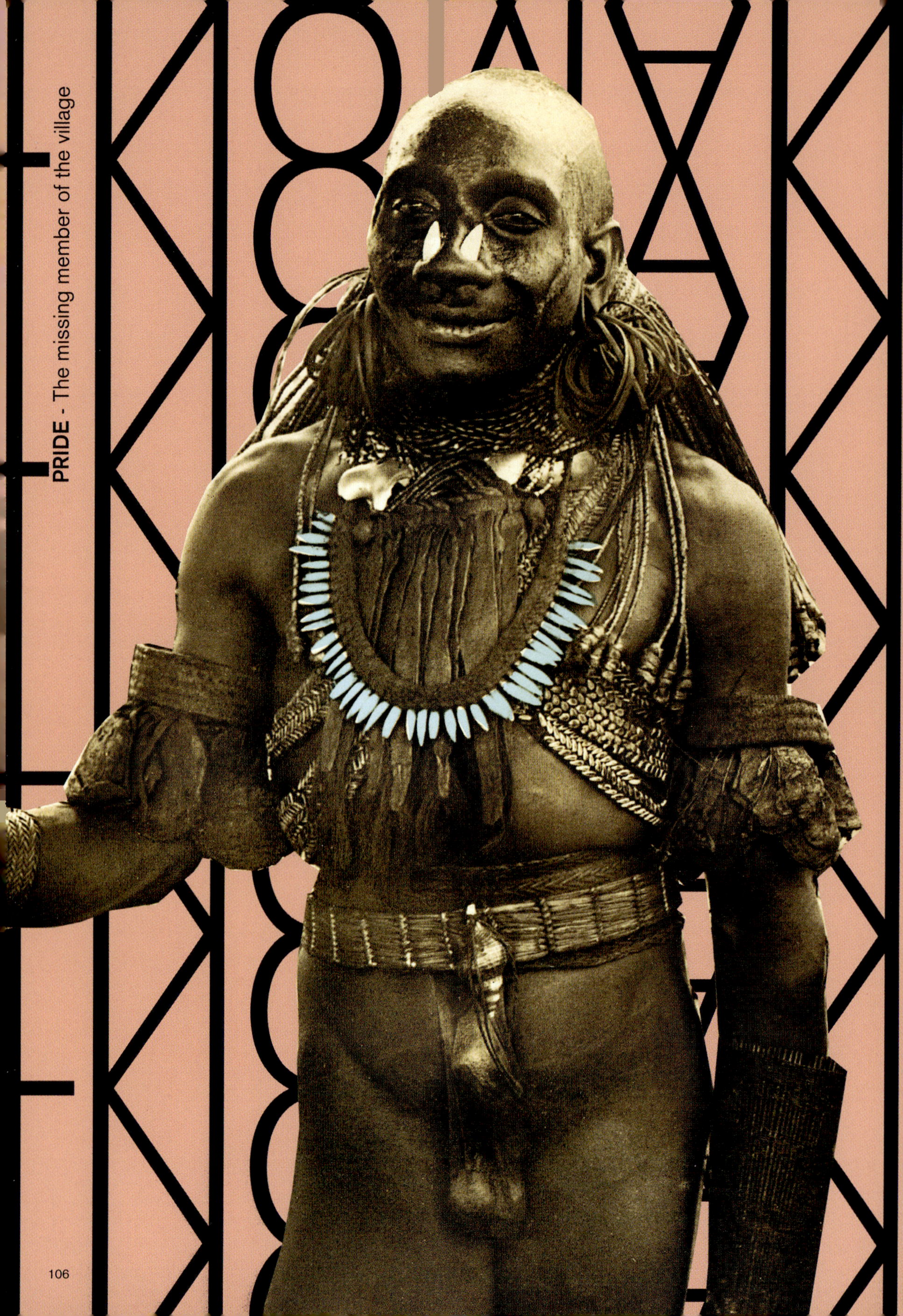

PRIDE - The missing member of the village

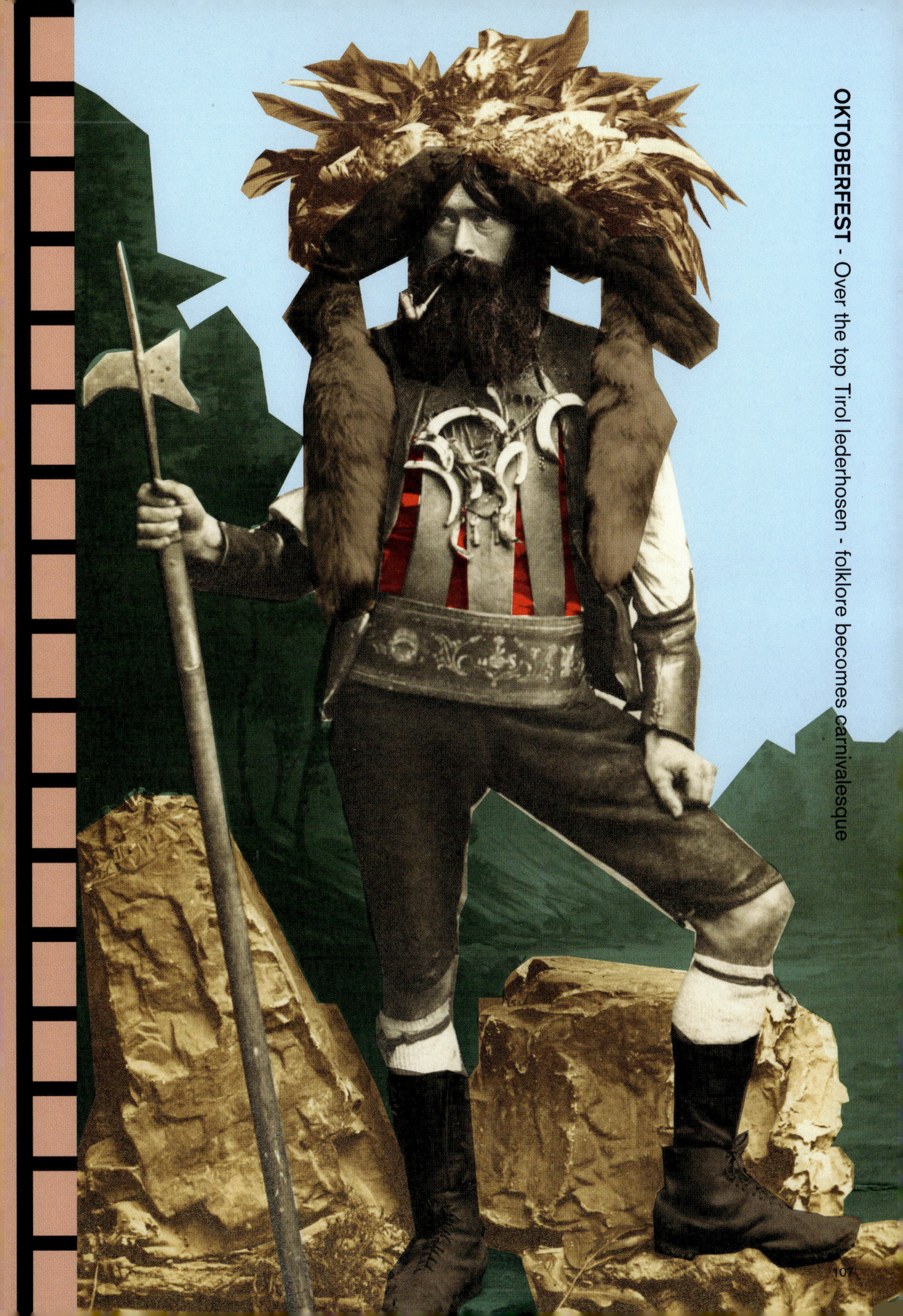
OKTOBERFEST - Over the top Tirol lederhosen - folklore becomes carnivalesque

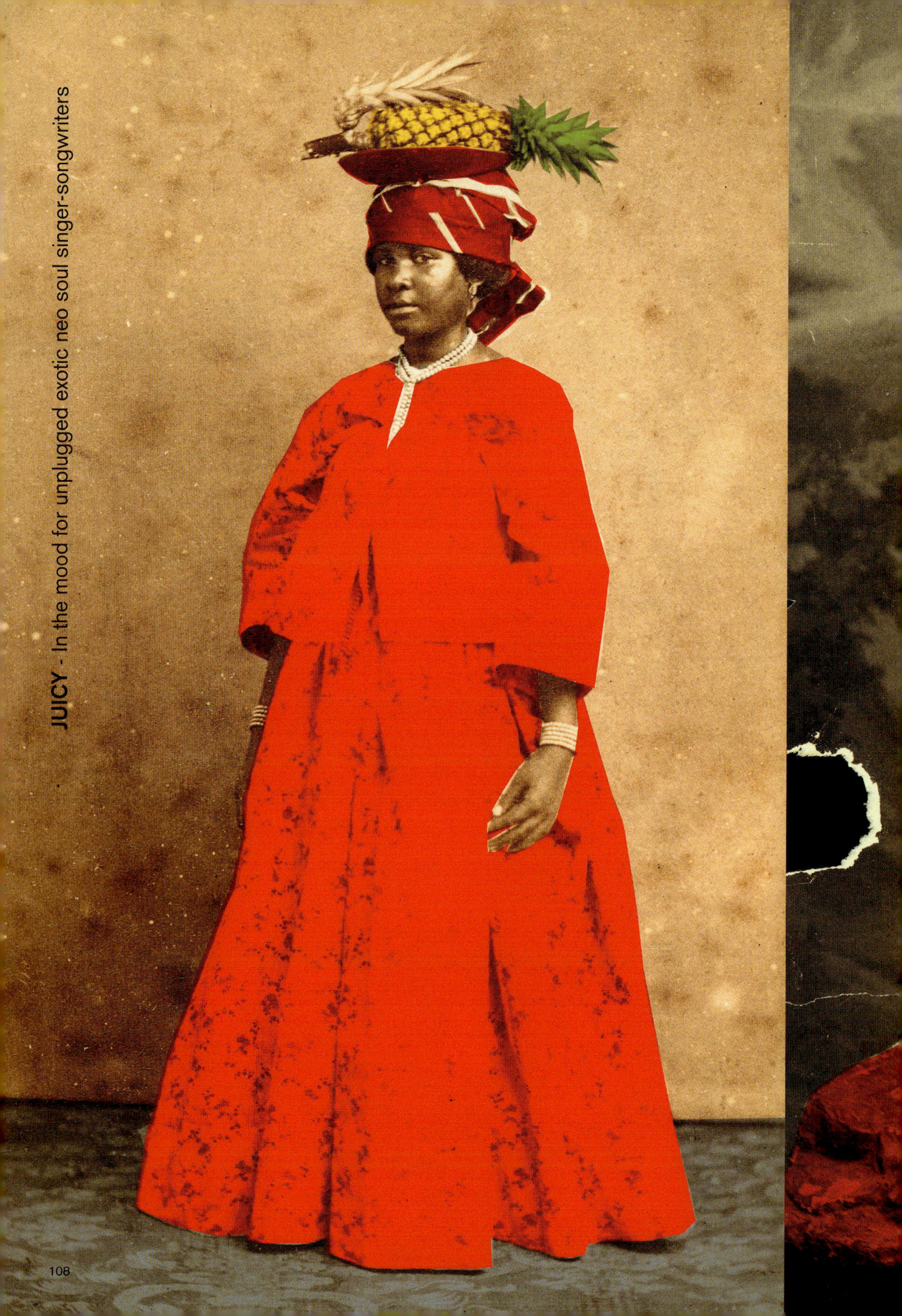

JUICY - In the mood for unplugged exotic neo soul singer-songwriters

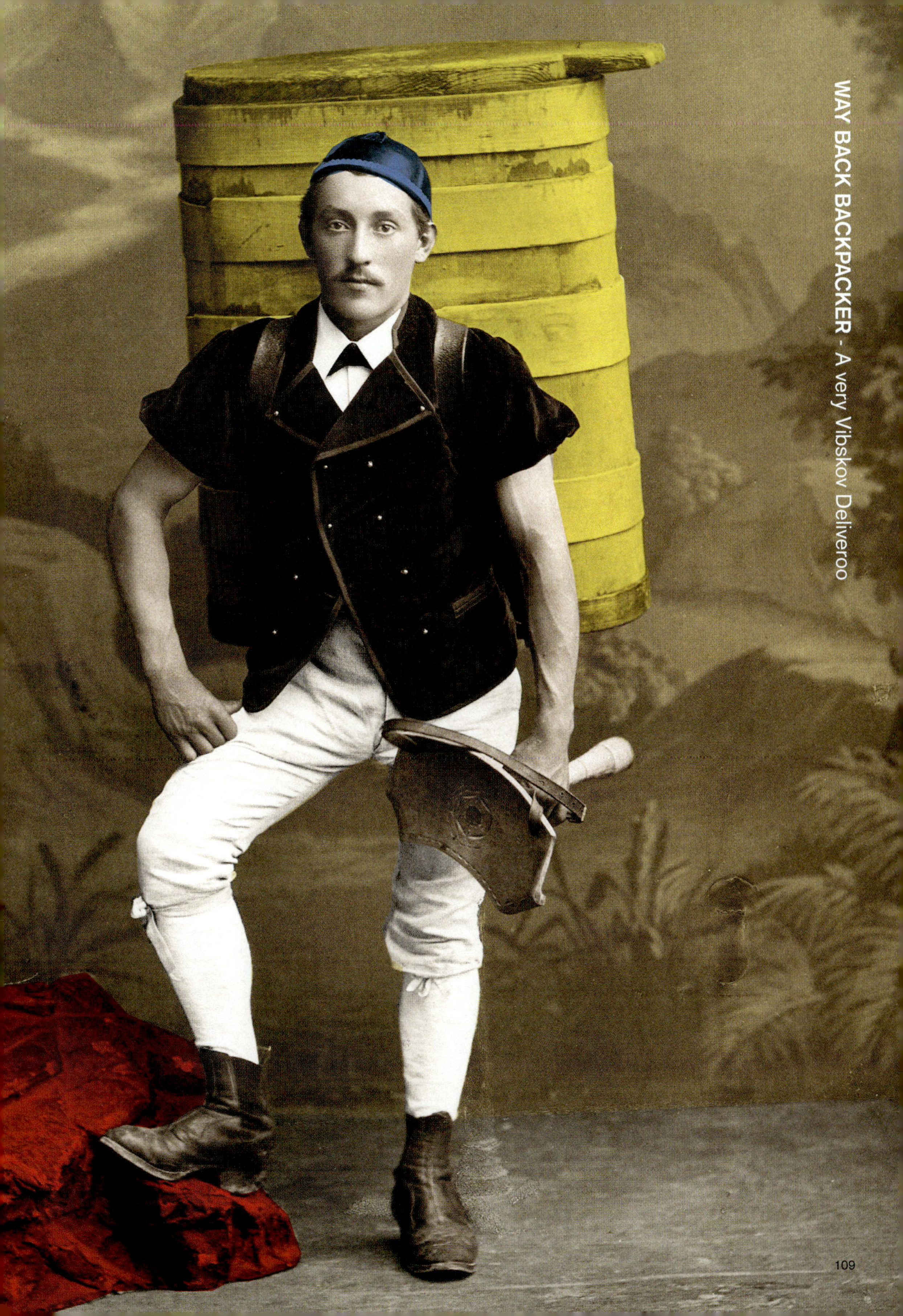
WAY BACK BACKPACKER - A very Vibskov Deliveroo

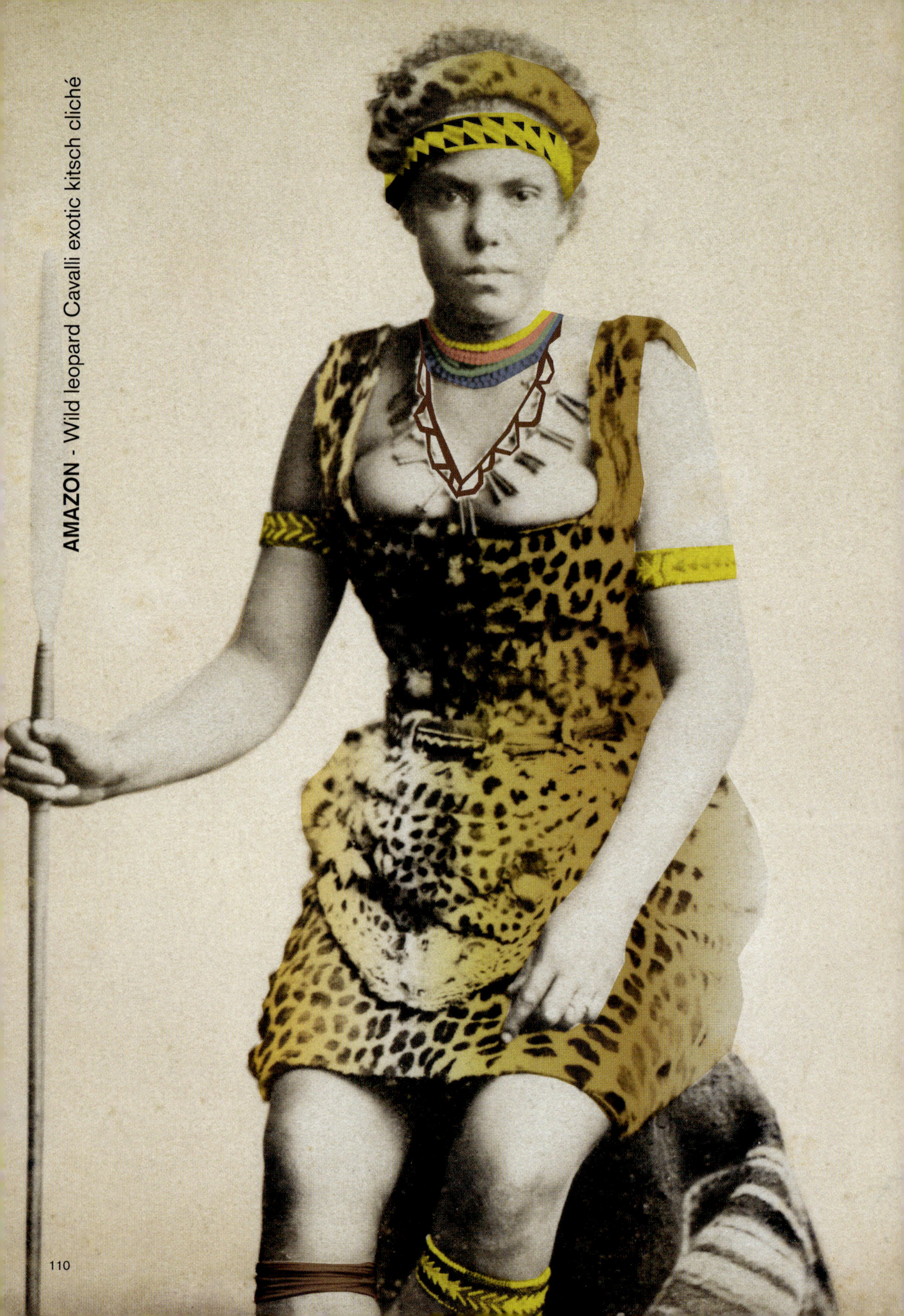

AMAZON - Wild leopard Cavalli exotic kitsch cliché

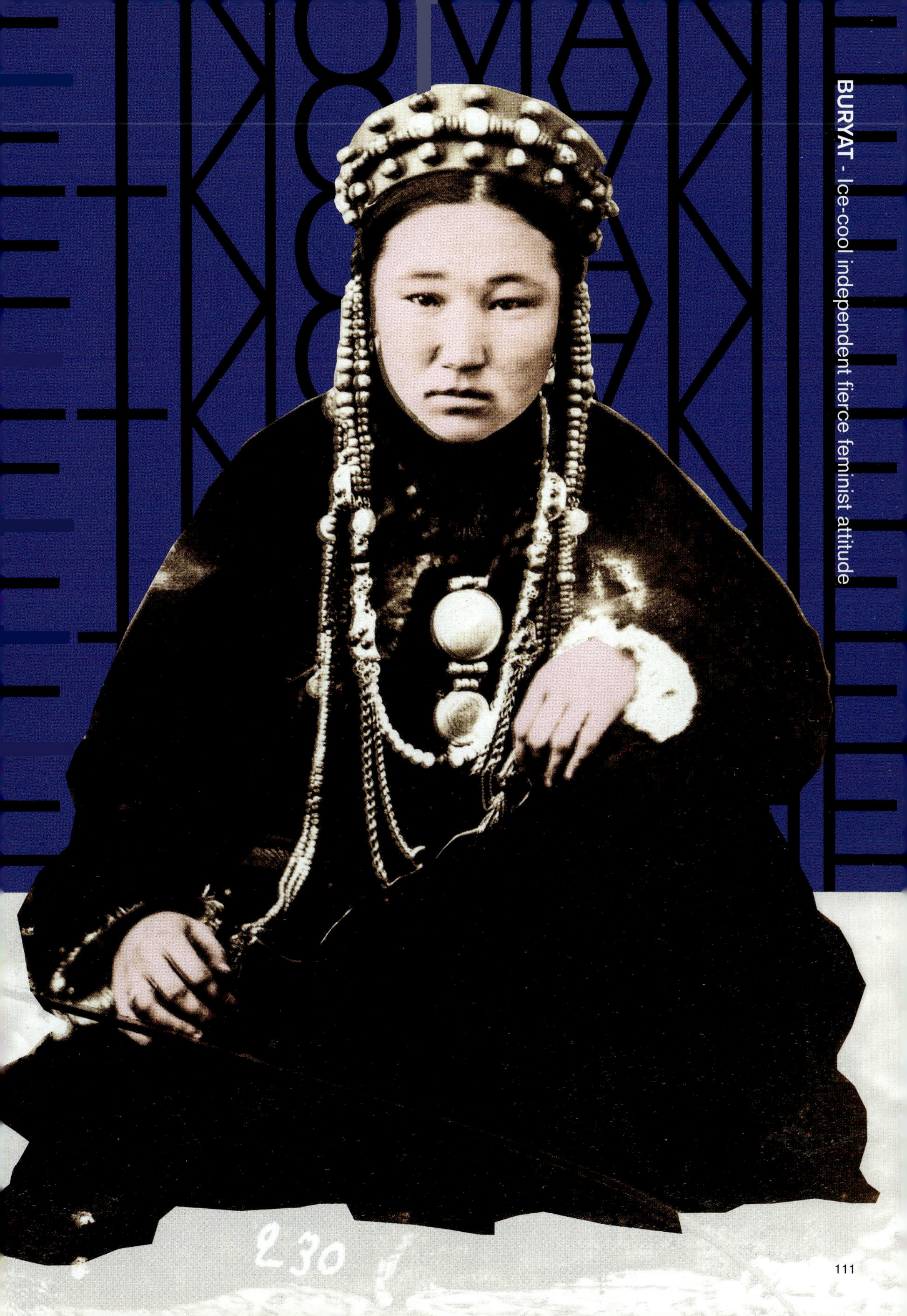
BURYAT - Ice-cool independent fierce feminist attitude

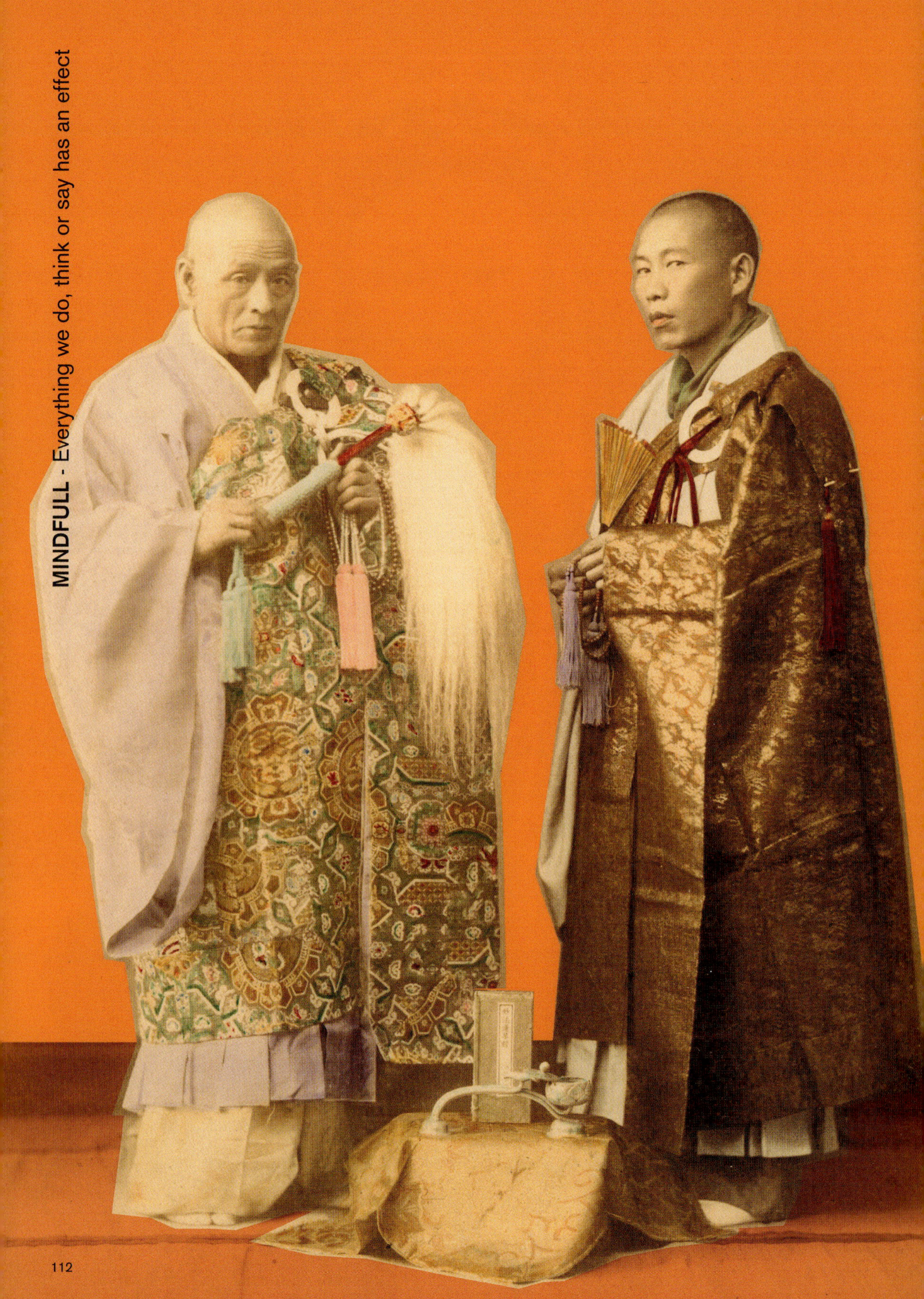

MINDFULL - Everything we do, think or say has an effect

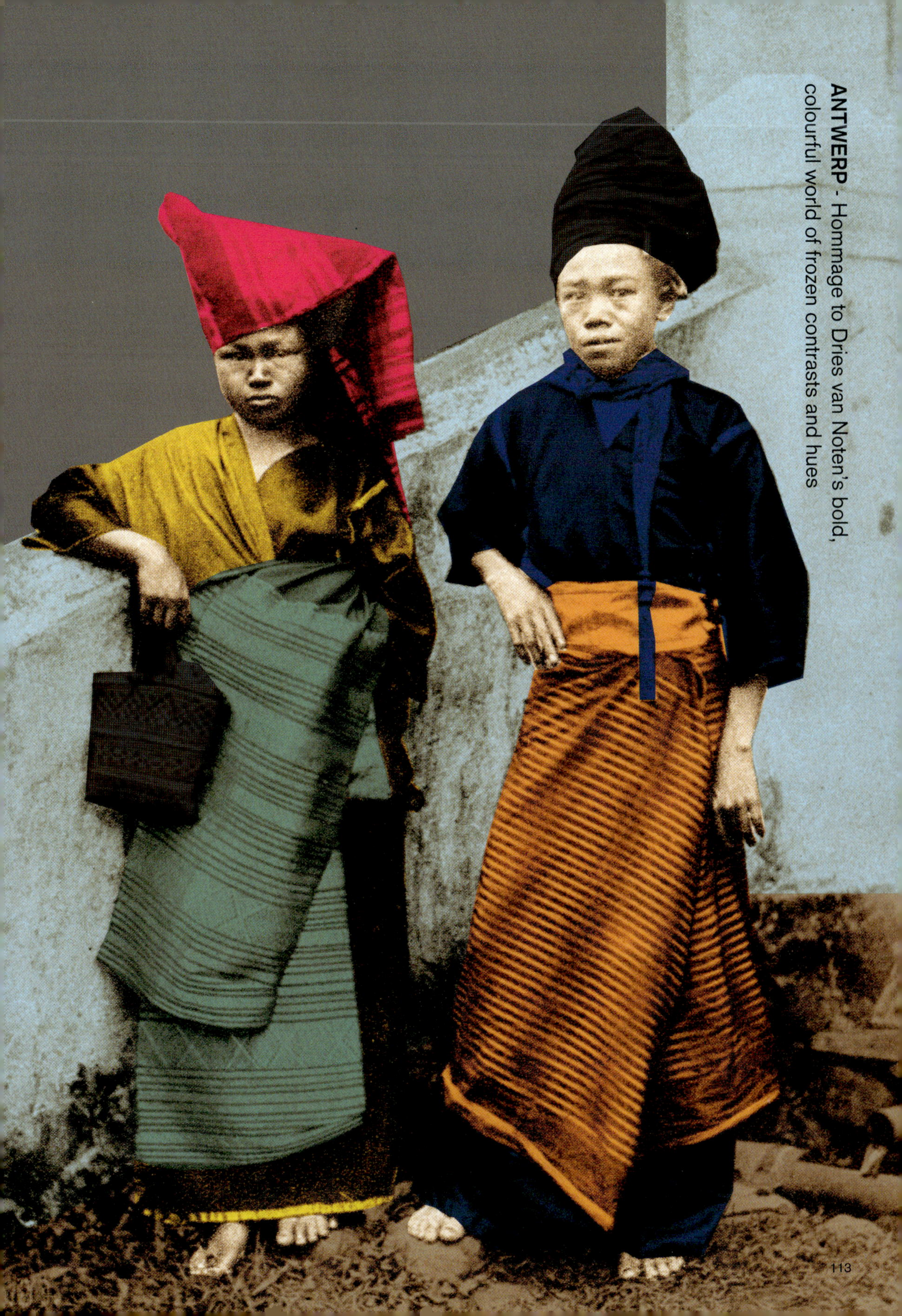

ANTWERP - Hommage to Dries van Noten's bold,
colourful world of frozen contrasts and hues

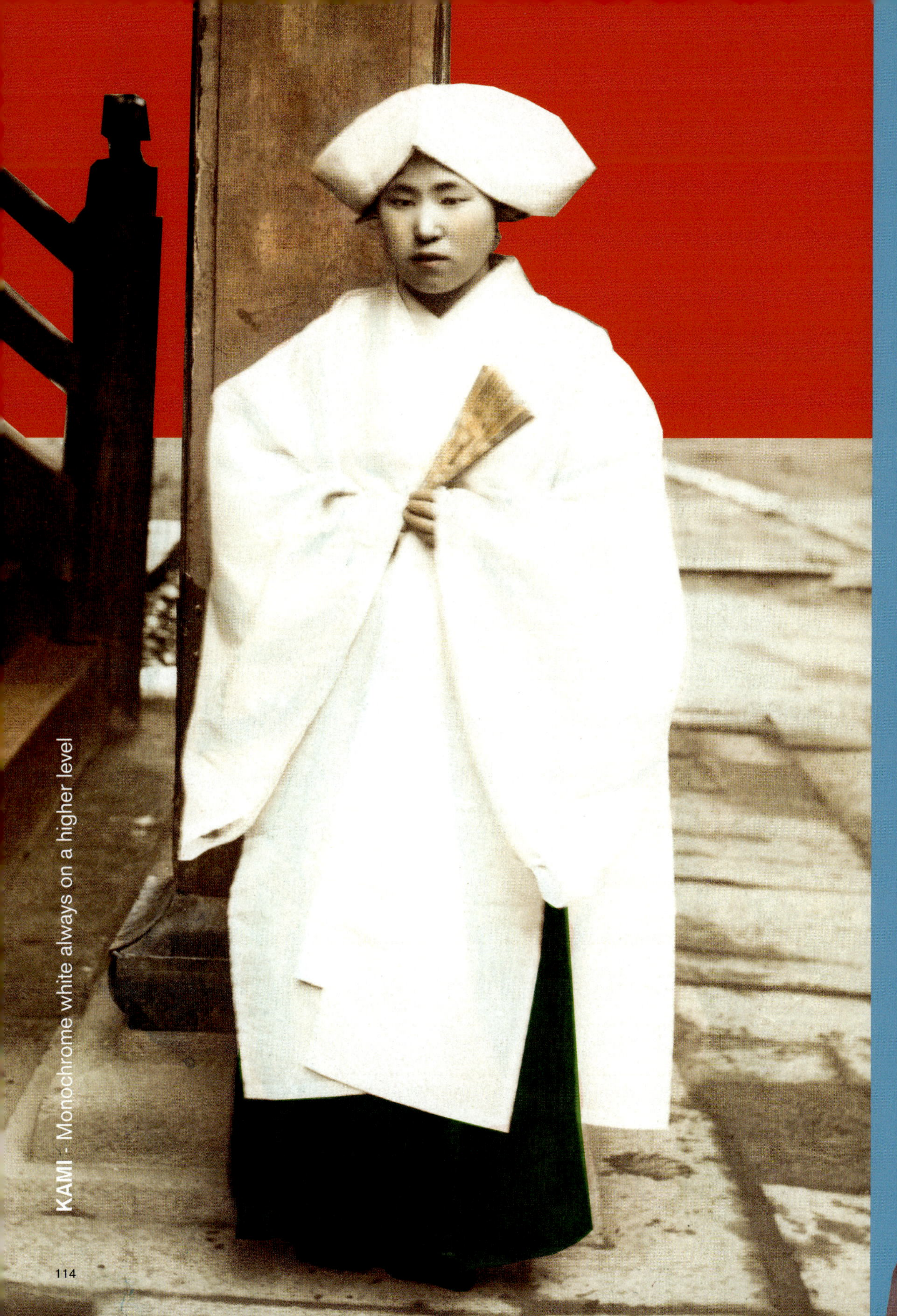

KAMI - Monochrome white always on a higher level

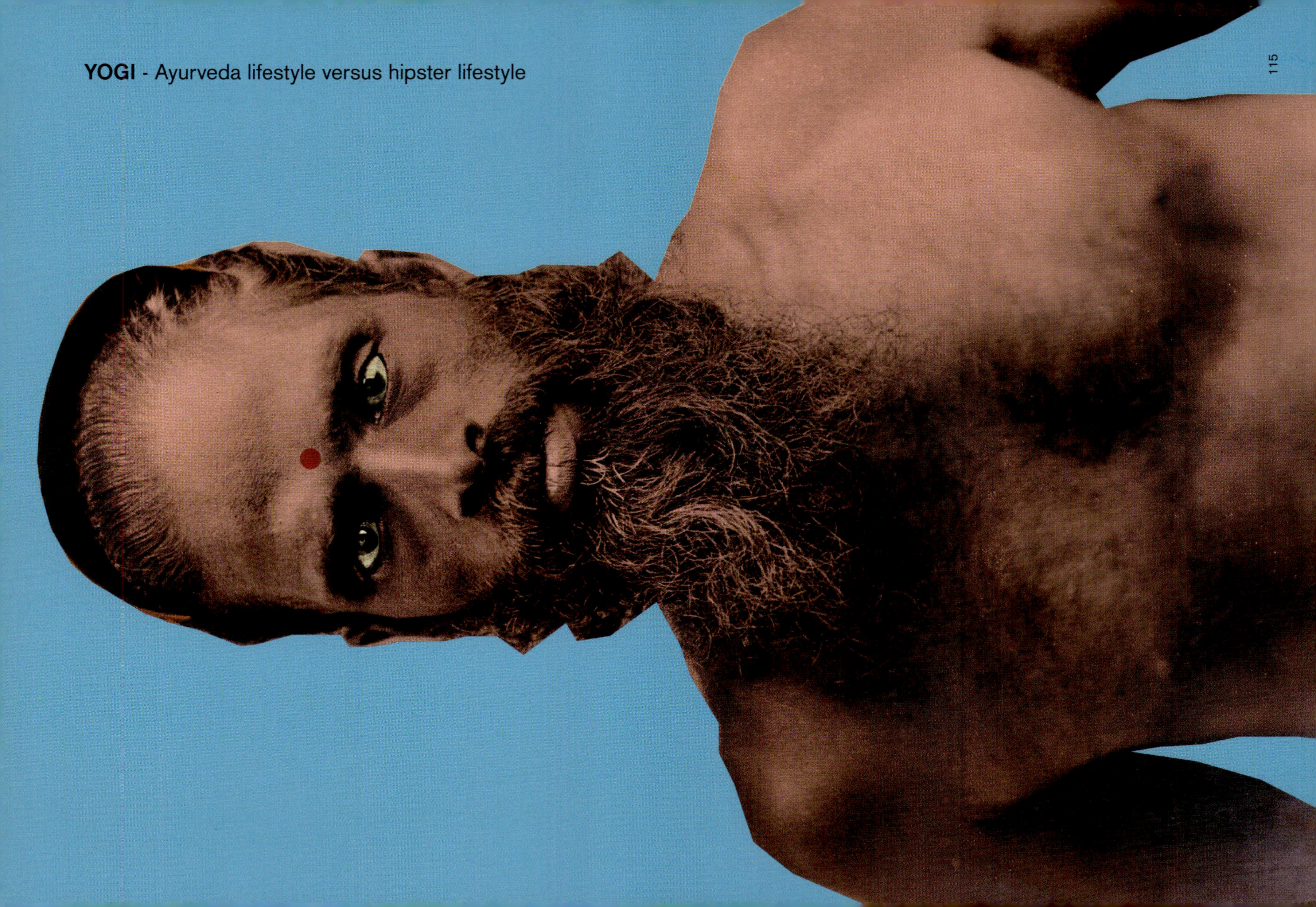
YOGI - Ayurveda lifestyle versus hipster lifestyle

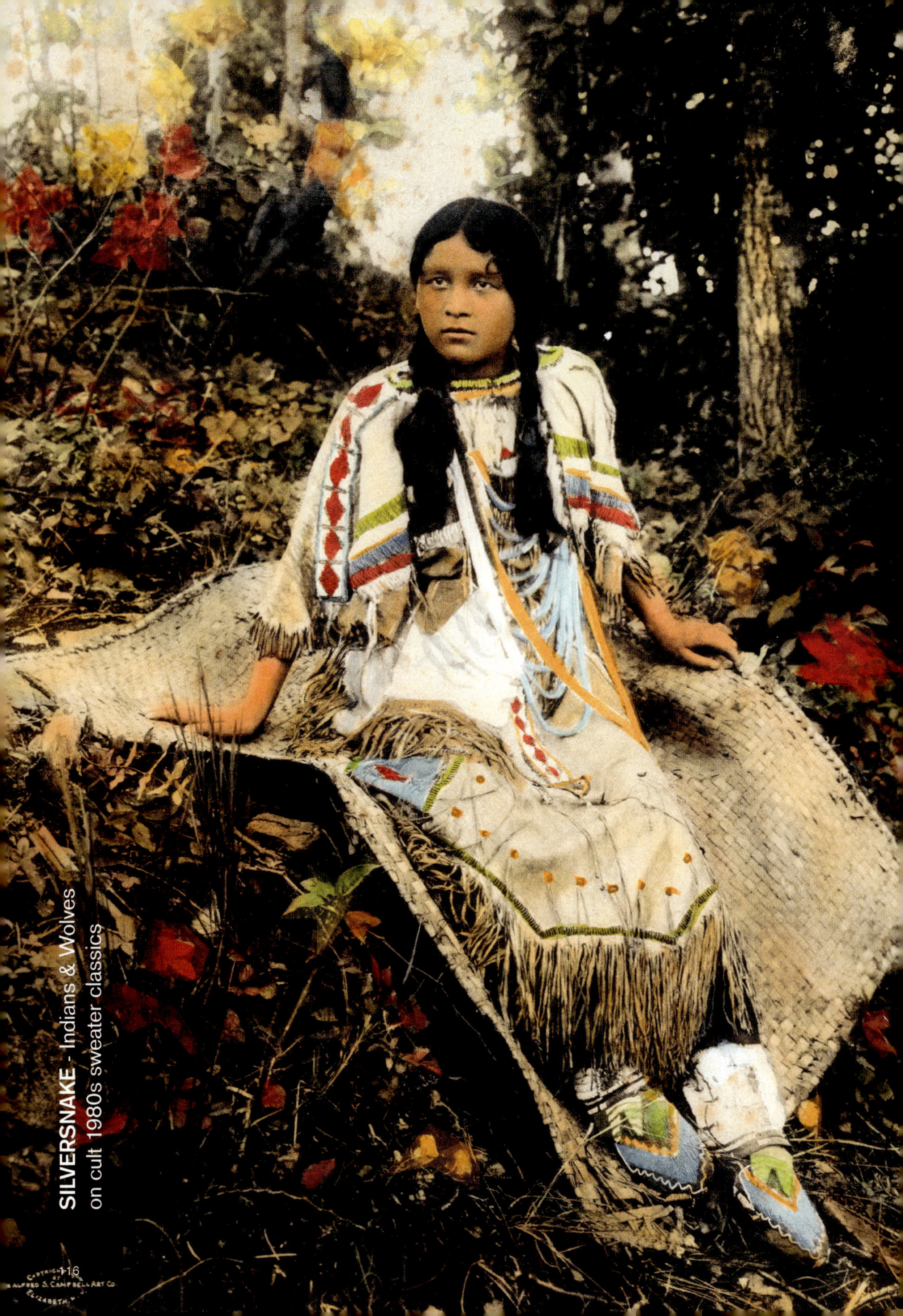

SILVERSNAKE - Indians & Wolves
on cult 1980s sweater classics

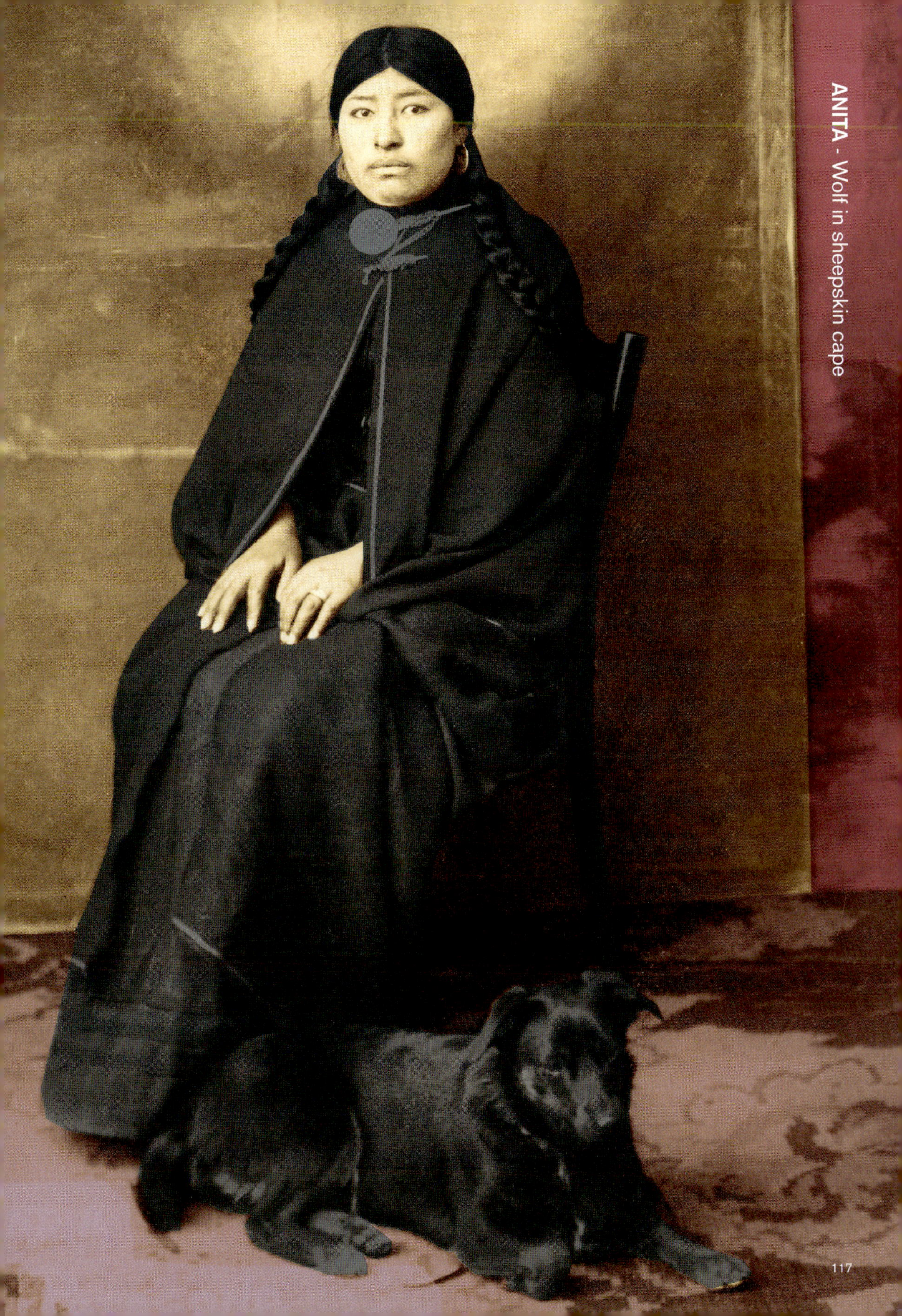

ANITA - Wolf in sheepskin cape

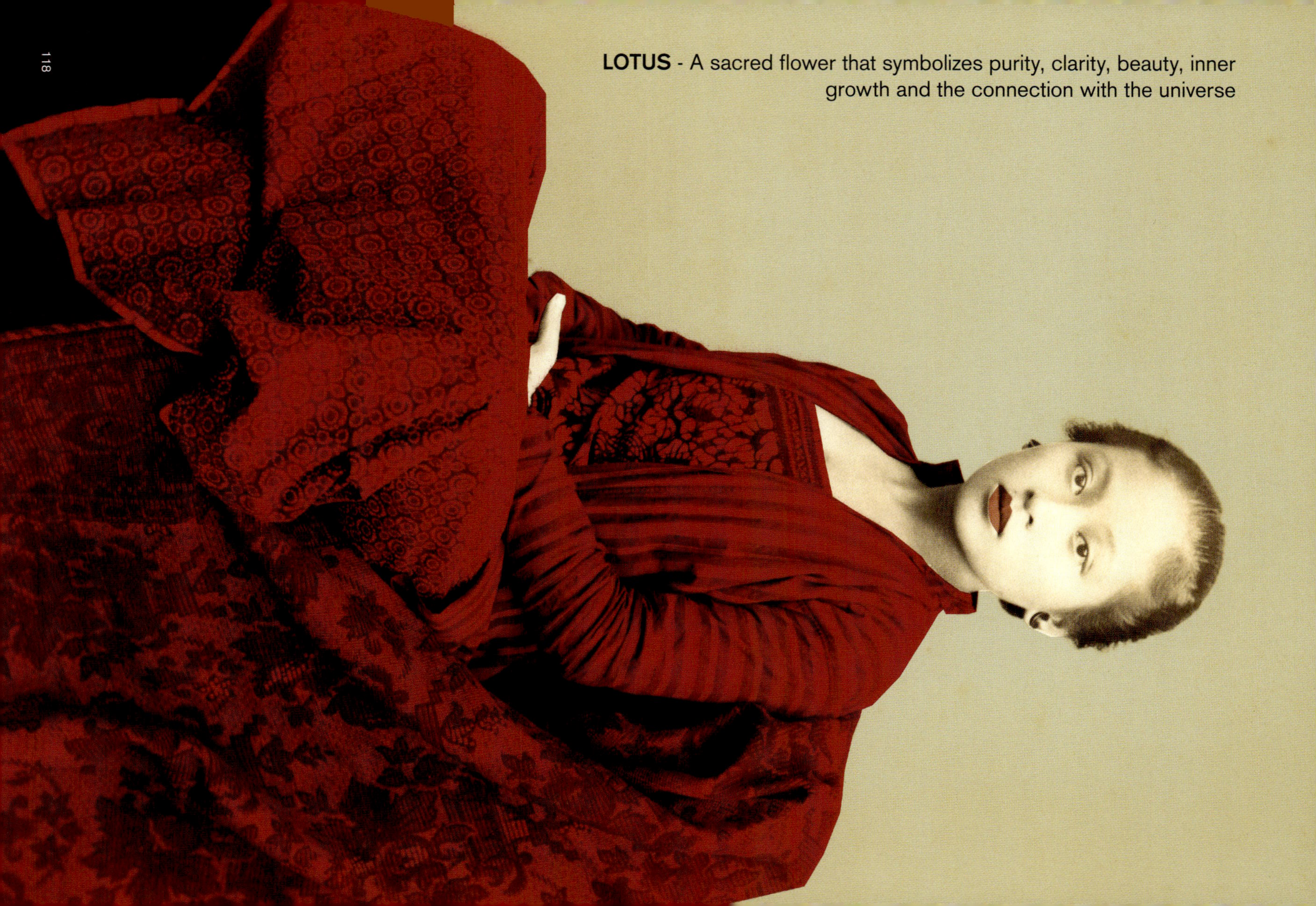

LOTUS - A sacred flower that symbolizes purity, clarity, beauty, inner growth and the connection with the universe

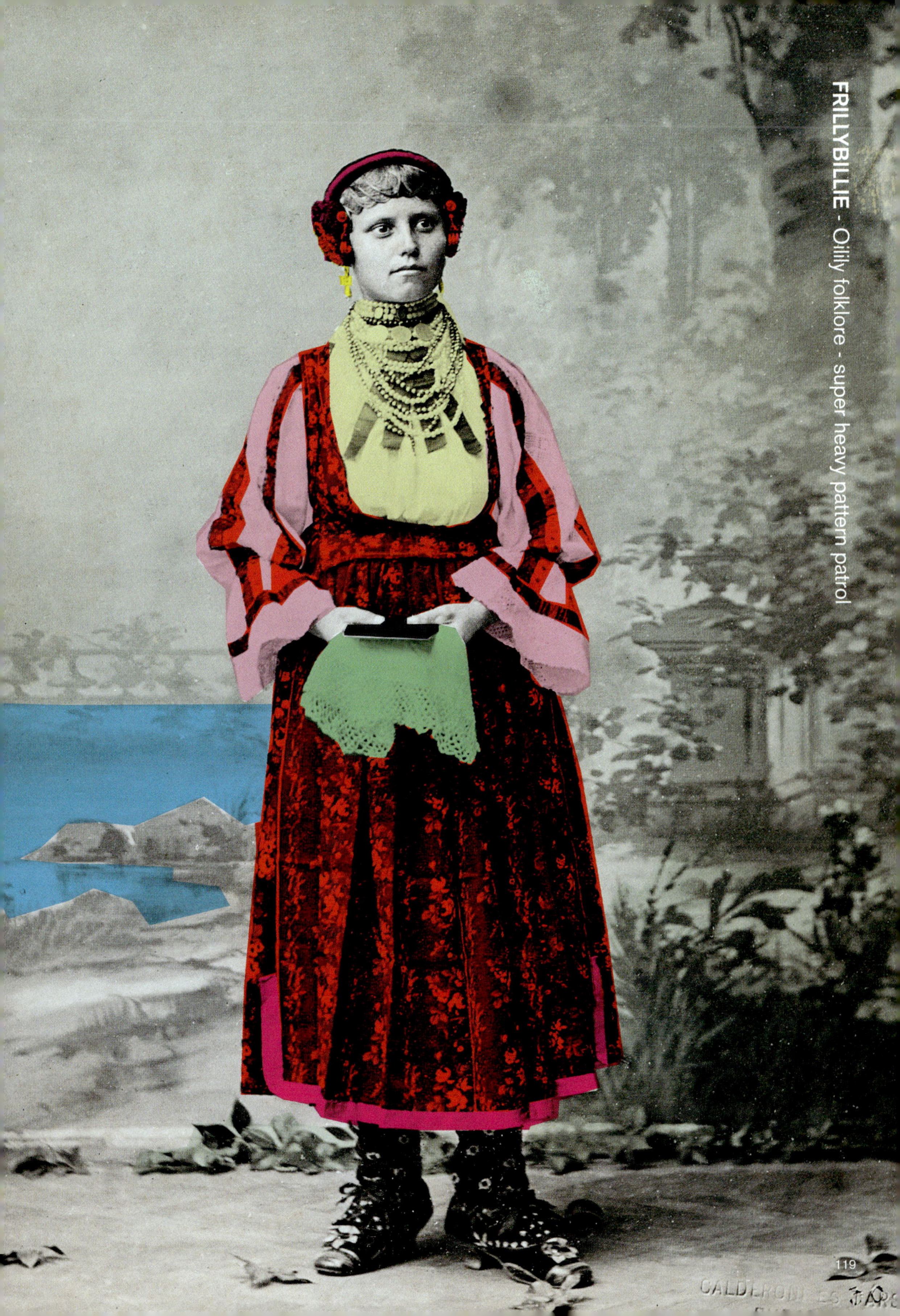

FRILLYBILLIE - Oilily folklore - super heavy pattern patrol

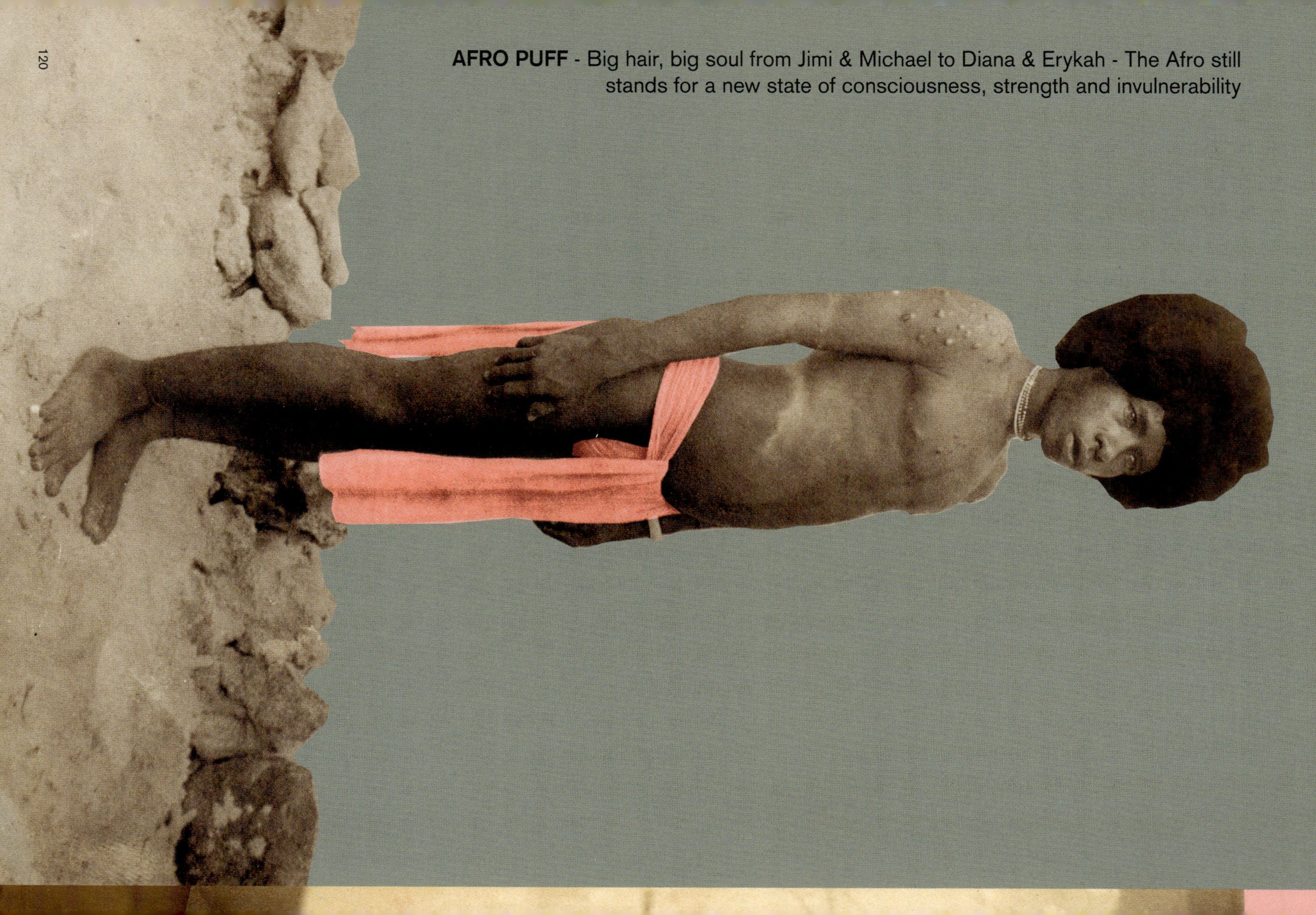

AFRO PUFF - Big hair, big soul from Jimi & Michael to Diana & Erykah - The Afro still stands for a new state of consciousness, strength and invulnerability

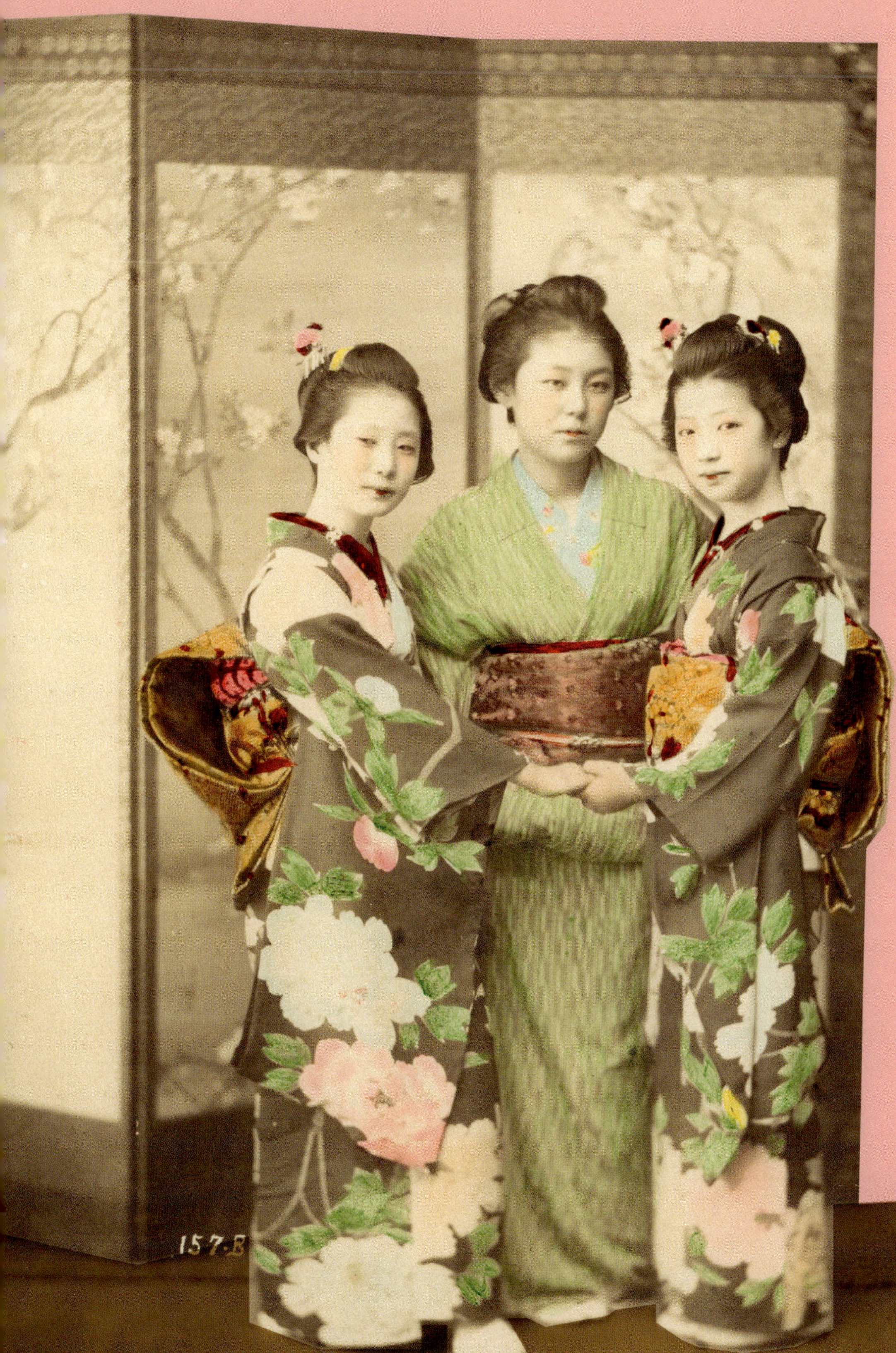

KAWAII TRIO - Girly girly Japanese Hello Kitty homebase

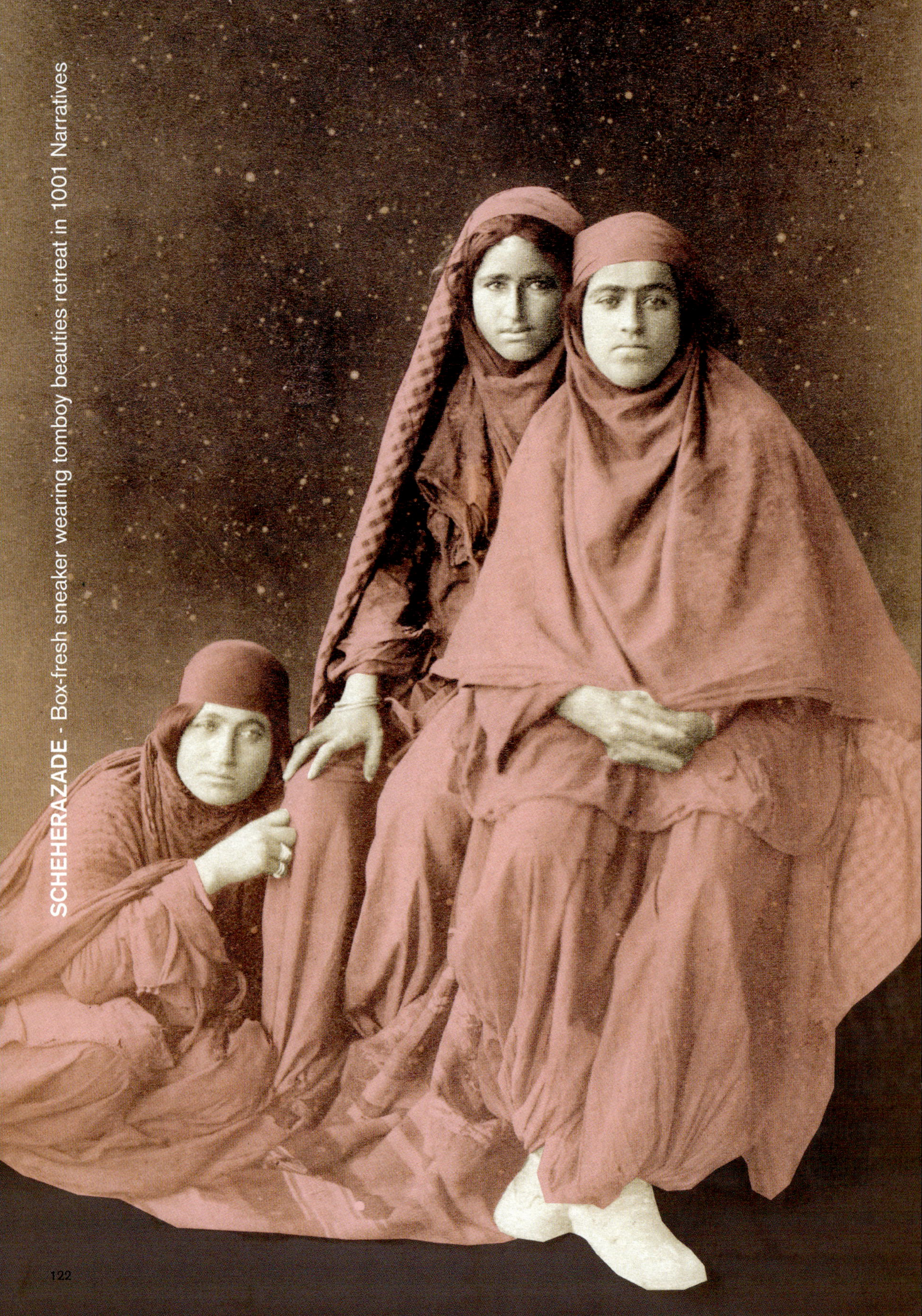

SCHEHERAZADE - Box-fresh sneaker wearing tomboy beauties retreat in 1001 Narratives

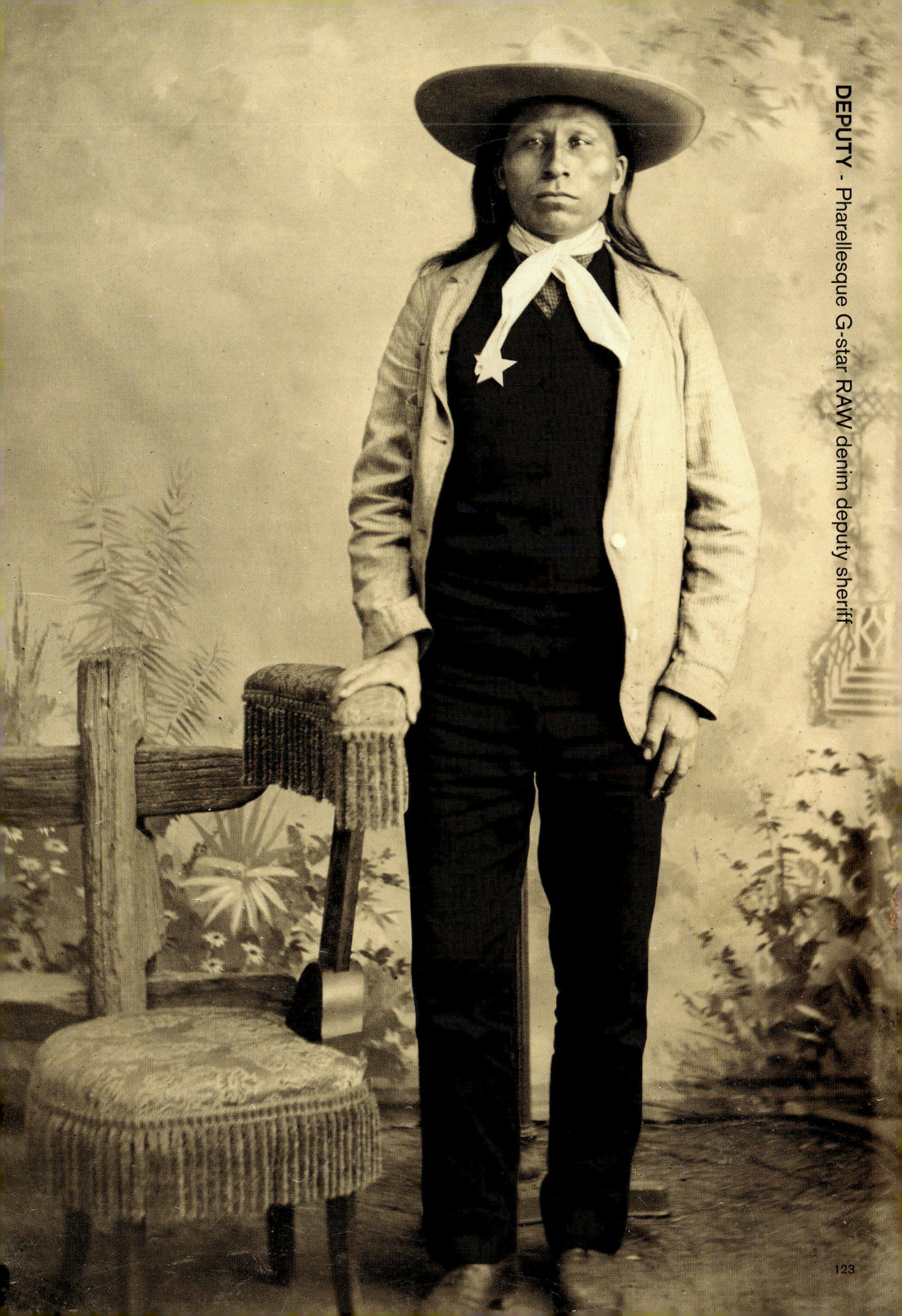

DEPUTY - Pharellesque G-star RAW denim deputy sheriff

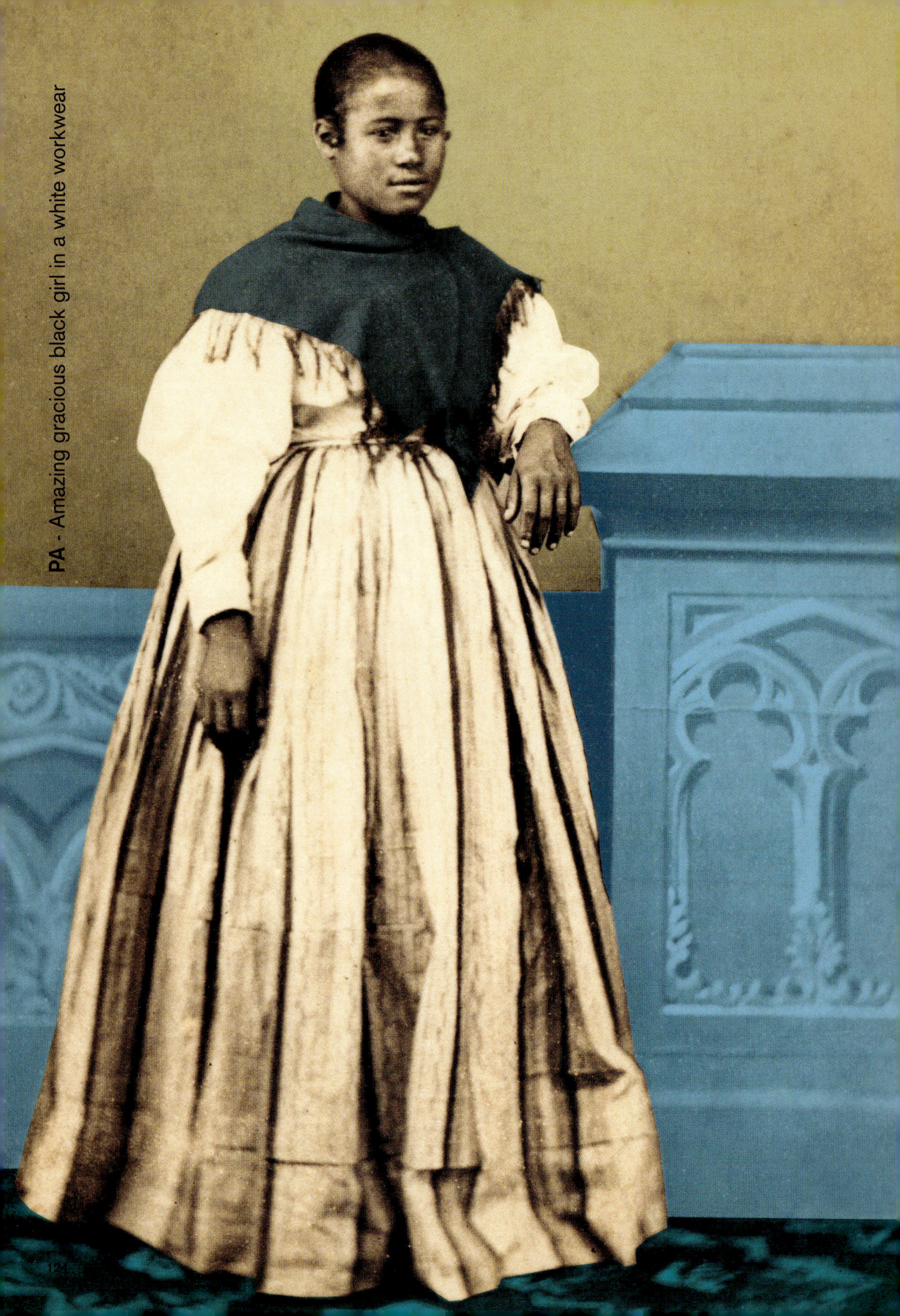

PA - Amazing gracious black girl in a white workwear

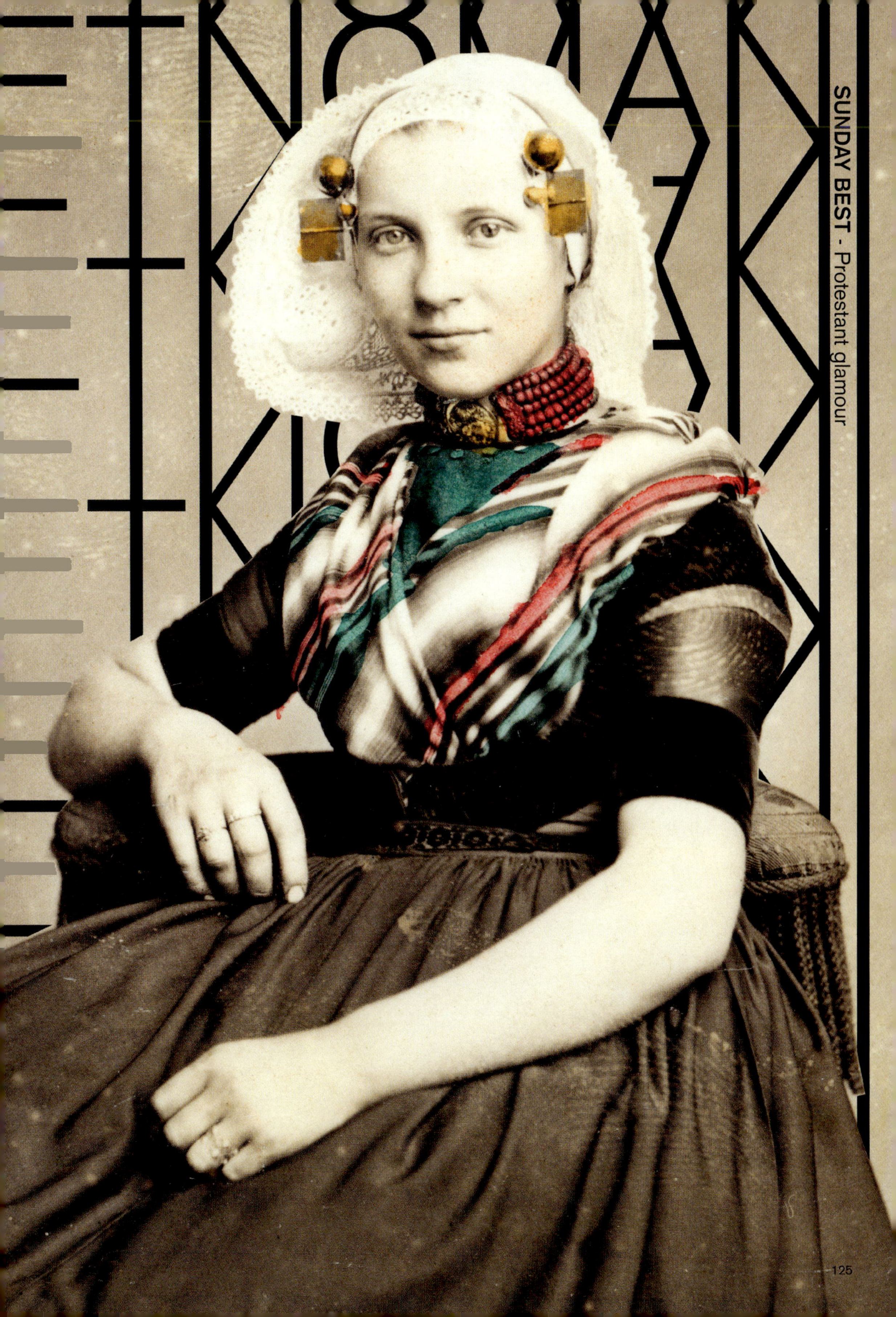

ETNOMANIK
SUNDAY BEST · Protestant glamour
125

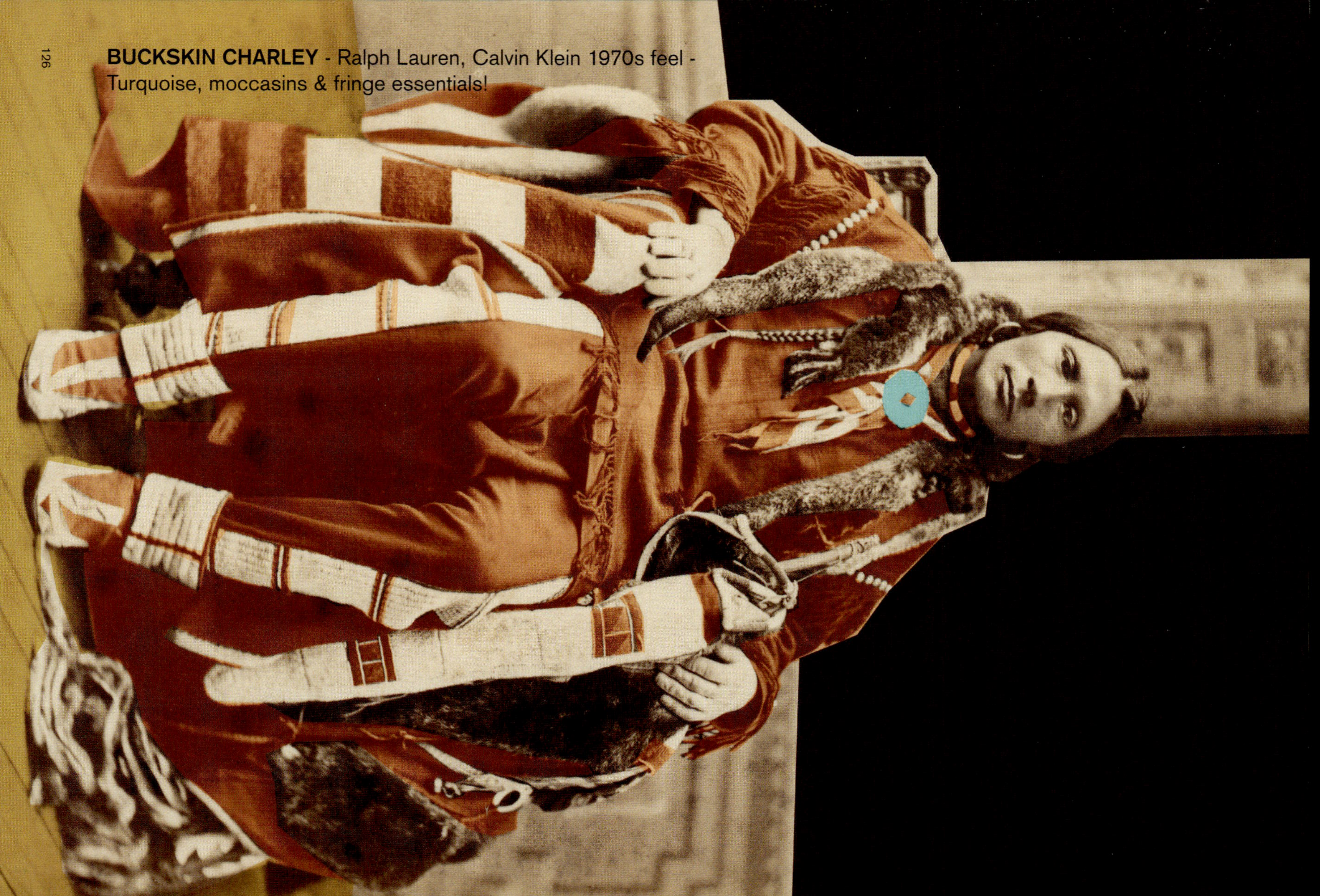

126
BUCKSKIN CHARLEY - Ralph Lauren, Calvin Klein 1970s feel -
Turquoise, moccasins & fringe essentials!

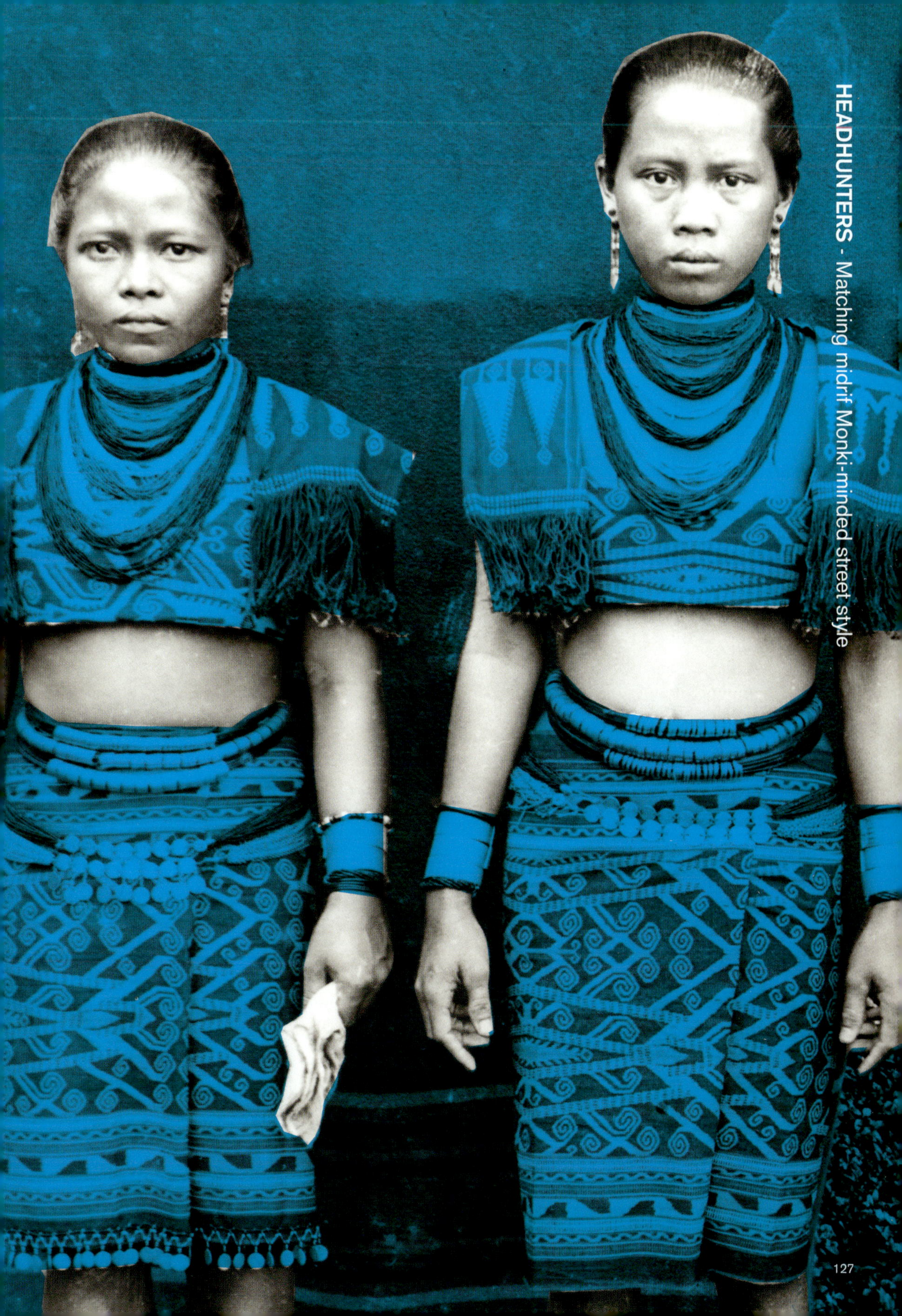

HEADHUNTERS - Matching midrif Monki-minded street style

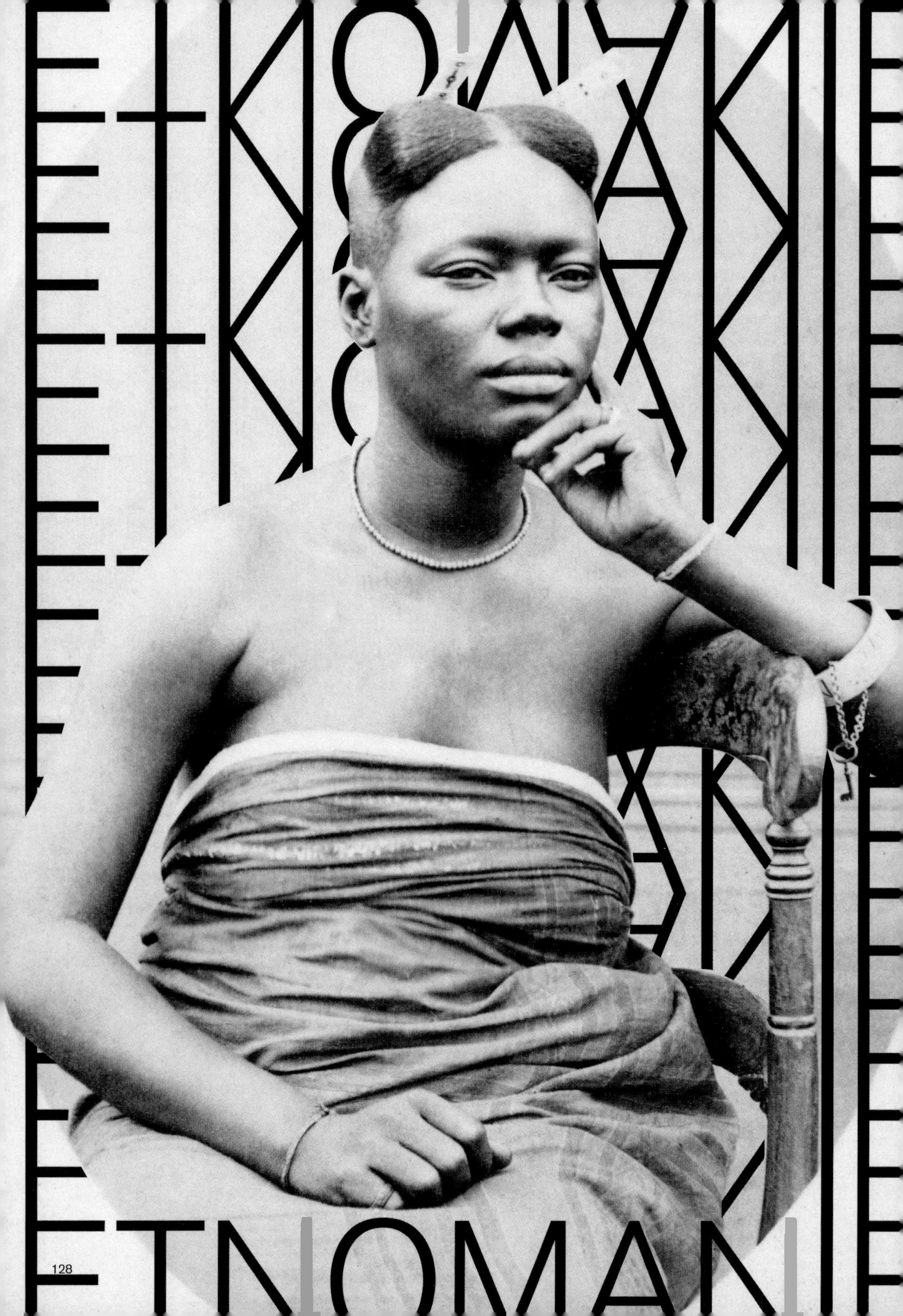

ETNOMANIE

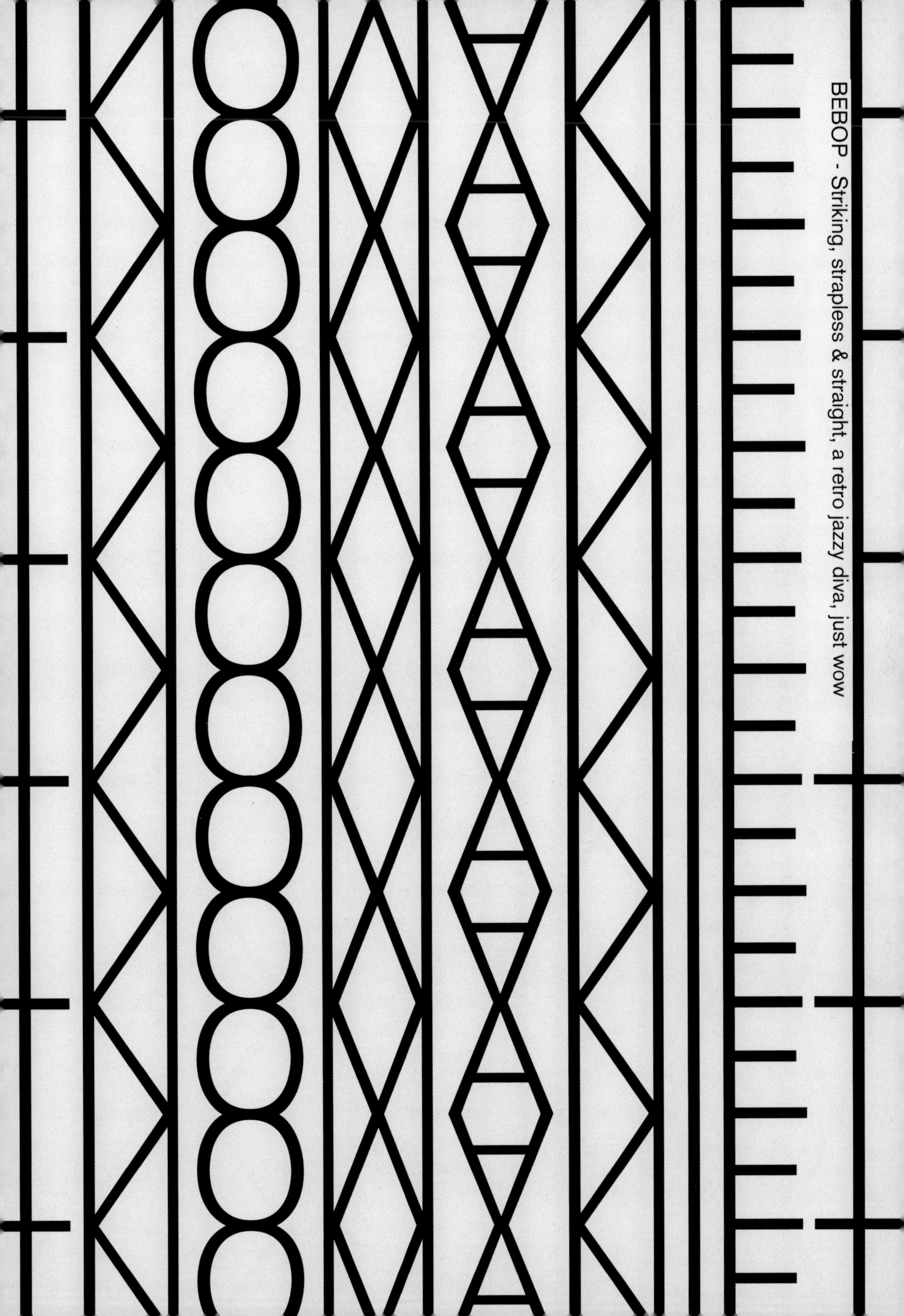

BEBOP - Striking, strapless & straight, a retro jazzy diva, just wow

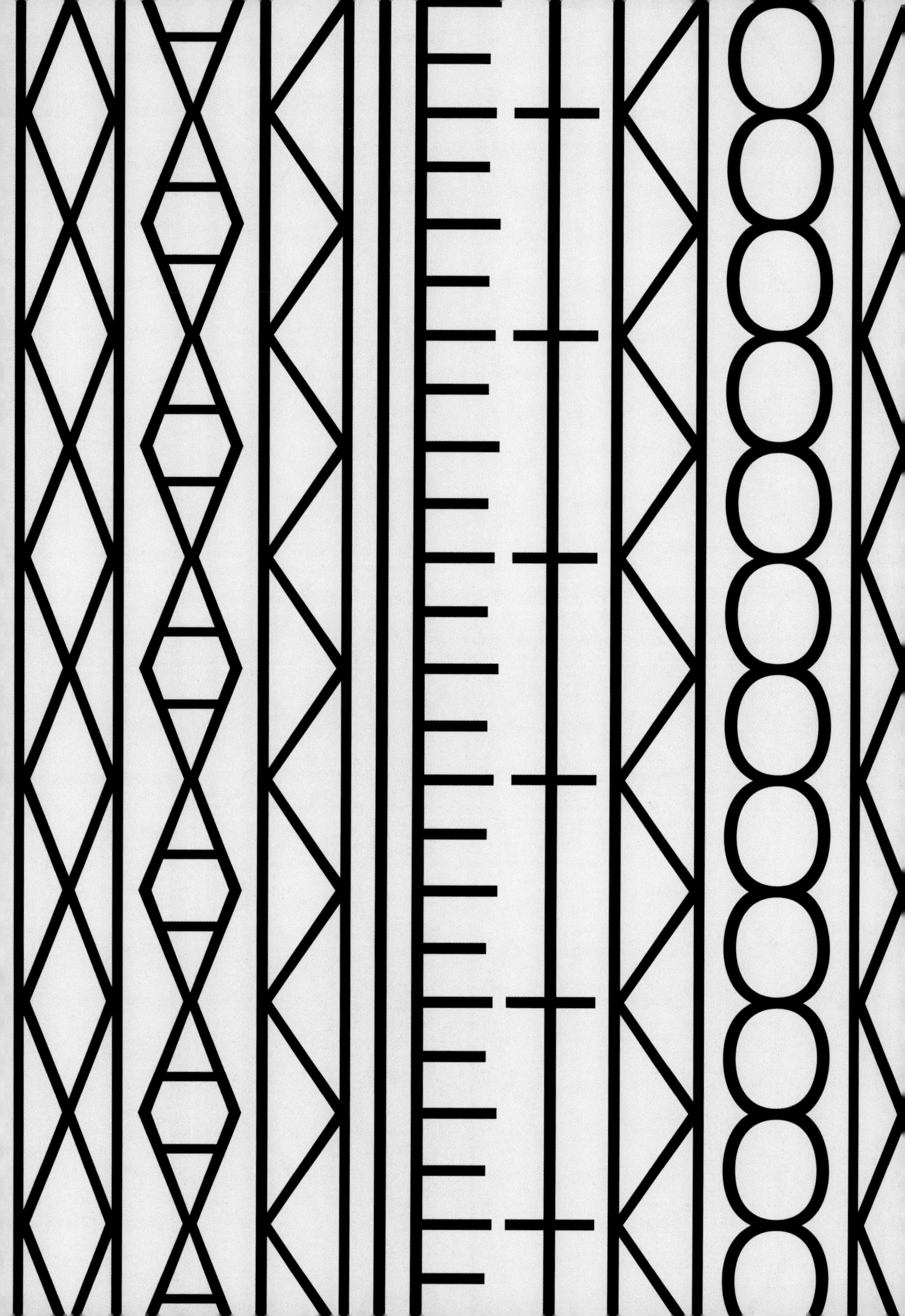

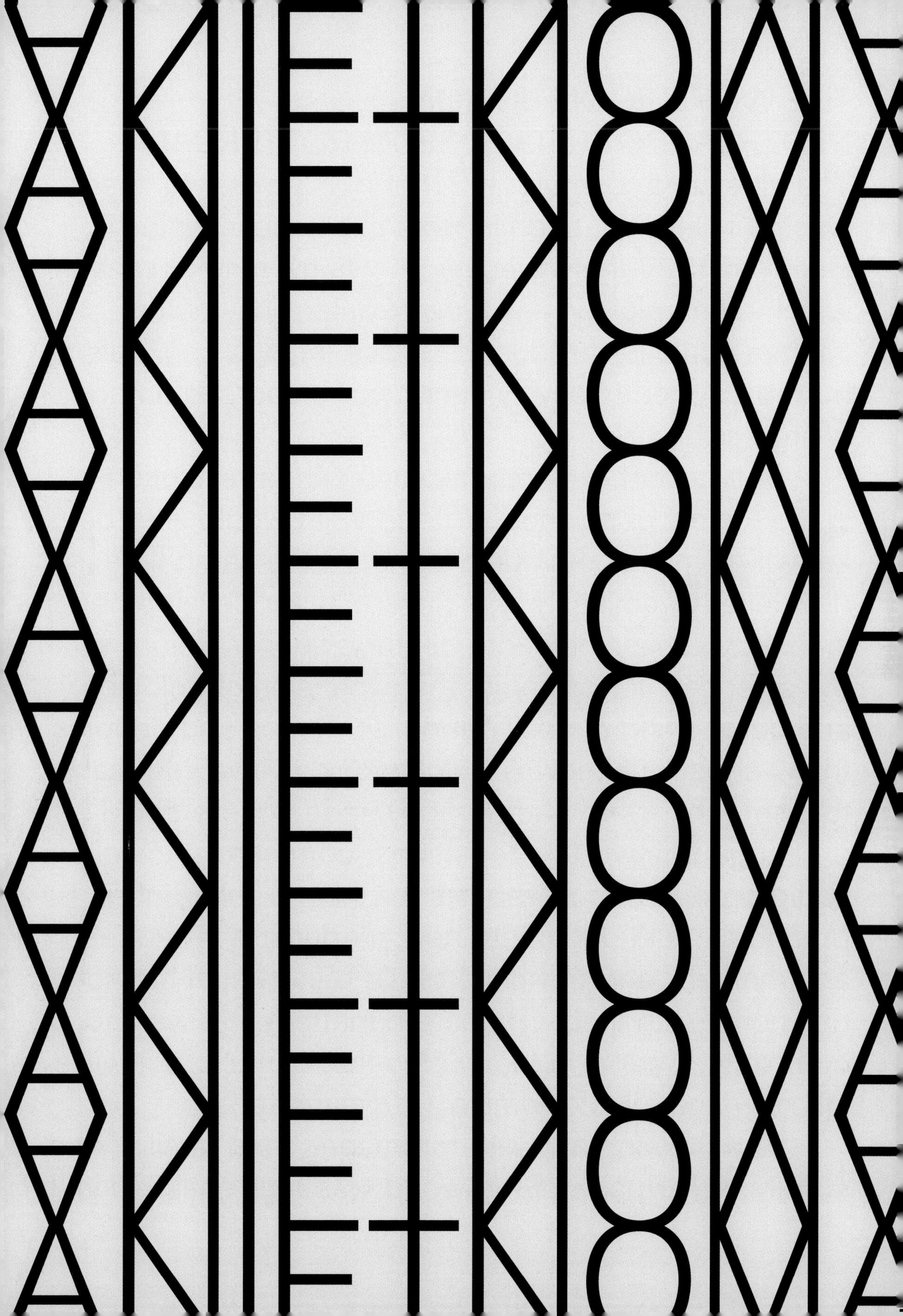

THE WORLD COLLECTION
NEDERLANDS FOTOMUSEUM ROTTERDAM

The nineteenth century: Internet didn't exist yet, there was no television, and film was still to be invented. But from 1839 there was photography, a medium with which a completely new type of ostensibly factual images could be produced. These images could also be reproduced relatively easily and dispersed among a large public.

The advent of photography meant a revolution in the realms of science, art and what would later be known as mass communications. At the same time it dovetailed seamlessly with several other developments in that dynamic nineteenth century: specialization within the sciences, for example, the expansion of colonies, and burgeoning curiosity about territories and peoples that were still unknown, which would evolve into mass tourism. Thanks to photography, researchers could exchange trustworthy depictions, commercial travellers could produce visual reports for their clients, entrepreneurs could document new production territories and markets, and travellers could bring visual memories home with them. These are matters that we find completely normal in the twenty-first century, but were still new and full of promise 150 years ago.

The growing appetite for images from familiar and still unfamiliar parts of the world was thus satisfied with

photographs. Collecting photographs also became
a popular pursuit among those who stayed at home.
That applied for expensive, richly decorated, leather-
bound albums with splendid prints that were pasted
onto cardboard, as much as for mass-reproduced
photos of exotic landscapes, people, animals, monu-
ments and world wonders. The invention of photography thus formed a sturdy boost for the mass
'discovery of the world'.

The founding of the 'Museum voor Land- en
Volkenkunde' – Museum for Geography and Ethnology
– in Rotterdam in 1885 is easy to understand in the
context of this burgeoning interest in other countries
and peoples. Now known as the Wereldmuseum, this
museum immediately started to amass photographs as
soon as it was established. It presented these images
almost immediately in exhibitions and publications. The
initiators had an educational goal in mind, namely to
'give the young merchant an impression of the life and
work of foreign peoples'. The two-volume 1903 work
'De Volken der Aarde' ('Peoples of the Earth'), which
is richly illustrated with photographs, provides a hand-
some example of this that speaks of a Zeitgeist in
which scientific exhaustiveness seemed be as great
a truth as the connectedness of all people. Today,
in 2017, young businesspeople and many others
can revel in an international collection of more than

100,000 photographs in which humans and their environment take centre stage. The majority were taken in Asia, the Middle East, North Africa and North America, but Europe is featured as well. In 2012 this 'World Collection' was transferred to the Nederlands Fotomuseum, the national photography museum of the Netherlands. There it forms an important counterpart to the existing collection of more than 5 million images by photographers, primarily Dutch, from the nineteenth and twentieth centuries.

Almost every conceivable genre, such as war, costume and portraits, is represented in the World Collection, but it also includes art photography. That should be no surprise, when we realize that the photographs originate from many different corners of the world and from a diversity of suppliers. Among the latter were diplomats and missionaries, but also entrepreneurs, researchers and 'normal' enthusiasts, and it goes without saying that these included people from Rotterdam. In 1894, for example, the museum acquired a highly unique 'art album' from businessman Hendrik Veder, a wooden piece of furniture that is more like a library cabinet, with 500 photographs from Europe, Egypt, Israel, Morocco and Turkey pasted onto cardboard. Rotterdam merchant Hendrik Muller was active in Africa, and encouraged amateur photographers by issuing grants, to zoologist Johan Büttikofer, for instance. Albert Hotz was a Rotterdam merchant who took photographs in Persia (now Iran) between 1874 and 1892, and Gerrit Verschuur was a 'globetrotter' who bequeathed a collection of almost 1,500 photographs by the most heterogeneous photographers from various parts of the world, from Felice Beato (Japan) to the Burton Brothers (New Zealand). Other examples of unusual donors include physician-anthropologist Herman ten Kate, who as a scientific researcher took anthropometric portraits of North American Indians, and Daniël Veth, who from 1877 to 1887 was active as an explorer in Central Sumatra.

This short enumeration, which hardly does justice to the World Collection's diversity and scope, shows that the collection does not form a harmonious entity. The photographs were once taken, purchased and collected for widely divergent reasons. Scientific, economic and tourist interest alternate with a fascination for the exotic or a love of art. It is this great diversity that makes the World Collection so special.

In this collection a whole world is still waiting to be discovered.

Ethnography – the science of peoples and cultures – used to be called ethnology and is now known as anthropology. The World Collection is an ethno-historical photo collection. It clarifies how 'the other' has been regarded over the course of time and interconnects the histories of different peoples and communities (migrant and indigenous) over the last 175 years.

Photos cannot be regarded independently of their origin and the purpose they once served. The World Collection includes photos that tell painful stories, about colonialism, exploitation, racism or slavery. These images must be faced up to and cannot be denied or explained away. It is necessary that they continue to be part of today's social debate, in which the historical component is unmissable. At the same time these photos possess the potential to tell different stories as well, stories that have more to do with their visual and poetic qualities, the associations that they evoke or the way in which they can inspire.

In order to discover and demonstrate this, the Nederlands Fotomuseum granted 'carte blanche' to Rotterdam-based style profiler Ellie Uyttenbroek to create an exhibition with the World Collection. She digitally styled a selection of a hundred portraits from the collection in conjunction with graphic designer Mary Pelders Vos. They concentrated on posed, frontally shot portraits in which individual expression is strongly foregrounded and aspects of clothing, style, attitude or silhouette are clearly visible. Introducing colour into the images, the people portrayed and their clothing makes them seem to be of our time.

Uyttenbroek explains her perspective on these images in short texts. For her style is timeless: 'I look at the people in these photos in the same way I look at people in the contemporary streetscape. On this basis I make concise style profiles.'

ETNOMANIE is an exhibition and a book about style, compiled with a nod to the street and fashion looks of today: from tribal hipsters to zen vagabonds and from floral crossdressers to oversized fashionistas. According to Uyttenbroek, fashion is always repeating itself. The title is a term that she coined herself. Thanks to her day-to-day work as a style profiler, she looks at Rotterdam as an 'ethnomaniac' city where countless cultures and subcultures live together without noteworthy problems. That is possible, she believes, not despite but rather thanks to the many ethnic and other differences.

ETNOMANIE builds two bridges in one go: one between history and our time, and a second between the collection and the city.

Frits Gierstberg

Curator Nederlands Fotomuseum

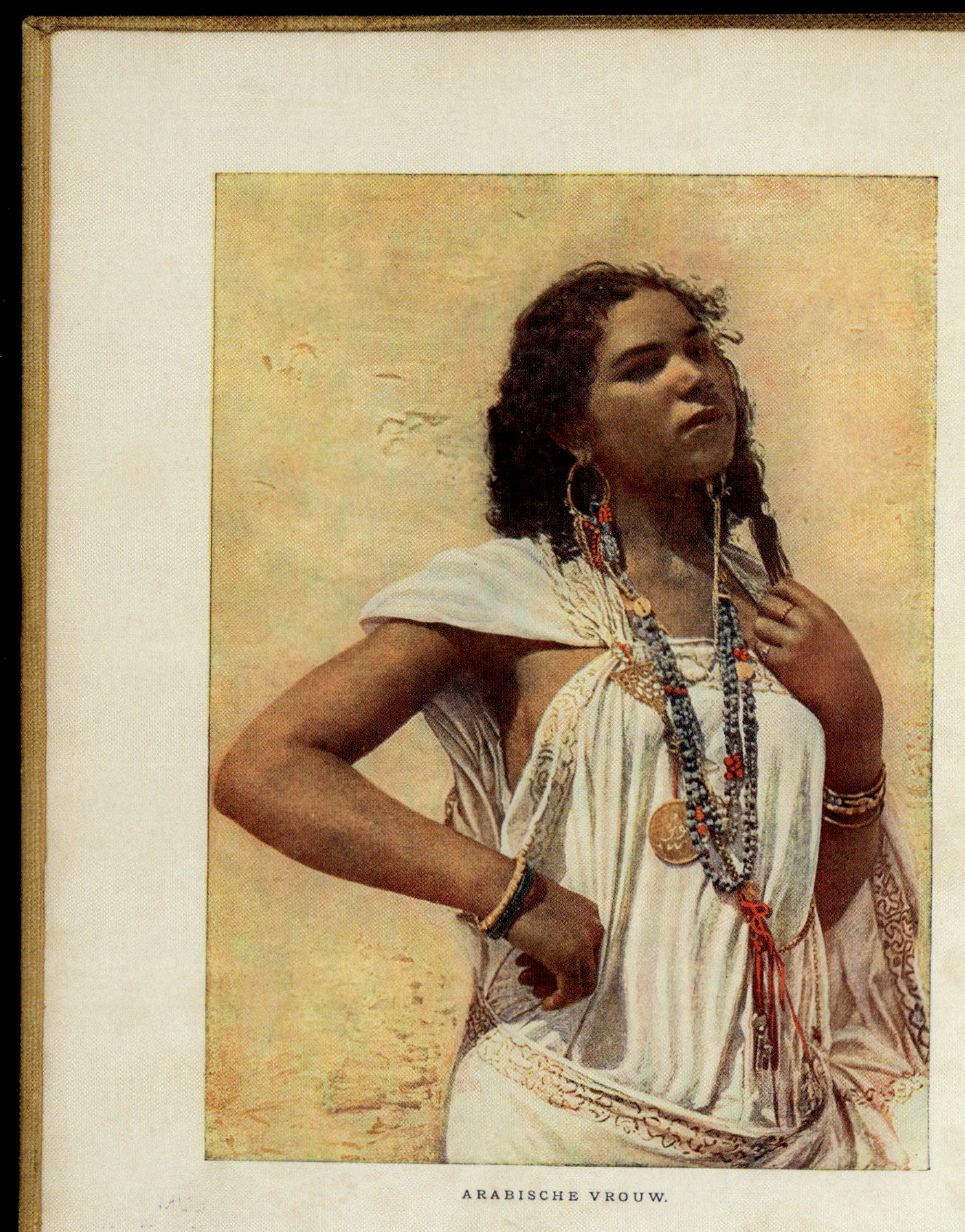

ARABISCHE VROUW.

DE VOLKEN DER AARDE

DOOR

JOH. F. SNELLEMAN,

MET MEER DAN

800 AFBEELDINGEN,

BEVATTENDE DUIZENDEN PORTRETTEN, FOTOGRAFISCH
OPGENOMEN OVER DE GEHEELE AARDE.

DEEL I.

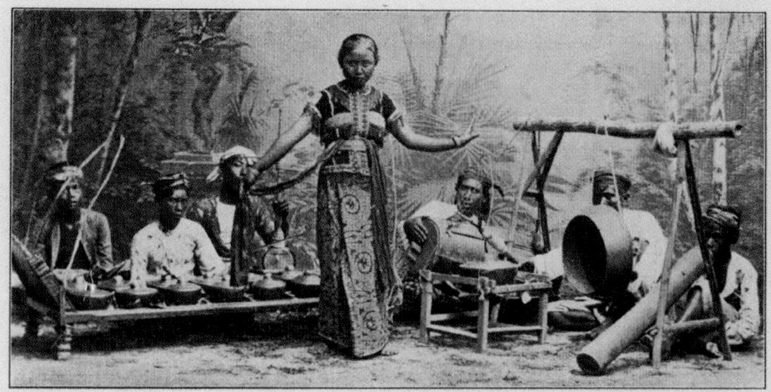

AMSTERDAM,
SCHELTEMA & HOLKEMA'S BOEKHANDEL.

Johan François Snelleman, The peoples of the earth. With over 800 illustrations including portraits, photographed around the world. (Amsterdam: Scheltema en Holkema's Boekhandel, 1903), 2 vols.

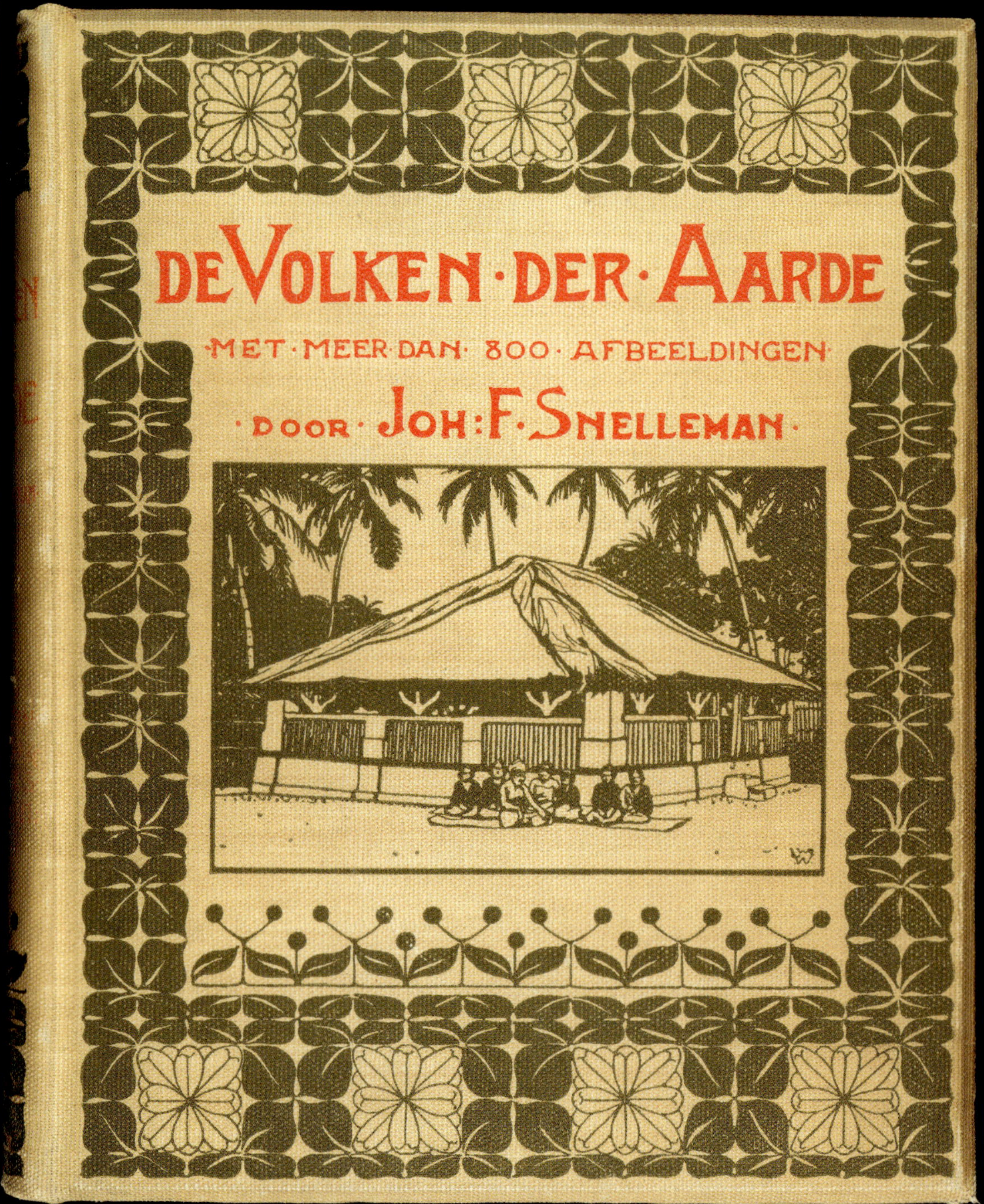

DE VOLKEN · DER · AARDE
MET · MEER · DAN · 800 · AFBEELDINGEN
· DOOR · JOH: F. SNELLEMAN ·

BOOKS ON THE WORLD COLLECTION

Series - Photography from the Collection of the Museum of Ethnology

Paul Faber and Anneke Groeneveld
<u>Images of the Orient, Photography and Tourism, 1860-1900</u>
vol. 1
Amsterdam: Uitgeverij Fragment, 1986

Anneke Groeneveld and Hardwicke Knight
<u>Burton Brothers, Photographers in New Zealand, 1866-1898</u>
vol. 2
Amsterdam: Uitgeverij Fragment, 1987

Anneke Groeneveld, Steven Wachlin and Ineke Zweers
<u>Toekang Potret, 100 Years of Photography in the Dutch Indies 1839-1939</u>
vols. 3 & 4
Amsterdam: Uitgeverij Fragment, 1989

Anneke Groeneveld and Rosemarijn Höfte
<u>Photography in Surinam 1839-1939</u>
vol. 5
Amsterdam: Uitgeverij Fragment, 1990

Anneke Groeneveld and Pieter Hovens
<u>Odagot, Photographs of American Indians 1860-1920</u>
vol. 6
Amsterdam: Uitgeverij Fragment, 1992

John Falconer, Anneke Groeneveld and Steven Wachlin
<u>From Bombay to Shanghai, Historical Photography in South and Southeast Asia</u>
vol. 7
Amsterdam: Uitgeverij Fragment, 1994

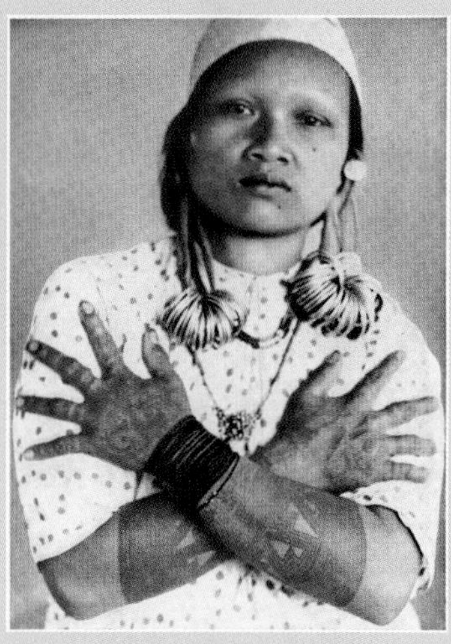

Hendrik Freerk Tillema (1870-1952)
Apo-Kajan, film of a journey to and in Central
Borneo, 336 images, H.F. Tillema (1933)
Offset lithograph
Donation Hendrik Freerk Tillema, ca. 1933
> Cover

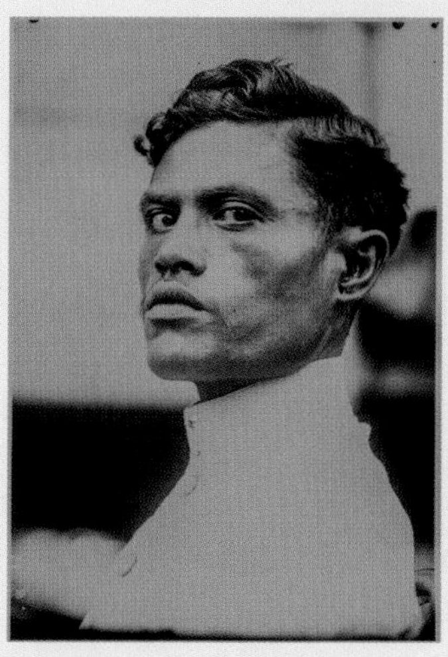

Piet (Petrus) Drabbe (1887-1970)
Minister of the church, Tanimbar, Moluccas
(1915-1935)
Gelatin developing-out paper
Provenance unknown
> p. 3

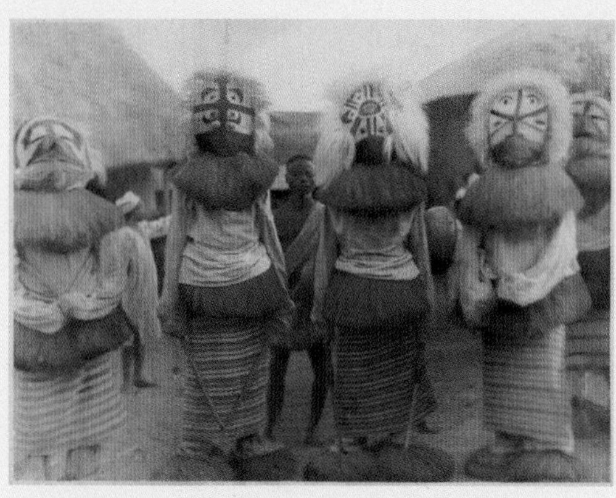

Anonymous
Ngafagoti (secret society), Sierra Leone
(1890-1910)
Gelatin printing-out paper
Provenance unknown
> p. 6

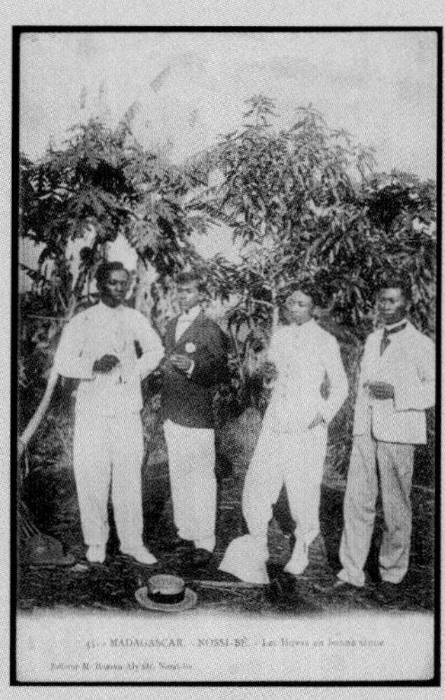

M. Hassan Aly fils (act. 1900-1910)
Hova (free commoners) from the island of
Nosy Be, Madagascar (1890-1920)
Collotype
Provenance unknown
> p. 8

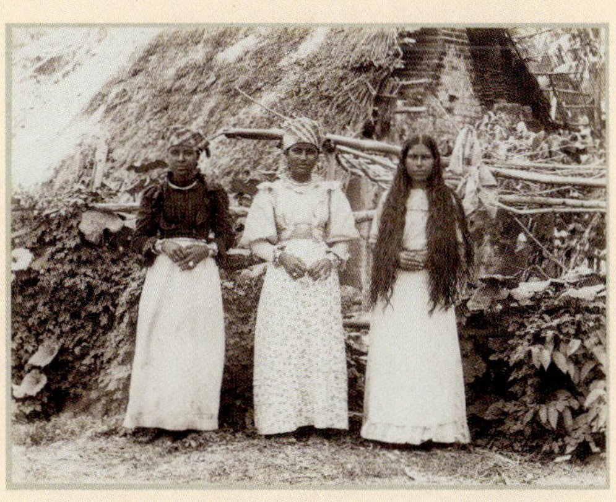

Adolphe Duperly & Sons (act. 1842-1922)
Women in front of a house, Jamaica
(1876-1903)
Gelatin printing-out paper, toned
Legacy - Gerrit Verschuur, 1907
> p. 10

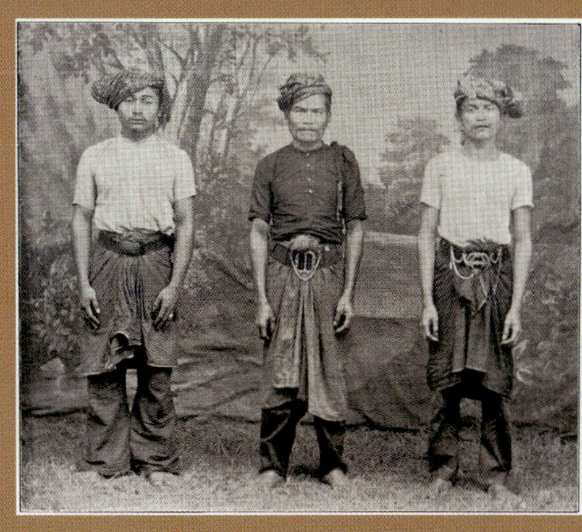

Christiaan Benjamin Nieuwenhuis (1863-1922)
Muslims from the Gajo land, Aceh, Sumatra,
Indonesia (1903)
Offset lithograph
Provenance unknown
> p. 12

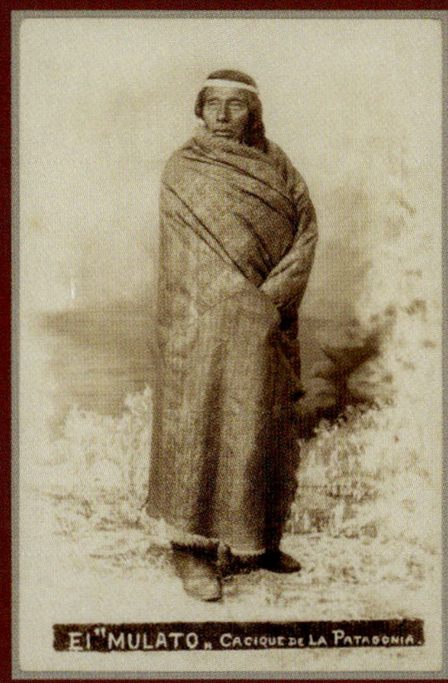

John Bell Hatcher (1861-1904)
Chümjalu, a.k.a. El Mulato, cacique (chief) of
the Tehuelche, Patagonia (c. 1896)
Albumen print
Donation - Peter A. de Bruyne, 1906
> p. 16

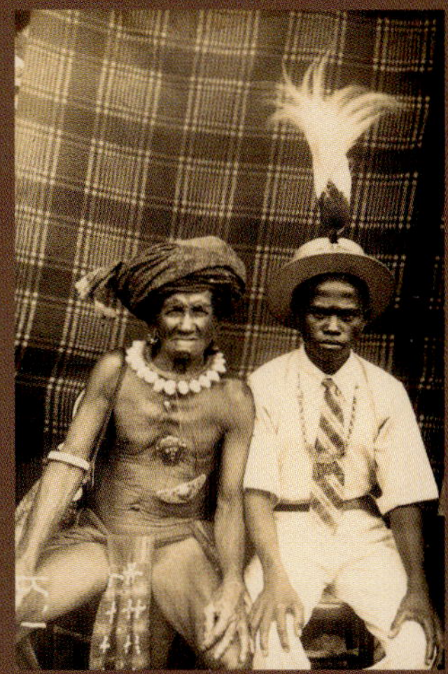

Piet (Petrus) Drabbe (1887-1970)
Aristocratic man with son studying to be a
shaman, Tanimbar, Moluccas (1915-1935)
Gelatin developing-out paper
Provenance unknown
> p. 17

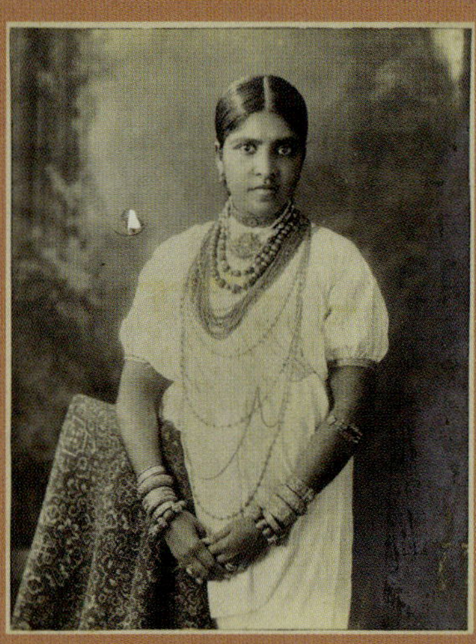

William Louis Henry Skeen & Co. (1847-1903)
Young Singalese from wealthy family, Sri Lanka
(1890-1900)
Gelatin developing-out paper
Legacy - Gerrit Verschuur, 1907
> p. 18

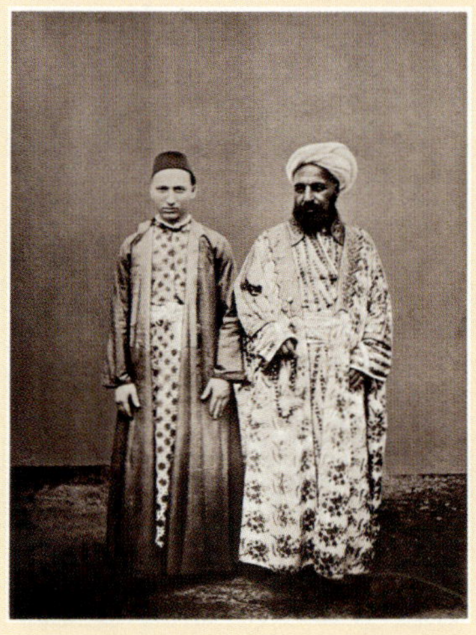

Christiaan Snouck Hurgronje (1857-1936)
Distinguished merchant with his Circassian
slave (from the Caucasus), Mecca, Saudi
Arabia (1885)
Collotype
Provenance unknown
> p. 19

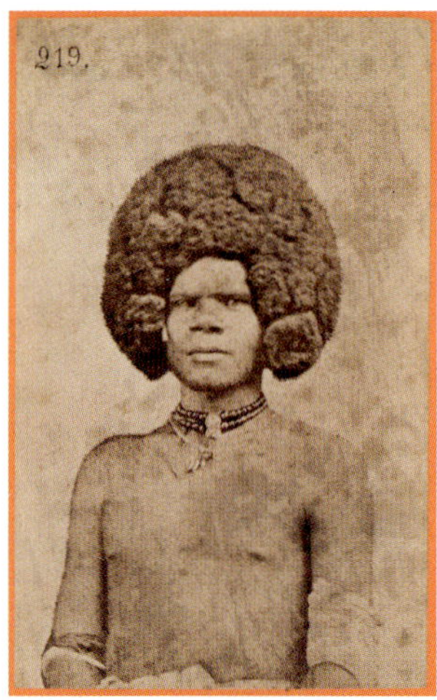

Andrew Garrett (1823-1878)
Loto, a mountain inhabitant of the island of
Viti-Levu with a wig-like hairdo, Fiji (1866-1870)
Albumen print
Donation - Herman ten Kate, 1910
> p. 20

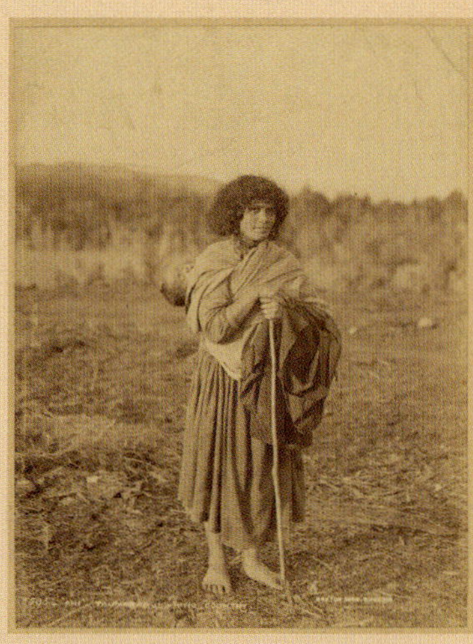

Burton Brothers (act. 1866-1898)
Ani, Maori of tutua (commoner) rank,
Taumarunui, King Country, New Zealand
(1885)
Albumen print
Legacy - Gerrit Verschuur, 1907
> p. 21

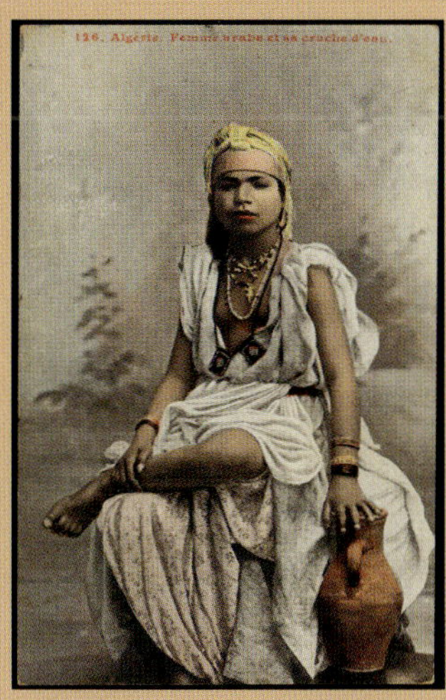

Aqua-Photo L.V.S. (act. 1900-1915)
Woman with water jar, Algeria (1900-1915)
Offset lithograph
Provenance unknown
> p. 22

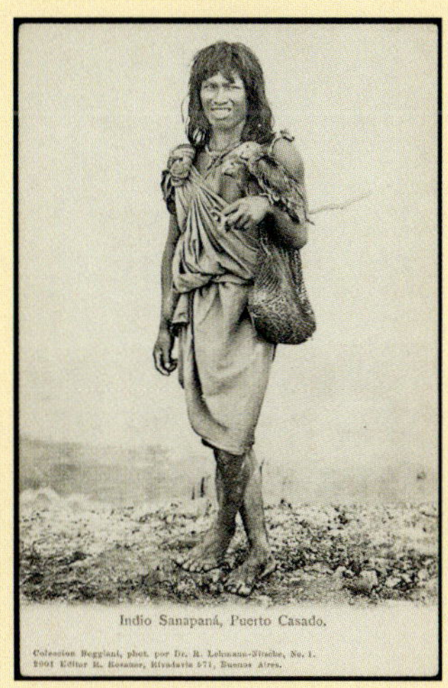

Guido Boggiani (1861-1902)
Young man aged 25-30 from the Sanapaná
people in Puerto Casado, Paraguay
(1896-1901)
Collotype
Donation - Herman ten Kate, 1910
> p. 23

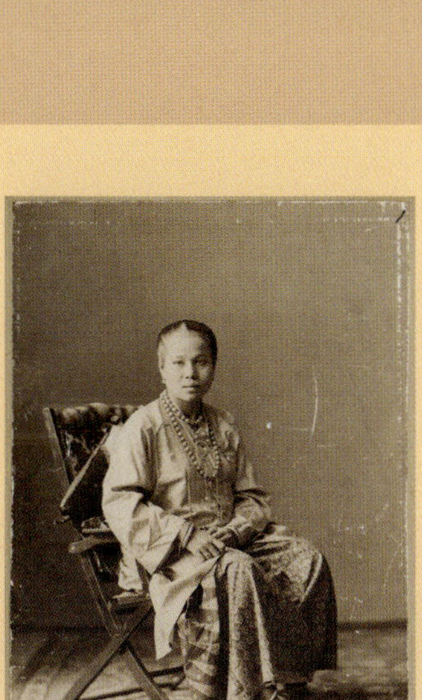

Carl Josef Kleingrothe (1864-1925)
Chinese woman, Medan, Sumatra, Indonesia
(1898-1915)
Platinotype
Donation - Herman ten Kate, 1910
> p. 24

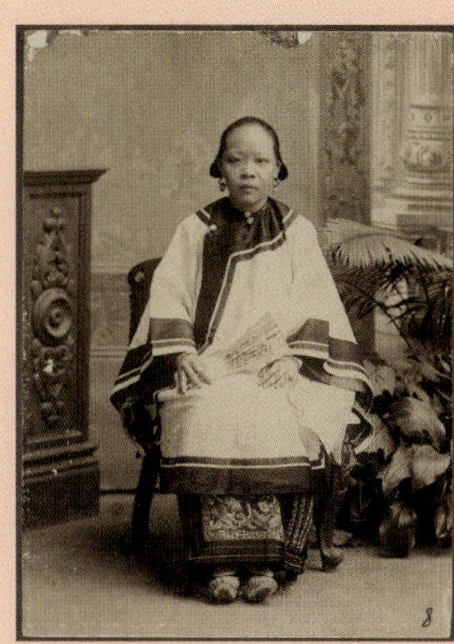

Carl Josef Kleingrothe (1864-1925)
Chinese woman from the British Crown colony
of Straits Settlements, Medan, Sumatra,
Indonesia (1898-1915)
Collodion printing-out paper
Donation - Herman ten Kate, 1910
> p. 25

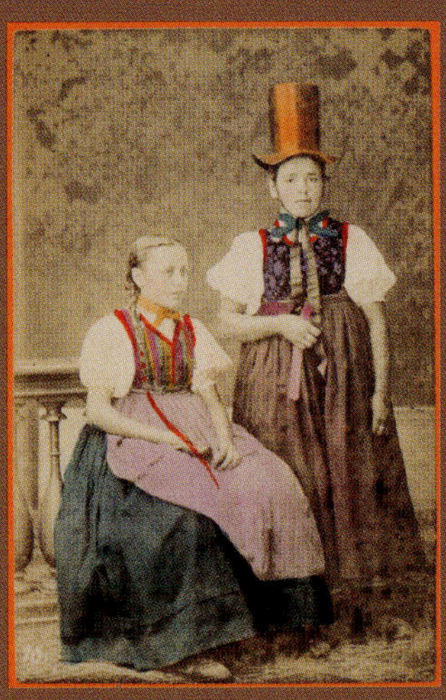

F. Willmann & Johann Bleibel (act. 1860-1864)
Woman in local costume of Elzach, Germany
(1864)
Albumen print, hand-coloured
Donation - Herman ten Kate, 1910
> p. 26

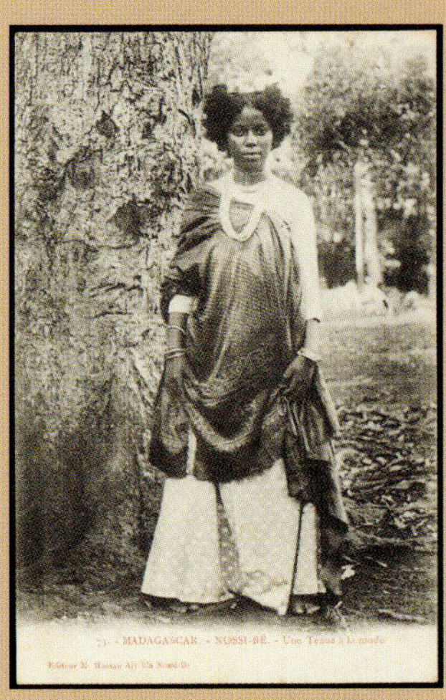

M. Hassan Aly fils (act. 1900-1910)
Woman from the island of Nosy Be, dressed
in the latest fashion, Madagascar (1890-1920)
Collotype
Provenance unknown
> p. 27

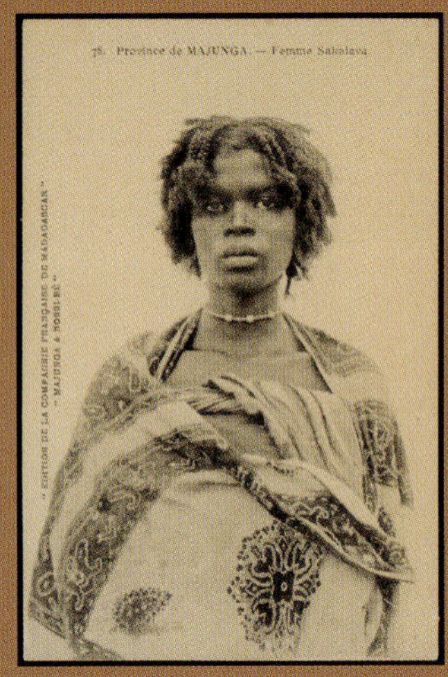

Compagnie Française de Madagascar (act.
1880-1920)
Sakalava wearing a lamba (colourful wrap-
around), Madagascar (1880-1920)
Collotype
Provenance unknown
> p. 28

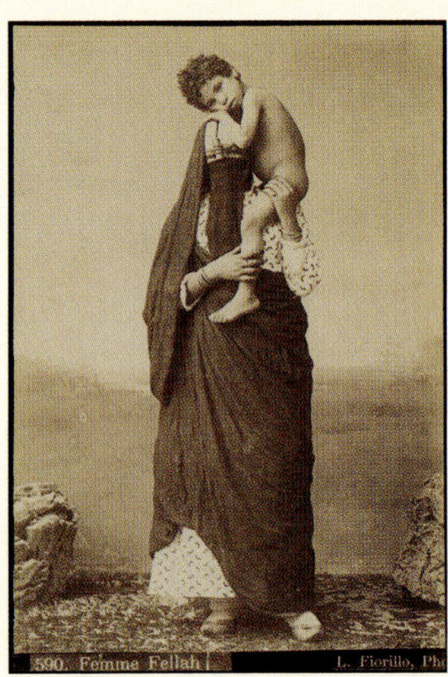

Luigi Fiorillo (?-1898)
Veiled peasant woman with child, Egypt
(1870-1890)
Albumen print
Donation - Hendrik Veder, 1894
> p. 29

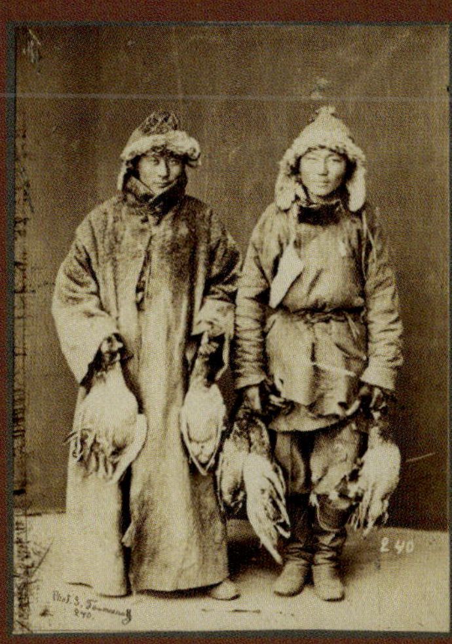

S.B. Toumanoff (act. 1870-1879)
Buryat hunters, Adygeya, Russian Federation
(1870-1879)
Albumen print
Donation - Herman ten Kate, 1910
> p. 30

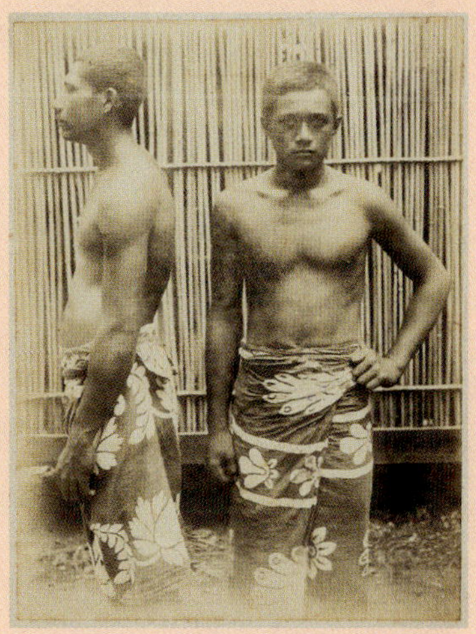

Herman Frederik Carel ten Kate (1858-1931)
Anthropometric study of young men, Tahiti
(1892)
Albumen print
Donation - Herman ten Kate, 1910
> p. 31

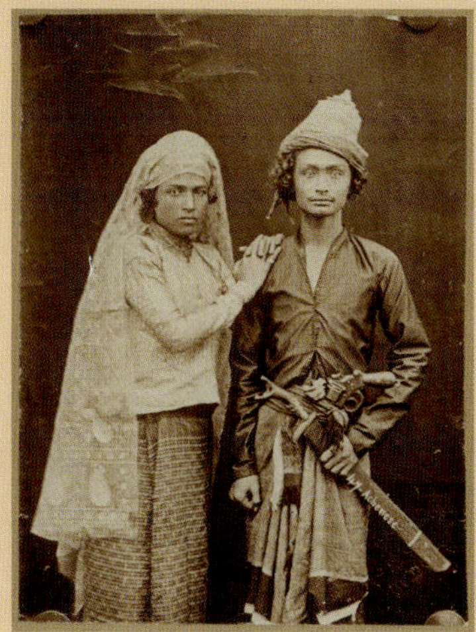

Gustav Richard Lambert & Co. (1846-1907)
Bride and groom from Aceh, Sumatra,
Indonesia (1883-1918)
Gelatin printing-out paper, toned
Donation - Herman ten Kate,1910
> p. 32

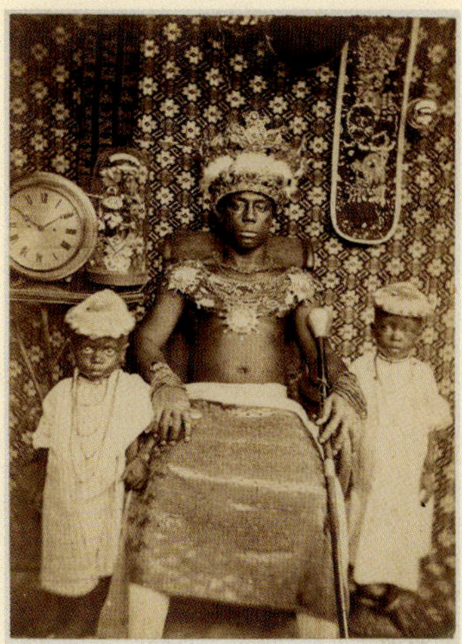

José Augosto da Cunha Moraes (1855-1933)
Prince Eyamba of Calabar, Nigeria (1870-1889)
Albumen print
Donation - J.P. Verdoorn, 1906
> p. 33

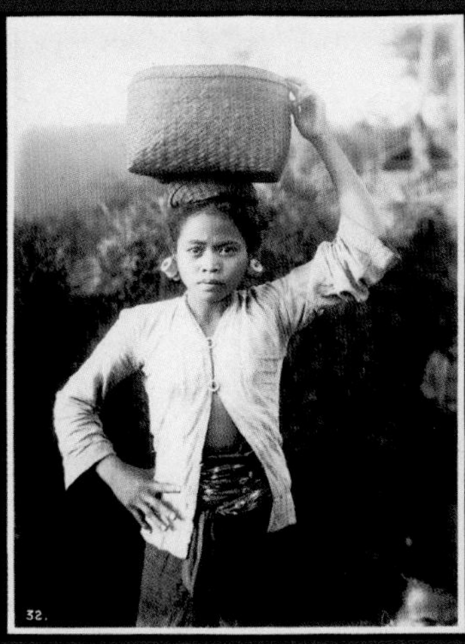

Thilly Weissenborn (1889-1964)
Girl from rural area, Bali, Indonesia (1917-1929)
Gelatin printing-out paper, toned
Provenance unknown
> p. 34

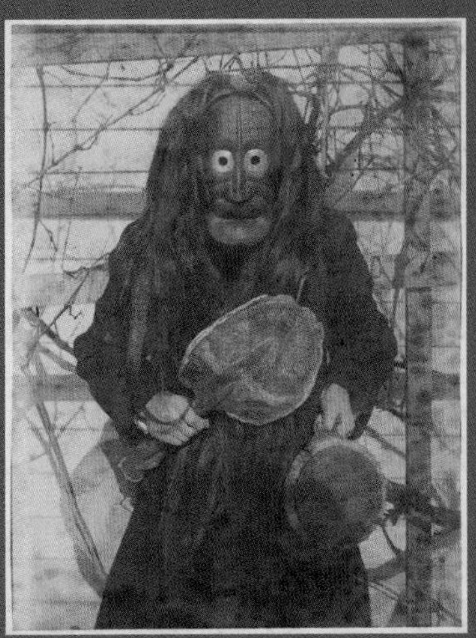

J.W. Sanborn (act. 1889)
Iroquois shaman, New York State, United States (1889)
Albumen print
Donation - Herman ten Kate, 1910
> p. 35

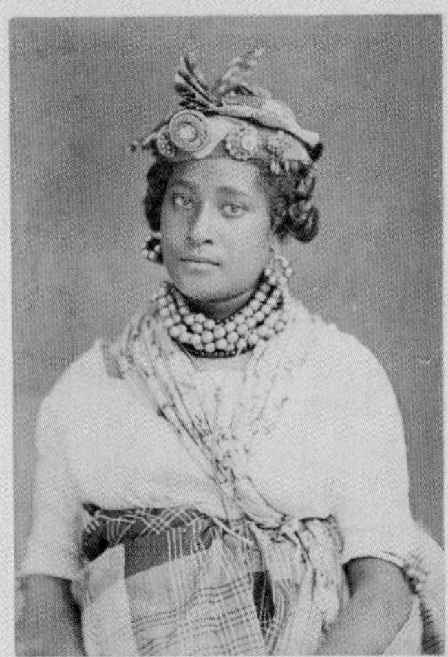

Félix Morin (act. 1865-1900)
Women from Martinique (1880-1886)
Albumen print
Donation - Herman ten Kate, 1910
> p. 36

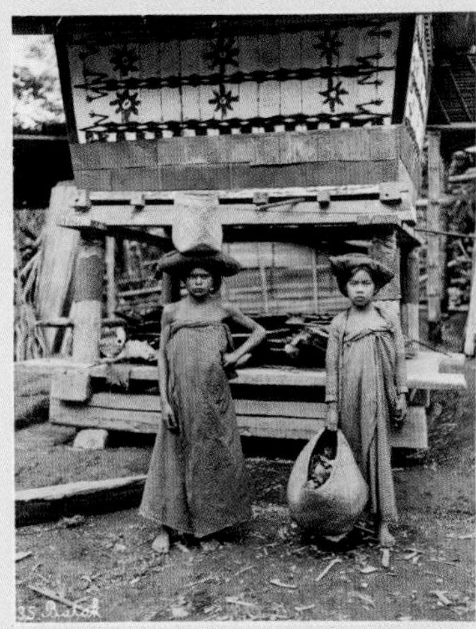

Gustav Richard Lambert & Co. (1846-1907)
Young Batak women in front of rice barn, with the harvest of indigofera leaves, used to make indigo, Sumatra, Indonesia (1883-1918)
Collodion printing-out paper, toned
Provenance unknown
> p. 37

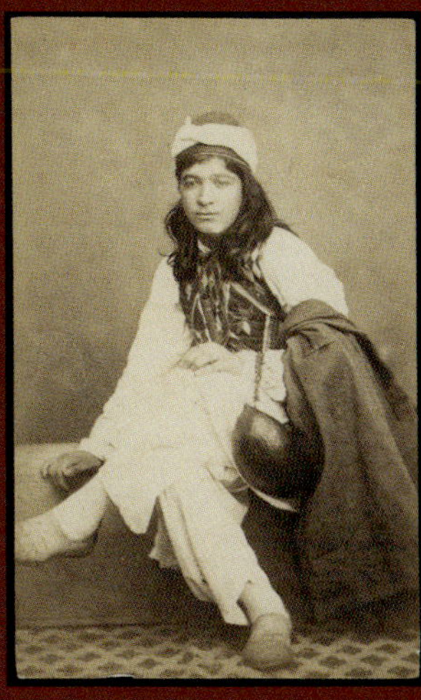

Pascal Sébah (1823-1886),
studio act. 1856-1888
Dervish (mendiant monk) with begging bowl,
Turkey (1856-1888)
Albumen print
Donation - Hendrik Veder, 1894
> p. 38

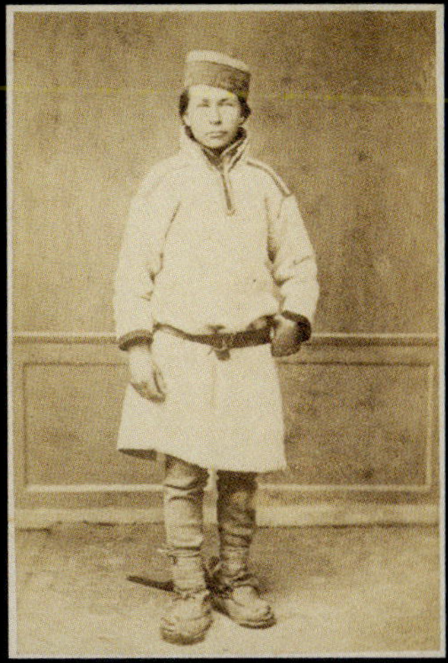

Anonymous
Young Sami, Lapland, Norway (1880-1884)
Albumen print
Donation - Herman ten Kate, 1910
> p. 39

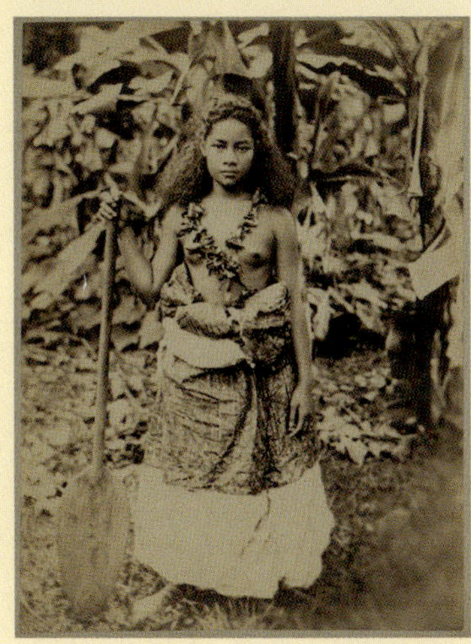

John Davis (1831-1903)
Young woman with necklace of fruit stones,
Samoa (1879-1903)
Albumen print
Donation - Anatomisch-Embryologisch
Laboratorium der R.U. Leiden, 1987
> p. 40

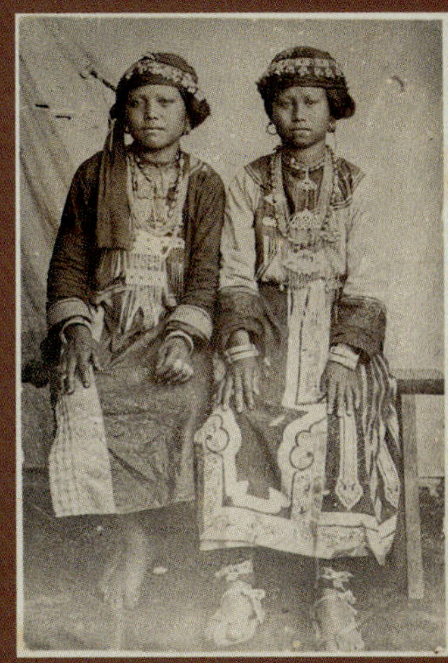

Anonymous
Taiwanese girls (1895-1910)
Gelatin printing-out paper, toned
Donation - Herman ten Kate,1910
> p. 41

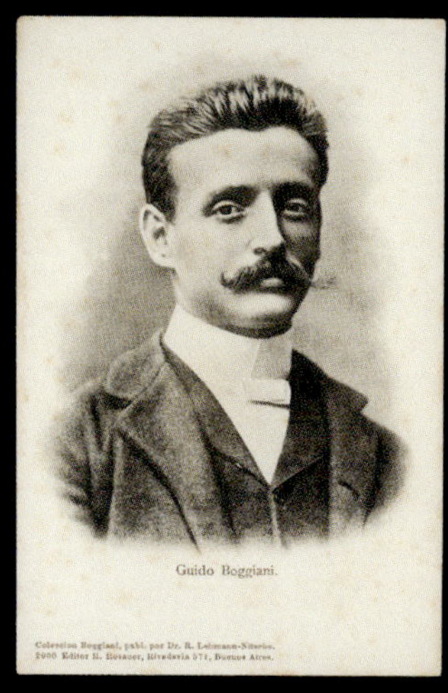

Guido Boggiani (1861-1902)
Guido Boggiani, a painter, draughtsman,
photographer and ethnologist, Paraguay
(1888-1901)
Collotype
Donation - Herman ten Kate,1910
> p. 42

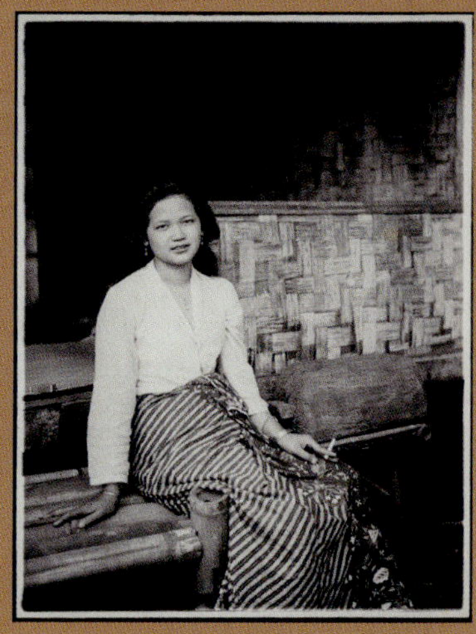

Wijnand Elbert Kerkhoff (1886-1974)
Village woman with cigarette, Java, Indonesia
(1919-1930)
Carbon print
Donation - Loek Bakhuizen, 1988
> p. 43

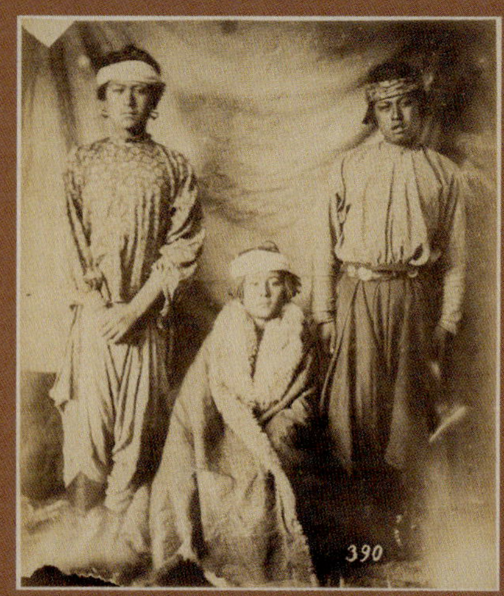

Julio German (Jules) Koslowsky (1846-1923)
Brothers Tsalhuaik, Cajaï and Cánel, Tehuelche
from Patagonia, Argentina (1896)
Albumen print
Donation - Herman ten Kate, 1910
> p. 44

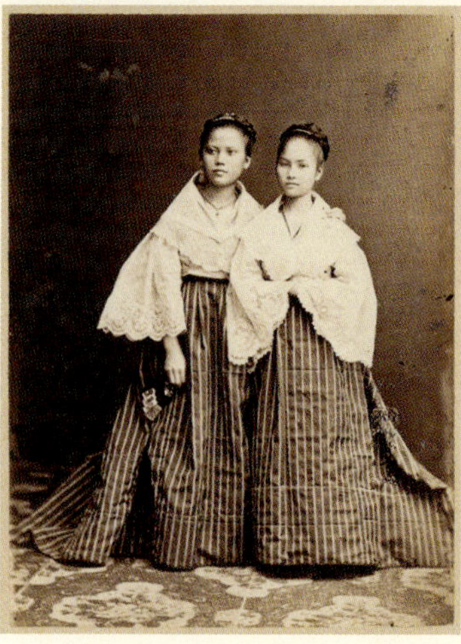

Francisco van Camp (act. 1874-1880)
Tagalog women, Manila, Philippines
(1875-1880)
Albumen print
Provenance unknown
> p. 45

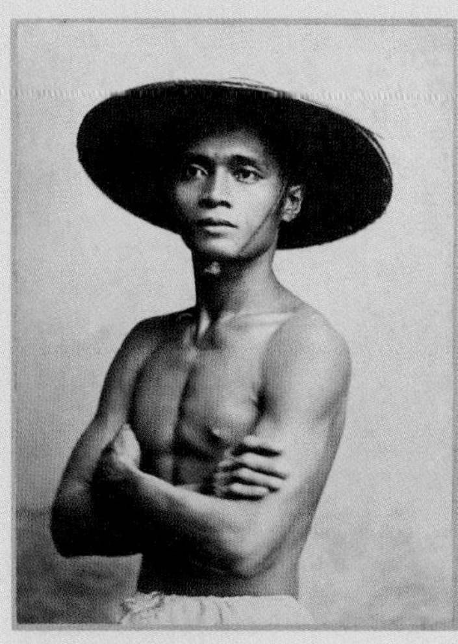

Francisco van Camp (act. 1874-1880)
Tagalog, Manila, Philippines (1875-1880)
Albumen print
Provenance unknown
> p. 46

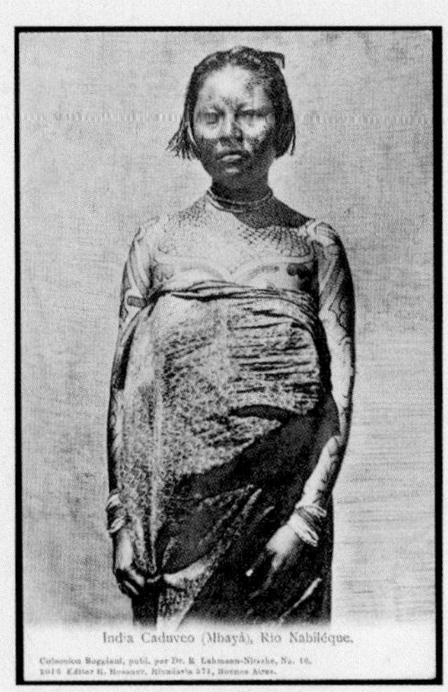

Guido Boggiani (1861-1902)
Guaicurú woman, with face and body painting
of the Kadiweu people, Rio Nabiléque,
Paraguay (1896-1901)
Collotype
Donation - Herman ten Kate,1910
> p. 47

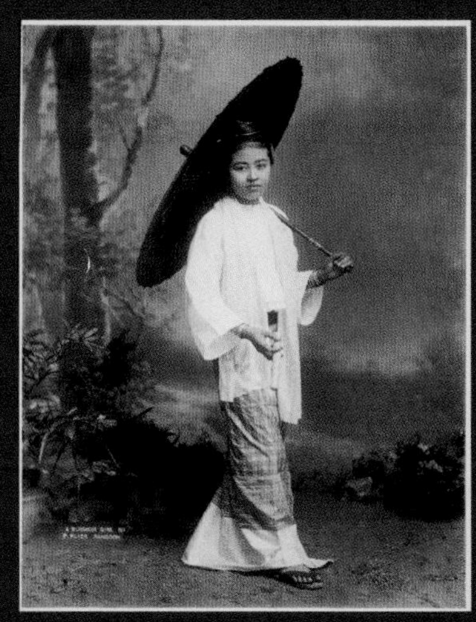

Philip Adolphe Klier (1845-1911)
Girl with cheroot (cigar), Burma
(c. 1880-1890)
Albumen print
Legacy - Gerrit Verschuur, 1907
> p. 48

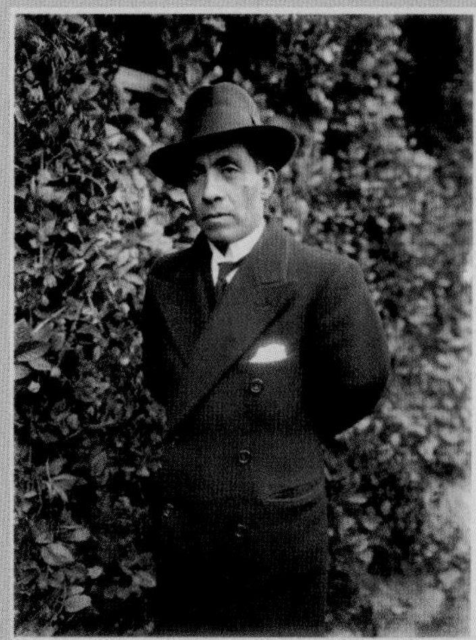

Martín Chambi (1891-1973)
Luis M. Sanchez Cerro, President of Peru
from 1931 to 1933 (1929-1931)
Gelatin developing-out paper
Purchase - Wereldmuseum, 1990
> p. 49

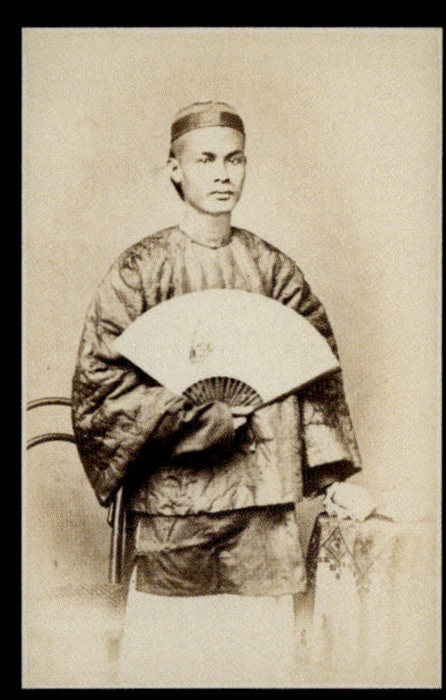

Anonymous
Young man holding fan, Singapore (c. 1870)
Albumen print
Legacy - Gerrit Verschuur, 1907
> p. 50

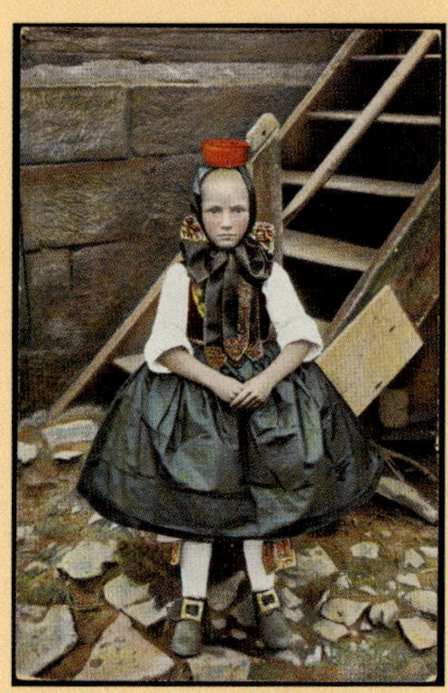

Siegfried Bäcker (act. 1900-1920)
Girl in costume of Hesse, Germany
(1900-1918)
Offset lithograph
Donation - J.F. van Leeuwen, 1911
> p. 51

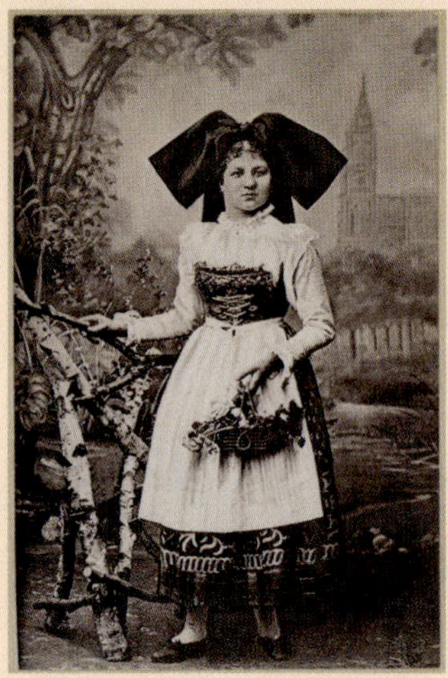

Anonymous
Girl in Alsatian costume, France (c. 1900)
Collotype
Donation - Herman ten Kate, 1910
> p. 52

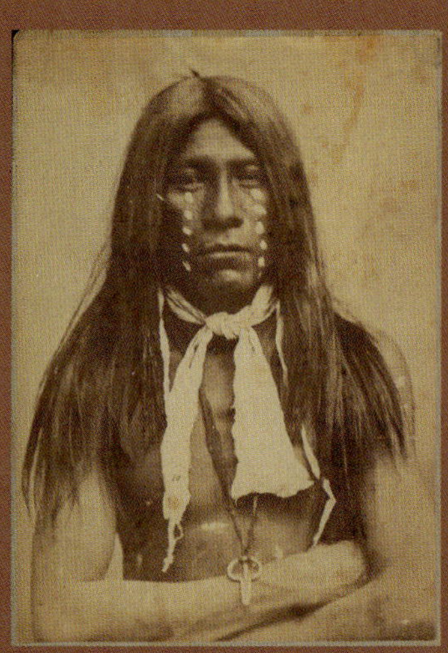

Henry Buehman (1851-1912)
Yuma from Arizona, United States (c. 1883)
Albumen print
Donation - Herman ten Kate, 1910
> p. 53

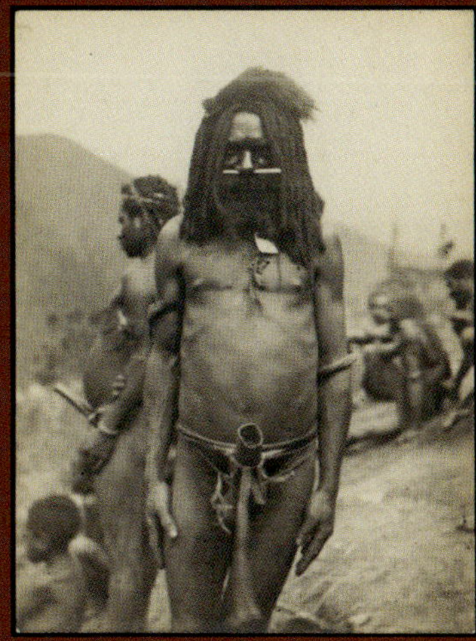

W. Jan Jongejans (1883-1939)
Uringgup wearing penis sheath and nose
ornament, Central New Guinea (1920-1921)
Gelatin developing-out paper
Provenance unknown
> p. 54

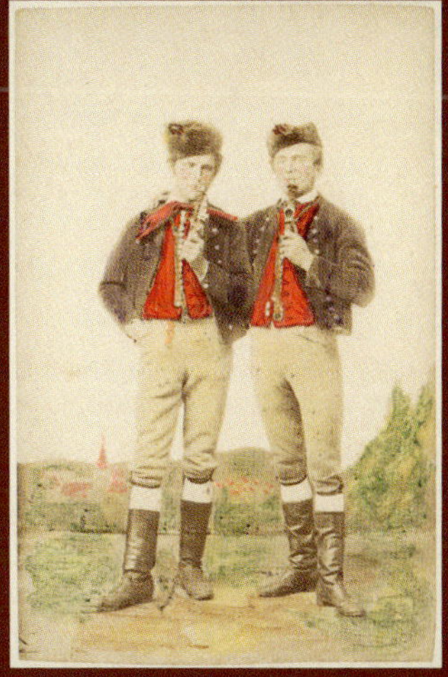

Paul Sinner (1838-1925)
Men from Tübingen, Germany (1864-1881)
Albumen print
Donation - Herman ten Kate, 1910
> p. 55

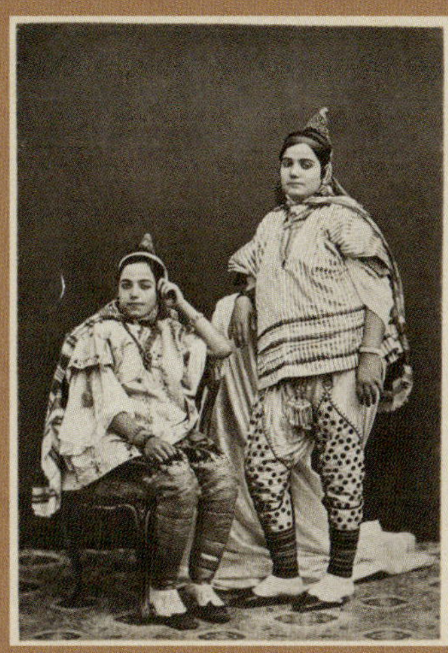

J. André Garrigues (1848-1923)
Jewish women, Tunis, Tunisia (1875-1900)
Collodion printing-out paper
Donation - Herman ten Kate, 1910
> p. 56

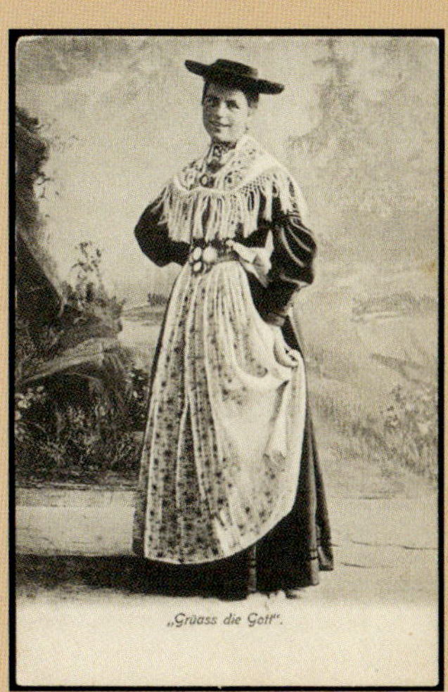

Bernhard Johannes (1846-1899),
studio act. 1880-1940
Woman in traditional Bavarian costume,
Garmisch-Partenkirchen, Germany
(1900-1910)
Collotype
Donation - J.F. van Leeuwen, 1911
> p. 57

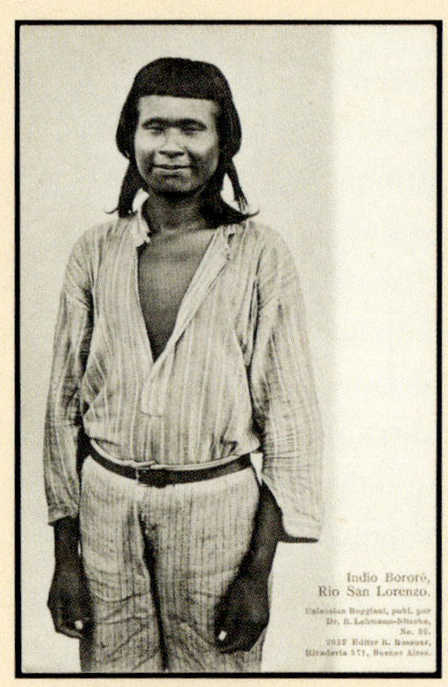

Guido Boggiani (1861-1902)
Boe or Bororo aged 16 or 17, in Western
dress, Rio San Lorenzo, Paraguay (1896-1901)
Collotype
Donation - Herman ten Kate, 1910
> p. 58

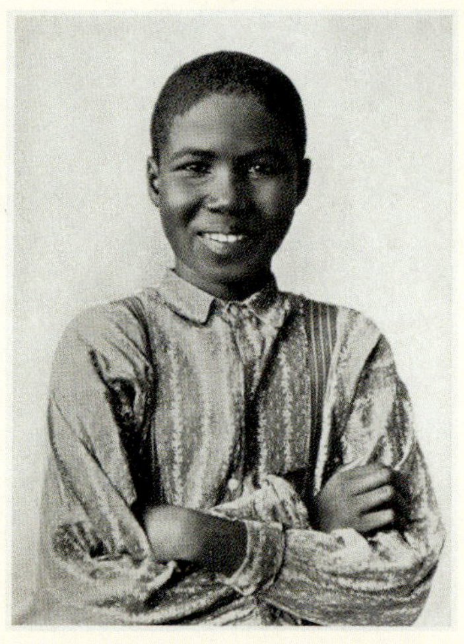

Anonymous
Boy from Curaçao, Curaçao (1900-1911)
Offset lithograph
Reproduction - Wereldmuseum, 1911
> p. 59

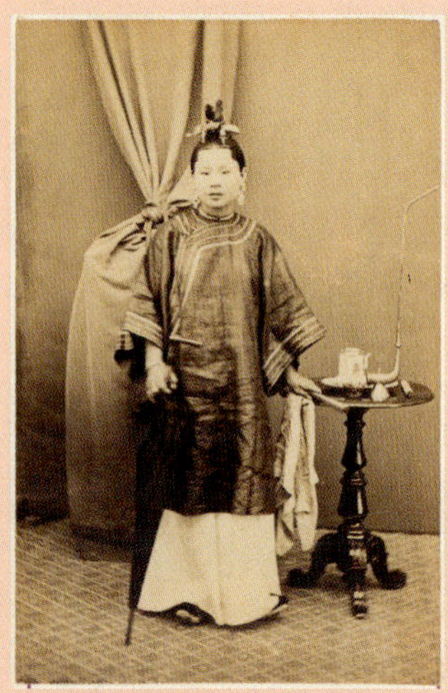

August Sachtler (act. 1863-1874)
Distinguished Chinese woman in Singapore
(1863-1874)
Albumen print
Legacy - Gerrit Verschuur, 1907
> p. 60

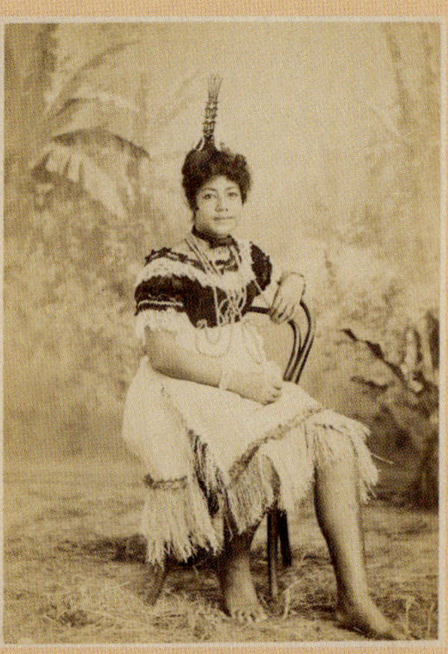

John Davis (1831-1903)
Woman in traditional skirt and headdress
worn with Western blouse and necklaces,
Apia, Samoa (1879-1903)
Albumen print
Donation - Anatomisch-Embryologisch
Laboratorium der R.U. Leiden, 1987
> p. 61

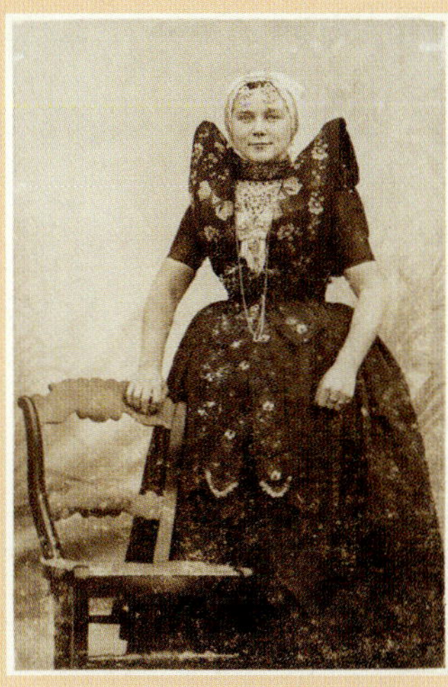

Honoré Feijen (1873-1956)
Woman in Axel costume, Zeeland,
Netherlands (1870-1879)
Gelatin printing-out paper, toned
Purchase - Nederlands Fotomuseum, 2005
> p. 62

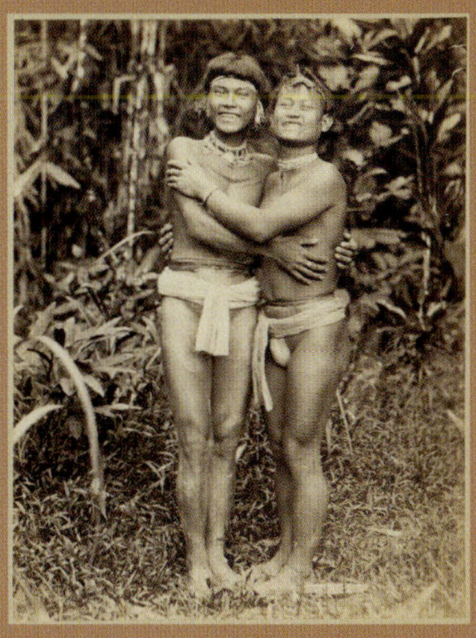

Christiaan Benjamin Nieuwenhuis (1863-1922)
Young men from the Mentawai Islands,
Sumatra, Indonesia (1895)
Albumen print
Provenance unknown
> p. 63

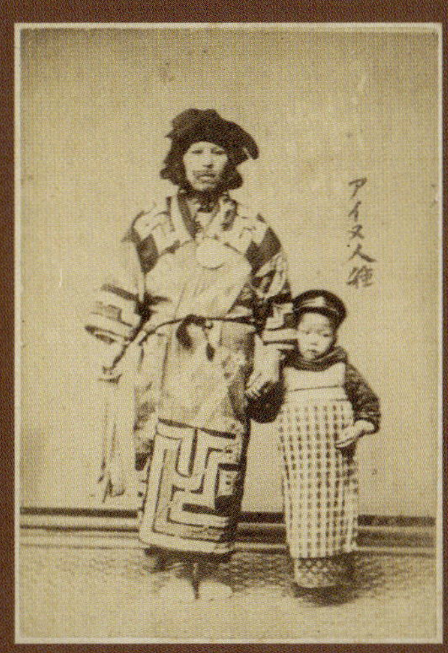

Anonymous
Aino woman and child in a Human Zoo,
Osaka, Japan (1903)
Albumen print
Donation - Herman ten Kate, 1910
> p. 64

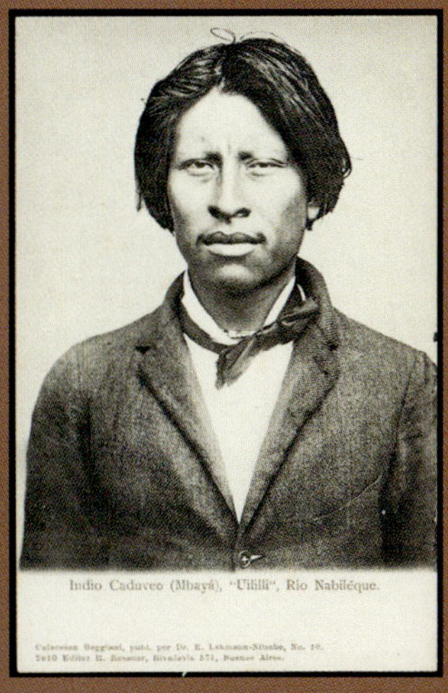

Guido Boggiani (1861-1902)
Uilili, a Kadiweu man aged 25-30,
wearing Western dress, Rio Nabiléque,
Paraguay (1896-1901)
Collotype
Donation - Herman ten Kate, 1910
> p. 65

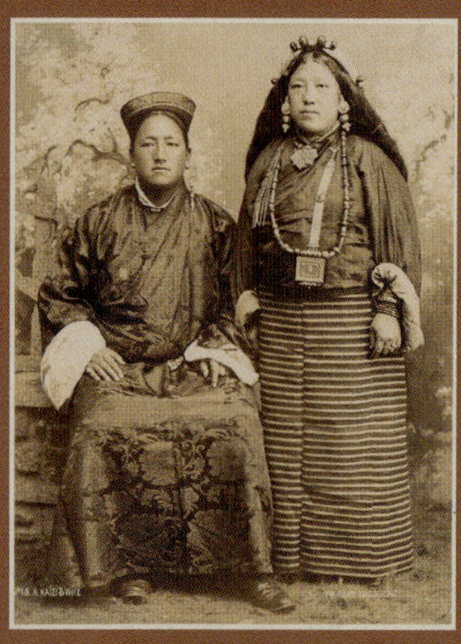

Theodore Paar (act. 1870-1890)
Khasi couple, Darjeeling, India (c. 1890)
Gelatin printing-out paper
Legacy - Gerrit Verschuur, 1907
> p. 66

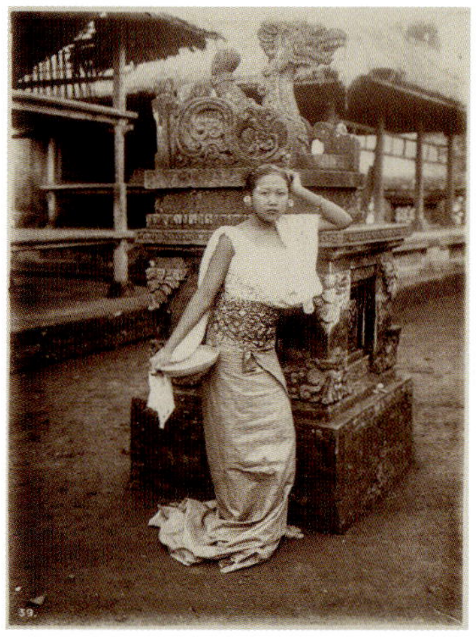

Thilly Weissenborn (1889-1964)
Aristocratic woman in temple complex,
Bali, Indonesia (1917-1929)
Gelatin printing-out paper, toned
Provenance unknown
> p. 67

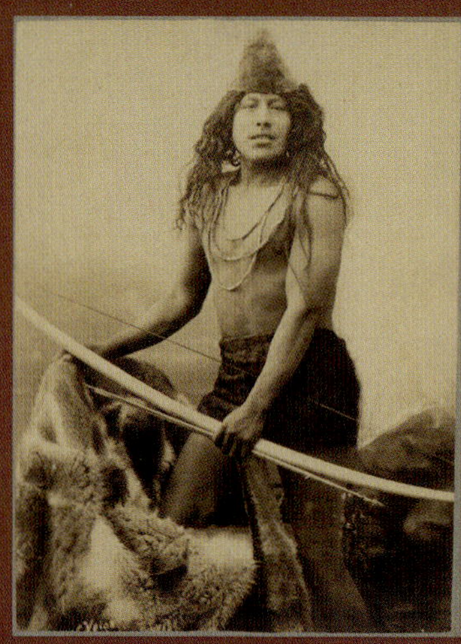

John Bell Hatcher (1861-1904)
Vaios, a Yaghan from Tierra del Fuego,
Punta Arenas, Argentina (c. 1896)
Albumen print
Donation - Peter A. de Bruyne, 1906
> p. 68

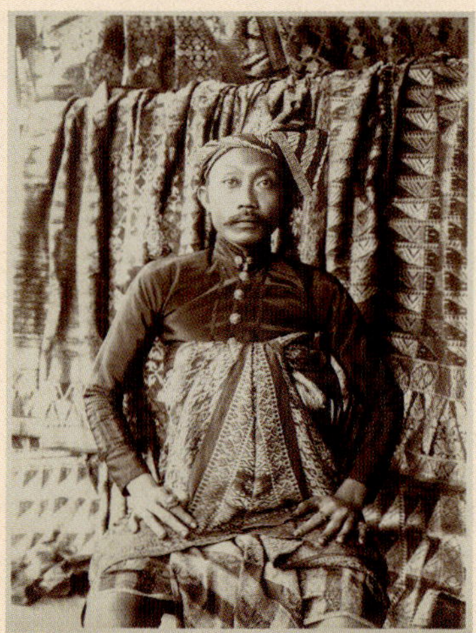

Thilly Weissenborn (1889-1964)
Bridegroom, Bali, Indonesia (1917-1929)
Gelatin printing-out paper, toned
Provenance unknown
> p. 69

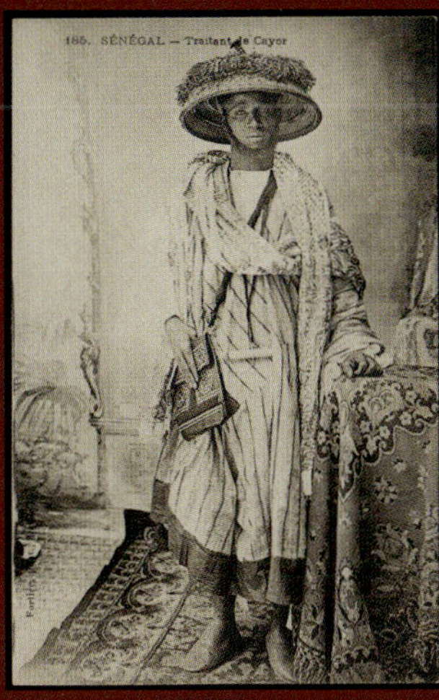

François-Edmond Fortier (1862-1928)
Shaman from Cayor, Senegal (1900-1910)
Collotype
Donation - J.P. Verdoorn, 1906
> p. 70

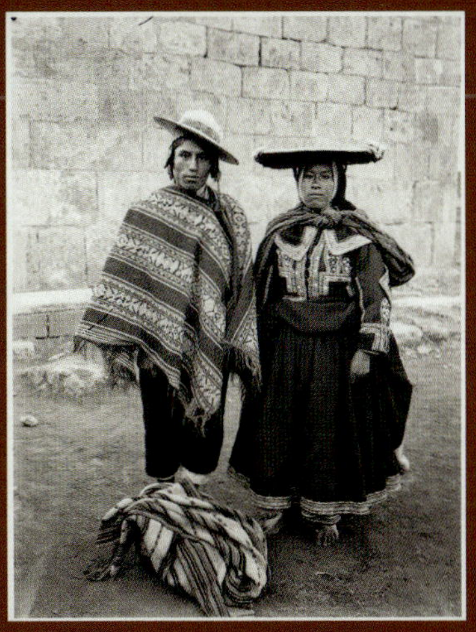

Martín Chambi (1891-1973)
Married couple from Tinta, Peru (c. 1932)
Gelatin developing-out paper
Purchase - Wereldmuseum, 1990
> p. 71

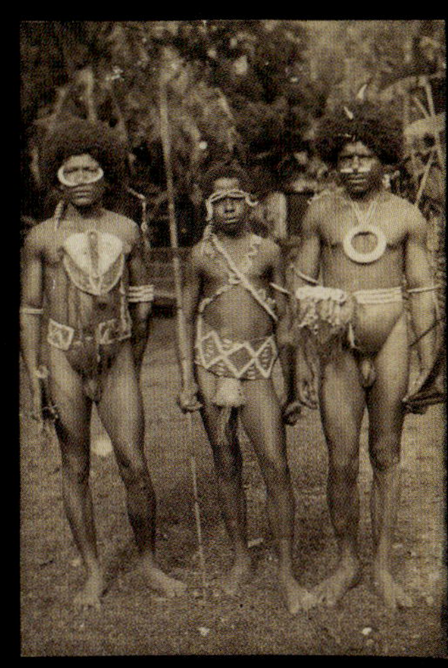

Anonymous
Papuans from Humboldt Bay, New Guinea
(c. 1910)
Gelatin printing-out paper
Provenance unknown
> p. 72

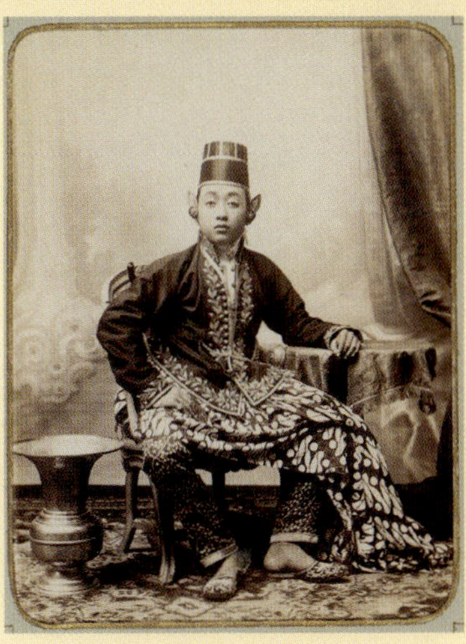

Kassian Céphas (1845-1912)
Prince of the court of Yogyakarta, Java,
Indonesia (1871-1890)
Albumen print
Provenance unknown
> p. 73

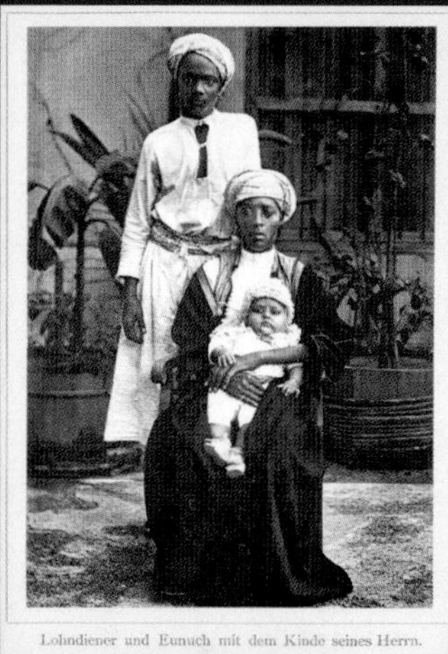

Christiaan Snouck Hurgronje (1857-1936)
Servant (eunuch) with the children of his
master (on pilgrimage in Mecca), Saudi Arabia
(1885)
Collotype
Provenance unknown
> p. 74

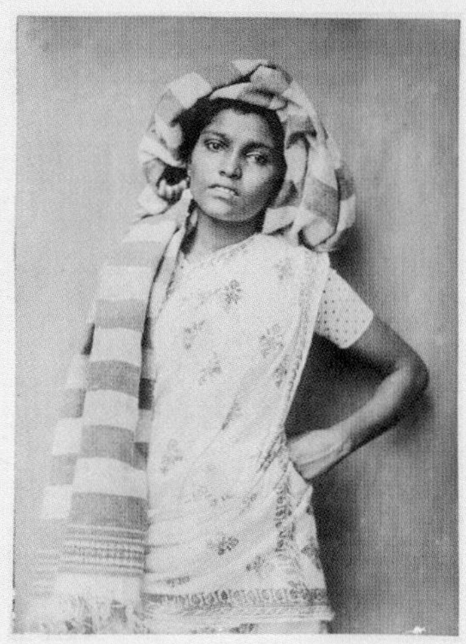

William Louis Henry Skeen & Co.
(1847-1903)
Young Tamil, Sri Lanka (1868-1897)
Gelatin developing-out paper
Legacy - Gerrit Verschuur, 1907
> p. 75

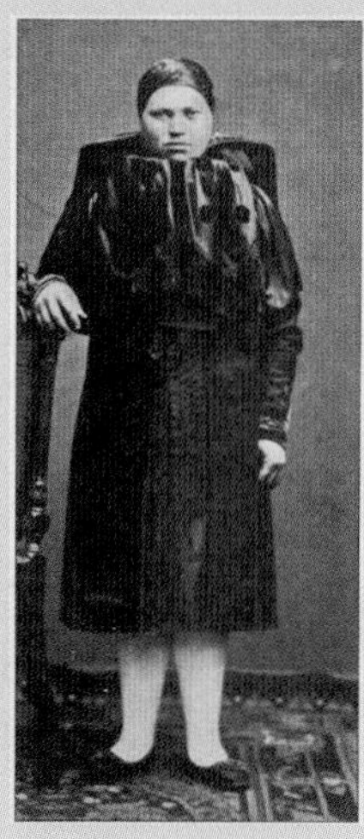

A. Schüler (act. 1890-1920)
Local women's costume, Wenden, Altenburg,
Germany (1890-1920)
Offset lithograph
Donation - Johan François Snelleman, 1911
>p. 76

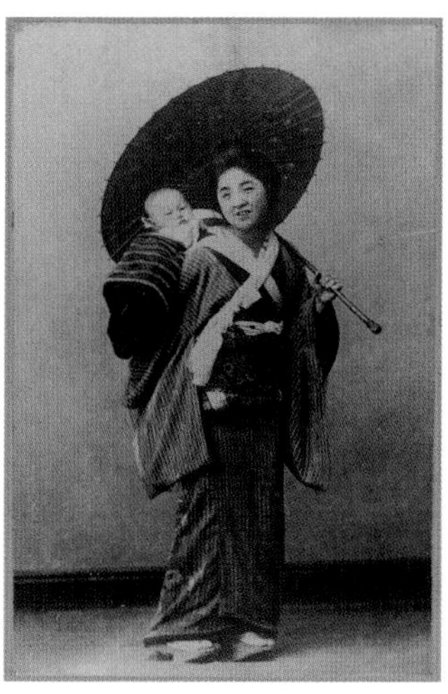

Anonymous
Woman with baby, Japan (1890-1900)
Collodion printing-out paper
Provenance unknown
> p. 77

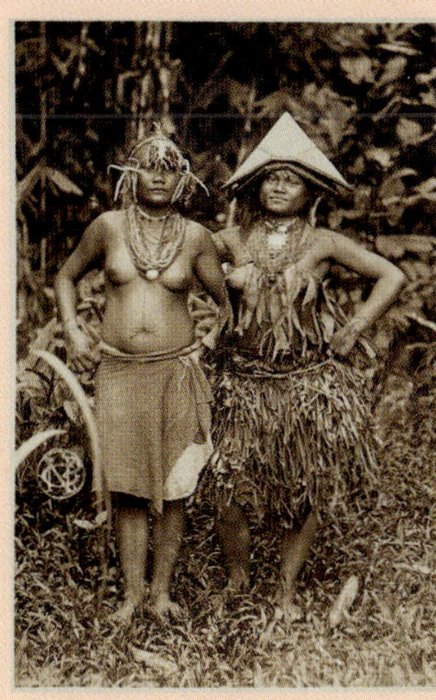

Christiaan Benjamin Nieuwenhuis
(1863-1922)
Women from the Mentawai Islands,
Indonesia (1895)
Rotogravure
Provenance unknown
> p. 78

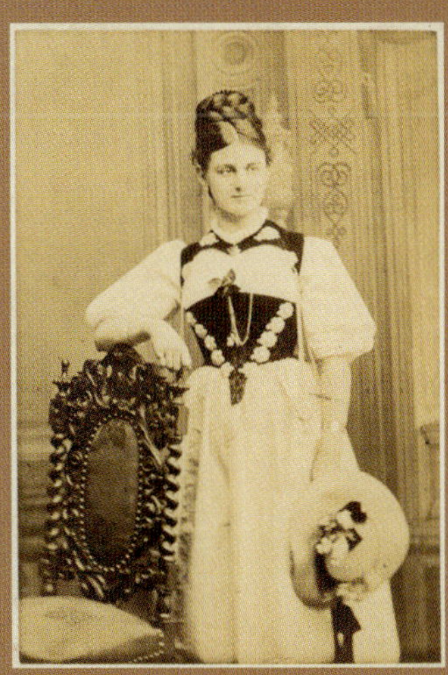

C. Lichtenberger (act. ca. 1870-1896)
Swiss woman, Interlaken, Switzerland
(1870-1896)
Albumen print
Donation - Herman ten Kate, 1910
> p. 79

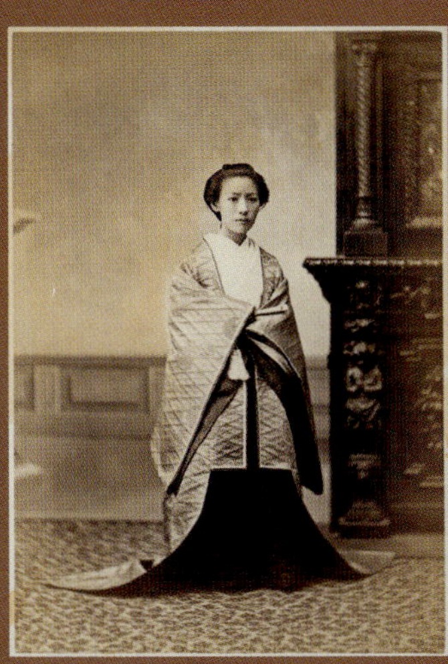

Shin'ichi Suzuki (1835-1918)
Wife of Ito Hirobumi, first prime minister of
Japan, Tokyo, Japan (1870-1890)
Albumen print, toned
Donation - dr. J.E. van der Pot, 1951
> p. 80

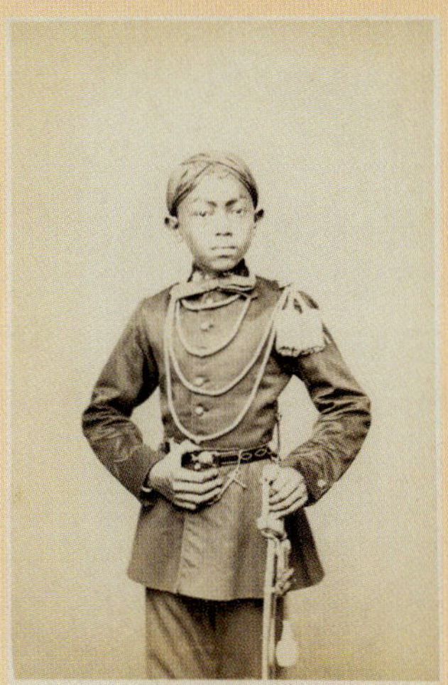

Woodbury & Page (act. 1857-1896)
Young prince, Java, Indonesia (1857-1863)
Albumen print
Purchase - Wereldmuseum, 1989
> p. 81

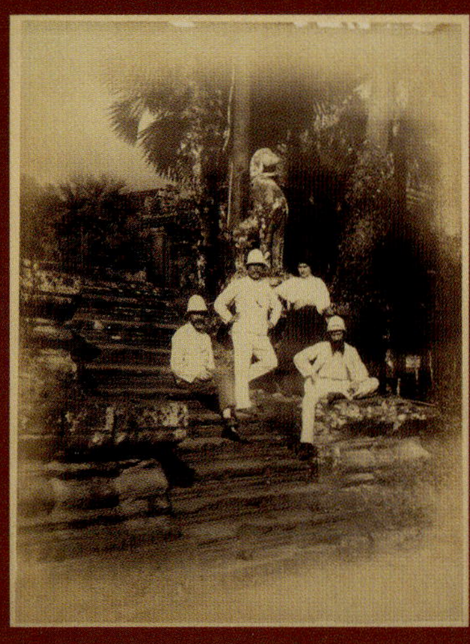

C. Basset (act. 1896-1897)
Globetrotting photo collector Gerrit Verschuur
with travelling companions at temple of
Angkor Wat, Cambodia (1896)
Albumen print
Legacy - Gerrit Verschuur, 1907
> p. 82

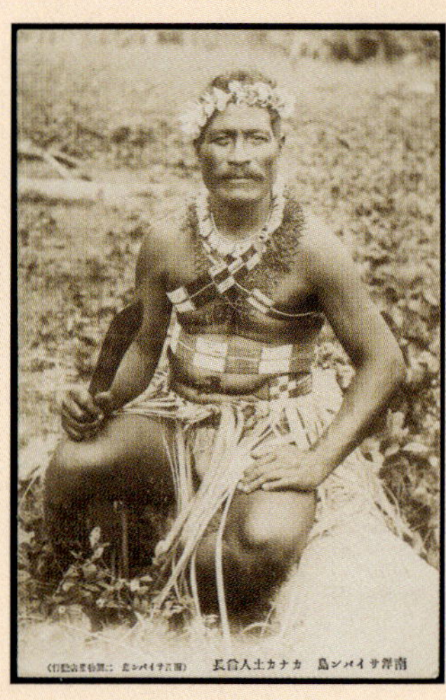

Sendai Saito Printing Co. (act. 1900-1910)
Man in traditional clothing, Hawaii
(1900-1910)
Collotype
Provenance unknown
> p. 83

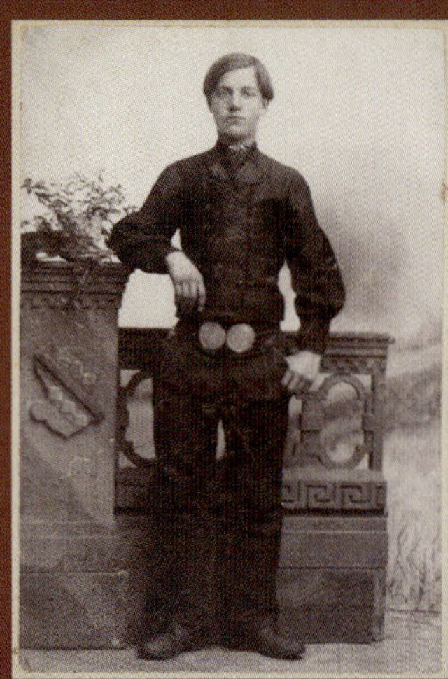

Sytze Reinder Elzinga (1863-1912)
Peasant in local costume, Zeeland,
Netherlands (1883-1903)
Collodion printing-out paper
Purchase - Nederlands Fotomuseum, 2005
> p. 84

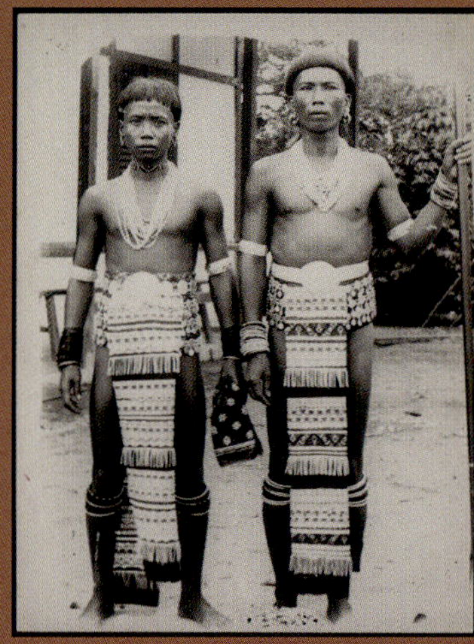

Paters Capucijnen (act. 1905-1933)
Segai Dayak with long beaded apron,
Balongan, Kalimantan (Borneo), Indonesia
(1905-1933)
Gelatin developing-out paper
Provenance unknown
> p. 85

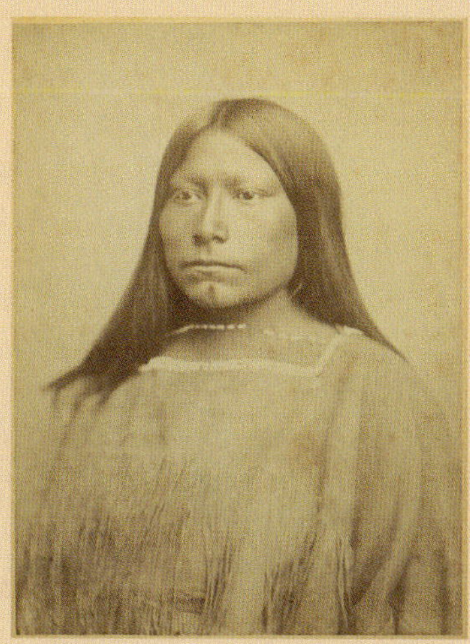

Will (William Stinson) Soule (1836-1908)
Kiowa captive in Fort Sill, Oklahoma,
United States (1869-1874)
Albumen print
Donation - Herman ten Kate, 1910
> p. 86

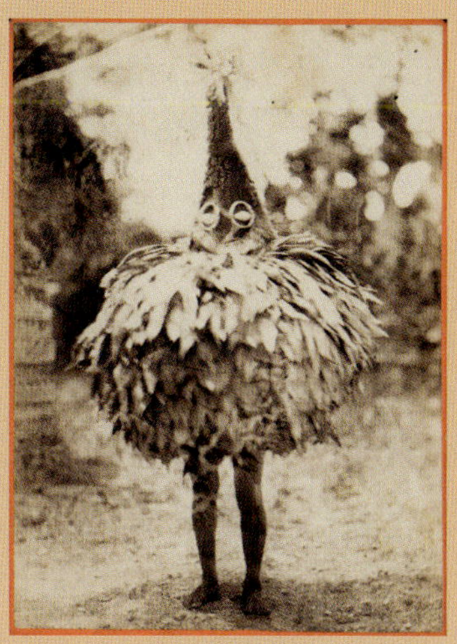

Johann Theodor Kleinschmidt (1834-1881)
Duk-Duk dancer, member of a secret society,
wearing a mask of leaves, New Britain
(1875-1881)
Albumen print
Donation - Herman ten Kate, 1910
> p. 87

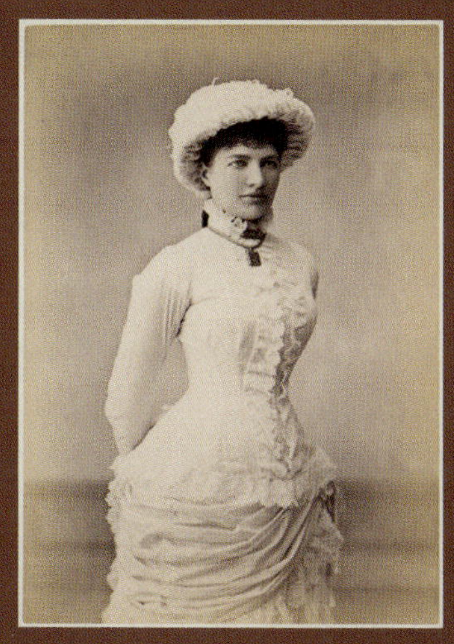

Shin'ichi Suzuki (1835-1918)
European or American woman in summer
attire, a resident of Japan (1870-1890)
Albumen print, toned
Donation - dr. J.E. van der Pot, 1951
> p. 88

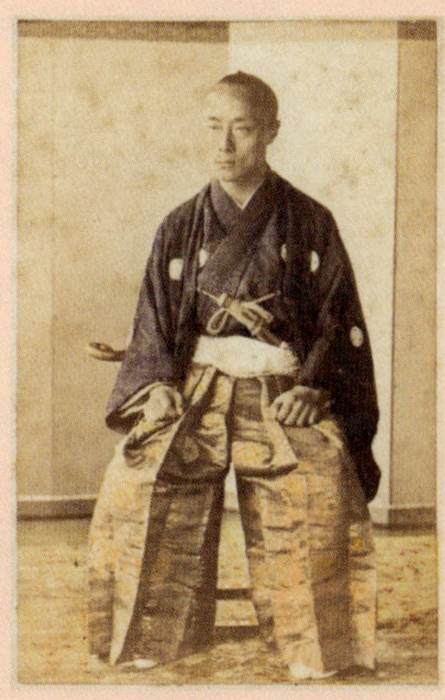

Frederick William Sutton (1832-1888)
Hitotsubashi Keiki (1837-1913), a.k.a.
Tokugawa Yoshinobu, the last Shogun,
Osaka, Japan (1864)
Albumen print, hand-coloured
Donation - dr. J.E. van der Pot, 1951
> p. 89

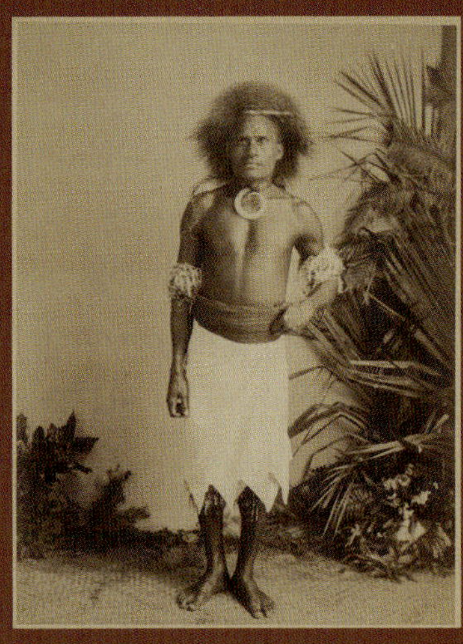

Frank (Francis Herbert) Dufty (1846-1910)
Fijian man (1871-1892)
Albumen print
Provenance unknown
> p. 90

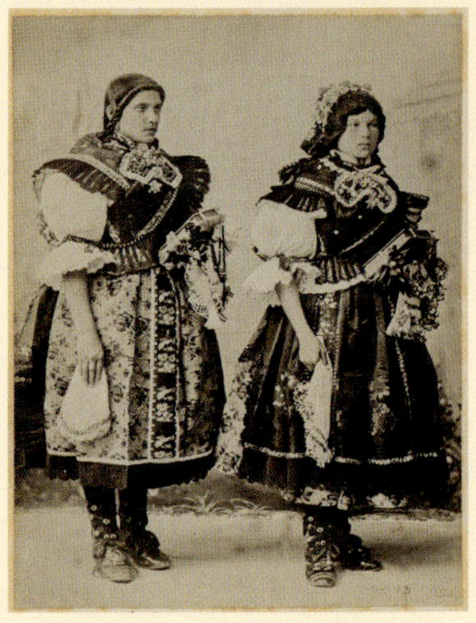

Calderoni & Co. (act. 1870-1885)
Peasant women in local costume, Hungary
(c. 1885)
Albumen print
Donation - Herman ten Kate, 1910
> p. 91

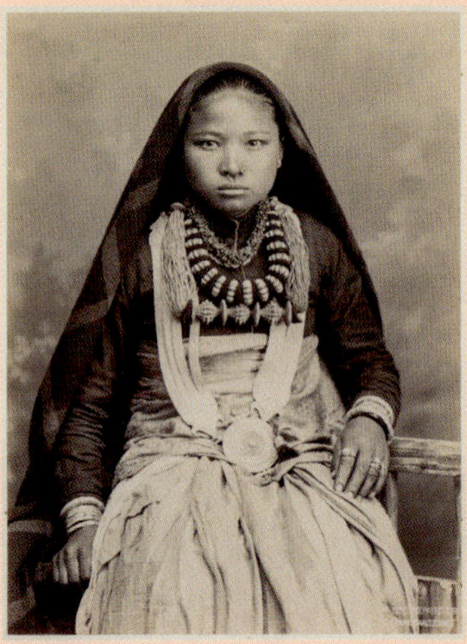

Theodore Paar (act. 1870-1890)
Nepalese girl in Darjeeling, India (c. 1890)
Gelatin printing-out paper
Legacy - Gerrit Verschuur, 1907
> p. 92

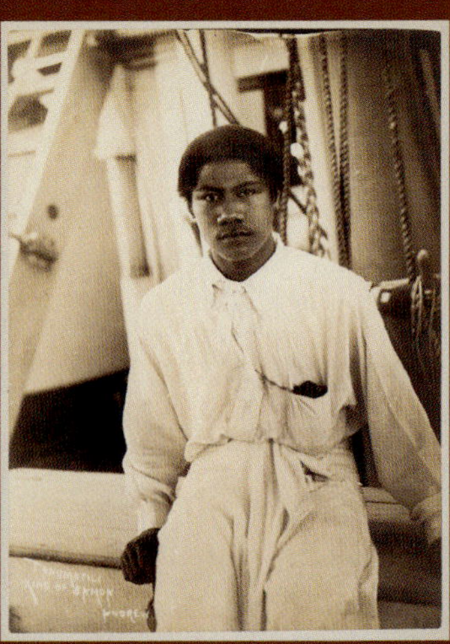

Thomas Andrew (1885-1939)
Tanumafili I (1879-1939), malietoa (king) of
Samoa since 1898 (c. 1898)
Albumen print, toned
Donation - Anatomisch-Embryologisch
Laboratorium der R.U. Leiden, 1987
> p. 93

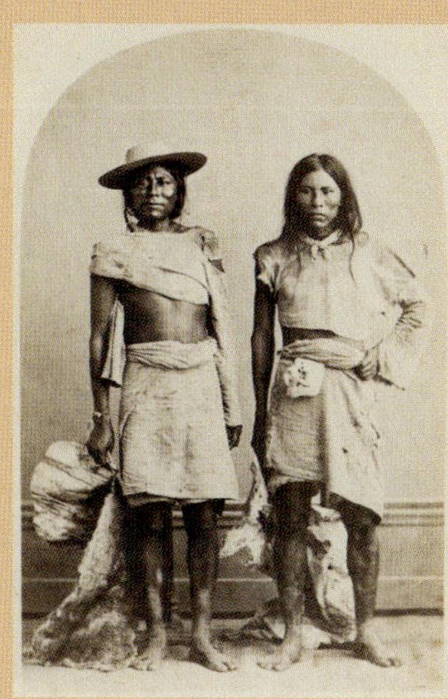

Alfredo Laurent (?-1888)
Seris from the state of Sonora, photographed
in Guaymas, Mexico (c. 1865)
Albumen print
Donation - Herman ten Kate, 1910
> p. 94

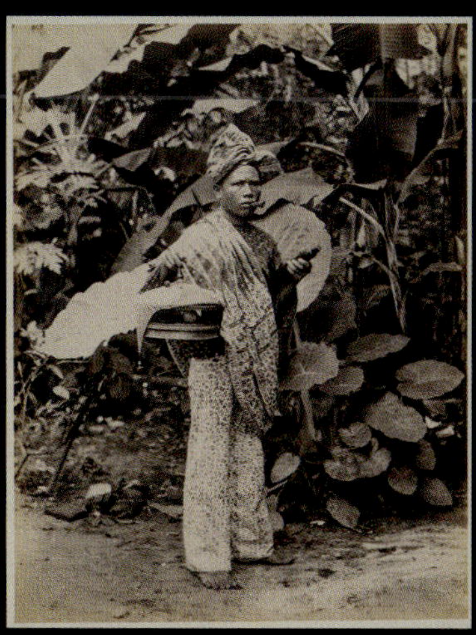

Gustav Richard Lambert & Co. (1846-1907)
Minangkabau man with fighting bird,
Bukittinggi, Sumatra, Indonesia (1883-1918)
Albumen print
Provenance unknown
> p. 95

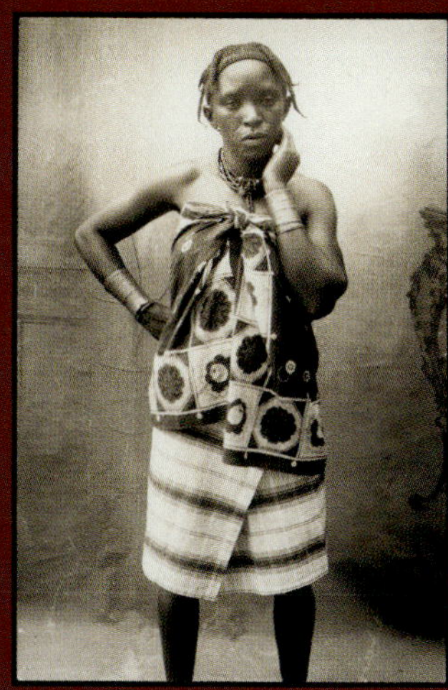

Augusta Curiel (1873-1937)
Maroon wearing a pangi (wrap skirt) and
scarification tattoos (decorative scarring),
Suriname, Paramaribo (c. 1910)
Gelatin developing-out paper
Permanent loan - Koninklijke Nedlllyd Groep,
1987
> p. 96

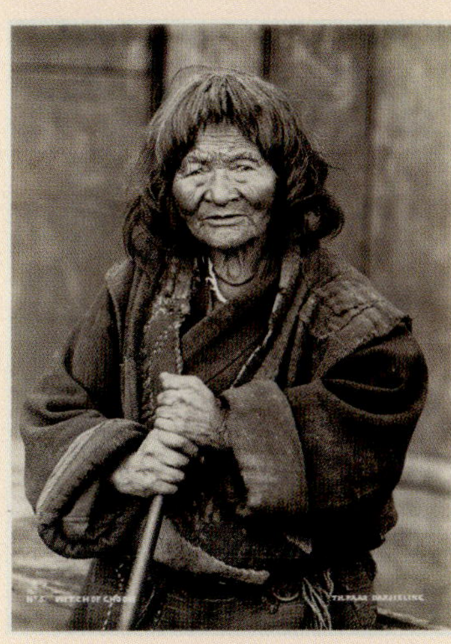

Theodore Paar (act. 1870-1890)
Buddhist nun from Ghoom, Darjeeling,
India (c. 1890)
Gelatin printing-out paper
Legacy - Gerrit Verschuur,1907
> p. 97

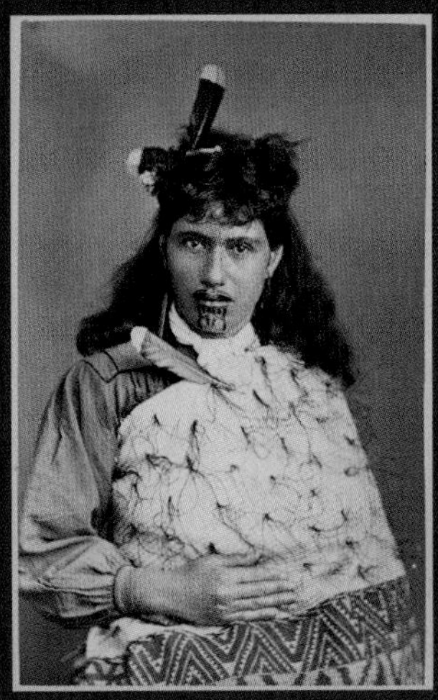

John McGarrigle, American Photographic
Company (act. 1865-1874)
Maori with a chin tattoo reserved for
aristocratic women, New Zealand (c. 1867)
Albumen print
Provenance unknown
> p. 98

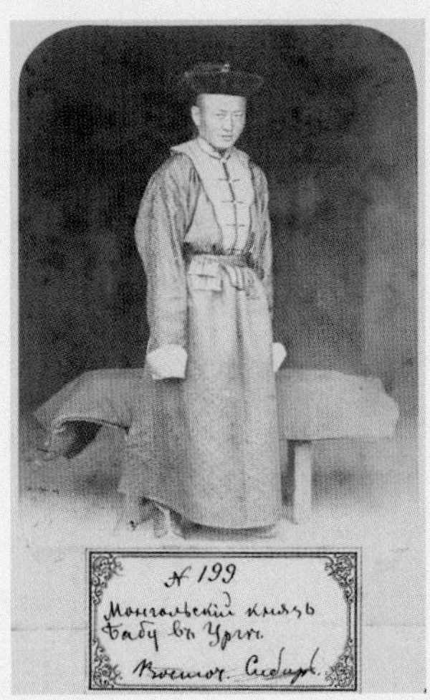

S.B. Toumanoff (act. 1870-1879)
Prince Nabon, Ulaanbaatar, Mongolia
(1870-1879)
Albumen print
Donation - Herman ten Kate, 1910
> p. 99

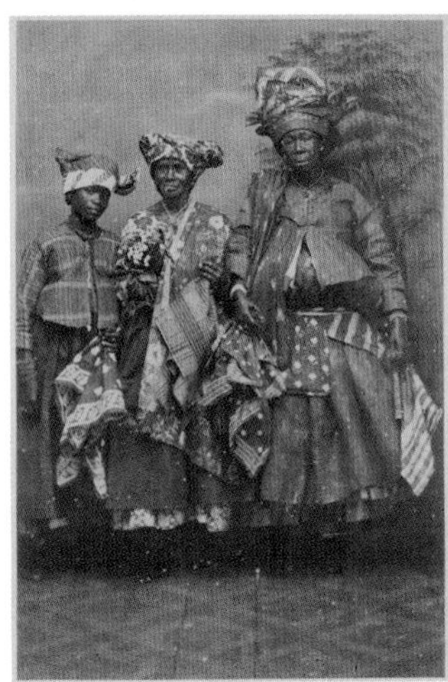

Julius Eduard Muller (1846-1902)
Creole women wearing kotomisi (left) and
partomisi (centre and right), Paramaribo,
Suriname (1883-1892)
Albumen print
Donation Herman ten Kate, 1910
> p. 100

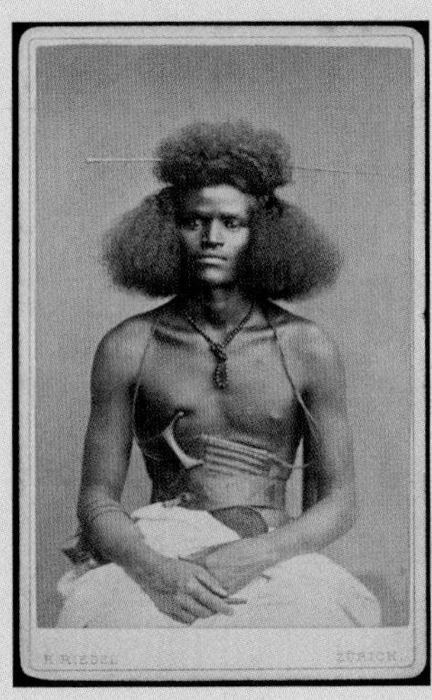

R. Riedel (act. 1865-1880)
Nubian, on tour with a Human Zoo, Zurich,
Switzerland (1880)
Albumen print
Donation - Herman ten Kate, 1910
> p. 101

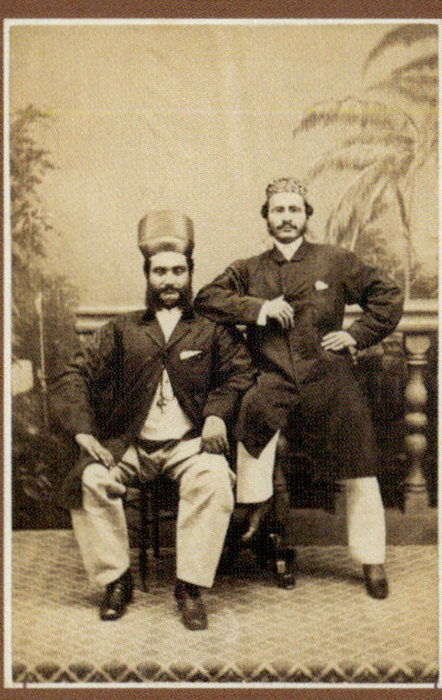

August Sachtler (act. 1863-1874)
Parsi merchants from India or Iran, in
Singapore (1863-1874)
Albumen print
Legacy - Gerrit Verschuur,1907
> p. 102

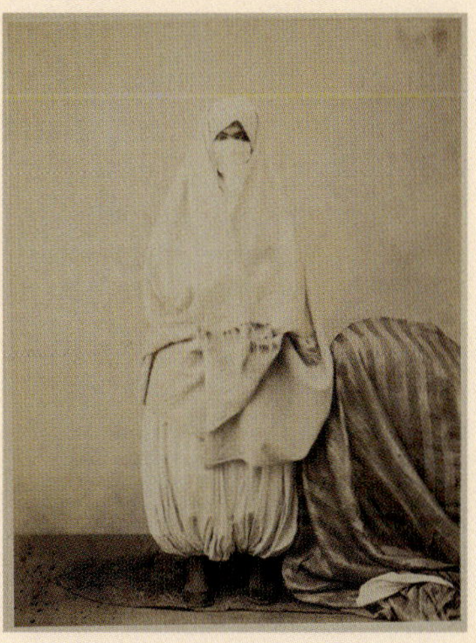

Félix-Jacques Antoine Moulin (1802-1879)
Veiled woman, Algeria (1856-1858)
Albumen print
Provenance unknown
> p. 103

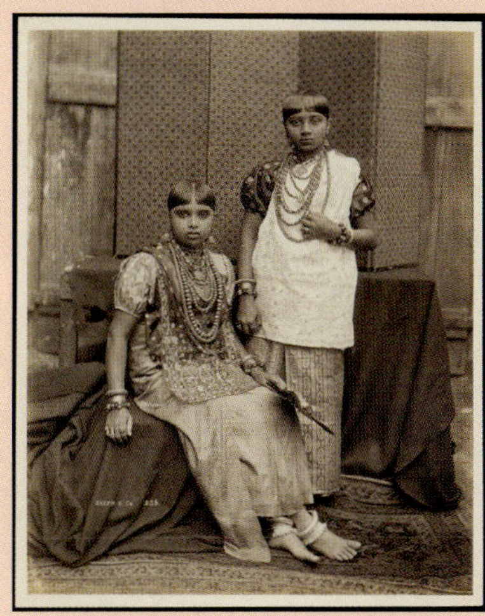

William Louis Henry Skeen & Co.
(1847-1903)
Girls from Kandy, Sri Lanka (1868-1897)
Albumen print, toned
Legacy - Gerrit Verschuur,1907
> p. 104

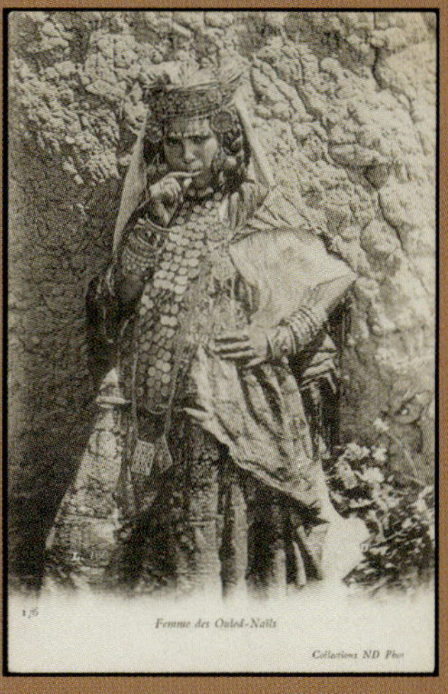

Lehnert & Landrock (act. 1904-1930)
Ouled-Naïl woman, Algeria (1904-1930)
Collotype, chromolithographic
Provenance unknown
> p. 105

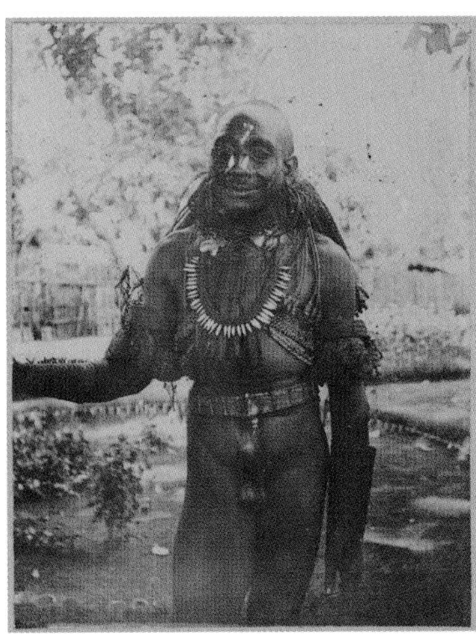

Anonymous
An ewati (marriageable man), identifiable by
his headdress of artifical hair and ornaments,
Merauke, Western New Guinea (c. 1890)
Collodion printing-out paper, matte, toned
Provenance unknown
> p. 106

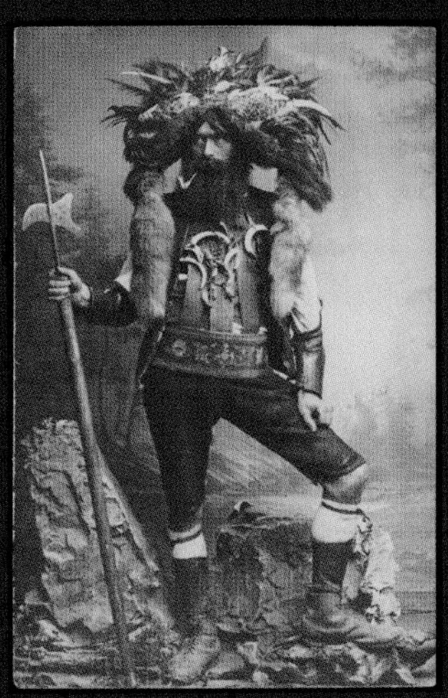

F. Peter (act. 1906-1910)
Vineyard-keeper from the Meran area, Tirol,
Italy (1906-1910)
Gelatin printing-out paper
Donation - J.F. van Leeuwen, 1911
> p. 107

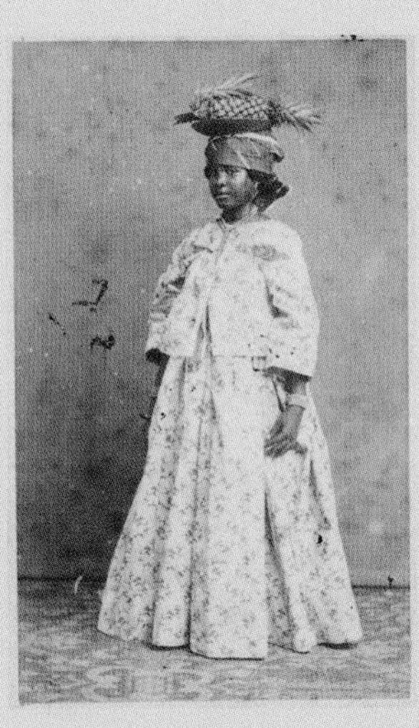

Anonymous
Creole woman in paletomisi, Paramaribo,
Suriname (1865-1880)
Albumen print
Donation - Herman ten Kate, 1910
> p. 108

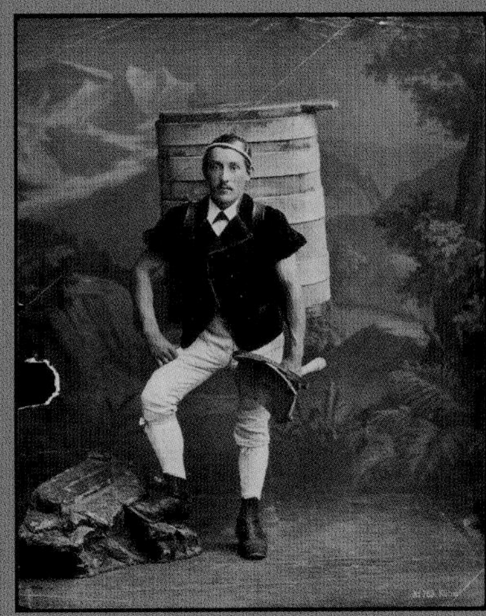

Schroeder & Co. (act. 1894-1895)
Cowherd, Switzerland (1890-1900)
Gelatin developing-out paper
Donation - Gemeentearchief Barneveld, 1990
> p. 109

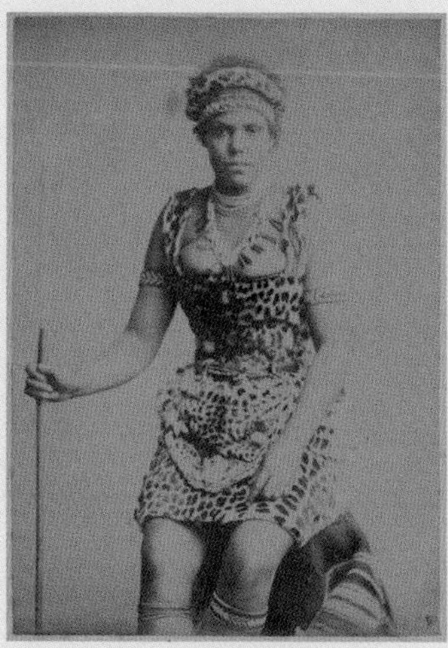

Carl Günther (act. 1865-1884)
Zulu, wearing a tiger skin dress, in a
Human Zoo in Berlin, Germany (1884)
Albumen print
Donation - Herman ten Kate, 1910
> p. 110

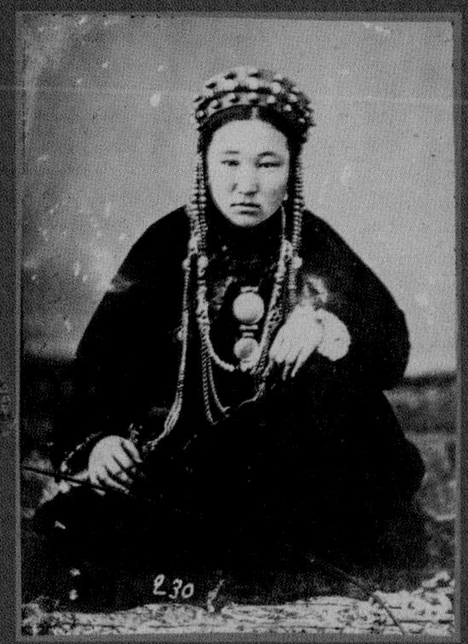

S.B. Toumanoff (act. 1870-1879)
Young woman from Buryatia in Adygeya,
Russian Federation (1870-1879),
Albumen print
Donation Herman ten Kate, 1910
> p. 111

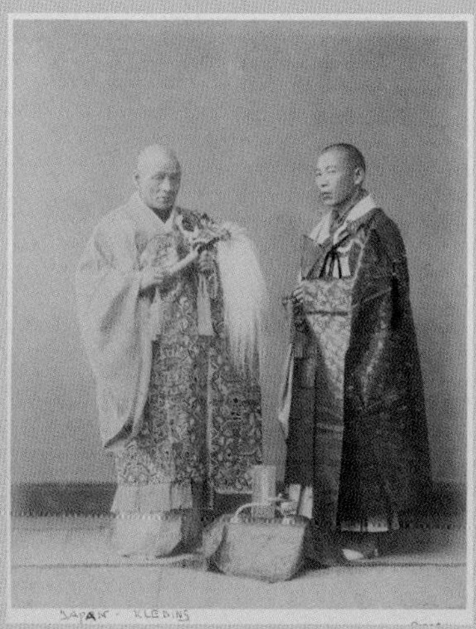

Kozaburo Tamamura (1856-1923?)
Buddhist priests, Japan (1874-1916)
Albumen print, hand-coloured
Provenance unknown
> p. 112

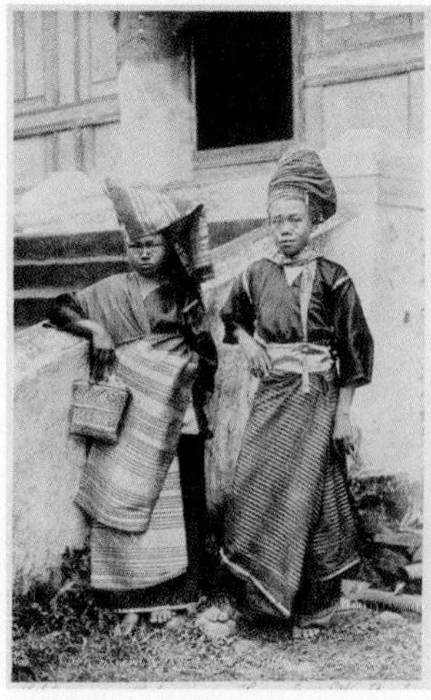

Christiaan Benjamin Nieuwenhuis (1863-1922)
Married couple, Bukittinggi, Sumatra,
Indonesia (1922)
Rotogravure
Donation - Elisabeth Wilhelmina Dijkstra-Viruly
Verbrugge, 1923
> p. 113

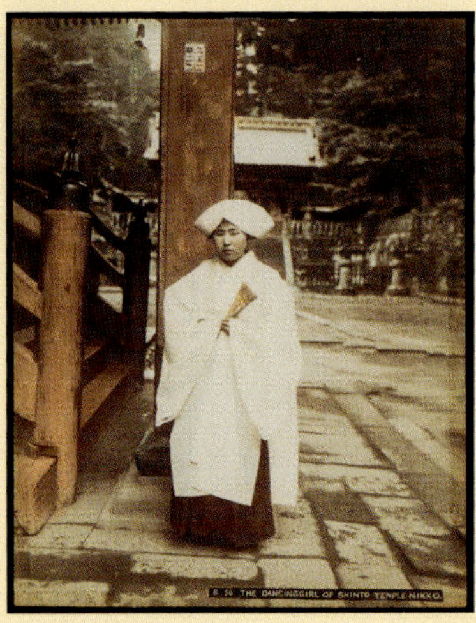

Seibei Kajima (1866-1924)
Female servant from a Shinto shrine, Nikko,
Japan (1895-1913)
Albumen print, hand-coloured
Provenance unknown
> p. 114

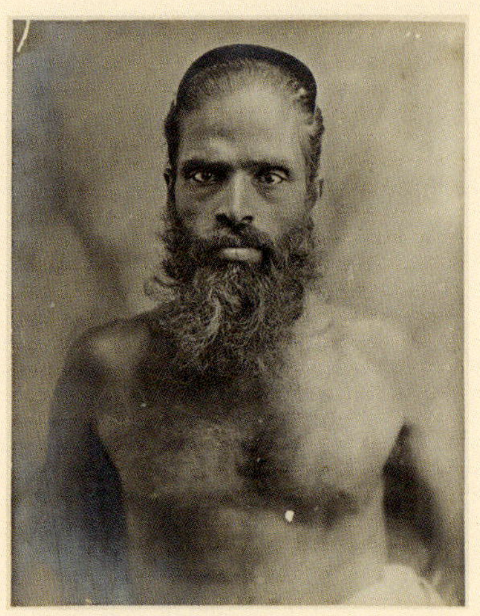

William Louis Henry Skeen & Co.
(1847-1903)
Middle-aged man, Sri Lanka (1868-1897)
Gelatin developing-out paper
Provenance unknown
> p. 115

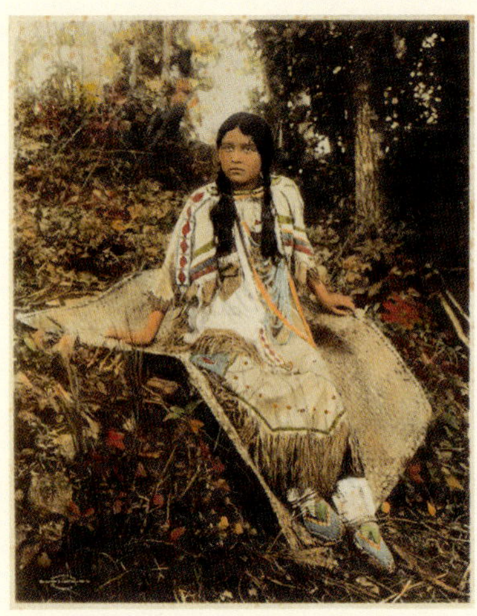

Alfred S. Campbell (1840-1912)
Ojibwa, Great Lakes region, United States
and Canada (1902)
Collotype, applied color
Donation - Herman ten Kate, 1910
> p. 116

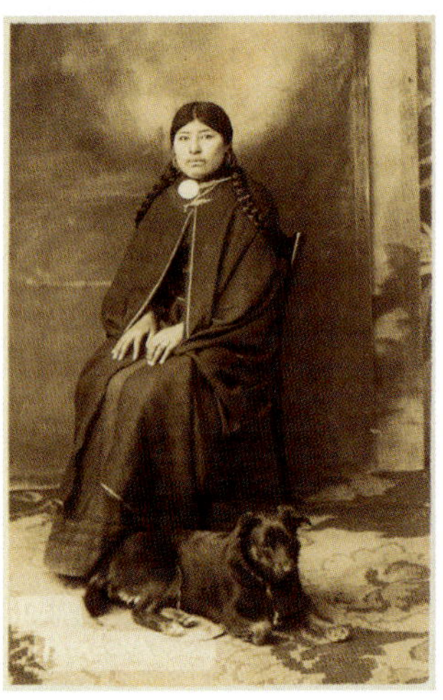

John Bell Hatcher (1861-1904)
K'ooküchüm, a.k.a. Anita, niece of Chümjalu,
Tehuleche chief. She is dressed like the
Araucanian women who live in the same
region, Patagonia (c. 1896)
Albumen print
Donation - Peter A. de Bruyne, 1906
> p. 117

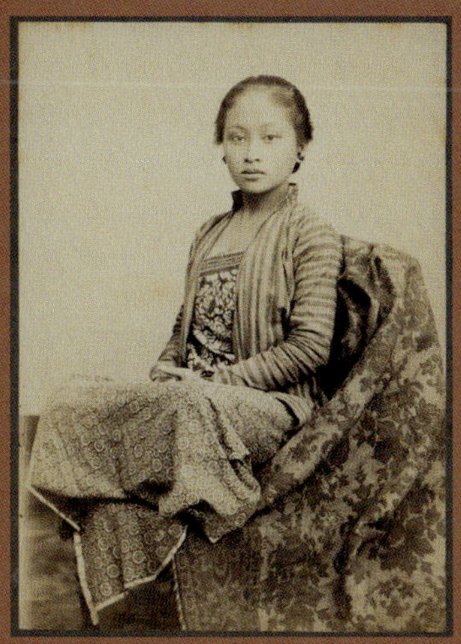

Isidore van Kinsbergen (1821-1905)
Princess of the court of Yogyakarta,
Indonesia (1862)
Albumen print
Donation - A.W. Dupont, 1900
> p. 118

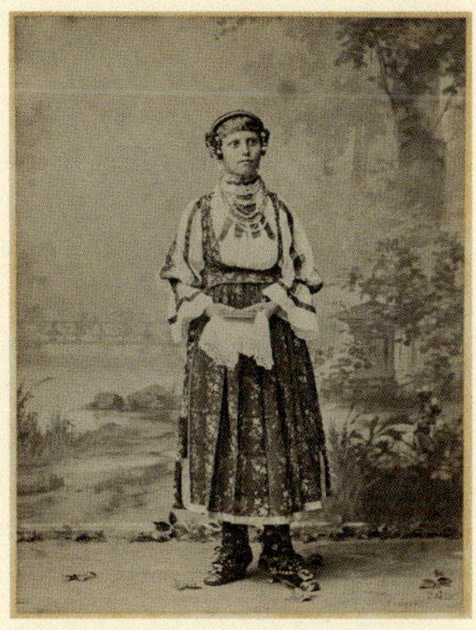

Calderoni & Co. (act. 1870-1885)
Schokaz girl (Schokaz people), Hungary
(c. 1885)
Albumen print
Donation - Herman ten Kate, 1910
> p. 119

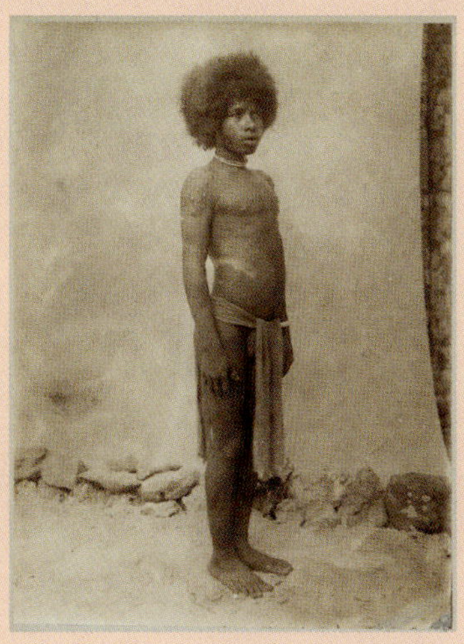

Missiehuis van het Heilig Hart, Tilburg
(act. 1905-1912)
Young man, Fakfak, Western New Guinea
(1908)
Collodion printing-out paper
Reproduction - Missiehuis van het Heilig Hart,
Tilburg, 1912
> p. 120

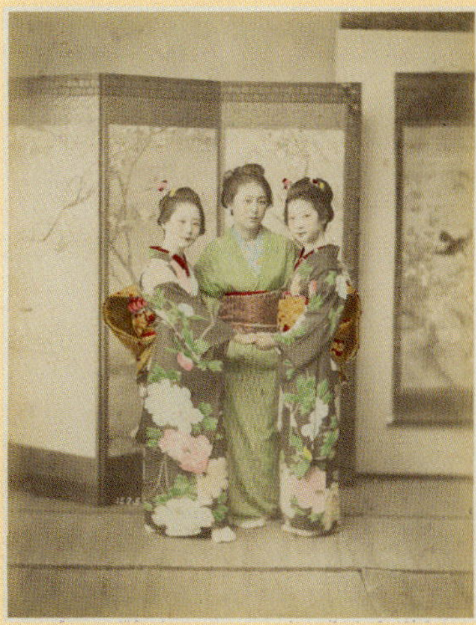

Baron Raimund von Stillfried-Rathenitz
(1839-1911)
Kimono-clad women posing as the three
graces in front of a screen, Yokohama, Japan
(1863-1885)
Albumen print, hand-coloured
Provenance unknown
> p. 121

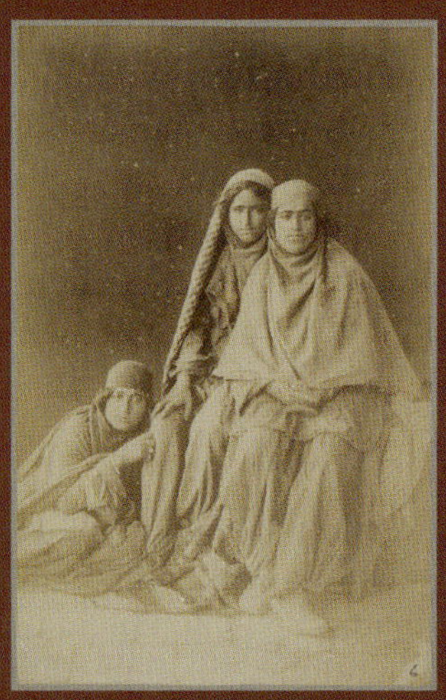

Antoin Sevruguin (1830-1933)
Women from Loristan, Iran (1870-1885)
Albumen print
Donation - Albert Hotz, 1885
> p. 122

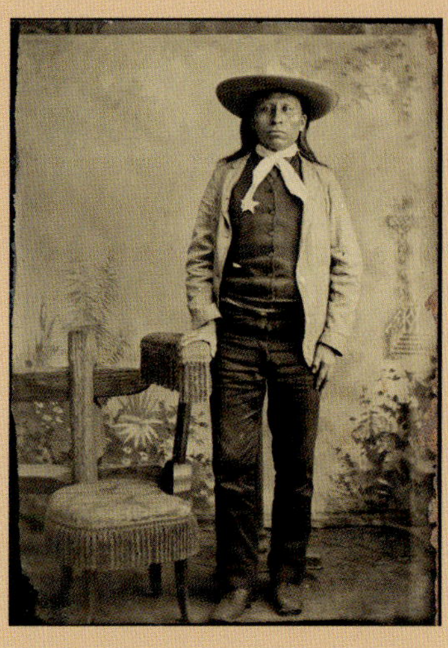

J.M.B. Fowler (act. 1883)
Cherokee from the Indian Terrritory,
Oklahoma, United States (1883)
Ferrotype
Donation - Herman ten Kate, 1910
> p. 123

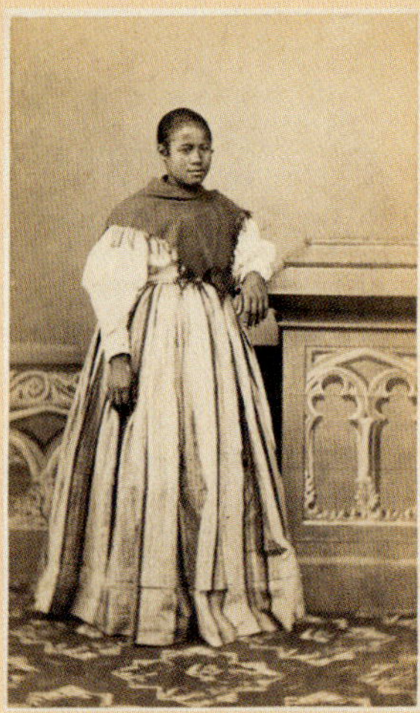

Anonymous
Female servant, Cape of Good Hope,
South Africa (1860-1880)
Albumen print
Donation - J.P. Verdoorn, 1906
> p. 124

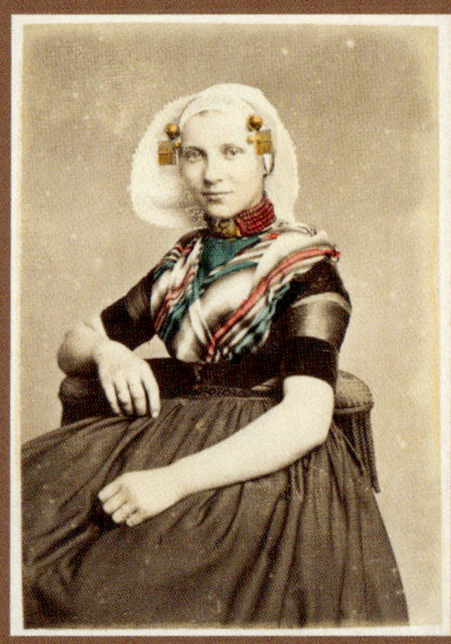

Andries Jager (1825-1905)
Woman in Protestant costume of South
Beveland, Goes, Zeeland,
Netherlands (1860-1869)
Albumen print, hand-coloured
Purchase - Nederlands Fotomuseum, 2005
> p. 125

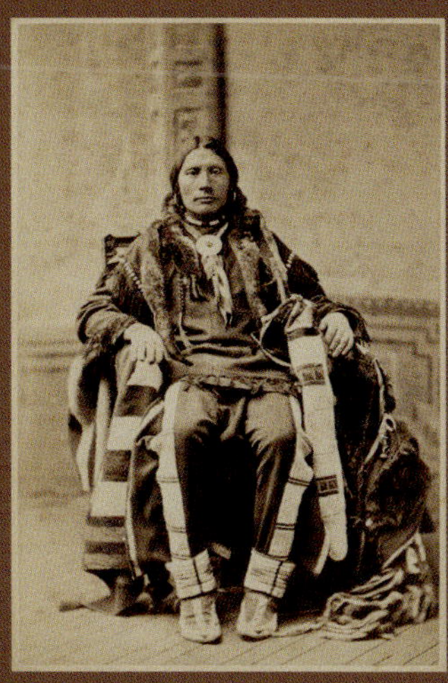

Mathew Benjamin Brady (1823-1896)
Buck Skin Charley, Ute chief, in Washington,
United States (c. 1880)
Albumen print
Donation - Herman ten Kate, 1910
> p. 126

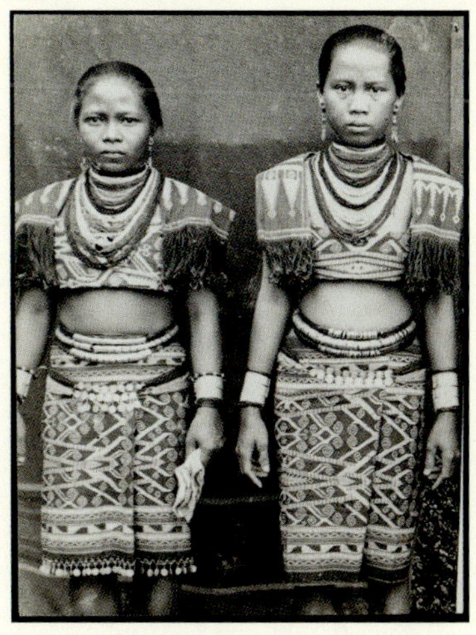

Paters Capucijnen (act. 1905-1933)
Kantuk Dayak, Kalimantan (Borneo), Indonesia
(1905-1933)
Gelatin developing-out paper
Provenance unknown
> p. 127

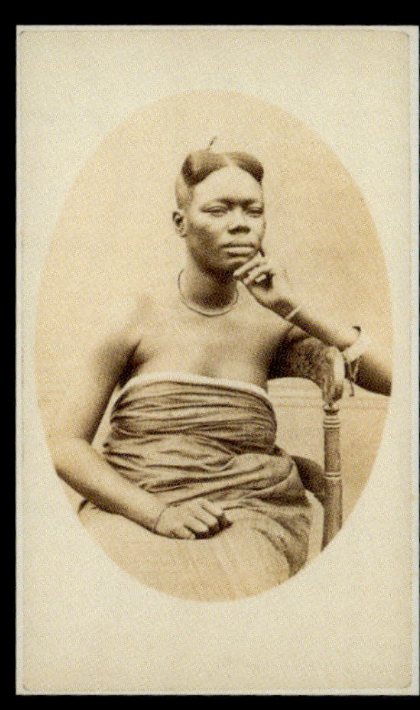

Francis W. Joaque (1845-1900)
Woman from Gabon (c. 1870)
Albumen print
Donation - J.P. Verdoorn, 1906
> p. 128

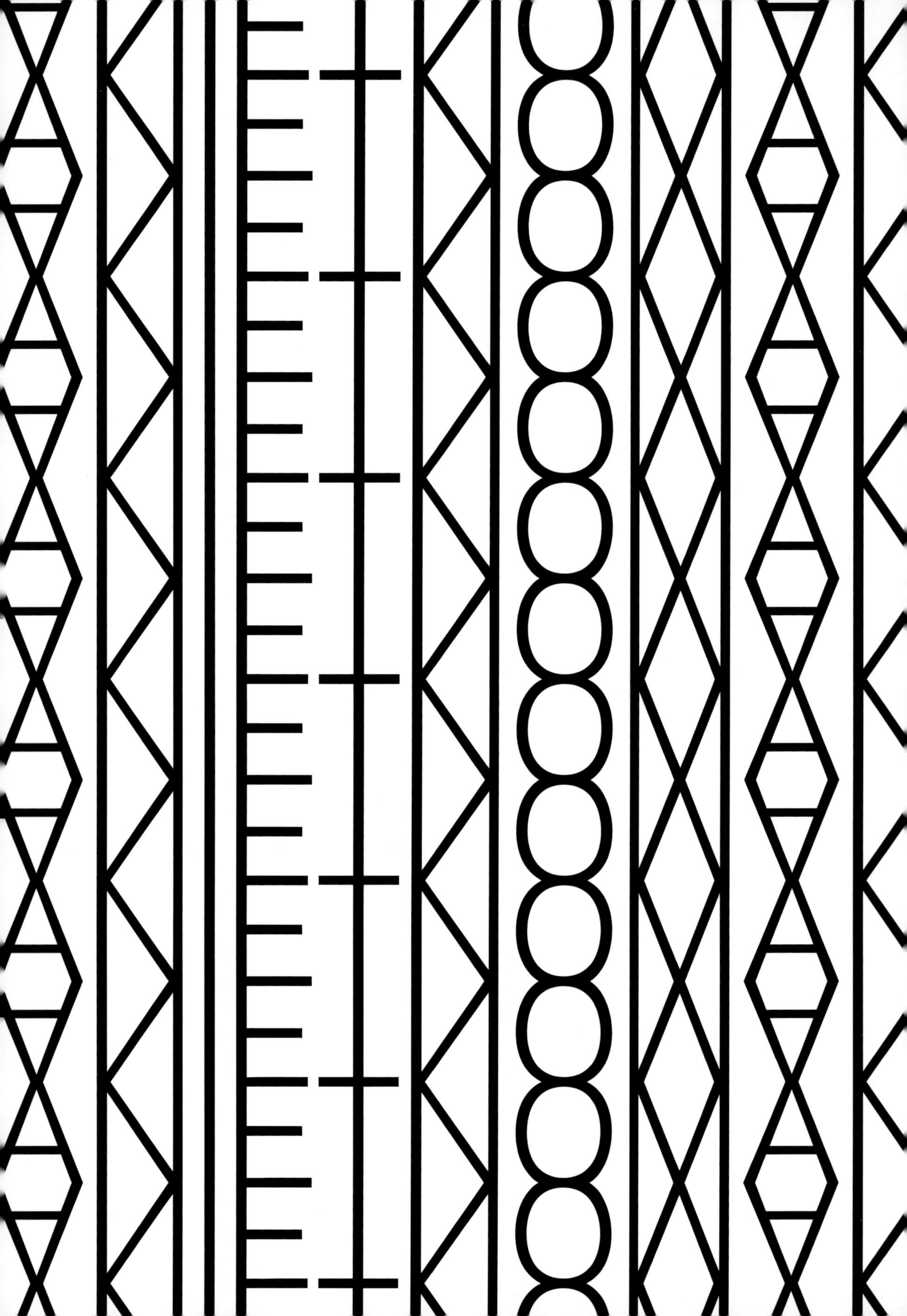

CREDITS
This book was published in association with the Nederlands Fotomuseum for the exhibition ETNOMANIE in the Nederlands Fotomuseum, Rotterdam.

Edited by - Ellie Uyttenbroek. Photo editing - Ellie Uyttenbroek & Mary Pelders Vos. Captions ETNOMANIE - Ellie Uyttenbroek. Captions World Collection - Anneke Groeneveld. Text - Charlotte Dwyer, Frits Giersberg. Translation - Joseph Hughes (captions ETNOMANIE), Andrew May (text Frits Giersberg), Janey Tucker (captions World Collection). Copy editing - D'Laine Camp. Design - Mary Pelders Vos. Printing and lithography - Wilco Art Books Printing and Binding. Lithography - BFC, Bert van der Horst. Production - Brecht Bleeker. Publisher - Eelco van Welie, nai010 publishers.

This publication was made possible by financial support from Fonds 21, VSBfonds, J.E. Jurriaanse Stichting/Stichting Bevordering van Volkskracht, Erasmusstichting. Acknowledgements: Nationaal Museum van Wereldculturen, Mr. and Mrs. Leguit.

The Nederlands Fotomuseum in Rotterdam is the leading national museum of photography in the Netherlands. The museum shows every facet of photography: documentary and experimental, contemporary and historical. It has an impressive collection of 5.5. million photographic images, which comprises an important part of the Netherlands' visual heritage.

nai010 publishers is an internationally orientated publisher specialized in developing, producing and distributing books in the fields of architecture, urbanism, art and design. www.nai010.com.

nai010.com - nederlandsfotomuseum.nl

Printed and bound in the Netherlands
ISBN 978-94-6208-363-9

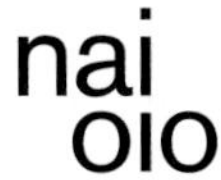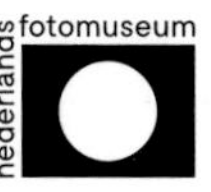

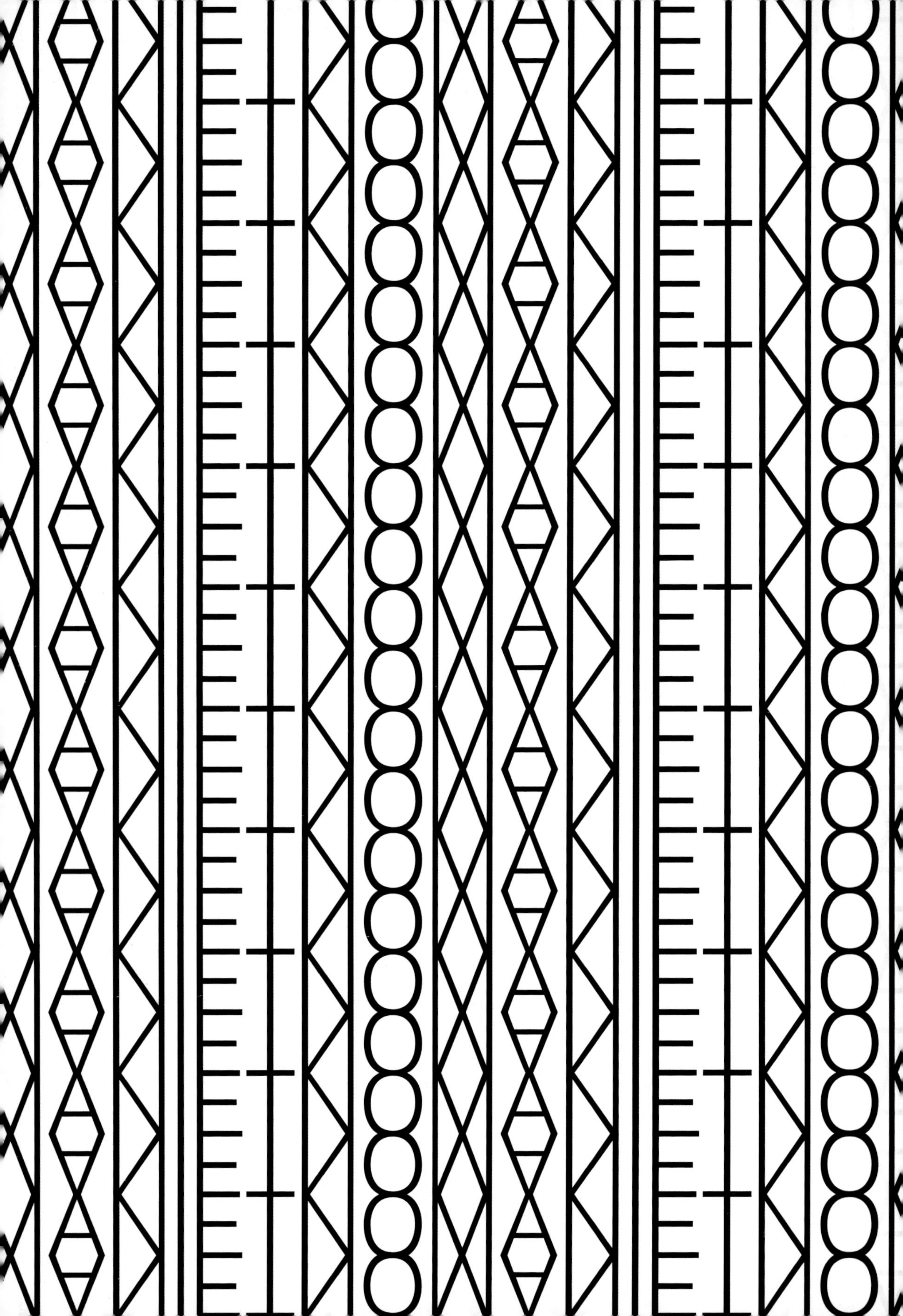

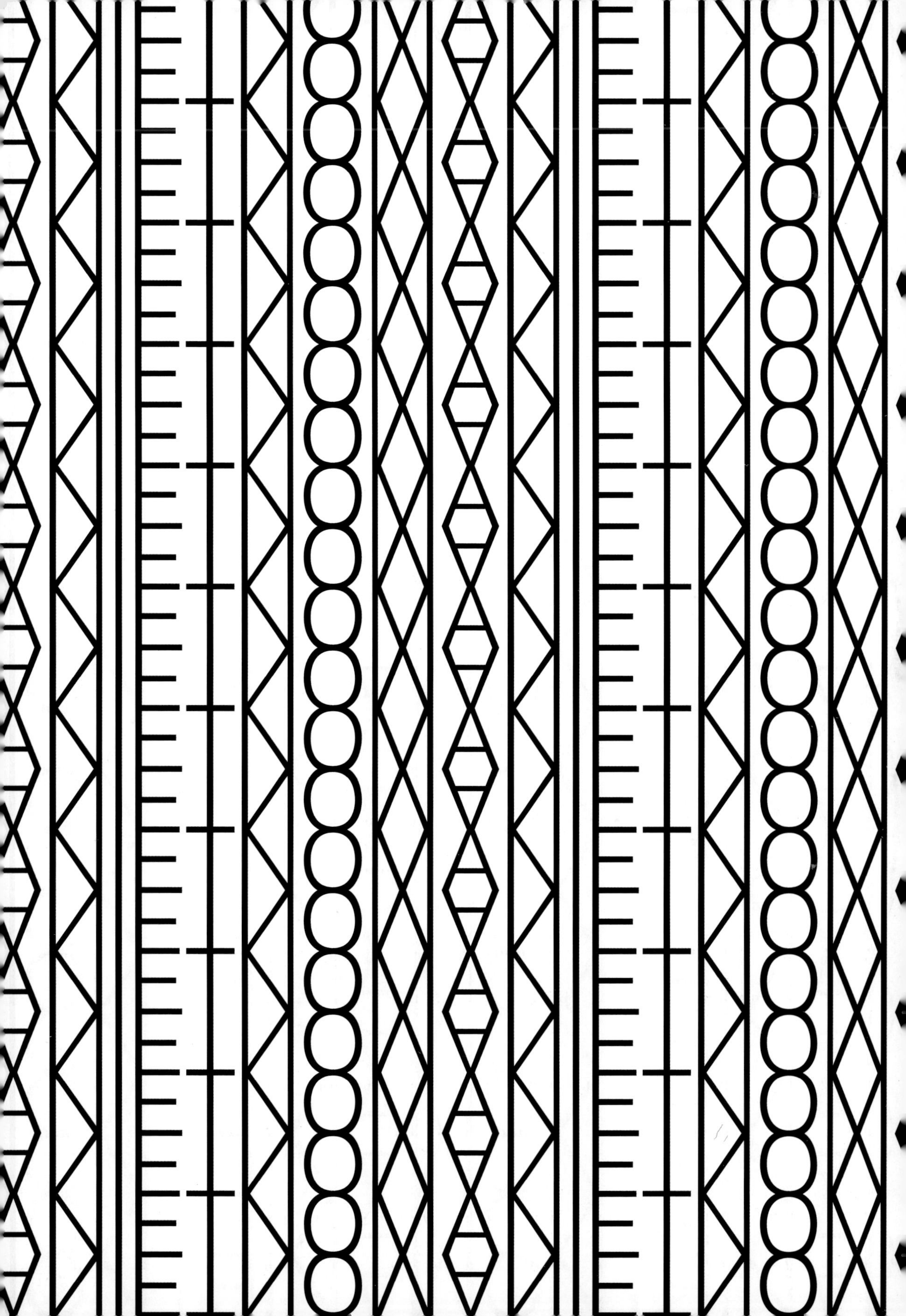

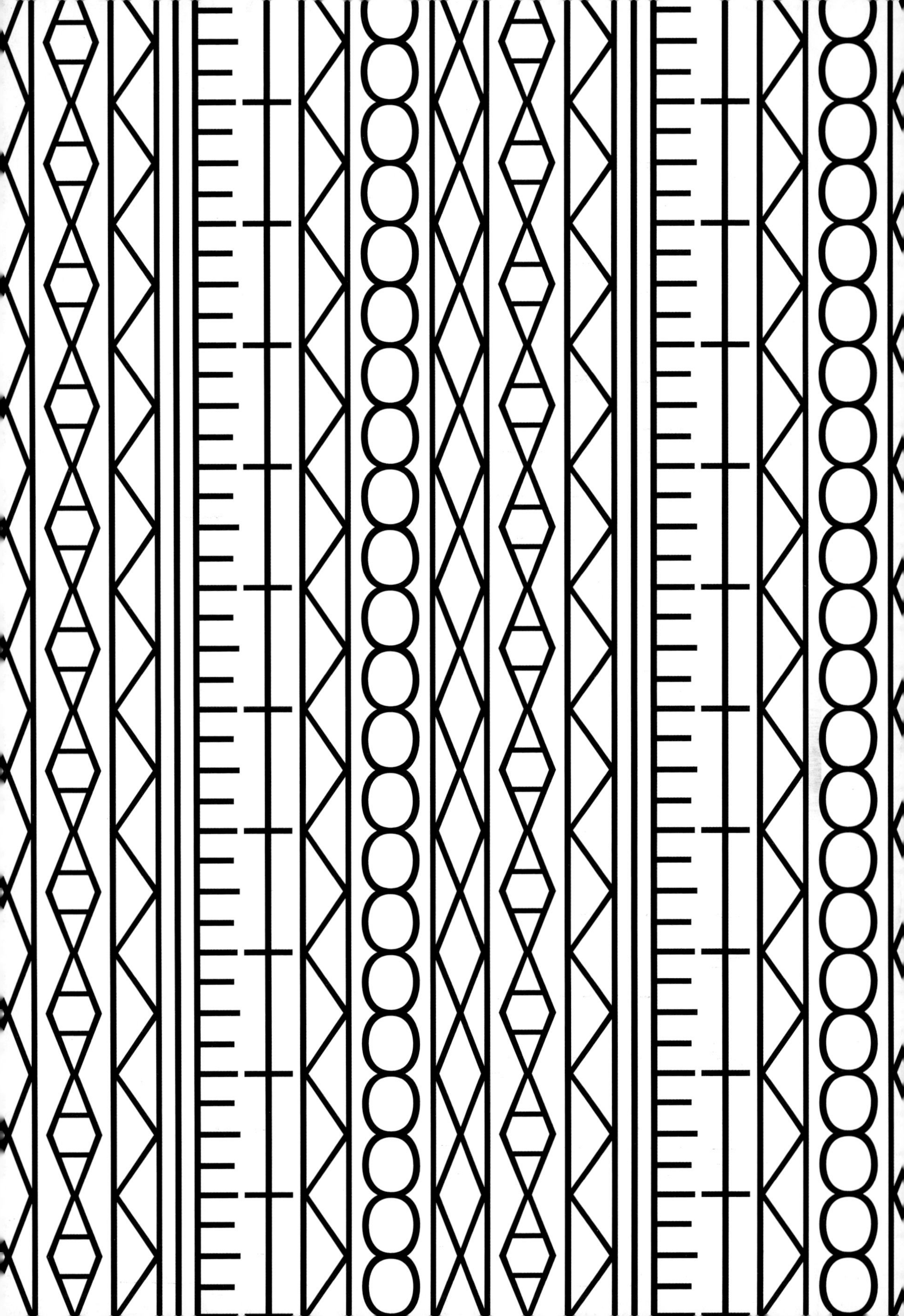